FINANCE IN A NUTSHELL

FT Prentice Hall

FINANCIAL TIMES

In an increasingly competitive world, we believe it's quality of thinking that will give you the edge – an idea that opens new doors, a technique that solves a problem, or an insight that simply makes sense of it all. The more you know, the smarter and faster you can go.

That's why we work with the best minds in business and finance to bring cutting-edge thinking and best learning practice to a global market.

Under a range of leading imprints, including *Financial Times Prentice Hall*, we create world-class print publications and electronic products bringing our readers knowledge, skills and understanding, which can be applied whether studying or at work.

To find out more about our business publications, or tell us about the books you'd like to find, you can visit us at **www.pearsoned.co.uk**

PEARSON

Education

FINANCE IN A NUTSHELL

A no-nonsense companion to the tools and techniques of finance

Javier Estrada

FT Prentice Hall
FINANCIAL TIMES

An imprint of Pearson Education

London • New York • Toronto • Sydney • Tokyo • Singapore
Hong Kong • Cape Town • New Delhi • Madrid • Paris • Amsterdam • Munich • Milan

PEARSON EDUCATION LIMITED

Edinburgh Gate
Harlow CM20 2JE
Tel: +44 (0)1279 623623
Fax: +44 (0)1279 431059

Website: www.pearsoned.co.uk

First published in Great Britain in 2005

ISBN 0 273 67540 0

British Library Cataloguing in Publication Data
A catalogue record for this book is available from the British Library

Library of Congress Cataloging-in-Publication Data
Estrada, Javier.
    Finance in a nutshell: a desktop companion to the tools and techniques of finance
        p. cm. — (Corporate finance)
    Includes index.
    ISBN 0–273–67540–0
    1. Business enterprises—Finance—Handbooks, manuals, etc. 2.
Corporations—Finance—Handbooks, manuals, etc. I. Title. II. Corporate finance
(Financial Times Prentice Hall)

    HG4027.3.E88 2005
    658.15—dc22

10 9 8 7 6 5 4 3 2 1
09 08 07 06 05

Typeset in 10/14pt Century ITC by 70
Printed and bound in Great Britain by Bell and Bain Ltd, Glasgow

The Publishers' policy is to use paper manufactured from sustainable forests.

CONTENTS

Preface   vii

PART I: RISK AND RETURN   1

1   Returns I: Basic concepts   3

2   Returns II: Mean returns   14

3   Risk I: Total risk   26

4   Risk and return I: Portfolios   35

5   Risk II: Diversification   45

6   Risk III: Systematic risk   56

7   Risk and return II: The CAPM and the cost of capital   67

8   Risk and return III: Alternatives to the CAPM   84

9   Risk IV: Downside risk   96

10   Risk and return IV: Risk-adjusted returns   109

11   Risk and return V: Optimal portfolios   124

12   Risk and return VI: The long run   136

PART II: VALUATION   153

13   Stocks I: The dividend discount model   155

14   Stocks II: The WACC model   168

15   Stocks III: Other DCF models   181

16   Stocks IV: Reverse valuation   193

17   Stocks V: Relative valuation   203

18   Bonds I: Prices and yields   213

19   Bonds II: Default risk and market risk   227

20   Bonds III: Duration and convexity   239

PART III: OTHER IMPORTANT TOPICS   **253**

21 NPV and IRR   255

22 Real options   270

23 Corporate value creation   281

24 Options   292

25 Futures and forwards   304

26 Currencies   317

PART IV: STATISTICAL BACKGROUND   **331**

27 Stats I: Summary statistics   333

28 Stats II: Normality   346

29 Stats III: Non-normality   358

30 Stats IV: Regression analysis   370

Index   383

PREFACE

I always thought I'd write a book but never quite knew when or on what topic. I never felt the need of doing it and, to be honest, I never set it as a goal for myself. But eventually I got to a point when I decided to surrender to the evidence: too many people were asking for the same thing, and the market, in my opinion, had not delivered. So I thought I'd deliver it myself.

A brief history of this book

It happened many times. During the course of an executive education program, I'd come in to give a few sessions on finance topics. After finishing those sessions, someone would come to me and say something like, 'Listen, this was very interesting and, though my job is only marginally related to finance, I'd like to know more about it. What would you advise me to read?' Or something like, 'Hey, I work in finance but my job is so specialized that I feel I need to refresh my knowledge of the basics. Can you recommend some book that covers a wide range of essential topics?'

Depending on the topic I had discussed in the program and what the participant had asked, I usually did one (or both) of the following: recommend a few short books that, when put together, would cover a wide range of topics; or recommend a textbook, which as you are well aware usually contains between 600 and 900 pages and chapters no less than 20 pages long. Often, I would show the recommended references to the inquiring participant.

And that's when I started getting the two standard replies. If I recommended the few short books, the reply would be something like, 'Well, all these books look very interesting, but isn't there *one* book that tackles all these topics?' If I recommended the textbook, the reaction would be something like, 'Listen, I'm sure this book is very good, but I really have no time to read so many pages, or even half of them. Plus, you don't expect me to carry this book with me, do you? They'd charge for excess baggage at the airport!' (OK, I'm dramatizing a bit.) I can't really tell how many times I went through similar exchanges, but I do know that eventually there was a straw that broke the camel's back.

But wait, it wasn't then that I decided to write this book. In fact, it was then that I decided to do something that would take a lot less of my time: I decided to look for a book I could recommend to all these people. I made a mental list of the characteristics that were in high demand and started my search. And, to my surprise, such a book didn't exist. Or maybe I didn't find it. Either way, it was then, and only then, that I thought I had to write this book.

Distinctive features

The stylized story above happened many times, give or take a few details, in many executive programs. It also happened many times while teaching in MBA and executive MBA programs. And it happened often while talking with former students who needed to refresh or broaden their knowledge of finance. After failing in my search for a book to recommend, and starting to think that maybe I should write the book myself, I thought long and hard about the characteristics of the book the market had, in my opinion, failed to deliver. This was, more or less, my list:

- *The book needs to be comprehensive.* It doesn't have to address a few issues in depth; rather, it should cover a wide variety of topics, concepts, and tools that professionals forget, find hard to understand, and need or would like to know more about.

- *The book needs to be easy to read.* Professionals are put off by academic books written in academic style. There is a need for a book written in a way that sounds pretty much like having an instructor talking right in front of them.

- *The book needs to be relatively short.* Not an 800-page, 5-pound book, but one that could be easily taken around from the office to home, and from the hotel to the airport. Something that could be always at hand, like a desktop companion.

- *The book needs to have relatively short chapters.* Most professionals dislike starting a chapter and not being able to finish it after two or three sittings. There is a need for a book with short chapters that can be read in one sitting. Short chapters would also make it easy for readers to quickly grasp the essentials of a concept or tool.

- *The book needs to contain some elementary theory and many real-world examples.* It's a lot easier to understand and remember concepts and tools when an elementary conceptual framework and its application are discussed together. And if the application is not hypothetical but about an actual situation the reader can quickly identify with, even better.

- *The book needs to explain how to implement things in Microsoft® Excel.* Spreadsheets have become an inseparable tool for finance, and the book needs to show how to implement in Excel all the concepts and tools discussed.

- *The book needs to have a few short problems at the end of each chapter.* Many books have them, to be sure, but this book would have just two or three that go to the heart of the issues discussed in the chapter.

- *The book needs to be self-contained.* Other than some elementary math, no other previous knowledge should be required.

Well, that's a long list! But I promised myself that I wouldn't start writing a book before making sure I could deliver one that had *all* of the characteristics above. I trust the book you have in your hands does. So, if I had to define this book in one paragraph, it would be this:

Many professionals have long forgotten some key financial concepts or tools; others never learned them properly; some need to broaden the scope of their financial knowledge; others need a desktop companion for quick reference; and most of them have neither the time nor the motivation to dig into either several books or an 800-page textbook. This book solves all these problems in 30 short, easy-to-read, very practical chapters full of real-world examples and applications in Excel.

Target audience and intended use

Let me tell you first what this book is *not*. First, it is not a textbook; I didn't write it as a required reference for a specific course. Second, it is not a specialized book; it's not for those who want to acquire a deep knowledge of one or two topics. And third, it is not a cookbook; I didn't write it for those who want to blindly follow a few steps to solve a problem without understanding what's going on. If you're looking for a book to satisfy any of these needs, you've picked the wrong one.

The distinctive features of this book outlined above should give you an idea of who this book is for. Again, it was born as an answer to the demand of professionals who wanted to broaden their knowledge of finance; refresh their memory of some topics; learn other topics from scratch; or simply have a light desktop companion covering a wide range of essential topics in finance. And all that subject to the constraints of limited time and lack of patience to read an academic textbook.

I firmly believe that executives, professionals, and practitioners in different areas unrelated to finance will find this book useful. Their need to understand financial concepts and tools at the user level was constantly in my mind as I wrote this book. I also firmly believe that finance professionals such as investment bankers, portfolio managers, brokers and security analysts will find this book valuable. Their need for a reference book to quickly get up to speed on many different issues was also in my mind. In this regard, participants of executive education programs, and MBA and executive MBA students and former students, all of them in both finance and non-finance jobs, provided invaluable feedback.

I also trust the individual investor will find this book valuable. It provides the tools to value assets, assess risk, diversify and optimize portfolios, evaluate performance, and invest for retirement, to name just a few issues interesting to investors and covered in the book. And it discusses these and many other issues from scratch, showing how to implement everything in Excel.

Finally, I think that academics in finance and economics will find this book useful. It could be used as a complementary or recommended reference in many general courses such as corporate finance or investments; or in more specific courses dealing with asset pricing, stocks, bonds, and portfolio analysis, among other topics. I also think academics themselves will find the book useful as a personal desktop companion, a reference book to consult on a wide range of finance topics.

Organization of the book

The book is divided into four parts. The first, entitled 'Risk and return,' covers a wide range of issues that deal with different definitions of returns, different ways of assessing risk, different ways to put risk and return together, and the optimization of portfolios.

The second part, entitled 'Valuation,' focuses on stocks and bonds. It covers different models of stock valuation, including several versions of the DCF model, reverse valuation, and relative valuation. It also covers issues related to fixed-income securities, including pricing, sources of risk, duration, and convexity.

The third part, entitled 'Other important topics,' puts together several issues that no book of finance essentials could ignore. These include project evaluation through NPV, IRR, and real options, as well as derivatives such as options, futures, and forwards.

Finally, the fourth part, entitled 'Statistical background,' contains a refresher of essential statistical topics for practitioners, including summary statistics, the calculation of probabilities with the normal and lognormal distributions, and regression analysis. The discussion includes the implementation of all these concepts and tools in Excel.

How to read this book

I wrote the book thinking of professionals who needed to jump in for a specific issue. As a result, I wrote the chapters as independent of each other as possible. This means that this is not a book that you need to start reading at Chapter 1 and finish at Chapter 30. Some readers will not need to read the statistical background and others will find it essential reading. Some readers will be interested in stocks and others in bonds. Others may want to focus on issues related to investing or corporate finance.

Every chapter concludes with an Excel section and a Challenge section. The Excel sections aim to show how to implement in Excel the concepts and tools discussed in the chapter. These sections range from discussing some elementary functions, such as logs and exponentials, to more complex implementations, such as multiple regression analysis and portfolio optimization programs. If you're not fully familiar with Excel, I think you will find these sections essential. And if you are familiar with Excel, these sections will probably take you a few steps further.

The Challenge sections aim to test the essential concepts and tools discussed in each chapter. The problems are few, short, and go straight to the key points. Most of them are based on data from well-known companies so that you can not only test what you've learned but also learn a bit about the companies too. Some people may find these sections useful and others will probably ignore them. It's your choice.

Finally, if you want to reproduce precisely all the calculations discussed in the book, it is important that you use the data in the accompanying Excel file (see www.pearsoned.co.uk/estrada). I have performed all calculations in Excel, which 'remembers' many more decimals than would be wise to report in a book. That's why you may find 'rounding errors,' particularly in calculations based on previous calculations. Similarly, if you go over the problems in the Challenge sections, you may want to use the data in the accompanying Excel file rather than that provided in the tables and exhibits.

Take a good look at the index and a quick look at the rest of the book. I trust you will find the scope comprehensive, the chapters short, the style engaging, the approach practical, and the discussions easy to follow. You will also find loads of information on many companies that are household names, which are used throughout to keep your feet firmly on the ground.

Acknowledgments

My deepest gratitude goes to the long list of participants in executive education programs, MBA students, executive MBA students, and former students who directly or indirectly encouraged me to write this book. Most of them did not actually ask me to write a book; but their search for a book that the market had not provided was the main reason for writing this one.

I'm also indebted to my research assistant, Alfred Prada, who read every chapter, checked every formula, double checked every table, and triple checked every calculation. He put up with all my demands, which were not few, and delivered every time he had to. Needless to say, he is in no way responsible for any errors that may remain in this book. Those are, of course, my sole responsibility.

Finally, I want to dedicate this book to my dad, who was alive when I started writing it but did not live to see me finish it. I know he would have been even prouder than I am for having written this, my first book. I'm sure he would have read it just because I wrote it, and I'm sure he would have told me that *even he* could understand what I was writing about. And of course, I also dedicate this book to my mom, who will most likely not read it, but will proudly and insistently show it to every single person that passes by within a mile of her house.

A final word

Time will tell whether I have delivered the book that so many people seem to have been looking for. I certainly hope so. And yet I'm also sure it can be improved. For this reason, if you have any comments or suggestions, feel absolutely free to send me an email at *jestrada@iese.edu*. I would be more than glad to know your opinion.

This concludes what for me has been a long journey. And as much as I wanted to finish, I now realize that I'll miss working on this book. It was, above all, a whole lot of fun. I certainly hope you enjoy reading it as much as I enjoyed writing it.

Barcelona, March 2005

part I:

RISK AND RETURN

1

RETURNS I: BASIC CONCEPTS

Simple returns

Compounding

Continuously compounded returns

Multiperiod simple and continuously compounded returns

The big picture

Excel section

Challenge section

We will start easy, with a few concepts, definitions, and notation we use throughout the book. We will define and discuss simple returns and its components, compounding, continuously compounded returns, and multiperiod returns. This is just a warm-up.

Simple returns

Table 1.1 shows the stock price (p) of Coca-Cola at the end of the years 1994 to 2003, and the annual dividend per share (D) paid by the company (both adjusted by stock splits). Suppose we had bought a share of Coca-Cola at the end of 2002 and had sold it at the end of 2003. What would have been our one-year return?

TABLE 1.1

Year	p ($)	D ($)	R (%)	r (%)
1994	25.75	0.39		
1995	37.12	0.44	45.9	37.8
1996	52.63	0.50	43.1	35.9
1997	66.69	0.56	27.8	24.5
1998	67.00	0.60	1.4	1.4
1999	58.25	0.64	−12.1	−12.9
2000	60.94	0.72	5.9	5.7
2001	47.15	0.72	−21.4	−24.1
2002	43.84	0.80	−5.3	−5.5
2003	50.75	0.88	17.8	16.4

That's easy. We bought at $43.84, sold at $50.75, and received a dividend of $0.88 along the way. Hence, our return would have been

$$\frac{(\$50.75 - \$43.84) + \$0.88}{\$43.84} = 17.8\%$$

More generally, the **simple return (R)** from holding a share of stock over any given period is given by

$$R = \frac{(p_E - p_B) + D}{p_B} \qquad (1.1)$$

where p_B and p_E denote the stock price at the beginning and at the end of the period, respectively, and D denotes the dividend per share received during the period. The fourth column of Table 1.1 shows annual returns for Coca-Cola between 1995 and 2003 calculated this way.

Note that simple returns have two components: (1) a **capital gain or loss** given by the change in price during the period, relative to the price paid for the share; that is, $(p_E - p_B)/p_B$; and (2), a **dividend yield** given by the dividend per share received during the period, again relative to the price paid for the share, that is, D/p_B.

Note, finally, that simple returns can go by other names such as **arithmetic returns** or **holding-period returns**. All three are different names for the same concept and we will use them interchangeably throughout the book.

Compounding

Let's now go to the bank. Suppose that we see an ad in the local bank that offers an annual rate of 10%. This means that, if we deposit $100 today, one year later we will withdraw $110, that is, $100 \cdot (1 + 0.10) = 110. Simple enough.

Now let's go across the street. The other local bank has a similar ad offering an annual rate of 10% but offers *semiannual compounding*. This is just a fancy way of saying that the bank will pay half of the rate offered half way into the year, and the other half at the end of the year. Will we then obtain $10 in interest and end up the year with $110? Not really. We will end up with more than that. Let's see why.

If the bank pays 5% half way into the year, we will receive $5 then. *But left in the bank those $5 of interest will earn interest during the second half of the year.* Hence, the 5% the bank will pay us in interest for the second half of the year will not be calculated over our initial $100 but over the $105 outstanding at the beginning of the second half. Therefore, at the end of the second half we will receive $105 \cdot (0.05) = 5.25 in interest, which amounts to a total interest of $10.25 for the year, and a $110.25 withdrawal at the end of the year.

Let's suppose now that the bank in the corner also offers a 10% annual rate but with *quarterly compounding*. If we deposit $100 in this bank, how much money will we withdraw one year down the road? The answer is $110.3813, and you shouldn't find it difficult at this point to figure out why.

This bank pays a quarter of the 10% annual interest at the end of the first quarter ($2.5), which means that coming into the second quarter our interest would be calculated on $102.5. Hence, at the end of the second quarter we would be paid an additional $102.50 \cdot (0.025) = \$2.5625$. Following the same line of reasoning, it is not difficult to establish that we would be paid $2.6266 at the end of the third quarter, and $2.6922 at the end of the fourth quarter, for a total of $10.3813 in interest for the whole year. The $110.3813 we will withdraw at the end of the year follows directly.

One final bank? Alright, but you fill in the blanks. What if the bank down the street offers an annual rate of 10% with *monthly compounding*. You should have no difficulty at this point to calculate that, if we were to deposit $100 today, we would withdraw from this bank $110.4713 one year down the road.

Now, let's put all these numbers together in Table 1.2 and see what we make out of them. The first column simply shows that we are considering the same initial deposit (W_0) in all four banks, and the second that all four banks offer the same 10% interest rate. (We'll clarify the notation shortly.) The third column shows the compounding period (CP), which is different in each of the four banks. And the fourth column shows the amount of money we will withdraw one year down the road (W_1) from each of the four banks. (We'll get to the last column shortly.)

TABLE 1.2

W_0 ($)	I (%)	CP	W_1 ($)	EI (%)
100	10	Annual	110.0000	10.00
100	10	Semiannual	110.2500	10.25
100	10	Quarterly	110.3813	10.38
100	10	Monthly	110.4713	10.47

Note that if we compare our initial deposit with our final withdrawal, in all banks but the first we get *more* than a 10% return. Also, note that the more frequent the compounding, the more money we get at the end of the year. The 10% interest rate paid by all banks is usually called the **nominal interest rate** (I); the rate we actually get when we compare our deposit with our withdrawal is usually called the **effective interest rate** (EI).

The relationship between these two rates is given by

$$EI = \left(1 + \frac{I}{N}\right)^N - 1 \tag{1.2}$$

where N is the number of compounding periods per year (one in the first bank, two in the second, four in the third, and twelve in the fourth). The numbers in the last column show the effective interest rate obtained in each bank calculated with equation (1.2), which, again, can be thought of as the return we actually get if we compare our deposit with our withdrawal.

Note, also, that we can calculate all the numbers in the fourth column (that is, the amount of money we withdraw from each bank) by using either the nominal interest rate or the effective interest rate. That is,

$$W_1 = W_0 \cdot \left(1 + \frac{I}{N}\right)^N = W_0 \cdot (1 + EI) \tag{1.3}$$

One final thing: how would you calculate for each of the four banks above the amount of money we would withdraw in two years? What about in three years? What about, more generally, in T years? Very easy. Let W_T be the withdrawal in T years, then

$$W_T = W_0 \cdot \left(1 + \frac{I}{N}\right)^{T \cdot N} \tag{1.4}$$

And what is the effective interest rate we get when comparing our deposit with our withdrawal after T years (EI_T)? Again, fairly easy. It is

$$EI_T = \left(1 + \frac{I}{N}\right)^{T \cdot N} - 1 \tag{1.5}$$

Just to make sure you're on top of all these definitions and how they relate to each other, make sure you work out problem 2 in the Challenge section at the end of the chapter.

Continuously compounded returns

If you followed all the calculations above, you have no doubt noticed that the more frequently interest is paid, the more money we withdraw at the end of the year. Does this mean that if money compounds frequently enough we will be able to withdraw an 'infinite' amount of money one year down the road? Unfortunately not.

No matter how frequently our money compounds, we will never withdraw more than \$110.5171. If you're curious, this is because as N approaches infinity, the expression $(1 + I/N)^N$ approaches e^I, where $e = 2.71828$. If you're not curious, then you can simply take notice of the fact that, when money compounds continuously, the amount of money we will withdraw one year, and, more generally, T years down the road, is respectively given by

$$W_1 = W_0 \cdot e^I \tag{1.6}$$

and

$$W_T = W_0 \cdot e^{T \cdot I} \tag{1.7}$$

and the effective interest rates we will get are respectively given by

$$EI = e^I - 1 \tag{1.8}$$

and

$$EI_T = e^{T \cdot I} - 1 \tag{1.9}$$

Let's now go back to Coca-Cola and the 17.8% *simple* return we could have obtained by holding this stock during 2003. Notice that we could have turned \$43.84 into \$51.63 (the closing price plus the dividend) if our money had continuously compounded at 16.36%, that is, $\$43.84 \cdot (e^{0.1636}) = \$51.63$. In other words, we can measure the change in wealth from one period to the next either by using simple returns or by using **continuously compounded returns (r)**. The relationship between these two types of returns is given by the following expressions:

$$r = \ln(1 + R) \tag{1.10}$$

and

$$R = e^r - 1 \tag{1.11}$$

where 'ln' denotes a natural logarithm. These two expressions provide a way to calculate the continuously compounded return of any investment if we know its simple return, and the simple return if we know its continuously compounded return.

In the case of Coca-Cola over the year 2003, if we knew that Coca-Cola delivered a 17.8% simple return, we can immediately infer that it also delivered a $\ln(1 + 0.178) = 16.4\%$ continuously compounded return. Alternatively, if we knew that Coca-Cola delivered a 16.4% continuously compounded return, we can immediately calculate that it also delivered an $e^{0.164} - 1 = 17.8\%$ simple return.

Think of simple returns and continuously compounded returns simply as two different types of returns. You may think that simple returns are enough for most investors' purposes, and that is true. Investors do care about the amount of money they start with and the amount of money they end up with, and that is straightforwardly measured by the simple return. Continuously compounded returns, however, are also important and widely used in finance and we'll return to them later in the book.

For the time being, let's briefly mention here three more things. First, note that the smaller the change in wealth, the smaller the difference between these two types of returns. This is due to the fact that, for any small x, it is the case that $\ln(1 + x) \oplus x$. That is relevant to our discussion because, for small changes in wealth, it is the case that $r = \ln(1 + R) \oplus R$. (See problem 3 in the Challenge section at the end of the chapter.) Conversely, for large changes in wealth, the difference between these two types of returns can be large. (In this context, think of 'small' changes and 'large' changes as those under and over 25–30%, respectively.)

Second, continuously compounded returns also go by the name of **logarithmic returns**. Both are different names for the same concept and we will use them interchangeably throughout the book. And third (and important), if throughout the book we refer to 'returns' without specifying whether they are simple or continuously compounded, we'll be referring to *simple* returns.

Multiperiod simple and continuously compounded returns

One more thing and we'll finish this warm-up. Many times, we won't be interested only in a one-period investment but in an investment over several periods. In this case it is important to keep in mind that although we calculate multiperiod simple returns by *multiplying* simple (one-period) returns, we calculate multiperiod continuously compounded returns by *adding* continuously compounded (one-period) returns. Formally, multiperiod returns over a T-year period are given by

$$R(T) = (1 + R_1) \cdot (1 + R_2) \cdot \ldots \cdot (1 + R_T) - 1 \qquad (1.12)$$

and

$$r(T) = r_1 + r_2 + \ldots + r_T \qquad (1.13)$$

where $R(T)$ and $r(T)$ represent **multiperiod simple returns** and **multiperiod continuously compounded returns**, respectively.

Going back to our previous example, if we had invested $100 in Coca-Cola at the end of 1994 (and we had reinvested all the dividends received), how much money would we have had at the end of 2003? One way of calculating this is by using the multiperiod simple return; that is,

$$R(9) = (1 + 0.459) \cdot (1 + 0.431) \cdot \ldots \cdot (1 + 0.178) - 1 = 120.4\%$$
$$\Rightarrow \$100 \cdot (1 + 1.204) = \$220.4$$

Another way to arrive at the same number is by using the multiperiod continuously compounded return; that is,

$$r(9) = 0.378 + 0.359 + \ldots + 0.164 = 79.0\%$$
$$\Rightarrow \$100 \cdot (e^{0.790}) = \$220.4$$

Finally, note that the same relationship we've seen above between annual simple returns and annual continuously compounded returns also applies to multiperiod returns. That is, $r(9) = \ln\{1 + R(9)\} = \ln\{1 + 1.204\} = 79.0\%$ and $R(9) = e^{r(9)} - 1 = e^{0.790} - 1 = 120.4\%$.

The big picture

Just in case this distinction between simple returns and continuously compounded returns sounds a bit confusing, let's stress again a couple of things we mentioned before. First, think of simple returns and continuously compounded returns simply as two different types (definitions) of returns. Second, investors are largely interested in simple returns. And third, continuously compounded returns play an important role in the background of many financial calculations.

In plain English this means that, for most practical purposes, we will still focus on simple returns. That, in turn, means that we'll keep on calculating annual and multiperiod changes in wealth by using simple returns. As investors, we are usually not interested in the continuously compounded returns generated by a stock, which we calculated above with the sole purpose of making clear the relationship between this type of returns and simple returns.

In short, for investment purposes stick to simple returns, but remember that there is another definition of returns that plays an important role in the background of many financial calculations.

Excel section

There is little mystery here; the magnitudes discussed in this chapter can be calculated in Excel by applying their definitions straightforwardly. For example, you can compute both simple and continuously compounded returns by using equations (1.1) and (1.10), respectively. Having said that, you may want to take into account the following:

- To get the e number in Excel you need to use the 'exp' function. For example, if you type '=**exp(1)**' and hit 'Enter,' you will obtain the value of the e number; that is, 2.71828. In the same fashion, by typing '=**exp(x)**' and hitting 'Enter,' you can find the value of e raised to any number x.

- To get a natural logarithm in Excel you need to use the 'ln' function. For example, if you type '=**ln(1)**' and hit 'Enter,' you will obtain 0. In the same fashion, by typing '=**ln(x)**' and hitting 'Enter,' you can find the natural log of any number x.

Challenge section

1 Given the stock price of General Electric (GE) at the end of the years 1994–2003, and the annual dividend per share paid during those years (both adjusted by stock splits) shown in Table 1.3, fill the blanks of the fourth column by computing GE's annual simple returns.

▶

TABLE 1.3

Year	p ($)	D ($)	R (%)	r (%)
1994	8.50	0.25		
1995	12.00	0.27		
1996	16.48	0.31		
1997	24.46	0.35		
1998	34.00	0.40		
1999	51.58	0.47		
2000	47.94	0.55		
2001	40.08	0.64		
2002	24.35	0.72		
2003	30.98	0.76		

2 Given an initial deposit of $100 and the data in Table 1.4, which shows the nominal interest rate and the compounding period offered by five banks, fill in the blanks of the third and the fifth columns by computing your withdrawal from each bank one year and five years down the road. Then fill in the blanks in the fourth and sixth columns by computing the effective interest rate you would get from each bank after one year and five years.

TABLE 1.4

I (%)	CP	W_1 ($)	EI (%)	W_5 ($)	EI_5 (%)
15	Annual				
15	Semiannual				
15	Quarterly				
15	Monthly				
15	Continuous				

3 Go back to Table 1.3 and fill in the blanks of the fifth column by computing GE's annual continuously compounded returns. Then think: in which years is the difference between simple and continuously compounded returns large? In which years is it small? What do you make of this comparison?

4 Go back again to Table 1.3 and assume you invested $100 in GE at the end of 1994 (and reinvested all the dividends received). How much money would you have had at the end of 2003? What would have been your nine-year holding period return? What about your nine-year continuously compounded return?

2

RETURNS II: MEAN RETURNS

Arithmetic mean returns

An example: Russia, 1995–98

Geometric mean returns

Another example: Exxon Mobil *v.* Intel

The dollar-weighted return

The big picture

Excel section

Challenge section

I n the previous chapter we discussed, among other things, how to compute returns on a period-by-period basis. Now, if you think about it, staring at several years of monthly returns of any asset, or even looking at a chart of those returns, is not of much help. Most of the time, we need to *summarize* information about risk and return. In this chapter, we will discuss two ways to summarize returns and the relationship between the two.

Arithmetic mean returns

Go back momentarily to Table 1.1 and the annual returns of Coca-Cola between 1995 and 2003. As you can see in the table, those returns fluctuated significantly over time from a high of 45.9% in 1995 to a low of –21.4% in 2001. Can we somehow aggregate all these returns into one number that summarizes the return performance of Coca-Cola stock during the 1995–2003 period? You bet.

A straightforward way to summarize return performance is to simply average the relevant returns; that is, to add them all up and then to divide the sum by the number of returns. In general, the **arithmetic mean return (AM)** of any series of returns is given by

$$AM = \frac{R_1 + R_2 + \ldots + R_T}{T} \tag{2.1}$$

where R denotes returns and T the number of returns. In our case, the arithmetic mean return of Coca-Cola during the 1995–2003 period is

$$\frac{0.459 + 0.431 + \ldots + 0.178}{9} = 11.4\%.$$

Although some issues related to the interpretation of this magnitude are a bit tricky, this much we can safely say. First, we can think of the 11.4% mean return in the same straightforward way we usually think of any other average. Second, under some conditions (basically, a symmetric distribution of returns), the arithmetic mean yields the most likely return to occur one period forward. And third, this magnitude does *not* properly describe the rate at which capital invested evolved over time.

As an illustration of this last point, consider the following example. Suppose we invest $100 for two years in a stock that returns –50% over the first year and 50% over the second year. What is the arithmetic mean return of this stock over this two-year period? That's easy, it's (−0.50+0.50)/2 = 0%. But do we have after two years the same $100 we started with as the 0% mean return seems to indicate? Not really.

Note that at the end of the first year, after losing 50% of our capital, our initial $100 have been reduced to $50. And after a 50% return over the second year we end up the two-year period with $75. So by investing in this stock with an arithmetic mean return of 0% we lost 25% of our money! What is going on? Simply that, as mentioned above, the arithmetic mean return does not properly describe the rate at which capital invested evolves over time.

A bit confused? That's alright, just read on.

An example: Russia, 1995–98

Consider the end-of-year values and implied returns of the Morgan Stanley index for the Russian market (in dollars and accounting for both capital gains and dividends) between 1994 and 1998 displayed in Table 2.1.

TABLE 2.1

Year	Index	Return (%)
1994	100.00	
1995	72.91	−27.1
1996	184.40	152.9
1997	391.16	112.1
1998	66.53	−83.0

Suppose that in an article in the financial press I argue that, 'between 1995 and 1998 the Russian stock market delivered a 38.7% mean annual return.' A reader could not be blamed for thinking that, had he invested $100 at the beginning of 1995, he would have $370.5 at the end of 1998, that is, $100 · (1 + 0.387)^4 = 370.5. If asked to defend my answer, I could readily provide the four annual returns for the years 1995–98 and the calculation of the mean return.

Now suppose that in another article I argue that, 'between 1995 and 1998 the Russian stock market delivered a *negative* 9.7% mean annual return.' A reader of this article could not be blamed for thinking that, had he invested $100 at the beginning of 1995, he would have $66.5 at the end of 1998, that is, $100 · (1 − 0.097)^4 = 66.5. And again, if asked to defend my answer, I could readily provide the four annual returns for the years 1995 to 1998 and the calculation of the mean return.

What's going on here? How can I truthfully argue, at the same time, that between 1995 and 1998 the Russian stock market delivered a positive 38.7% and a negative 9.7% mean annual return? Very simple: the first number is the *arithmetic* mean return, and the second number is the *geometric* mean return.

The first one, the arithmetic mean return, we know by now how to calculate: add up the four annual returns and divide the sum by 4 to obtain the 38.7% mean return mentioned above. Does that number properly describe how capital invested in the Russian market evolved between 1995 and 1998? Not really.

By way of proof, consider an initial investment of $100 and the four annual returns between 1995 and 1998, and then compute the multiperiod (1995–98) return. You should have no difficulty at this point calculating that, after four years, an initial investment of $100 would have been reduced to $66.5. That is a far cry from the $370.5 that the 38.7% arithmetic mean return over this period seems to imply. In other words, as anticipated above, the arithmetic mean return does *not* properly describe how wealth evolves over time.

Geometric mean returns

This is a good time to introduce a different way of computing mean returns. The **geometric mean return (GM)** of any series of returns is given by

$$GM = \{(1 + R_1) \cdot (1 + R_2) \cdot \ldots \cdot (1 + R_T)\}^{1/T} - 1 = \{\Pi_t (1 + R_t)\}^{1/T} - 1 \tag{2.2}$$

where the symbol 'Π' indicates 'the product of' the quantities that follow it. Alternatively, there is an equivalent (and easier) way to compute a geometric mean return, and it is by using the expression

$$GM = (p_T/p_1)^{1/T} - 1 \tag{2.3}$$

where p_T is the terminal price (or terminal value of the index, or terminal capital) and p_1 is the initial price (or initial value of the index, or initial capital invested). Equations (2.2) and (2.3) are mathematically equivalent and yield the exact same results. (However, be careful when using (2.3) with dividend-paying stocks: if the prices are not adjusted by the dividends paid, we would underestimate the mean return. Most data providers do offer 'total return' indices, which adjust prices by taking into account dividends.)

Now for the interpretation of this geometric mean. Let's first go back to our hypothetical stock that returned –50% in the first period and 50% in the second. Recall that, although the arithmetic mean return of this stock over the two periods considered was 0%, we had actually lost 25% of the $100 investment and ended the two-year period with $75. Let's now calculate the geometric mean return of this stock. According to equations (2.2) and (2.3) it is given by

$$\{(1 - 0.50) \cdot (1 + 0.50)\}^{1/2} - 1 = \{\$75/\$100\}^{1/2} - 1 = -13.4\%$$

One way of interpreting the –13.4% is as follows. If we had invested in this stock over the two years considered, we would have lost capital at the *compounded* annual rate of 13.4%. That is just a fancy way of saying that we would have lost 13.4% *on top of* 13.4%. Furthermore, note that $\$100 \cdot (1 - 0.134)^2 = \$75$. In other words, the geometric mean return does appropriately describe what happened to the capital we invested over the two-year period considered: we started with $100, lost money over two years at a compounded annual rate of 13.4%, and ended up with $75.

Just to drive this point home, let's go back to the Russian market during the years 1995 to 1998. The geometric mean return during this period is given by

$$\{(1 - 0.271) \cdot (1 + 1.529) \cdot (1 + 1.121) \cdot (1 - 0.830)\}^{1/4} - 1 = \\ \{66.53/100.00\}^{1/4} - 1 = -9.7\%$$

In other words: if we had invested money in the Russian market during the years 1995 to 1998, we would have lost money at the compounded annual rate of 9.7%. Had that been the case, our initial $100 would have turned into $100 · $(1 - 0.097)^4 = \$66.5$.

Note, finally, that a geometric mean return also goes by the name of **mean compound return**. Both are different names for the same concept and we will use them interchangeably throughout the book.

Another example: Exxon Mobil v. Intel

Let's now briefly discuss the relationship between arithmetic and geometric mean returns. Consider the returns generated by Exxon Mobil and Intel between the years 1994 and 2003 displayed in Table 2.2. Note that the difference between the arithmetic and the geometric mean return for Intel (over

TABLE 2.2

Year	Exxon (%)	Intel (%)
1994	0.9	3.4
1995	38.4	78.2
1996	26.3	131.3
1997	28.4	7.4
1998	22.4	69.0
1999	12.6	39.1
2000	10.2	−26.9
2001	−7.6	4.9
2002	−8.9	−50.3
2003	20.6	106.6
AM	14.3%	36.3%
GM	13.3%	23.8%

12 percentage points) is far larger than that for Exxon (1 percentage point). What are the factors that determine the difference, for any given asset, between the arithmetic mean and the geometric mean? The answer is simple: volatility.

Although we have not yet formally defined this concept (we will do so in the next chapter), for the moment think of volatility as variability or uncertainty. Look at Intel first. As you can see, this stock delivered very large (positive and negative) returns. This huge variability in returns obviously makes investors very uncertain about future returns. Exxon returns, by contrast, fluctuated much less. Hence, the difference between the arithmetic and the geometric mean return is much larger for Intel than for Exxon.

One final thing: note that, in all the examples we have discussed so far, for any given series of returns, its arithmetic mean was larger than its geometric mean. This is no coincidence; it is always the case. To be more precise, the arithmetic mean is always larger than or equal to the geometric mean. In fact, only in the hypothetical case in which the return series does not fluctuate at all would these two magnitudes be equal.

The dollar-weighted return

Now that hopefully you're at ease with the two different ways of calculating mean returns, let's introduce a *third* one! Yes, another one, and here's why. One thing is the return delivered *by an asset*, and another is the return obtained *by an investor* in that asset. These two returns can be different, and this is the issue we'll briefly explore in this section. (To understand what follows, you need to be familiar with the concepts of present value and internal rate of return. If you're not, you may want to take a look at these concepts in Chapter 21.)

You know by now how to assess the mean return of an asset. If our focus is on the past performance of the asset, and on how capital invested in it evolved over time, then we assess its performance with the geometric mean return. This is fine for a passive (buy-and-hold) strategy in which we make an investment and let it ride (without buying and selling any more shares, and reinvesting the dividends if any) until we cash out. In this case, the mean return of the asset and the mean return of our investment on the asset will be the same.

But the story changes if we buy or sell shares in the asset over time. Consider the simple example in Table 2.3. At the end of year 0 a stock is trading at $5 a share, one year later it goes up to $10 (for a 100% return), and in year 2 it goes back down to $5 (for a –50% return). The arithmetic and geometric mean return of this stock over this two-year period are 25% and 0%, respectively.

TABLE 2.3

| | Price | Return | | Passive strategy | | | Active strategy | |
| | | | | CF | Wealth | | CF | Wealth |
Year	($)	(%)	Shares	($)	($)	Shares	($)	($)
0	5		+100	−500	500	+100	−500	500
1	10	100.0	0	0	1,000	+100	−1,000	2,000
2	5	−50.0	−100	500	500	−200	1,000	1,000
AM		25.0%						
GM		0.0%						
DWR				0.0%			−26.8%	

Suppose we buy 100 shares of this stock at $5 a share at the end of year 0. At that point in time we'll have a negative cash flow (CF) of $500 and wealth of $500 invested in the stock. If we pursue a passive strategy and do nothing until the end of year 2 when we sell the 100 shares, we'll then receive a positive cash flow of $500, which is also our wealth (now in cash) at that point in time. The internal rate of return (IRR) of our cash flow, then, solves from the equation and

$$-\,\$500 + \frac{\$0}{(1 + IRR)} + \frac{\$500}{(1 + IRR)^2} = 0 \qquad (2.4)$$

is equal to 0%. Unsurprisingly, the internal rate of return of our investment is equal to the geometric mean return of the stock. This is the case because we simply bought some shares in the stock, passively let the investment ride, and cashed out two years later.

Let's introduce a definition and generalize this result. The **dollar-weighted return (DWR)** is the discount rate that sets the present value of a series of cash flows equal to 0, that is,

$$CF_0 + \frac{CF_1}{(1 + DWR)} + \frac{CF_2}{(1 + DWR)^2} + \ldots + \frac{CF_T}{(1 + DWR)^T} = 0 \qquad (2.5)$$

where CF_t denotes the cash flow in period t, and T is the number of periods we have invested in the asset. Note that, by definition, *the dollar-weighted return is the internal rate of return of our investment*. Note, also, that the dollar-weighted return of a passive strategy will always be equal to the geometric mean return of the investment.

If we always followed passive strategies, there would be no need to introduce the concept of dollar-weighted returns; the geometric mean return of an asset return would appropriately describe our mean return. But, of course, we actively buy and sell assets many times, and it is then that the concept of dollar-weighted return becomes important. To see this point, consider the last three columns of Table 2.3.

We now pursue an active strategy in which we make an initial investment of 100 shares at $5 a share at the end of year 0 (just like before), but now we buy another 100 shares (at $10) at the end of year 1 (at which time we'll have a negative cash flow of $1,000 and wealth invested in the asset of $2,000). Then, at the end of the second year, we sell our 200 shares at $5 and pocket $1,000. The geometric mean return of the asset has obviously not changed; it remains at 0%. But what about *our* return in this asset?

The dollar-weighted return of our active strategy solves from the equation

$$-\,\$500 - \frac{\$1,000}{(1 + DWR)} + \frac{\$1,000}{(1 + DWR)^2} = 0 \qquad (2.6)$$

and is equal to −26.8%. That's quite a difference from 0%! But it is the dollar-weighted return that appropriately captures *our* return. Note that the key difference from the passive strategy is that now we add 100 shares at a 'bad' time, that is, at the end of year 1 when the stock price is 50% higher than it is at the time we finally cash out.

Just to make sure you're on top of this important concept, let's go over one more example, but this time not hypothetical as the stock in the previous exhibit. Table 2.4 shows the closing price of Sun Microsystems stock at the end of the years 1998 to 2003. During this time, Sun did not pay any dividends. A passive strategy of buying 100 shares of Sun at the end of 1998 at $10.70 a share, and then selling the 100 shares at the end of 2003 at $4.47 would have had a dollar-weighted return of −16%, equal to the geometric mean return of the stock. (Note that during this period Sun is another interesting case of positive arithmetic mean return and negative geometric mean return. See why many times it's pointless to talk about 'mean' returns?)

TABLE 2.4

			Passive strategy			Active strategy		
Year	Price ($)	Return (%)	Shares	CF ($)	Wealth ($)	Shares	CF ($)	Wealth ($)
1998	10.70		+100	−1,070	1,070	+100	−1,070	1,070
1999	38.72	261.9	0	0	3,872	+100	−3,872	7,744
2000	27.88	−28.0	0	0	2,788	0	0	5,576
2001	12.30	−55.9	0	0	1,230	0	0	2,460
2002	3.11	−74.7	0	0	311	0	0	622
2003	4.47	43.7	−100	447	447	−200	894	894
AM		29.4%						
GM		−16.0%						
DWR				−16.0%			−33.5%	

But what if instead of a passive strategy we had been a little more active? Suppose that, as the last three columns of Table 2.4 show, we had bought 100 shares at the end of 1998 (at $10.70 a share as before), and another 100 shares at the end of 1999 (at $38.72), to finally sell the 200 shares at the end of 2003 at $4.47. Note that, again, we'd be doing our second purchase at a 'bad' time when the stock price is high. And then, unsurprisingly, our dollar-weighted return (−33.5%) is lower than the stock's geometric mean return (which remains at −16%).

The big picture

The examples discussed in this chapter suggest that many times it doesn't make sense to speak simply of 'mean returns' without specifying whether we are referring to an arithmetic mean or to a geometric mean. This becomes particularly important when considering very volatile assets, such as emerging markets or internet stocks, because this is when the difference between arithmetic and geometric mean returns can be very large. The 'mean' performance of the Russian market between 1995 and 1998, or that of Sun between 1998 and 2003, made this point clear.

Until we get back to this issue in the next chapter, remember two things. First, for any given series of returns, the arithmetic mean return is always larger than the geometric mean return. And second, the higher the volatility of returns, the larger the difference between these two means.

It is also important to keep in mind that the return of an asset and the return an investor obtains from the asset may be different. When investors follow passive (buy-and-hold) strategies, both are properly described by the asset's geometric mean return. However, when investors pursue active strategies, the return obtained by investors is properly described by the dollar-weighted return.

Excel section

Calculating arithmetic and geometric mean returns in Excel is fairly simple and can be done in more than one way; here we'll address the easiest way. Suppose you have a series of ten returns in cells A1 through A10. Then, you do the following:

- To calculate the *arithmetic mean return*, simply type '=**average (A1:A10)**' in cell A11 and then hit 'Enter.'
- To calculate the *geometric mean return*, type '=**geomean(1+A1:A10)–1**' in cell A12. But note two important things. First, the 'geomean' command yields 1 plus the geometric mean return; hence, make sure you do subtract 1 as shown above. Second, we are using what in Excel is called an 'array.' This means that instead of typing an expression and hitting 'Enter' you must type the expression and hit 'Ctrl+Shift+Enter' *simultaneously*.

Excel also easily calculates internal rates of return. This calculation, as well as that of present values and net present values, are discussed in Chapter 21.

Challenge section

1 Given the annual returns of General Motors and Wal-Mart between 1994 and 2003 in Table 2.5, compute the arithmetic mean return and the geometric mean return of both stocks. For each stock, which one of these two means is larger? Is this finding specific to these two stocks or is it more general?

TABLE 2.5

Year	General Motors (%)	Wal-Mart (%)
1994	-22.00	-14.42
1995	28.68	5.56
1996	8.61	3.11
1997	19.21	74.72
1998	21.30	107.55
1999	25.74	70.45
2000	-27.84	-22.79
2001	-0.98	8.94
2002	-20.82	-11.76
2003	52.85	5.73

2 Suppose you had invested $100 in each of these two stocks (General Motors and Wal-Mart) at the end of 1993 and you had held the investment (and reinvested the dividends received) until the end of 2003. How much money would you have had in each stock at the end of this period?

3 Calculate the quantities $\$100 \cdot (1 + AM)^{10}$ and $\$100 \cdot (1 + GM)^{10}$ for General Motors, where AM and GM denote the arithmetic and the geometric mean returns, respectively. Which of these two magnitudes matches the terminal wealth you calculated in the previous question? Repeat the exercise for Wal-Mart. What do you make of the findings in this question?

4 Compute the absolute difference $(AM - GM)$ and the relative difference $(AM/GM - 1)$ between the arithmetic mean and the geometric mean of General Motors. Then do the same for Wal-Mart. In which stock are these differences larger? Why?

▶

5 Table 2.6 displays again the prices of Sun Microsystems at the end of the years 1998 to 2003. It also displays the share purchases of two active strategies. (Note that the second strategy just reverses the order of the purchases.) What is the dollar-weighted return of these two strategies? In which strategy is it higher? Why?

TABLE 2.6

Year	Price ($)	Return (%)	Active strategy 1			Active strategy 2		
			Shares	CF ($)	Wealth ($)	Shares	CF ($)	Wealth ($)
1998	10.70		50			800		
1999	38.72	261.9	100			400		
2000	27.88	−28.0	200			200		
2001	12.30	−55.9	400			100		
2002	3.11	−74.7	800			50		
2003	4.47	43.7	−1,550			−1,550		

3

RISK I: TOTAL RISK

What is risk?

Volatility of returns

The standard deviation of returns

Interpretations of the standard deviation

Mean returns and the standard deviation

The big picture

Excel section

Challenge section

So much for the 'good' stuff. In the previous chapter we focused on two ways of summarizing the return performance of an asset. Here comes the 'bad' stuff: in this chapter we'll focus on one way of summarizing an asset's risk. Keep this in mind, though: the concept of risk is hard to pin down, so we'll explore alternative definitions in forthcoming chapters.

What is risk?

Silly question? Well, not really. The fact is that, simple as it may sound, academics and practitioners in finance have been wrestling with this definition for many years. And it gets worse. Nobody seems to have provided an answer that everybody else agrees with. As is often heard, it may well be the case that risk, like beauty, is in the eyes of the beholder.

But don't throw up your arms in despair just yet. The fact that there is no universally accepted definition of risk doesn't mean that risk cannot be quantified in a variety of ways. Before we get into definitions and formulas, take a look at Exhibit 3.1, which depicts the indices for Exxon and Intel that generated the returns we discussed in the previous chapter. Just to make the comparison easier, the indices are normalized so that they both start at 100.

EXHIBIT 3.1
Intel v. Exxon, indices

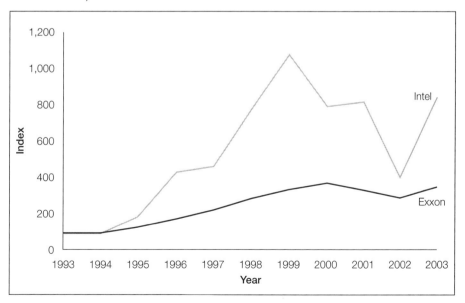

Although the concept of risk may be hard to pin down, your eyes probably won't fool you: while Exxon seems to have had a rather steady climb, Intel seems to have been on a roller coaster, with pronounced rises and falls. Just by looking at the picture, most reasonable people would agree that Intel seems to be riskier (that is, more volatile or more unpredictable) than Exxon.

Think about it this way: the more a price fluctuates over time, the greater the uncertainty about where that price may be at some point in time in the future. And the greater that uncertainty, the greater the risk. Does that make sense? If it does, then read on for a similar and complementary way of thinking about risk.

Volatility of returns

Instead of thinking about prices, as in Exhibit 3.1, we can think of risk in terms of returns. Exhibit 3.2 depicts the annual returns of Exxon and Intel during the 1994–2003 period. These are the same returns as those reported in Table 2.2.

EXHIBIT 3.2
Intel v. Exxon, returns

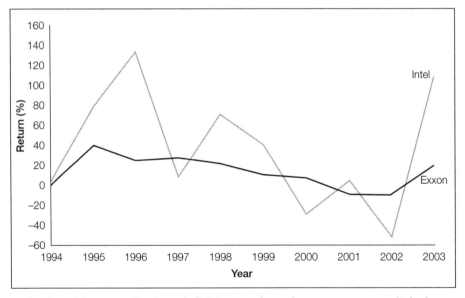

Again, without getting into definitions or formulas, your eyes won't fool you. At the same time that Exxon consistently delivered returns between, roughly, –10% and 40% (no small range, to be sure), Intel delivered far more volatile returns, with annual gains in excess of 130% and annual losses in excess of 50%.

By looking at Exhibit 3.2, most reasonable people would again conclude that Intel is riskier than Exxon.

The standard deviation of returns

Now it is time to formalize the concept of risk. Let's focus on Exhibit 3.2. As we just discussed, an obvious way of thinking about risk is in terms of volatility (or variability) in returns, which led us to conclude that Intel is riskier than Exxon.

One way to formally capture this volatility is to compute the **standard deviation of returns (SD)**, which is (hold on to your seat) the square root of the average quadratic deviation from the arithmetic mean return. If after reading that again it still sounds like Sylvester Stallone speaking Chinese, stop reading this chapter and go to the stats review in Chapter 27. Otherwise, keep reading for a bit of extra insight on this measure of risk.

The standard deviation of a series of returns is formally given by the expression

$$SD = \sqrt{(1/T) \cdot \sum_{t=1}^{T} (R_t - AM)^2} \tag{3.1}$$

where R represents returns, AM represents the (arithmetic) mean return of the series of returns, t indexes time, and T is the number of observations. (Note that sometimes the standard deviation is calculated by dividing the sum of quadratic deviations by $T-1$ instead of by T. For practical purposes, you don't really have to worry about this distinction.)

Let's take a quick look at the calculation of the standard deviation of returns of Intel. Table 3.1 shows the returns in the second column, the deviations from the mean return in the third, and the square of those numbers in the fourth. The average of the numbers in the fourth column is the *variance* of returns, but it is not widely used as a measure of risk. The number in the intersection between the last row and the last column, the square root of the average of quadratic deviations, is the standard deviation of returns, which in the case of Intel is 55.8%.

TABLE 3.1

Year	R (%)	R – AM (%)	(R – AM)²
1994	3.4	–32.9	0.1080
1995	78.2	41.9	0.1754
1996	131.3	95.0	0.9029
1997	7.4	–28.8	0.0831
1998	69.0	32.8	0.1073
1999	39.1	2.8	0.0008
2000	–26.9	–63.1	0.3986
2001	4.9	–31.4	0.0985
2002	–50.3	–86.6	0.7497
2003	106.6	70.3	0.4948
Average	**36.3%**		**0.3119**
Square root			**55.8%**

Of course, you don't have to go through all these calculations to estimate a standard deviation; Excel calculates this magnitude in the blink of an eye and in just one cell. But the table shows where the number that Excel calculates comes from.

Interpretations of the standard deviation

Let's focus now on the interpretation of the standard deviation as a measure of risk. The easiest way to think about it is as follows: the larger this number, the riskier the asset. This way of thinking of the standard deviation confirms our previous argument that Intel appears to be riskier than Exxon; the standard deviation of the former is 55.8% and of the latter only 15.0%. (You will be asked to calculate this last number in the Challenge section at the end of the chapter.)

Basically, a small standard deviation indicates that returns fluctuate 'closely' around the mean return, and a large standard deviation indicates the opposite. In other words, the larger the standard deviation, the more that returns tend to depart from the mean return.

Another way to think about the standard deviation is to recall that, under normality, 68.3% of the returns cluster one standard deviation around the mean. It is also the case that 95.4% and 99.7% of the returns cluster two and three standard deviations around the mean, respectively. (See Chapter 28 if you need to refresh your memory.) Keeping this in mind, think of two hypothetical stocks, both with a mean return of 20%, and standard deviations of 5% (stock 1) and 30% (stock 2).

Note that there is a 95% probability that the returns of stock 1 fluctuate between 10% and 30%, that is, two standard deviations around the mean. However, in the case of stock 2, returns will fluctuate, with a 95% probability, in the interval [–40%, 80%], a range so large as to be basically useless. We could drive a train sideways between these two numbers.

This simple example illustrates another way of thinking about the standard deviation: we can use it to estimate the interval within which returns will fluctuate with any chosen probability. The larger the interval, the larger the uncertainty, and the riskier the stock.

Going back to Exxon and Intel, our previous line of reasoning would suggest that there is a 95% probability that the returns of Exxon fluctuate between –15.6% and 44.3%, and those of Intel between –75.4% and 148.0%. Because the range between the lower and the higher ends of the interval in the case of Intel (over 220%) is far larger than that for Exxon (under 60%), we confirm the fact that Intel is riskier than Exxon. (Note, however, that the intervals calculated are valid under normality, which may be a questionable assumption in this context.)

Mean returns and the standard deviation

We intuitively know that risk is 'bad,' and the discussion in the previous section attempts to explain why the standard deviation may be a good measure of how 'bad' an asset may be. Essentially, the standard deviation is a measure of volatility and uncertainty, both of which, most investors would agree, are 'bad.'

Now we'll take another (usually less explored) look at why volatility is bad for an investor. Consider the six hypothetical stocks in Table 3.2, all of which have an arithmetic mean return (AM) of 10% but different volatility (SD). Note that, as we move from stock A to stock F, volatility increases, so that, as we move from left to right, the stocks become riskier.

TABLE 3.2

Year	A (%)	B (%)	C (%)	D (%)	E (%)	F (%)
1	10.0	12.0	15.0	20.0	25.0	40.0
2	10.0	8.0	5.0	0.0	−5.0	−20.0
3	10.0	12.0	15.0	20.0	25.0	40.0
4	10.0	8.0	5.0	0.0	−5.0	−20.0
5	10.0	12.0	15.0	20.0	25.0	40.0
6	10.0	8.0	5.0	0.0	−5.0	−20.0
7	10.0	12.0	15.0	20.0	25.0	40.0
8	10.0	8.0	5.0	0.0	−5.0	−20.0
9	10.0	12.0	15.0	20.0	25.0	40.0
10	10.0	8.0	5.0	0.0	−5.0	−20.0
AM	10.0%	10.0%	10.0%	10.0%	10.0%	10.0%
SD	0.0%	2.0%	5.0%	10.0%	15.0%	30.0%
GM	10.0%	10.0%	9.9%	9.5%	9.0%	5.8%
TW	$25,937	$25,895	$25,671	$24,883	$23,614	$17,623

Now take a look at the geometric means (*GM*). As we move from left to right, the arithmetic mean return remains constant, volatility increases, *and the geometric mean return decreases*. This is sometimes referred to as the 'variance drag,' which is just a fancy way of saying that volatility has a negative impact on mean compound returns.

As you'll remember from our discussion in the previous chapter, an investment does not compound over time at its arithmetic mean return but at its geometric mean return. So here we have another way to rationalize why volatility is bad: because it lowers the compound return of an investment, thus having a negative impact on its terminal value.

Table 3.2 illustrates this point. An initial investment of $10,000, compounded over 10 years at the geometric mean returns reported in the next-to-last row, yields the terminal wealth (*TW*) reported in the last row. To state the obvious: the terminal value of an investment is negatively related to the volatility of the asset's returns.

Formally, for any series of returns the relationship between the arithmetic mean, the geometric mean, and volatility is given by the expression

$$GM \oplus \exp\left\{ \ln(1 + AM) - (1/2) \frac{SD^2}{(1 + AM)^2} \right\} - 1 \qquad (3.2)$$

which holds well, as an approximation, for returns not much larger than ±30%. This expression is, in fact, a better approximation to the geometric mean than the more widely used (and simpler) approximation given by $GM \oplus AM - (1/2) \cdot (SD^2)$.

The big picture

Risk is one of the most elusive concepts in finance. One of the most widely accepted ways to define it, however, is as volatility measured by the standard deviation of returns. This volatility can be thought of as uncertainty about the future price of an asset, or as dispersion around the asset's mean return.

Volatility also causes a drag on mean compound return, which is one of the reasons we consider it detrimental. In other words, the higher the volatility of an asset, the lower the asset's ability to compound wealth over time.

Excel section

Just as in the Excel sections of the previous two chapters, the stuff in this section is rather straightforward.

■ To calculate a square root in Excel you need to use the 'sqrt' function. With it, calculating the square root of any number x is as simple as typing '=**sqrt(x)**' and hitting 'Enter.'

Calculating a standard deviation in Excel is also very simple. Suppose you have a series of ten returns in cells A1 through A10. Then, you do the following:

■ To calculate a standard deviation that divides the average of squared deviations from the mean by T, simply type '=**stdevp(A1:A10)**' in cell A11 and hit 'Enter.'

■ To calculate a standard deviation that divides the average of squared deviations from the mean by $T - 1$, simply type '=**stdev(A1:A10)**' in cell A11 and hit 'Enter.'

Challenge section

1 Given the returns of Exxon shown in Table 2.2, confirm that (as suggested in the text) the standard deviation of those returns is 15.0%.

2 Given the returns of American Express (Amex) between 1994 and 2003 shown in Table 3.3, calculate the standard deviation of returns. (Just for the sake of completeness, calculate this number with respect to both T and $T - 1$.) Is Amex riskier than Exxon? Is it riskier than Intel?

TABLE 3.3

Year	Return (%)
1994	13.5
1995	42.8
1996	39.8
1997	59.9
1998	15.7
1999	63.4
2000	–0.3
2001	–34.5
2002	0.2
2003	37.7

3 Given the returns of Amex during the period 1994–2003, calculate the (arithmetic) mean return. Then, assuming normality, estimate the interval within which Amex returns should fluctuate with a probability of 95%. How does this interval compare with those discussed in the text for Exxon and Intel?

4 Calculate the geometric mean return of Amex in the way discussed in the previous chapter. Then, using equation (3.2) in this chapter, calculate the approximate geometric mean return for Exxon, Intel, and Amex. Does the approximation seem to work? Does it work in some cases better than in others? Why?

4

RISK AND RETURN I: PORTFOLIOS

Two assets: Risk and return

Two assets: Other concepts

Three assets

n assets

The big picture

Excel section

Challenge section

ost investors don't hold all their wealth in just one asset; virtually all of them hold portfolios of securities with different degrees of diversification. This makes it necessary to estimate the risk and return of portfolios (as opposed to those of an individual security), which is the issue we'll discuss in this chapter. We'll also discuss a few related concepts, such as feasible sets, efficient sets, and the minimum variance portfolio.

Two assets: Risk and return

It's usually convenient to start with the simplest possible scenario, and in this case that means a two-asset portfolio. Consider then the returns of Bank of America (BoA) and IBM between the years 1994 and 2003, displayed in panel A of Table 4.1. As the table shows, IBM delivered a higher mean return (26.7% versus 18.8%) with higher volatility (33.1% versus 23.4%) than BoA.

TABLE 4.1

	Panel A		Panel B			
Year	BoA (%)	IBM (%)	x_1 (%)	x_2 (%)	Risk (%)	Return (%)
1994	−4.4	32.2	100.0	0.0	23.4	18.8
1995	59.8	25.7	90.0	10.0	22.2	19.6
1996	44.4	67.7	80.0	20.0	21.5	20.4
1997	27.9	39.3	70.0	30.0	21.4	21.2
1998	1.3	77.5	60.0	40.0	21.8	22.0
1999	−14.0	17.6	50.0	50.0	22.8	22.7
2000	−4.5	−20.8	40.0	60.0	24.2	23.5
2001	42.7	43.0	30.0	70.0	26.0	24.3
2002	14.5	−35.5	20.0	80.0	28.2	25.1
2003	20.1	20.5	10.0	90.0	30.5	25.9
AM	18.8%	26.7%	0.0	100.0	33.1	26.7
SD	23.4%	33.1%				

Let's consider first the calculation of the annual return of a portfolio containing these two markets. Obviously, the returns of such a portfolio would depend on how much we invest in each market. Let's call the proportion of money invested x_i (that is, the amount of money invested in asset i divided by the total amount of money invested in the portfolio), and R_i the return of asset i. Then, the **return of the portfolio (R_p)** in any given period would be given by

$$R_p = x_1 \cdot R_1 + x_2 \cdot R_2 \tag{4.1}$$

where $x_1 + x_2 = 1$. (This implies that, given the amount of money to be invested in a portfolio, we invest all of it in the two assets considered. This assumption extends to all portfolios regardless of the number of assets; that is, given a portfolio of n assets, and weights $x_1 \ldots x_n$, the usual assumption is that $x_1 + \ldots + x_n = 1$.)

For example, in 2003, the return of a portfolio invested 60% in BoA and 40% in IBM delivered a $(0.60)(0.201) + (0.40)(0.205) = 20.3\%$ return. Simple enough. If we had held this 60/40 portfolio during the years 1994 to 2003, then we would have obtained a $(0.60)(0.188) + (0.40)(0.267) = 22.0\%$ mean annual return. Again simple enough. There is really no mystery in how to calculate the return of a two-asset portfolio.

Now, what about its risk? That's a bit more complicated, but not too bad in the two-asset case. The **standard deviation of a portfolio (SDp)**, which is a measure of its risk, is given by

$$SD_p = \{(x_1)^2(SD_1)^2 + (x_2)^2(SD_2)^2 + 2x_1x_2SD_1SD_2Corr_{12}\}^{1/2} \tag{4.2}$$

where SD_p is the standard deviation (risk) of the portfolio, SD_i is the standard deviation of asset i, and $Corr_{12}$ is the correlation between assets 1 and 2 (BoA and IBM, in our case). Note that because, by definition, $SD_1 \cdot SD_2 \cdot Corr_{12} = Cov_{12}$, where Cov_{12} is the covariance between assets 1 and 2, then you may occasionally find the third term of the right-hand side of equation (4.2) written as $2x_1x_2Cov_{12}$. (If your knowledge of covariances and correlations is a bit rusty, you may want to read Chapter 27 before continuing.)

Back to the 60/40 portfolio, note that we know at this point all the numbers in equation (4.2) except for one, the correlation between BoA and IBM, which is a rather low 0.28. (You could try to calculate it for yourself from the data in the table.) With this number, the 60/40 weights, the standard deviations in Table 4.1, and equation (4.2), we get that the volatility of the 60/40 portfolio over the 1994–2003 period was

$$SD_p = \{(0.60)^2(0.234)^2 + (0.40)^2(0.331)^2 + 2(0.60)(0.40)(0.234)(0.331)(0.28)\}^{1/2} = 21.8\%$$

In short, calculating the risk and return of a two-asset portfolio is simple, even using a handheld calculator. However, as we will see below, the computational burden increases exponentially with the number of assets, which means that for portfolios larger than three or four assets, spreadsheets become essential. Before we discuss portfolios of more than two assets, however, let's take a look at a few useful definitions in the two-asset case.

Two assets: Other concepts

Now that we know how to compute the risk and return of a two-asset portfolio, let's take a look at panel B of Table 4.1. Using equations (4.1) and (4.2), you should have no difficulty replicating the numbers in this panel, which shows the risk and return of several combinations of BoA and IBM. Note that if we invest 100% of our money in either stock, the portfolio reflects the risk and return of that stock. Note, also, that although the numbers in the 'Return' column are the weighted average of the returns of BoA and IBM, the numbers in the 'Risk' column are *not* the weighted average of the risks of these two stocks. (This is due to the diversification effect, which we'll discuss in the next chapter.)

The last two columns of Table 4.1 are depicted in Exhibit 4.1. This line is called the **feasible set**, and it's simply the set of all the possible combinations (portfolios) between BoA and IBM. The points labeled BoA and IBM indicate a 100% investment in each of these stocks, and all the points in between indicate (infinite) other combinations between these two stocks. Point A, for example, indicates a portfolio invested 90% in BoA and 10% in IBM, and point B indicates a portfolio invested 90% in IBM and 10% in BoA.

Note that each point along the feasible set is a portfolio, and each of these portfolios has a different risk–return combination. Note, also, that the feasible set could go beyond the points labeled BoA and IBM in the presence of short-selling (that is, allowing an investor to borrow one asset, to sell it, and to invest more than 100% of his capital in the other asset).

For all the obvious reasons, the point of the feasible set farthest to the left is called the **minimum variance portfolio (MVP)**. Of all the possible combinations between BoA and IBM, this is the one that minimizes the risk of the portfolio. In the two-asset case, in fact, the equation to find it is not too difficult and is given by

$$x_1 = \frac{(SD_2)^2 - Cov_{12}}{(SD_1)^2 + (SD_2)^2 - 2Cov_{12}} \qquad (4.3)$$

EXHIBIT 4.1
IBM v. BoA, feasible set

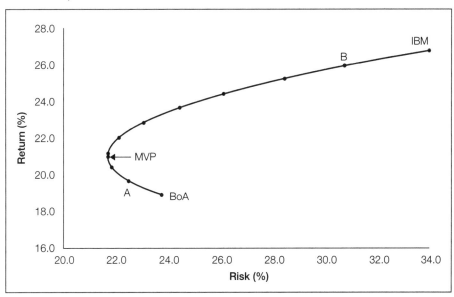

Note that, in our case, $Cov_{12} = SD_1 \cdot SD_2 \cdot Corr_{12} = (0.234)(0.331)(0.28) = 0.0216$. Therefore, the proportion of money to be invested in BoA (x_1) in order to minimize the risk of the portfolio is equal to 72.6%, leaving 27.4% to be invested in IBM. You should have no difficulty calculating that this portfolio has a risk of 21.4% and a return of 21.0%. (Actually, the risk is 21.38%, just slightly lower than the risk of the 70/30 portfolio, which is 21.40%.)

Finally, the **efficient set** is the upper half of the feasible set, beginning at the MVP. Take another look at Exhibit 4.1. Would you choose a portfolio in the lower branch of the feasible set (that is, the branch that goes down from the MVP)? Of course not. For each portfolio in the lower branch, you could choose one with the same level of risk but higher return in the upper branch. That's why it's called the *efficient* set: because it's the set of portfolios that, for any chosen level of risk, offers the highest possible return.

Three assets

Before considering the general *n*-asset case, let's take a quick look at a three-asset portfolio. The return of this portfolio is straightforward; it is (again) the weighted average of the returns of all the assets in the portfolio (three in this case). That is,

$$R_p = x_1 \cdot R_1 + x_2 \cdot R_2 + x_3 \cdot R_3 \qquad (4.4)$$

Now for the bad news. The inclusion of just one more asset complicates the calculation of the risk of the portfolio quite a bit. It's not difficult, just messy. Let's start with the expression, which is given by

$$SD_p = \{(x_1)^2(SD_1)^2 + (x_2)^2(SD_2)^2 + (x_3)^2(SD_3)^2 + 2x_1x_2Cov_{12} + 2x_1x_3Cov_{13} + 2x_2x_3Cov_{23}\}^{1/2} \qquad (4.5)$$

It looks a bit scary but there's really nothing to it. Let's compare it with equation (4.2) and think about both a bit.

Note, first, that equation (4.2) has four terms (the third term is multiplied by 2, so it's actually two identical terms) and equation (4.5) has nine terms (again, the last three terms are multiplied by 2 and each is made up of two identical terms). Can you see the pattern? The expression for the risk of a portfolio has as many terms as the square of the number of assets in the portfolio; that is, $2^2 = 4$ in the two-asset case and $3^2 = 9$ in the three-asset case.

Note, also, that for each asset in the portfolio we'll have a 'variance term' that consists of a weight multiplied by a standard deviation, both squared; these are the $(x_i)^2(SD_i)^2$ terms. To determine the number of 'covariance terms' $(x_ix_jCov_{ij})$, we just count all the different combinations of assets and multiply this number by 2. In the two-asset portfolio, we find only one combination (1-2), so there should be two covariance terms $(2x_1x_2Cov_{12})$. In the three-asset portfolio, we find three combinations (1-2, 1-3, and 2-3), so there should be six covariance terms $(2x_1x_2Cov_{12}, 2x_1x_3Cov_{13},$ and $2x_2x_3Cov_{23})$.

In the three-asset case, the feasible set is no longer a line as it is in the two-asset case. In fact, it is a bullet-shaped *surface*, as shown in Exhibit 4.2. The MVP is still the point farthest to the left of this feasible set, and the efficient set is the upper border of the feasible set, beginning at the MVP.

EXHIBIT 4.2
Feasible set, efficient set and MVP

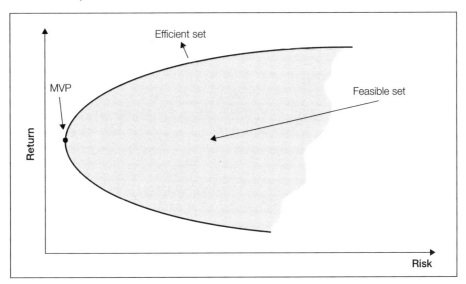

n assets

Now for the general case. Regardless of the number of assets, the return of a portfolio is always equal to the weighted average of returns of all the assets in the portfolio. That is,

$$R_p = x_1 \cdot R_1 + x_2 \cdot R_2 + \ldots + x_n \cdot R_n \qquad (4.6)$$

No trouble there. Perhaps it's convenient to add at this point that, in order to calculate the *expected* return of a portfolio, we simply replace in (4.6) the observed returns of the assets by their respective expected returns. (This doesn't mean that estimating expected returns is simple. We briefly discuss this issue in Chapter 11.)

The risk of an *n*-asset portfolio, however, is much more difficult to estimate, particularly when the number of assets is large. As we've seen above, even for a very small portfolio of three assets the expression to estimate its risk is not all that simple. Formally, the standard deviation of an *n*-asset portfolio can be written as

$$SD_p = \left\{ \sum_{i=1}^{n} \sum_{j=1}^{n} x_i x_j Cov_{ij} \right\}^{1/2} \tag{4.7}$$

It doesn't look that scary, but that may be simply because the two sum signs are hiding the burden. In a relatively small portfolio of 20 assets, equation (4.7) implies that we have to come up with 400 terms. For all practical purposes, we may as well forget this expression, which is just another way of saying that, when calculating the standard deviation (risk) of a portfolio, we'd better have a spreadsheet at hand.

However, even with a spreadsheet, we need to know what to do. The Excel program to optimize portfolios discussed in Chapter 11 provides a simple way to estimate both the risk and return of a portfolio for any number of assets. In any case, when calculating the standard deviation of a portfolio, it's important to keep in mind the following. First, we write down as many 'variance terms,' $(x_i)^2 (SD_i)^2$, as we have assets in the portfolio. Second, we determine every possible combination of assets (1-2, 1-3, ... 1-n, 2-3, 2-4, ... 2-n, ...) and write down *two* 'covariance terms' for each, that is, $2x_1 x_2 Cov_{12}$, ... $2x_1 x_n Cov_{1n}$, $2x_2 x_3 Cov_{23}$, ... $2x_2 x_n Cov_{2n}$, ... Third, we add up all the terms. And fourth, we take the square root of the sum.

Sometimes it may help to visualize the variance–covariance matrix, including all the relevant weights. In the general, n-asset case, this matrix looks like the one displayed in Table 4.2.

TABLE 4.2

	1	2	3		n
1	$(x_1)^2(SD_1)^2$	$x_1 x_2 Cov_{12}$	$x_1 x_3 Cov_{13}$	. . .	$x_1 x_n Cov_{1n}$
2	$x_2 x_1 Cov_{21}$	$(x_2)^2(SD_2)^2$	$x_2 x_3 Cov_{23}$	. . .	$x_2 x_n Cov_{2n}$
. . .	. . .	. . .	. . .	. . .	. . .
n	$x_n x_1 Cov_{n1}$	$x_n x_2 Cov_{n2}$	$x_n x_3 Cov_{n3}$	. . .	$(x_n)^2(SD_n)^2$

Note that, at the end of the day and regardless of the number of assets, *the variance of a portfolio is given by the sum of all the elements in this matrix* (and the standard deviation simply by the square root of this variance). Think about this matrix a bit and relate it to the discussion above. If you were able to follow the discussion, you should have no trouble writing down this matrix for any number of assets.

Finally, note that the feasible set, efficient set, and MVP of an n-asset portfolio, when n is larger than 2, look just like those in Exhibit 4.2. In other words, the feasible set is a bullet-shaped surface, the MVP is the point farthest to the left of the feasible set, and the efficient set is the upper border of the feasible set beginning at the MVP.

The big picture

Calculating the risk and return of a portfolio may be time consuming without a spreadsheet or other software package. However, the intuition behind the calculations is relatively simple. The same applies to some portfolios in which investors may be particularly interested, such as those in the efficient set or the minimum variance portfolio. In Chapter 11 we discuss an Excel program that quickly and easily estimates all the magnitudes and portfolios we have just discussed.

Note that this chapter is mostly about mechanics, that is, about *how to calculate* the risk and return of different portfolios. But we still haven't discussed *why* investors may want to form portfolios. That is the issue we discuss in the next chapter.

Excel section

There are two new concepts to implement in Excel in this chapter, covariance and correlation. Both are very easy to deal with. Suppose you have two series of ten returns each, the first in cells A1 through A10 and the second in cells B1 through B10. Then you do the following:

- To calculate the *covariance* between the assets, type '**=covar(A1:A10,B1:B10)**' in cell A11 and then hit 'Enter.'
- To calculate the *correlation coefficient* between the assets simply type '**=correl(A1:A10,B1:B10)**' in cell A12 and then hit 'Enter.'

You may also find it useful to know that in Excel you can not only sum numbers along a row or a column but also over a whole matrix (such as the variance–covariance matrix discussed above). Suppose you have a 3×3 variance–covariance matrix in the range A1:B3. Then you do the following:

- To sum all the elements in the matrix, type '**=sum(A1:B3)**' in cell D4 and then hit 'Enter.'

Challenge section

1 Consider the annual returns of Pepsi and Hewlett-Packard (HP) during the years 1994 to 2003 in panel A of Table 4.3. Then calculate:

(a) The mean annual return of both companies.

(b) The annual standard deviation of returns of both companies.

(c) The correlation of returns between the two companies. (Is it high? Low? What do you make of it?)

TABLE 4.3

| | Panel A | | | Panel B | | |
Year	Pepsi (%)	HP (%)	x_P (%)	x_{HP} (%)	Risk (%)	Return (%)
1994	−9.5	28.1	100.0	0.0		
1995	56.7	69.4	90.0	10.0		
1996	6.2	21.1	80.0	20.0		
1997	36.6	25.3	70.0	30.0		
1998	14.3	10.7	60.0	40.0		
1999	−12.5	67.7	50.0	50.0		
2000	42.6	−28.6	40.0	60.0		
2001	−0.5	−34.0	30.0	70.0		
2002	−12.1	−13.9	20.0	80.0		
2003	12.0	34.5	10.0	90.0		
			0.0	100.0		

2 Given the weights for Pepsi and HP in panel B of Table 4.3, calculate the risk and return of those ten portfolios. Then:

(a) Make a graph of the feasible set.

(b) Of the ten portfolios calculated, which is the one with the lowest risk?

(c) Calculate now the MVP using equation (4.3). Is it too different from the portfolio you found in the previous question?

3 Consider, finally, a four-asset portfolio and a five-asset portfolio. In both cases, write the expressions for the risk and the return of each portfolio.

5

RISK II: DIVERSIFICATION

Three hypothetical stocks

The correlation coefficient

Three views on diversification

Another view on diversification: Risk-adjusted returns

The role of mutual funds

The big picture

Excel section

Challenge section

The idea that an asset's risk can be thought of as the volatility of its returns measured by the standard deviation seems plausible, doesn't it? Well, the problem is that it doesn't extend well when assets are combined, among other reasons because the volatility of a two-asset portfolio is not equal to the sum of the volatilities of each individual asset. It's a bit more complicated than that. But not that complicated. You most likely heard the expression 'Don't put all your eggs in one basket.' Well, at the end of the day, this chapter may be as simple as that.

Three hypothetical stocks

Let's consider the returns of the three hypothetical stocks in Table 5.1. We know by now how to calculate their (arithmetic) mean return and standard deviation, which are also reported in the table. And we also know that, given those numbers, stock 1 (SD = 10.0%) is riskier than stock 3 (SD = 5.0%), which in turn is riskier than stock 2 (SD = 1.5%).

TABLE 5.1

Year	Stock 1 (%)	Stock 2 (%)	Stock 3 (%)
1	25.0	21.3	32.5
2	5.0	24.3	22.5
3	22.5	21.6	31.3
4	6.0	24.1	23.0
5	17.5	22.4	28.8
6	4.0	24.4	22.0
7	31.0	20.4	35.5
8	5.5	24.2	22.8
9	24.0	21.4	32.0
10	4.0	24.4	22.0
AM	14.5%	22.8%	27.2%
SD	10.0%	1.5%	5.0%

Now, instead of thinking of each of these stocks individually, let's think of combinations of them. Let's combine, for example, stocks 1 and 2. So suppose that at the beginning of year 1 we had invested $1,000, 13% in stock 1 and the rest (87%) in stock 2. We know by know how to calculate, period by period, the return of that portfolio.

The return for the first period is given by (0.13)(0.250) + (0.87)(0.213) = 21.7%. If we calculate in the same fashion the returns of the portfolio in all subsequent periods we will find . . . surprise! The return of the portfolio in each and every period is the exact same 21.7%.

Take a look at Exhibit 5.1, which plots the returns of stocks 1 and 2, as well as the return of the proposed portfolio (the dotted line). Although stocks 1 and 2 fluctuate from period to period, the return of the portfolio remains constant at the calculated 21.7% return. Magic? Not really. But before we discuss what's going on, let's think of another combination of these hypothetical stocks.

EXHIBIT 5.1
Perfect diversification

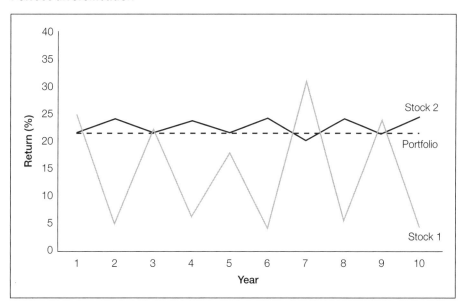

Suppose now that, at the beginning of the first year, we had split our money equally between stocks 1 and 3. Exhibit 5.2 plots the returns of stocks 1 and 3, as well as the return of this equally weighted portfolio (the dotted line). Pretty different picture, huh?

If we compare the two-stock portfolios in Exhibits 5.1 and 5.2, it is obvious that they are very different: the first has no volatility, though it results from the combination of two volatile stocks, whereas the second seems very volatile. If you're wondering what is the main driver of the difference between these two portfolios, you're asking the right question.

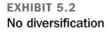

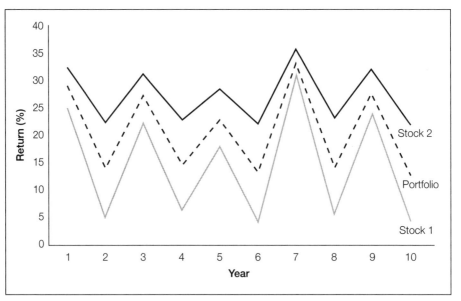

EXHIBIT 5.2
No diversification

The correlation coefficient

So if we combine two stocks, what determines that in one case we end up with a portfolio that locks a fixed return, while in the other we end up with a very volatile portfolio? It all comes down to one parameter: the correlation coefficient.

This coefficient, which is also discussed in Chapter 27, measures the strength of the (linear) relationship between two variables. When the coefficient is positive the two variables tend to move in the same direction, and when it's negative they tend to move in opposite directions. It can take a maximum value of 1 and a minimum value of –1, with these two extremes indicating a perfect linear relationship (positive in the first case and negative in the second).

For reasonably long periods of time, however, it is virtually impossible to find a negative correlation (or a correlation very close to 1) between two stocks within a market, or between two equity markets. We'll explore why in the next chapter, but for now keep in mind that the *empirical* values of the correlation coefficient are within a much narrower band than its theoretical extremes.

Back to our hypothetical stocks now. What's going on between stocks 1 and 2? Simply that they exhibit a perfect negative correlation; that is, a correlation equal to –1. In such situations, a combination between two stocks that enables the investor to lock a return (and obtain a portfolio with 0 volatility) can always be found. But, however interesting this may sound, it has little or no practical importance. As mentioned above, it's virtually impossible to find two stocks with a negative correlation, let alone with a correlation equal to –1.

What's going on, in turn, between stocks 1 and 3? Pretty much the opposite. They exhibit a perfect positive correlation (that is, a correlation equal to 1) and, in such situations, the risk of the portfolio is simply given by the average volatility of the two stocks in the portfolio (weighted by the proportion of wealth invested in each stock). In other words, in terms of risk reduction, there is nothing to gain by combining these two stocks. (In fact, the *only* case in which the risk of a two-stock portfolio is equal to the weighted average of risks is when the correlation between them is 1. In every other case, the risk of the portfolio is *lower* than the weighted average of the risks.)

If the goal is to reduce the risk of a portfolio, we should look for stocks with low correlations to each other. This is particularly important when the portfolio has few assets. Remember, the lower the average correlation across stocks in the portfolio, the larger the reduction of risk. That is, the larger the difference between the weighted average of risks (a situation in which nothing is gained by combining stocks, from a risk-reduction point of view) and the actual risk of the portfolio.

One final word on the correlation coefficient before we move on. Don't think of it as a statistical magnitude with little practical importance. The correlation does in fact determine the extent to which risk can be reduced by combining stocks. Think for example of emerging markets as an asset class. Though emerging markets are very volatile, their correlation to developed markets is relatively low; hence, they may lower substantially the volatility of a portfolio of assets in developed markets. Something similar could be said, for example, about venture capital funds, which are very volatile but also have a low correlation to the market. In short, don't underestimate the *practical* importance of the correlation coefficient.

Three views on diversification

So, what is diversification? It is simply the combination of assets into a portfolio with the goal of reducing risk. Having said that, beware of this popular definition. As we discuss below, diversification can be thought of in other ways, and its ultimate goal is a bit more complicated than just reducing risk.

And why do investors usually diversify? If the first answer that comes to your mind is 'to reduce risk,' you're obviously right. Most people avoid putting all their money in one stock (or even in a few stocks) to avoid a situation in which the stock unexpectedly tanks and takes their whole portfolio with it. Think Enron, where many employees had over 90% of their pension money invested in Enron stock. That's a lesson on diversification learned the hard way!

But diversification can be thought of in at least three other ways, all useful though usually less explored. Take a look at panel A of Table 5.2, which shows the returns of Disney and Microsoft during the years 1994 to 2003. During this period, Microsoft delivered a higher return with a higher risk than Disney, as the numbers in the last two rows show. The correlation coefficient between these two stocks (not reported in the table) is a very low 0.05, which points to potentially high diversification benefits.

TABLE 5.2

	Panel A				Panel B		
Year	Disney (%)	Microsoft (%)	x_D (%)	x_M (%)	Risk (%)	Return (%)	RAR
1994	8.7	51.6	100.0	0.0	23.7	8.5	0.361
1995	29.0	43.6	90.0	10.0	22.2	11.7	0.526
1996	19.1	88.3	80.0	20.0	21.9	14.8	0.676
1997	42.9	56.4	70.0	30.0	22.9	17.9	0.781
1998	−8.5	114.6	60.0	40.0	25.1	21.0	0.838
1999	−1.7	68.4	50.0	50.0	28.2	24.2	0.858
2000	−0.4	−62.8	40.0	60.0	31.8	27.3	0.857
2001	−27.7	52.7	30.0	70.0	36.0	30.4	0.845
2002	−20.3	−22.0	20.0	80.0	40.4	33.5	0.830
2003	44.4	6.8	10.0	90.0	45.0	36.6	0.814
AM	8.5%	39.8%	0.0	100.0	49.8	39.8	0.798
SD	23.7%	49.8%					

Let's consider some combinations between Disney and Microsoft, such as those shown in panel B of Table 5.2. The first two columns show different portfolio allocations to Disney (x_D) and Microsoft (x_M), the next two columns the risk and return of the different portfolios, and we'll get to the last column in a minute.

An interesting question would be: what is the combination between Disney and Microsoft that yields the lowest possible risk (that is, the MVP)? That's very simple to find in the two-asset case, as we saw in the previous chapter. By investing 82.9% in Disney and the rest (17.1%) in Microsoft, we would obtain a portfolio with a standard deviation of 21.8%, just slightly lower than the risk of the 80/20 portfolio in the Table (21.9%). The return of this portfolio, on the other hand, would be 13.9%.

Which brings us to a second reason for diversifying. If we're happy holding Disney stock, we should be even happier to hold the MVP. This is simply because it enables us to lower our risk by 1.9% (= 23.7% – 21.8%) and to increase our returns by 5.4% (= 13.9% – 8.5%), both with respect to holding Disney by itself. In short, here's a second way of thinking about diversification: *it may enable us to lower our risk and increase our returns at the same time*.

Now, let's go back to assuming that we're happy holding Disney, which means that we accept the level of risk of this stock. Having said that, if someone offered us an asset with the same volatility but a higher return, wouldn't we want it? Of course we would, and that is just what we can obtain through diversification.

Take a look at Exhibit 5.3, which shows the feasible set between Disney and Microsoft. These numbers, of course, follow from panel B of Table 5.2. Besides the MVP we already discussed, the exhibit highlights another portfolio, labeled A. Given the choice between putting our money in Disney or putting it in portfolio A, what would you choose?

EXHIBIT 5.3
Disney v. Microsoft, feasible set

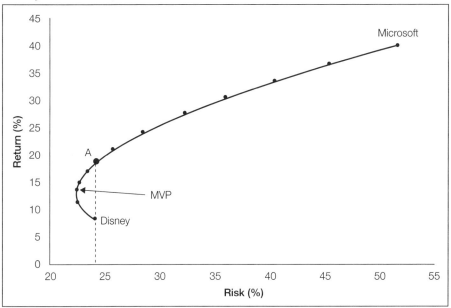

Portfolio A consists of an allocation of 65.9% in Disney and 34.1% in Microsoft and, by construction, has the same level of risk as Disney. However, this portfolio has a 19.2% return, which is 10.7% higher than Disney's return. That's quite a difference, and is as close to a 'free lunch' as we can get in financial markets. Why would we ever hold Disney by itself if, at the same level of risk, portfolio A has a much higher return? Which brings us to a third way of thinking about diversification: *it may enable us to increase our returns given an acceptable level of risk.*

Now, it seems that convincing someone who's happy holding Disney to diversify would be an easy task. But here's a challenge: how would you convince someone who's happy holding *Microsoft* to diversify? It doesn't look as if we can pull off the same 'trick' as before. We cannot offer this investor a portfolio with lower risk and higher return, or one with the same level of risk but a higher return. Is it, then, that diversification is not beneficial for someone who's happy holding Microsoft?

Another view on diversification: Risk-adjusted returns

Not really. Investors do not just care about the returns of their portfolio; they also care about its risk. In fact, what investors really care about is maximizing *risk-adjusted returns*. There are different ways of defining this concept (which we explore in Chapter 10), but for the time being let's simply think about a ratio that divides return by risk. This is exactly what the last column of Table 5.2 shows: the **risk-adjusted return (RAR)** defined as the 'Return' column divided by the 'Risk' column.

Can you see now why, even if we're happy holding all our money in Microsoft, it would be beneficial for us to diversify? Because we could increase the risk-adjusted return of our portfolio. In our case, the 'best' portfolio of those shown in Table 5.2 is a 50/50 split between Disney and Microsoft, simply because it has the highest RAR (0.858).

However, the portfolio with the highest possible RAR is not shown in the table. An investment of 46.1% in Disney and 53.9% in Microsoft would have an RAR of 0.859, just slightly higher than that of the 50/50 portfolio. The portfolio-optimization program discussed in Chapter 11 can find this optimal combination in the blink of an eye.

It will virtually never be the case that the highest RAR is found in a portfolio fully invested in one asset. Which brings us to a yet another way to see why diversification is beneficial: *it enables us to obtain the highest possible risk-adjusted returns*. And, don't forget, that's the most we could ever ask of any investing strategy.

Note that this last angle on diversification 'contains' all the others. We had agreed that both the MVP and portfolio A were better than putting all our money in Disney. The former enabled us to lower our risk and increase our return (relative to holding just Disney), thus increasing risk-adjusted returns. The latter enabled us to increase our return given the level of Disney's risk, again increasing risk-adjusted returns. And a portfolio invested 46.1% in Disney and 53.9% in Microsoft is better than investing just in Microsoft because, again, it increases (in this case, maximizes) risk-adjusted returns. In short, when grandma told us not to put all our eggs in one basket, she was, as usual, wiser than we probably gave her credit for.

The role of mutual funds

At this point you should have little or no doubts about the benefits of diversification. But in case any doubts remain, just look around you. The number of mutual funds has exploded throughout the world. In the US, in fact, there are more funds than individual stocks. And a lot of that explosive growth has to do with the fact that mutual funds provide investors with easy and low-cost diversification.

Think about the obstacles that a small investor faces when trying to diversify his portfolio broadly. First, he would have to choose wisely among hundreds (in some markets thousands) of stocks. That is no small task, to be sure.

Then he would have to decide how many stocks to include in the portfolio. That's tricky. How many stocks a properly diversified portfolio should contain is something that must be determined for a given market at a given point in time, and the estimates may vary widely.

And if this investor's capital is rather limited and he'd want to buy, say, some 20–30 stocks, he'd end up paying relatively high commissions. Much higher on a per-share basis, for sure, than the big boys in Wall Street.

Compare all that with buying shares in a mutual fund that aims to follow or outperform a benchmark of this investor's choice. By buying shares in this fund, our investor solves the problem of choosing among hundreds or thousands of shares and the problem of how many different stocks to buy, and does all that at a relatively low cost. Just one share in a fund may represent ownership in hundreds of companies. When it comes down to diversification, it doesn't get any better than investing through mutual funds.

The big picture

Most investors diversify their holdings, and they do so for a good reason: to lower the risk of their portfolios. But diversification is not just about risk reduction. At the end of the day, it is about achieving the ultimate goal of investors: the maximization of risk-adjusted returns.

A key magnitude in the process of diversification is the correlation coefficient. Far from being statistical magnitude with little practical importance, this coefficient plays a central role in the proper selection of assets to be included in portfolios. And it's also instrumental in properly assessing the risk of different assets.

If you're still not convinced that diversification is the way to go, there are two things you can do. First, just look around you at the explosive growth of the mutual fund industry worldwide. And second, read the next chapter, where we elaborate on the benefits of diversification.

Excel section

There is no new Excel material in this chapter; all the magnitudes we have discussed were covered in the Excel sections of previous chapters. The calculation of the portfolio that maximizes risk-adjusted returns is not trivial and we need more advanced tools to handle it. In Chapter 11 we'll discuss a portfolio-optimization program that will enable us to do that and more.

Challenge section

1 Consider the annual returns of the Norwegian and Spanish markets, both summarized by the MSCI indices (in dollars and accounting for both capital gains and dividends), displayed in panel A of Table 5.3. Then calculate:

   (a) The mean annual return of both markets.
   (b) The annual standard deviation of returns of both markets.
   (c) The correlation of returns between the two markets. (Is it high? Low? What do you make of it?)

TABLE 5.3

	Panel A		Panel B				
Year	Norway	Spain	x_N	x_S	Risk	Return	RAR
	(%)	(%)	(%)	(%)	(%)	(%)	
1994	24.1	−3.9	100.0	0.0			
1995	6.5	31.2	90.0	10.0			
1996	29.2	41.3	80.0	20.0			
1997	6.7	26.2	70.0	30.0			
1998	−29.7	50.6	60.0	40.0			
1999	32.4	5.3	50.0	50.0			
2000	−0.4	−15.5	40.0	60.0			
2001	−11.7	−11.0	30.0	70.0			
2002	−6.7	−14.9	20.0	80.0			
2003	49.6	59.2	10.0	90.0			
			0.0	100.0			

2 Given the weights for the Norwegian and Spanish markets in panel B of Table 5.3, calculate the risk, return, and risk-adjusted return (RAR) of those ten portfolios. Then:

(a) Make a graph of the feasible set.

(b) Calculate the MVP. Would you rather put all your money in Norway or in the MVP? Why?

(c) Would you rather put all your money in Norway, all your money in Spain, or all your money in a portfolio invested 40% in Norway and 60% in Spain? Why?

6

RISK III: SYSTEMATIC RISK

Total risk *v.* systematic risk

Diversification again

More on systematic risk

An example

A brief digression on covariances

A brief digression on international diversification

The big picture

Excel section

Challenge section

By now we know that there's more to risk than the volatility of individual assets. In this chapter we'll look into the factors that determine volatility and the role they play in the risk of a portfolio. And while doing all that, we'll end up redefining the concept of risk. We'll also explore further the role of correlations (or covariances) in portfolios, and briefly discuss the benefits of international diversification.

Total risk *v.* systematic risk

When discussing risk in Chapter 3 we stressed that, unlike the concept of return, which is easy to define, the concept of risk is far more slippery. That's one of the reasons why a few chapters of this book are allocated to discuss it from different points of view. Having said that, we have argued that a possible way to think about risk is as the standard deviation of the asset's returns. And, under some conditions, that is by far the most widely accepted way to think about risk.

What are the conditions? Basically that we consider the asset not as a part of a portfolio but in isolation. Yes, risk does depend on the context and that should come as no surprise. Giving darts to a monkey and setting him lose on the street may be dangerous, but giving him the darts in a crystal cage may be less so.

Let's think about volatility for a minute. We see stock prices changing all the time. Have you ever wondered why? Of course we can think of a million reasons, but let's try to fit all factors into two boxes. In one, let's put all the factors that are specific to the companies behind the stocks. You know, a new CEO, the introduction of a new product, the departure of a well-known executive, a competitor's release of a better technology . . . you get the picture. These and many others are all idiosyncratic factors that originate in the company (or perhaps the industry) and affect the company's stock price (and perhaps that of its competitors).

Having said that, there are of course many reasons why a company's stock price may fluctuate that have to do with factors unrelated to the company. Think, for example, about macroeconomic events, such as changes in interest rates, in expected inflation, or in the expected growth of the economy, to name but a few. Or think about political events, such as presidential elections. Or think, more generally, about events that affect the economy as a whole. These and many others are economy-wide factors that affect the stock price of all companies, at the same time, and in the same direction (though not necessarily in the same magnitude).

Let's give names to these two boxes before we go on. The idiosyncratic events that originate in the company are usually referred to as *unsystematic factors*; the economy-wide events exogenous to the company are usually called *systematic factors*. Most of the time we should have little trouble placing most of the events that affect stock prices into one of these two boxes. Which is another way of saying that volatility is determined by systematic and unsystematic factors. Or, put differently, total risk is the sum of **systematic (or market) risk** plus **unsystematic (or idiosyncratic) risk**.

Diversification again

In the previous chapters we discussed several reasons for which diversification is beneficial for investors. We'll discuss now yet another angle. Suppose we (unwisely) have invested all our money in one stock. Then the risk of our (one-asset) portfolio will be fully determined by the total risk of this stock, that is, by the standard deviation of its returns.

Now suppose we decide to add one other stock to our portfolio. Then the risk of our (now two-asset) portfolio should decrease. Why? Formally, because as long as the correlation between the two stocks is not exactly equal to 1, then the risk of our portfolio will be lower than the weighted average of the risks of the assets in our portfolio. (In other words, as long as the correlation is lower than 1, we will obtain *some* benefits from diversification.)

Intuitively, this happens for two reasons. First, because as we add another stock to the portfolio, the importance (weight) of each stock decreases. In a two-stock portfolio, events that affect the price of either stock only *partially* affect the risk of the portfolio. Second, because unless all the factors that affect one company also affect the other (at the same time, in the same direction, and in the same magnitude), the two stocks will not move exactly in sync. As long as that happens, we will obtain some diversification benefits.

What happens as we add more and more stocks to our portfolio? The same thing over and over again. That is, the more stocks we have, the more likely it becomes that the very many idiosyncratic factors that affect the price of the stocks in our portfolio cancel each other out. As information about idiosyncratic events flows into the market, the negative impact on some stocks will tend to be averaged out by the positive impact on others. In a fully diversified portfolio, the whole impact of unsystematic events vanishes and we're left bearing only systematic risk. In other words, diversification is a way of reducing (and, at the limit, eliminating) unsystematic risk.

Exhibit 6.1 displays a graphical representation of the preceding arguments. Note that the rate at which risk falls decreases as we increase the number of stocks, each additional stock reducing risk a bit less than the previous one. Eventually, adding more assets to the portfolio will reduce risk by a negligible amount, and that is when we have achieved a fully diversified portfolio. In that situation, all the unsystematic risk has been diversified away and we're left bearing only the systematic risk. It should come as no surprise, then, that unsystematic risk is sometimes referred to as *diversifiable* risk, and systematic risk as *undiversifiable* risk.

Why we can't diversify away the systematic risk should be obvious. As we discussed above, these are economy-wide factors that affect all companies, at the same time, and in the same direction. In other words, there's no escaping from the impact of these events. (International diversification, which we discuss below, may do the trick, though.)

EXHIBIT 6.1
Limits to diversification

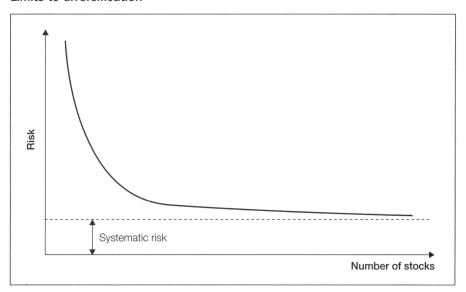

More on systematic risk

It should be clear from the previous discussion that systematic risk puts a limit on the benefits of diversification. That is, diversification enables us to reduce risk but never to eliminate it. How much risk we can diversify away, however, is an empirical question with a different answer across markets and over time. (As a very crude estimate, consider that an investor fully diversified in US stocks may bear some 25% of the volatility of the average stock.)

Much the same could be said about the number of stocks we need in order to achieve a fully diversified portfolio. Estimates vary widely across markets and over time. Some argue that full diversification in the US could be achieved with a careful selection of as few as 10–15 stocks, though others argue that the number is closer to 30 stocks. (And others think that the number is no less than 300.) Again, it's rather pointless to entertain an answer to this question without a specific market or point in time in mind.

It should also be clear now why finding stocks with a negative correlation is virtually impossible in practice. Although unsystematic factors may push different stocks in different directions, the systematic factor pushes all of them in the same direction. This induces a positive correlation among all stocks in the market, from which the limit on the benefits from diversification follows.

Now, how do we assess an asset's risk if instead of being considered in isolation we consider it within a diversified portfolio? The math of it is less than trivial and the intuition less than great, but the bottom line is this: the risk of a stock that is part of a diversified portfolio is measured by the *contribution* of the stock to the risk of the portfolio, which can be assessed in absolute or in relative terms. The absolute contribution is measured by the covariance between the stock and the portfolio, and the relative contribution by beta.

Like Sylvester Stallone speaking Chinese again? Fear not, an example's on the way.

An example

Panel A of Table 6.1 shows the returns of three companies, Apple, Home Depot (HD), and Procter & Gamble (P&G) over the years 1994 to 2003. According to our measure of (total) risk, the standard deviation of returns, Apple is the riskiest of the three (SD = 85.9%) and P&G the least risky (SD = 19.9%).

Let's now form an equally weighted portfolio of these three stocks by investing one-third of our money in each company. We know that the expected return of this portfolio is given by the weighted average of returns, that is, (1/3) · (0.300) + (1/3) · (0.256) + (1/3) · (0.174) = 24.3%. But right now we're more interested in its risk, for which we need standard deviations and covariances. The standard deviations are displayed at the bottom of Table 6.1, and the variances (the square of the standard deviations) and covariances in panel A of Table 6.2.

TABLE 6.1

	Apple (%)	HD (%)	P&G (%)
1994	35.2	16.9	11.3
1995	−17.3	4.3	36.8
1996	−34.5	5.4	32.2
1997	−37.1	76.9	50.5
1998	212.0	108.4	15.9
1999	151.2	69.0	21.6
2000	−71.1	−33.3	−27.1
2001	47.2	12.1	3.1
2002	−34.6	−52.7	11.5
2003	49.2	49.0	18.5
AM	30.0%	25.6%	17.4%
SD	85.9%	47.6%	19.9%

We know that the risk of any portfolio is given by the sum of all the elements in the variance–covariance matrix, which contains all the relevant variances, covariances, *and weights*. (Take a look at Chapter 4 if you don't remember.) That is precisely what is shown in panel B of Table 6.2. The 0.0820, for example, is calculated as $(1/3) \cdot (1/3) \cdot (0.7379)$; the 0.0338 is calculated as $(1/3) \cdot (1/3) \cdot (0.3038)$; and so on. The sum of these nine elements yields the variance of the portfolio (0.1905), and the square root of this number yields its standard deviation, 43.6%.

TABLE 6.2

Panel A	Apple	HD	P&G
Apple	0.7379	0.3038	0.0075
HD	0.3038	0.2265	0.0439
P&G	0.0075	0.0439	0.0396

Panel B	Apple	HD	P&G
Apple	0.0820	0.0338	0.0008
HD	0.0338	0.0252	0.0049
P&G	0.0008	0.0049	0.0044

Panel C	Apple	HD	P&G
Sum	0.1166	0.0638	0.0101
Proportion	0.61	0.34	0.05

Note that the risk of the portfolio, 43.6%, is lower than the weighted average of the risks, which is $(1/3) \cdot (0.859) + (1/3) \cdot (0.476) + (1/3) \cdot (0.199) = 51.1\%$. This reduction in risk is the result of diversification. In other words, when we put these three stocks together in a portfolio, part of their unsystematic risk vanishes and the risk of the portfolio is lower than the weighted average of the individual risks. It then follows, as a mathematical necessity, that each stock is contributing to the risk of the portfolio *less* than its total risk.

Let's look at the numbers, but, for convenience, instead of focusing on the standard deviation of the portfolio let's focus on its variance (0.1905). The row labeled 'Sum' in panel C of Table 6.2 is the vertical sum of the rows in panel B. (For example, $0.0820 + 0.0338 + 0.0008 = 0.1166$.) Each of these numbers represents the *absolute contribution* of each stock to the risk of the portfolio. In other words, if we add up these numbers, we obtain the risk of the portfolio $(0.1166 + 0.0638 + 0.0101 = 0.1905)$.

The row labeled 'Proportion,' on the other hand, is simply made up of the numbers in the row above divided by the variance of the portfolio. (For example, $0.1166/0.1905 = 0.61$.) Each of these numbers represents the *relative contribution* of each stock to the risk of the portfolio. In other words, if we add up these three numbers we obtain 1 $(0.61 + 0.34 + 0.05 = 1)$. These numbers suggest that Apple, HD, and P&G contribute 61%, 34%, and 5%, respectively, to the risk of our equally weighted portfolio.

That is the way we measure the risk of a stock that is part of a portfolio: by its (absolute or relative) contribution to the risk of the portfolio. Now for the names. Each number in the row labeled 'Sum' is the *covariance* between each stock and the portfolio; each number in the row labeled 'Proportion' is the *beta* of each stock relative to the portfolio. (We'll define formally and discuss the beta of a stock in the next chapter, but for the time being note, as the discussion above suggests, that it's obtained from the covariance between the stock and the portfolio divided by the variance of the portfolio.)

A brief digression on covariances

Most investors, perhaps for no good reason, tend to think of risk as volatility usually measured by the standard deviation of an asset's returns. However, as we just discussed, that is not the proper measure of risk of an asset in a portfolio, particularly when the portfolio is properly diversified. Put differently, the larger the number of assets in a portfolio, the less relevant the total risk of each asset (measured by its standard deviation), and the more relevant the asset's contribution to the risk of the portfolio (measured by the covariance between the asset and the portfolio).

The example above illustrates why this is the case. And there are two other quick ways of reinforcing this idea. First, think that as the number of assets in a portfolio grows, the number of covariances grows much faster than the number of variances. In a two-asset portfolio, we have two variances and two covariances; in a 20-asset portfolio we have 20 variances and 380 covariances; in a 100-asset portfolio we have 100 variances and 9,900 covariances. Which do you think will have more impact on the risk of the portfolio, those few variances or those very many covariances?

Second, let's make a couple of assumptions that are not really needed to get to the final conclusion; we'll make them just to get the point across more easily. Assume, first, that all the n assets in a portfolio have the same variance (let's call it V); second, that the covariance between any two assets in the portfolio is the same (let's call it C); and third, that we invest an equal amount in each of the n assets (which makes all weights equal to $1/n$). Then, the risk of this portfolio, measured by its variance (Var_p), is given by

$$Var_p = n \cdot \left(\frac{1}{n}\right)^2 \cdot V + (n^2 - n) \cdot \left(\frac{1}{n}\right)^2 \cdot C = \left(\frac{1}{n}\right) \cdot V + \left(1 - \frac{1}{n}\right) \cdot C \quad (6.1)$$

If the expression above looks a bit complicated, just give it some thought. We have n assets, n variances, $n^2 - n$ covariances, the weight of each asset is $1/n$, all the variances are the same (V), and all the covariances are the same (C). Got it? OK then, now think what happens as we increase the number of assets in the portfolio. For a very large n, the expression $(1/n) \cdot V$ tends to 0, and the expression $(1 - 1/n) \cdot C$ tends to C. In other words, as the number of assets grows, the risk of the portfolio is largely determined by covariances and largely independent of variances.

A brief digression on international diversification

So far we have implicitly been thinking of portfolios of stocks within a given market. That's why, after obtaining a fully diversified portfolio that eliminates all the unsystematic risk, we are left bearing the (undiversifiable) systematic risk of the market of our choice. But think about it: why end there?

Suppose we have a fully diversified portfolio of US stocks and we're therefore subject to the systematic risk of the US economy. Now, there's no reason to think that the factors that affect Japanese stocks should be perfectly correlated to those that affect US stocks. In fact, there are good reasons to think otherwise. (Think of events in the US that would have no impact on Japanese stocks, and events in Japan that would have no impact on US stocks.) Which means that if we now add Japanese stocks to our portfolio, the risk of our portfolio should fall. That's good; but again, why end there?

What if we now consider European stocks? Same story. As long as the factors that affect European stocks are not perfectly correlated to those that affect American and Japanese stocks (and of course they never are), European stocks should provide diversification benefits. In other words, the risk of our portfolio should fall again.

Can you see where we're going? In the same way that within a market we add stocks to our portfolio until we are fully diversified in that market, we're now adding international stocks (or markets) to our portfolio until we are fully diversified internationally. And, needless to say, the volatility of a fully diversified portfolio of international stocks would be lower than that of a fully diversified portfolio of stocks in any one country. (As a very crude estimate, consider that an investor fully diversified in international stocks would bear some 10% of the volatility of the average stock.)

Now for the bad news, which you probably expected anyway. No matter how many stocks from how many countries we include in our portfolio, we will never be able to *eliminate* risk; we'll only be able to *reduce* it. In other words, even the world market is subject to systematic factors (wars, international crises, oil prices . . .) that will prevent us from eliminating completely the volatility of our portfolio.

One final comment. Note that we have discussed diversifying across stocks within a market, and diversifying across international *equity* markets. However, a good diversification strategy does not have to be restricted to stocks only. The portfolio may (perhaps even should) contain other assets, such as bonds, derivatives, real estate, and more. In short, put your eggs in different baskets, and make sure that the baskets come in many different colors and sizes.

The big picture

However volatile an asset might be, we don't have to bear all its risk. That's one of the mean reasons why we diversify. But diversification does not *eliminate* risk; it merely *reduces* risk. How much we can reduce risk and how many stocks make up a fully diversified portfolio, in turn, are empirical questions that depend on the time and place we ask the question. In both cases, the estimates vary widely across countries and over time.

Unlike an asset in isolation, the risk of an asset within a diversified portfolio is measured by the *contribution* of the asset to the risk of the portfolio. This contribution can be assessed in total terms by the covariance between the asset and the portfolio, or in relative terms by the asset's beta. And this relative contribution to portfolio risk is, as we'll discuss in the next chapter, the proper measure of risk in the most widely used asset pricing model.

Excel section

There is no new Excel material in this chapter; all the magnitudes discussed have already been covered in the Excel sections of previous chapters.

Challenge section

We'll do only one thing in this Challenge section: we'll explore how the risk of the portfolio changes as we add more and more stocks to it. In order to make the task manageable, let's make the following two assumptions: (1) All assets have a standard deviation of 30%; and (2) the covariance between any two stocks is 0.02. Note that the first assumption implies that all assets have a variance of 0.09. The second assumption, in turn, implies that the correlation between any two stocks is 0.5.

- Open an Excel spreadsheet and input in cells A1, B1, and C1 the labels 'Number of stocks in the portfolio,' 'Variance of the portfolio,' and 'Standard deviation of the portfolio,' respectively.

- In cells A2 through A31 input the numbers 1 through 30, representing the number of stocks in the portfolio.

- In cell B2 input the expression '=(1/A2)*0.09+(1–1/A2)*0.02' for the variance of the portfolio. Then copy this expression all the way down through cell B31.

- In cell C2 input the expression '=sqrt(B2)' and copy all the way down through cell C31.

▶

■ Make a graph with the number of stocks in the x-axis and the standard deviation of the portfolio in the y-axis.

1 What do you make out of the numbers and the picture? More precisely:

(a) As the number of stocks in the portfolio increases, does risk fall at a decreasing rate or at an increasing rate? Does this make sense? Why?

(b) At what number of stocks, roughly, does risk begin to fall negligibly?

(c) If you look at the risk of the 30-stock portfolio measured by its *variance*, how different is it from the average covariance across stocks? Does this make sense? Why?

7

RISK AND RETURN II: THE CAPM AND THE COST OF CAPITAL

Required returns

The CAPM: Overview

The CAPM: Interpretation

The CAPM: Two issues

The CAPM: Estimating the risk-free rate

The CAPM: Estimating the market risk premium

The CAPM: Estimating beta

The CAPM: Application

The cost of capital

The big picture

Excel section

Challenge section

t is obvious that no investor is willing to bear an increase in risk if he doesn't expect to be compensated with a higher return. The question is, how much more? That is precisely what one of the most widely used models in finance, the CAPM, is built to answer. The CAPM is also a critical component of the cost of capital, an essential variable in project evaluation, company valuation, and capital-structure optimization.

Required returns

Question: what return should we require from a one-year investment? Wait, that may be too broad; let's make it a bit more precise. What is the *minimum* return we should require from a *risk-free* investment before parting with our money for one year? That's better, so let's think a bit about it.

If we take $100 from our pocket to put in a risk-free investment opportunity for one year, the least we would require is not losing purchasing power. In other words, we would require that, one year down the road, we could still buy the same amount of goods and services that we can buy today with $100. Well, actually, maybe a bit more; otherwise, why bother reaching for our wallet? But not much more; after all, we're not really taking any risk.

In short, it looks like we should require a small compensation over and above the expected loss of purchasing power. And that is, roughly, the one-year rate we would get if we deposited our money in the bank for one year. It is also, roughly, the rate we would get if we bought a one-year Treasury bill. Both rates track very closely the expected (and ultimately the observed) rate of inflation. In fact, in the century 1900–2000, the mean annual rate of inflation in the US was 3.3% and the mean annual return of US Treasury bills was 4.1%.

Now, what if instead of risk-free the investment were risky, in the sense that we would be uncertain about the amount of money to be received one year down the road? Obviously, in this case we would require a higher return. How much higher? That depends on the risk or uncertainty of the investment; the higher the perceived risk, the higher the required return.

Let's formalize and generalize this discussion a bit and say that the required return on any asset is the sum of two components, a risk-free rate and a risk premium. The risk-free rate is the compensation for the expected loss of purchasing power, and the risk premium is the compensation for bearing the risk of the asset. More precisely, the **required return on asset i, $E(R_i)$**, is given by

$$E(R_i) = R_f + RP_i \qquad (7.1)$$

where R_f denotes the risk-free rate and RP_i the risk premium of asset i.

It is important to notice the subscript i on $E(R_i)$ and RP_i but not on R_f. Intuitively, this means that *regardless* of the asset in which we invest, we always require the same compensation for the expected loss of purchasing power. However, *depending* on the asset in which we invest, we require an additional compensation for bearing the risk of *that* asset. In other words, when estimating the required return on two different assets, in both cases we would start from the *same risk-free rate* and then add *different risk premiums* for each asset.

The CAPM: Overview

The capital asset pricing model (CAPM) is, almost certainly, the most widely used model in finance. And that is for a very simple reason: it yields an essential magnitude, the return investors should require from an asset given the asset's risk. Surprising as it may seem, until the CAPM was proposed in the mid-1960s, no model provided investors with such a critical estimate. Sure, academics and practitioners agreed that given two assets with different risk, investors should require a higher return from the riskier asset. But no model enabled investors to estimate of *how much more* they should require.

Take another look at equation (7.1). In order to calculate the required return on an asset we need a risk-free rate and a risk premium. The former is the same for all assets and the latter is specific to each asset. The CAPM defines a way to measure an asset's risk and makes the asset's risk premium a function of that definition of risk. Essentially, then, the CAPM is a model that provides investors with a formal way of estimating the risk premium of an asset. Here, in a nutshell, is how.

The CAPM begins with an investor whose goal is to maximize his utility, which depends on the risk and return of his portfolio. In equilibrium, this investor ends up splitting his money between two assets: part of his money is invested in a fully diversified basket of risky assets called the *market portfolio* (*M*) and part of his money is invested in a risk-free rate. The market portfolio is the optimal combination of *risky* assets in the sense that it maximizes risk-adjusted returns. It contains no unsystematic risk (which has been diversified away), and therefore the risk of each individual asset is measured by the contribution of the asset to the risk of this portfolio. That contribution, in turn, is measured by beta, defined as the covariance between the asset and the market portfolio divided by the variance of this portfolio. And that is, precisely, the CAPM's definition of risk.

Although the CAPM can in principle be used to estimate the required return on any asset, it is more often than not used to estimate the required return on *equity*. For that reason, from now on we'll focus the discussion on stocks. Formally, then, the **beta of stock i (β_i)** is defined as

$$\beta_i = \frac{Cov_{iM}}{Var_M} \tag{7.2}$$

where Cov_{iM} denotes the covariance between stock i and the market portfolio, and Var_M denotes the variance of the market portfolio. Although under the CAPM this beta is the appropriate measure of the risk of a stock, there is more to the risk *premium* than beta.

In fact, the CAPM defines the risk premium of stock i as

$$RP_i = \{E(R_M) - R_f\} \cdot \beta_i = MRP \cdot \beta_i \tag{7.3}$$

where $E(R_M)$ is the required return on the Market Portfolio and *MRP* denotes the *market* risk premium defined as $E(R_M) - R_f$. Combining (7.1) and (7.3) we get that according to the CAPM, the **required return on stock i, $E(R_i)$**, follows from the expression

$$E(R_i) = R_f + \{E(R_M) - R_f\} \cdot \beta_i = R_f + MRP \cdot \beta_i \tag{7.4}$$

which is sometimes expressed as

$$E(R_i) - R_f = \{E(R_M) - R_f\} \cdot \beta_i = MRP \cdot \beta_i \tag{7.5}$$

Equations (7.4) and (7.5) are two of the most widely used in finance and their importance can hardly be overstated. Let's think a bit about them then.

The CAPM: Interpretation

Let's start with the left-hand side of equation (7.4), which we defined before as the required return on stock i. In fact, the CAPM yields both the *required* and the *expected* return of a stock. This is because the CAPM is an equilibrium model, and in equilibrium what we expect from a stock and what we require from it *must* be the same. There's a simple way of seeing why this is the case.

Suppose that investors require a 10% annual return from a stock but they expect it to yield 15%. Then they would rush to buy this stock, driving its price up and its expected returns down. Conversely, suppose that investors require a 15% annual return from a stock but expect it to yield only 10%. Then they would rush to sell this stock, driving its price down and its expected return up. In short, an equilibrium is only possible when the required and the expected return from a stock are the same. For this reason, $E(R_i)$ denotes *both* the required and the expected return from stock i, and we'll use both expressions interchangeably.

Now to the right-hand side where we have two terms, the risk-free rate and the risk premium. The interpretation of the first is straightforward and we have already discussed it; it is a compensation for the expected loss of purchasing power. The other term, the risk premium, we have also discussed in general terms; it is a compensation for bearing risk. So let's see now how the CAPM proposes to estimate this risk premium.

According to the CAPM, the risk premium of a stock is given by the product of two terms, the market risk premium and the stock's beta. It is important to note that there is no i in the market risk premium. That means that, just like the risk-free rate, this magnitude will be the same regardless of the stock we're considering. Intuitively, the simplest way to think about the market risk premium is as the *additional* compensation required by investors for investing in risky assets as opposed to investing in risk-free assets. It then follows that this magnitude should be positive, $MRP = E(R_M) - R_f > 0$, and that there is a positive relationship between risk (measured by beta) and return.

Regarding beta, note first that, given its definition ($\beta_i = Cov_{iM}/Var_M$), it is an unbounded number. Because a variance is a non-negative number and a covariance can be positive or negative (or 0), then so can be beta, that is, $\beta_i \gtrless 0$. But that's just in theory. Empirically, it is very difficult to find a stock with a negative correlation to another or to the market (as we discussed in the previous chapter), which means that in practice we deal almost exclusively with positive betas.

There are two other ways of thinking about beta that are important. First, we can express the beta of stock i as

$$\beta_i = \frac{\Delta R_i}{\Delta R_M} \tag{7.6}$$

In other words, beta measures the sensitivity of the returns of stock i to changes in the returns of the market. If $\beta_i > 1$, the stock amplifies the fluctuations of the market, and if $\beta_i < 1$ the stock mitigates the fluctuations of the market. For example, a stock with a beta of 2 indicates that, as the market goes up and down 1%, this stock will (on average) go up and down 2%. A stock with a beta of 0.5, on the other hand, indicates that as the market goes up and down 1%, this stock will (on average) go up and down 0.5%. This is why beta is sometimes called a measure of *relative* volatility (as opposed to the standard deviation, which is a measure of *total* volatility): because it measures the volatility of a stock *relative to that of the market.*

Alternatively, replacing in equation (7.2) Cov_{iM} by $SD_i \cdot SD_M \cdot Corr_{iM}$ (see Chapter 27 if this is not entirely clear), we can express the beta of stock i as

$$\beta_i = \frac{SD_i}{SD_M} \cdot Corr_{iM} \tag{7.7}$$

where SD_i and SD_M denote the standard deviations of stock i and the market, respectively, and $Corr_{iM}$ denotes the correlation between stock i and the market. This way of looking at beta underscores why a very volatile asset does not necessarily have to be very risky: because its correlation to the market may be very low. As we discussed in Chapter 5, emerging markets and venture capital funds fall neatly into this description; they both are much more volatile than the market, but their correlation to the market is also very low.

Finally, let's put together both the market risk premium and beta, and let's consider first a stock with $\beta_i = 1$. We can think of this stock as having average risk (that of the market), and therefore we require from it an average return, that is, $RP_i = E(R_i) - R_f = E(R_M) - R_f$ and $E(R_i) = E(R_M)$. A stock with $\beta_i = 2$, on the other hand, is twice as risky as the market, and we then require a compensation for risk twice as high as that of the market, that is, $RP_i = E(R_i) - R_f = \{E(R_M) - R_f\} \cdot 2$. Finally, a stock with $\beta_i = 0.5$, is half as risky as the market, and we then require a compensation for risk half as high as that of the market; that is, $RP_i = E(R_i) - R_f = \{E(R_M) - R_f\} \cdot 0.5$.

In sum, the CAPM provides investors with a simple and intuitive way of estimating the required (or expected) return of a stock. It argues that investors should require compensation for the expected loss of purchasing power (R_f) and for bearing risk (RP_i). And it specifies that the compensation for risk should be measured by the risk premium required to the market (MRP) corrected by a factor specific to each stock, the latter assessing how much more or less risky that stock is relative to the market (β_i). All very simple and intuitive, and yet, as usual, the devil is in the detail.

The CAPM: Two issues

Before discussing each of the three inputs the CAPM requires, let's briefly address two important issues. First, it's important to note that the required (or expected) return of a stock is a *forward*-looking magnitude. This implies that we need forward-looking estimates of the risk-free rate, the market risk premium, and beta. Although this poses no problem with respect to the risk-free rate, forward-looking estimates of the market risk premium and beta are not easy to obtain. In fact, in practice, these estimates are almost always based on historical data. Whether or not this is the best we can do is controversial, but at least keep in mind that, ideally, we need to estimate *expected* market risk premiums and betas.

Second, it is important to highlight that, however simple it may look, the CAPM is not trivial to implement in practice. This follows from the fact that the CAPM is silent regarding the exact way to estimate the three magnitudes we need for its implementation. As we discuss below, the exact definition of a risk-free rate, a market risk premium, and beta is far from obvious. This, in turn, implies that rather than being able to defend a particular choice on theoretical grounds, more often than not we'll find ourselves defending our choice simply as being the consensus of (or the most common choice made by) practitioners.

The CAPM: Estimating the risk-free rate

It seems that putting a number on R_f shouldn't be too difficult. All we need to do is to open the *Wall Street Journal* and find the number we're looking for. And yet, the CAPM is silent about what exactly is the risk-free rate. Even if we agree that it is the yield on a government bond, is it a one-year rate, a ten-year rate, a 30-year rate, or somewhere between? The CAPM is silent on this issue so let's discuss some possibilities.

Consider first the yield on a one-year Treasury bill. Some argue that the CAPM is a one-period model and that we usually discount annual cash flows, so we should consider the yield on a one-year bill. In addition, some argue, this one-year yield is the 'real' risk-free rate; yields on longer-term government bonds are free from default risk but not from interest rate risk. (These two sources of risk are discussed in Chapter 19.)

However, this alternative has at least two drawbacks. First, if we use a one-year yield, then we would have to estimate the one-year yields to be obtained two, three, and more years down the road. This is problematic for two reasons. On the one hand, it is not at all clear that we can forecast these yields accurately. On the other hand, we would then have to deal with a time-varying discount rate (if R_f changes from period to period so does the required return on equity), which may complicate the discounting of cash flows substantially. Second, practitioners do not use one-year yields often.

What about the yield on a 30-year Treasury bond? It's not free from problems, either. Many companies that tend to invest in short-term or medium-term projects find this yield too high. In addition, the US government's decision on October 31, 2001, to stop issuing 30-year bonds decreased the appeal of this long yield substantially. Finally, just like the one-year yield, the 30-year yield is not very widely used by practitioners (though it is used more often than the one-year yield).

That leaves us with the two more widely accepted alternatives. One is to use the yield on a government bond with a maturity similar to that of the average maturity of a company's projects. For example, toy makers would tend to use short-term yields, and airplane manufacturers would tend to use long-term yields. Note that this alternative obviously implies that different companies would use yields of different maturity, and therefore different estimates of the risk-free rate. And of course there's nothing wrong with that.

The other (increasingly popular) alternative is to use the yield on ten-year notes. Part of the reason this alternative is appealing stems from the fact that benchmark rates for government bonds are increasingly based on ten-year rates. If you open the *Wall Street Journal* or the *Financial Times* to look for a quick summary of government bond yields, you will find the yield on ten-year notes.

Finally, in order to assess the magnitude of the differences in yields we've been discussing, take a look at Table 7.1, which shows rates for different maturities and countries at the end of 2003. As the table shows, different choices may lead to rather substantial differences in the required return on equity. In the US case, the difference between choosing a one-year rate and a 30-year rate is almost 4 percentage points.

TABLE 7.1

Maturity	US (%)	UK (%)	Japan (%)	Germany (%)
1 year	1.3	4.4	0.1	2.3
5 years	3.2	4.6	0.6	3.5
10 years	4.3	4.8	1.3	4.3
20 years	5.1	4.8	1.9	4.8
30 years	5.1	4.7	2.1	4.9

In sum, although it is difficult to defend theoretically the choice of any given risk-free rate, the consensus of practitioners seems to have converged around two alternatives: the yield on a bond with a maturity similar to that of the average maturity of a company's projects, or the yield on ten-year Treasury notes. If we want to compare required returns on equity across companies, the latter is probably the better alternative.

The CAPM: Estimating the market risk premium

The market risk premium, as we discussed before, attempts to measure the additional compensation required by investors for investing in risky assets as opposed to investing in risk-free assets. Almost always, it is measured as the average historical difference between the return on the market and the return on the risk-free rate. That much is clear and rather uncontroversial. But again, the CAPM is silent on the details. What 'market' should we consider? What risk-free rate? How many years should we include in the historical average? Should we calculate an arithmetic average or a geometric average? The CAPM doesn't really say, theory doesn't really help, and we're left (again) to consider different alternatives and to look for help in the consensus among practitioners.

In theory, the market portfolio should contain *all* risky assets, including assets such as real estate and human capital, which makes it seem as if calculating its return were an impossible task. And yet, in practice, the standard choice for the market portfolio is rather uncontroversial. The reason is that, for better or for worse, in most countries there is a widely accepted choice for the market portfolio, almost always being a broadly diversified index of *stocks* (rather than of all risky assets). In the US, for example, the virtually undisputed choice for the market portfolio is the S&P500. And wherever you're reading this, practitioners have most likely converged into another virtually undisputed choice for the market portfolio of that country.

We have already discussed alternatives for the risk-free rate but let's make two additional points. First, in most countries the risk premium is calculated with respect to both government bills and bonds, although their attributes vary from country to country. More often than not, however, the market risk premium based on bills is calculated with respect to one-year yields, and that based on bonds is calculated with respect to yields longer than ten years. Second, of these two possibilities, the calculation based on bonds seems to be the more widely accepted alternative.

The number of years we should include in the average is far from clear. Because the market risk premium is usually calculated as a 'historical' average, it is common to include as many years as possible. But again, both the CAPM and theory are silent on any guidance on the specific number of years. In the US, the usual choice is whatever is the number of years after 1926, for the sole reason that the S&P500 was created in that year. (More on this in a minute.)

Finally, having obtained historical returns on the market and the risk-free rate, and having calculated their annual differences, should we calculate the arithmetic mean or the geometric mean of these differences? Again, neither the CAPM nor theory are of much help. Some argue that the arithmetic mean is the more appropriate choice because it better captures the *expected* risk premium; others disagree and recommend using the geometric mean instead. The evidence seems to indicate that the arithmetic mean is more widely used than the geometric mean for the computation of the average historical risk premium.

Table 7.2 shows the market risk premium for several countries, for the period 1900–2000, calculated on the basis of both the arithmetic mean and the geometric mean, as well as with respect to bills and bonds. It is interesting to note that a very common choice for the market risk premium in the US is a number between 5% and 6%, a range that seems to be consistent with a geometric average. This contrasts with surveys that indicate that the arithmetic average is the more common choice.

In sum, although it is again difficult to defend a particular choice on theoretical grounds, the consensus of practitioners seems to have converged around a market risk premium based on whatever the widely accepted market portfolio is in each country (in the US, the S&P500); on long-term risk-free rates (yields longer than ten years); on as many annual observations as possible (in the US, whatever the number of years after 1926); and on an arithmetic average (though the range typically used in the US is more consistent with a geometric average).

TABLE 7.2

Country	With respect to bills		With respect to bonds	
	Geometric (%)	Arithmetic (%)	Geometric (%)	Arithmetic (%)
Australia	7.1	8.5	6.3	8.0
Belgium	2.9	5.1	2.9	4.8
Canada	4.6	5.9	4.5	6.0
Denmark	1.8	3.4	2.0	3.3
France	7.4	9.8	4.9	7.0
Germany	4.9	10.3	6.7	9.9
Ireland	3.5	5.4	3.2	4.6
Italy	7.0	11.0	5.0	8.4
Japan	6.7	9.9	6.2	10.3
Netherlands	5.1	7.1	4.7	6.7
South Africa	6.0	8.1	5.4	7.1
Spain	3.2	5.3	2.3	4.2
Sweden	5.5	7.7	5.2	7.4
Switzerland	4.3	6.1	2.7	4.2
UK	4.8	6.5	4.4	5.6
US	5.8	7.7	5.0	7.0
World	4.9	6.2	4.6	5.6

Source: Adapted from *Triumph of the Optimists: 101 Years of Global Investment Returns*, by Elroy Dimson, Paul Marsh, and Mike Staunton. Princeton University Press, New Jersey, 2002

The CAPM: Estimating beta

Just like the other two inputs of the CAPM, estimating betas may appear to be trivial but the devil is in the detail. Let's start with the uncontroversial part. Estimating the beta of stock i requires running a time-series regression between the risk premium of stock i and the market risk premium. That is,

$$R_{it} - R_{ft} = \beta_0 + \beta_1 \cdot (R_{Mt} - R_{ft}) + u_t \qquad (7.8)$$

where R_i and R_M denote the returns of stock i and the market, respectively, R_f denotes the risk-free rate, β_0 and β_1 are two coefficients to be estimated, u is an error term, and the subscript t indexes time. The slope of this regression (β_1) is the beta we want to estimate.

Many times, however, the estimation is made without the risk-free rate, which makes the data collection a bit less demanding. In that case, the regression run is between the returns of stock i and the returns of the market. That is,

$$R_{it} = \beta_0 + \beta_1 \cdot R_{Mt} + u_t \qquad (7.9)$$

where again the slope of the regression (β_1) is the beta we want to estimate. In theory, if the risk-free rate were constant over time, the beta estimated from equation (7.8) or (7.9) should be identical. In practice, however, because R_f varies a bit over time, the estimates of beta that follow from (7.8) or (7.9) may be slightly different.

Now for the tricky issues. We could start asking what the market portfolio is for which we need to collect returns, but we have already addressed that issue. Although the market portfolio is in theory a very broad concept, in practice there is an index of stocks in each country that has become the widely accepted alternative (like the S&P500 in the US). However, the CAPM is also silent on other important issues. For example, should we collect daily, weekly, monthly, or annual returns? Should we estimate betas over one year, five years, ten years, more years? Again, theory does not really help, so we'll look at the consensus reached by practitioners, which in this case is less controversial than in some of the issues we discussed before.

Regarding the frequency of the data, the most widely accepted alternative is to use *monthly* returns. Daily returns are too noisy (they capture a lot of volatility that is useless for the purposes of estimating the required return on equity) and annual returns usually give us too few observations. Most data providers and practitioners estimate betas using either weekly or monthly returns, the latter being the more common choice.

Regarding the time period for which betas should be estimated, five years seems to be a widely accepted alternative. With very short periods of time (one or two years), we run the risk of capturing an unusually good or bad period for the company, which we shouldn't really extrapolate into the future. With very long periods of time, on the other hand, we run the risk of using data that ceases being representative for the company. Think Nokia, a former conglomerate that transformed itself completely into a provider of cellular phones. If we used data from the time before this deep transformation took place, we would be capturing risk that has little to do with the current business of the company.

Five years, then, seems to be a compromise (however good) aimed at capturing the current situation of the company without being unduly weighted by its very short-term performance.

Note, finally, that the choice of monthly returns and a five-year time span leaves us with 60 observations to run the regression in either equation (7.8) or (7.9). Table 7.3 in the next section shows the beta of the components of the Dow estimated from monthly returns for the 1999–2003 period.

The CAPM: Application

Let's finally put all the pieces together and estimate the required return on equity for the 30 stocks of the Dow Jones Industrial Average based on the CAPM. In order to estimate the required return on any stock, equation (7.4) requires an estimate of the risk-free rate, another of the market risk premium (both common to all companies), and another of the stock's beta (specific to each company).

Consistent with our discussion above, we'll use the yield on ten-year US Treasury notes as our estimate of the risk-free rate. On December 31, 2003, the yield on these notes was 4.3%. For the market risk premium we'll use the mid-point of the widely used 5–6% range, that is, 5.5%. This estimate is roughly consistent with a long-term geometric average of the market risk premium based on both bonds and bills. Using these two estimates, we can rewrite equation (7.4) as

$$E(R_i) = 0.043 + 0.055 \cdot \beta_i \tag{7.10}$$

Finally, we'll estimate the beta for the 30 stocks of the Dow using equation (7.9), five years of monthly returns (January 1999–December 2003), and the S&P500 as a proxy for the market. Table 7.3 shows these betas, as well as the required returns on these companies that follow from equation (7.10).

Note that one company (P&G) has a slightly negative beta. This is, of course, an anomaly which would not be expected to hold over time. (In fact, the beta of P&G is statistically non-significant, which means that for all practical purposes it is 0.) Note, also, that only one company (Intel) has a beta larger than 2. Although some very volatile stocks, such as internet companies, may have betas a bit larger than 3, it would be highly unusual to find betas much larger than that. Note, finally, that the average required return on equity of these blue-chip companies (not reported in the table) is just under 10%.

TABLE 7.3

Company	β_i	$E(R_i)$ (%)	Company	β_i	$E(R_i)$ (%)
3M	0.6	7.5	Honeywell	1.3	11.6
Alcoa	1.8	14.2	Intel	2.1	15.7
Altria	0.3	5.8	IBM	1.4	12.3
American Express	1.1	10.6	Johnson & Johnson	0.3	5.7
American Intl.	0.8	8.9	JP Morgan Chase	1.8	13.9
Boeing	0.7	8.2	McDonald's	0.8	8.5
Caterpillar	1.0	9.9	Merck	0.3	6.0
Citigroup	1.4	12.2	Microsoft	1.7	13.6
Coca-Cola	0.3	5.8	Pfizer	0.4	6.4
DuPont	0.9	9.4	Procter & Gamble	−0.1	3.5
Exxon Mobil	0.4	6.5	SBC Comm.	0.8	8.8
General Electric	1.1	10.2	United Tech.	1.1	10.3
General Motors	1.3	11.3	Verizon	1.0	9.8
Hewlett-Packard	1.8	13.9	Wal-Mart	0.8	8.7
Home Depot	1.4	11.9	Walt Disney	1.0	10.0

The cost of capital

Few variables are as critical for a company as the cost of its capital, a magnitude needed for company valuation, project evaluation, and capital-structure optimization, to name but a few important activities. Essentially, the cost of capital measures the average return required on a company given the company's risk. And the required return on equity derived from the CAPM that we just discussed is one of its components.

Let's assume, for the moment, that a company finances its projects with only two financial instruments, debt (D) and equity (E). Investors will obviously require a compensation for investing in these two instruments, so let's call R_D the required return on debt (or the cost of debt) and R_E the required return on equity (or the cost of equity). Then, a company's **weighted-average cost of capital (R_{WACC})** is given by

$$R_{WACC} = (1 - t_c) \cdot x_D \cdot R_D + x_E \cdot R_E \qquad (7.11)$$

where $x_D = D/(D + E)$ and $x_E = E/(D + E)$ represent the proportions of debt and equity, respectively, t_c denotes the corporate tax rate, and $x_D + x_E = 1$.

If you think about equation (7.11), ignoring for the moment the corporate tax rate, it basically says that a company's cost of capital is the average return required on the financial instruments issued by a company, each weighted by the proportion in which the company uses each instrument. The inclusion of the corporate tax rate simply indicates that interest payments on debt (but not dividends on equity) are tax deductible, which lowers the cost of this source of financing. That's why, although the cost of debt is R_D, the *after-tax* cost of debt is $(1 - t_c) \cdot R_D$.

The required return on debt is usually captured by the *yield* on the debt issued by the company, not by the interest rate on this debt. (If this distinction is not clear, take a look at Chapter 18.) Similarly, x_D should be measured at *market* value rather than at book value. Note that there is wide agreement about both of these statements, and neither academics nor practitioners would find them controversial. If a company does not have any debt traded in the market, then R_D is measured by the rate at which the company could borrow funds from a bank. Finally, the debt considered in the estimation of the cost of capital is interest-bearing (usually long-term) debt.

The required return on equity, in turn, is usually estimated with the CAPM (although, as we will see in the next chapter, there exist alternative models). Note in this regard a fundamental difference between the cost of debt and the cost of equity. Whereas a manager can always assess at any point in time the company's cost of debt by simply observing the yield of the debt traded in the market (or the rate at which the company could borrow from a bank), the cost of equity is nowhere to be observed. That's why it must be estimated from some model, such as the CAPM. Note, also, that just as we discussed, x_D, x_E should be measured at market value, not at book value.

Although the cost of capital is usually as in equation (7.11), it can really have as many terms as the different financial instruments a company issues to finance its projects. For example, if a company issues debt, equity, and preferred equity (P), then the company's cost of capital would be calculated as

$$R_{WACC} = (1 - t_c) \cdot x_D \cdot R_D + x_E \cdot R_E + x_P \cdot R_P \qquad (7.12)$$

where $x_P = P/(D + E + P)$ is the proportion of preferred equity, R_P is the required return on the preferred equity, and $x_D + x_E + x_P = 1$.

One of the critical uses for the cost of capital is as a hurdle rate, that is, as the minimum return required on a project. Both NPV and IRR, two widely used rules for project evaluation (both discussed in Chapter 19), use this cost of capital as a necessary input to determine the viability of a project. The cost of capital is also used as the discount rate of one of the most widely used methods of company valuation (called, precisely, the WACC method and discussed in Chapter 14). And it's also used as the target variable in the optimization of capital structures, that is, the optimal combination of financial instruments that minimizes a company's cost of capital.

The big picture

The CAPM is, almost certainly, the most widely used model in finance, in part because it provides a simple answer to a critical question: what compensation should investors require from a stock given the stock's risk? Simple as the model appears to be, however, the devil is once again in the detail; the three inputs the model requires may be interpreted in a variety of ways. And, lacking theoretical guidance about the most appropriate choice for each input, we're left following the consensus of practitioners.

The CAPM is also a critical input in the estimation of the cost of capital, a critical magnitude for every company and used in the evaluation of projects and the valuation of companies, among other important uses. But the CAPM is not the only model devised to estimate required returns on equity. In the next chapter we'll discuss its main contender.

Excel section

Running regressions such as those in equations (7.8) and (7.9) is fairly simple in Excel. However, we discuss that issue in Chapter 30 and there is no need to do it again here. Having said that, let's consider here a shortcut to estimate the slope of a linear regression (which is what we need to estimate the beta of the CAPM). Suppose you have a series of ten observations on a dependent variable in cells A1:A10, and a series of ten observations on an independent variable in cells B1:B10. Then,

- To estimate the slope of the linear regression simply type '**=linest(A1:A10, B1:B10)**' in cell A11 and hit 'Enter.'

If you think, for example, of the dependent variable as the returns on stock i, and the independent variable as the returns on the market, a linear regression between these two variables is exactly what is shown in equation (7.9). And the result of using the 'linest' command as indicated above will be the beta of stock i.

Challenge section

1 Consider the annual returns of Berkshire Hathaway (BH), Cisco, Morgan Stanley (MS), and the S&P500 between the years 1994 and 2003 displayed in Table 7.4.
   (a) Calculate the mean (arithmetic) return of these three companies and the market during the 1994–2003 period.
   (b) Calculate the beta of each of these three companies with respect to the market (the S&P500).
   (c) Does there seem to be a positive relationship between risk (measured by beta) and return?

TABLE 7.4

Year	BH (%)	Cisco (%)	MS (%)	S&P500 (%)
1994	25.0	8.7	–0.8	1.3
1995	57.4	112.5	40.6	37.6
1996	6.2	70.5	43.2	23.0
1997	34.9	31.4	80.7	33.4
1998	52.2	149.7	21.6	28.6
1999	–19.9	130.8	103.1	21.0
2000	26.6	–28.6	12.2	–9.1
2001	6.5	–52.7	–28.3	–11.9
2002	–3.8	–27.7	–27.2	–22.1
2003	15.8	85.0	47.9	28.7

2 Using a risk-free rate of 4.3% (the yield on ten-year Treasury notes at the end of 2003) and a market risk premium of 5.5%, calculate the required return on equity of the three companies in question 1 using the CAPM.

8

RISK AND RETURN III: ALTERNATIVES TO THE CAPM

Risk and required return according to the CAPM

A brief digression

The size and value premiums

The three-factor model: Overview

The three-factor model: Implementation

The three-factor model: Application

The big picture

Excel section

Challenge section

The CAPM we discussed in the previous chapter argues that the *only* variable important for the estimation of required returns on equity is systematic risk measured by beta. That's a very strong statement. Particularly when the empirical evidence seems to point to other variables that are clearly correlated to returns. Two of these variables are a company's market capitalization and book-to-market ratio, which can be articulated (together with beta) into the increasingly popular three-factor model.

Risk and required return according to the CAPM

When it comes down to popularity, the CAPM beats the competition hands down: over 80% of practitioners claim to use the CAPM when calculating a company's required (or expected) return on equity. Does that make it the 'best' model? Not necessarily. It is by far the most popular, though which one is the best (whatever that means, anyway) remains an open question.

The difference across models used to estimate required returns on equity largely stems from the way each proposes to estimate the risk premium. Recall that the required return on any stock i, $E(R_i)$, can be thought of as the sum of the risk-free rate (R_f) and the stock's risk premium (RP_i); that is, $E(R_i) = R_f + RP_i$. Recall, also, that the CAPM essentially argues that this risk premium can be calculated as the product of the market risk premium, $MRP = E(R_M) - R_f$, where $E(R_M)$ is the required return on the market portfolio, and the stock's beta (β_i), that is, $RP_i = \{E(R_M) - R_f\} \cdot \beta_i = MRP \cdot \beta_i$.

The previous arguments collapse into the central message of the CAPM, which says that the required return on equity on any stock i can be expressed as

$$E(R_i) = R_f + \{E(R_M) - R_f\} \cdot \beta_i = R_f + MRP \cdot \beta_i \tag{8.1}$$

or, similarly, as

$$E(R_i) - R_f = \{E(R_M) - R_f\} \cdot \beta_i = MRP \cdot \beta_i \tag{8.2}$$

where beta captures systematic risk, the *only* relevant source of risk according to this model.

A brief digression

Now, *that* is a strong statement! Think about it. Total risk (volatility), currency risk, bankruptcy risk, and as many others sources of risk as you can imagine . . . they don't matter. They provide no information about the required or expected return on stocks. If this sounds strange, it's simply because it is.

And yet, a die-hard supporter of the CAPM would justify this strong argument in many ways, two of which we'll consider briefly. The first line of defense would be theoretical. He would claim that, unlike the vast majority of its contenders, the CAPM is solidly grounded in theory. More precisely, he would argue that in a model in which investors behave optimally, beta *must* be the only relevant source of risk. In other words, this 'strange' prediction of the CAPM is not an assumption but the *result* of a model of optimal behavior.

Very little can be argued against this line of reasoning. It is indeed true that the CAPM is supported by a solid theoretical background and that it results from a model of optimal investor behavior. And it is also true that the vast majority of its competitors are models in which the variables used to determine the required return on equity come from guesses or plausible stories, or worse, from the result of trying one variable after another until something that correlates with returns is found. And yet it could be argued that a theory is only as good as its predictions, and if the evidence does not support these predictions, then the theory should be discarded.

That takes us straight into the second line of defense, which is empirical. But this is a tricky one; we could fill a room with studies that test the validity of the CAPM, in different countries, over different periods of time, and with different methodologies. The problem is that there is a huge amount of evidence on *both* sides of the fence. Both those who defend the CAPM and those who defend alternative models could point to a vast amount of evidence supporting their position. As a result, the evidence doesn't go a long way toward clearly supporting either the CAPM or one of its contenders.

The size and value premiums

And yet, at least *some* empirical evidence is surprisingly consistent. Data for different countries and over different time periods shows a consistent *negative* relationship between market capitalization and returns. In other words, the evidence seems to clearly show that small companies tend to deliver higher returns than large companies. This empirical regularity is usually known as the *size effect*.

Similarly, data for different countries and over different time periods show a consistent *positive* relationship between book-to-market ratios (*BtM*) and returns. In other words, companies with high *BtM* tend to deliver higher returns than those with low *BtM*. This ratio, recall, is a measure of cheapness in the sense that high and low *BtM* indicate cheap and expensive stocks (relative to book value), respectively. So the evidence seems to clearly show that cheap (also called *value*) stocks tend to outperform expensive (also called *growth*) stocks. This empirical regularity is usually known as the *value effect*.

Now, however clear the evidence may be, there doesn't seem to be any good theoretical reason for the size and value premiums. In other words, no model of optimal investor behavior converges into a result in which stock returns depend on size and value. Some may not consider this a problem; they would claim that as long as we can isolate the variables that explain differences in returns, we should use them to determine expected returns. Yet others would argue that without a good theory behind, there is no point in using a model for this purpose. You can pick your side on this debate.

If you think a bit about it, though, at first glance these two risk premiums seem to make sense. Small companies are probably less diversified and less able to withstand negative shocks than large companies. And as for cheap companies, well, there must be a reason why they're cheap! Put simply, it's not very difficult to come up with some plausible story to explain why small stocks and cheap stocks are riskier than large stocks and expensive stocks, and therefore why they should deliver higher returns.

But those are just stories. Perhaps a better alternative is attempting to link empirically size and value to obvious sources of risk. The evidence on this seems to point to the fact that small companies and cheap companies are less profitable (have lower earnings or cash flow relative to book value) than large companies and expensive companies. In other words, small companies and cheap companies are distressed because of their poor profitability, and are therefore perceived as riskier by investors.

The CAPM argues that stocks with high systematic (market) risk should outperform those with low systematic risk. Complementary evidence shows that small stocks outperform large stocks, and that cheap (value) stocks outperform expensive (growth) stocks. Put all this together and we get the result that stock returns are affected by a *market* premium, a *size* premium, and a *value* premium. And that is, precisely, the message from the three-factor model.

The three-factor model: Overview

Estimating required returns from the three-factor model is just a tiny bit more difficult than doing it with the CAPM. That is simply because we need some additional data and we have to estimate two additional beta coefficients. Other than that, as we'll soon see, the model poses no difficult obstacles to practitioners.

According to the three-factor model, the **required return on stock i** follows from the expression

$$E(R_i) = R_f + MRP \cdot \beta_i + SMB \cdot \beta_i^S + HML \cdot \beta_i^V \tag{8.3}$$

where SMB (small minus big) and HML (high minus low) denote the size and value premiums, respectively, and β_i^S and β_i^V denote the sensitivities (betas) of stock i with respect to the size factor and the value factor, respectively. Let's think a bit about these magnitudes.

Recall that MRP, the market risk premium, seeks to capture the additional compensation required by investors for investing in risky assets as opposed to investing in risk-free assets. Recall, also, that it is measured by the average historical difference between the return of the market portfolio (some widely accepted benchmark index of stocks) and the risk-free rate. And recall, finally, that β_i measures the sensitivity of the returns of stock i to changes in the market risk premium (or, simply, to changes in the returns of the market).

Similarly, SMB, the size premium, seeks to capture the additional compensation required by investors for investing in small companies as opposed to investing in large companies. It is measured as the average historical difference between the returns of a portfolio of small stocks and those of a portfolio of large stocks. And the beta associated with this factor, usually called the size beta (β_i^S), measures the sensitivity of the returns of stock i to changes in the size premium, or, simply, the exposure of company i to size risk.

Finally, HML, the value premium, seeks to capture the additional compensation required by investors for investing in cheap stocks as opposed to investing in expensive stocks. It is measured as the average historical difference between the returns of a portfolio of stocks with high BtM and those of a portfolio of stocks with low BtM. And the beta associated with this factor, usually called the value beta (β_i^V), measures the sensitivity of the returns of stock i to changes in the value premium, or, simply, the exposure of company i to value risk.

Note that just as we stressed in the previous chapter about *MRP*, neither *SMB* nor *HML* in equation (8.3) has an i subscript. That means that the average size and value premiums, as well as R_f and *MRP*, are independent of the stock we're considering. Note, on the other hand, that the size beta (β_i^S) and the value beta (β_i^V), as well as β_i, all have a subscript i, indicating that they are specific to the company we're considering.

The three-factor model: Implementation

The three-factor model, just like the CAPM, is silent about several practical issues. What is a portfolio of small stocks? And one of large stocks? What is a portfolio of cheap (value) stocks? And one of expensive (growth) stocks? Should we estimate betas out of daily, weekly, monthly, or annual data? Over what period of time? Again, we'll find ourselves looking at the convergence among practitioners for guidance.

Let's start with what we already know from the previous chapter regarding the estimation of the CAPM. We need a risk-free rate that we approximate with the yield on 10-year Treasury notes (or with the yield on a bond of maturity equal to the average maturity of a company's projects). We need a market portfolio that we approximate with a widely accepted benchmark of stocks (such as the S&P500 in the US). We need a market risk premium that we calculate as the average historical difference between the returns on the benchmark of stocks and a long-term risk free rate; the time period is as long as the data allows and the average can be either arithmetic or geometric. And we need a company's beta, which we estimate with respect to the benchmark of stocks using monthly returns over a five-year period.

Because the three-factor model essentially adds two factors to the CAPM, we'll focus now on what we need to estimate the size and value premiums. But a quick comment first. The three-factor model was proposed by professors Eugene Fama and Kenneth French in a series of articles published in the 1990s; that's why you may occasionally find this model referred to as the Fama–French three-factor model. In the 'Data Library' of Ken French's web page (*http://mba.tuck.dartmouth.edu/pages/faculty/ken.french/*) you will find a wealth of information about this model, as well as data to implement it. For that reason, we'll focus here on the essentials; if you want to get into details, do visit that web page.

Let's start with the estimation of *SMB* and *HML*. To estimate *SMB* we need to calculate the average historical difference between the returns of a portfolio of small stocks and those of a portfolio of large stocks. The formation and rebalancing of each of these two portfolios is less than trivial but you don't have to worry about it. In Ken French's web page you'll find annual returns for the *SMB* portfolio from 1927 on. The third column of Table 8.1 displays these returns for the 1994–2003 period only. Note that, on average *since 1927*, small stocks outperformed large stocks by almost 4 percentage points a year.

TABLE 8.1

Year	MRP (%)	SMB (%)	HML (%)
1994	−4.1	0.4	−0.1
1995	31.0	−6.9	−3.5
1996	16.3	−1.9	0.2
1997	26.1	−3.7	11.1
1998	19.4	−23.3	−15.0
1999	20.2	11.7	−39.4
2000	−16.7	−5.7	21.4
2001	−14.8	28.4	27.3
2002	−22.9	4.4	3.7
2003	30.7	28.1	15.1
AM (1927–2003)	8.5%	3.9%	4.4%
GM (1927–2003)	6.4%	2.9%	3.4%

The estimation of *HML* is similar. We need to calculate the average historical difference between the returns of a portfolio of stocks with high *BtM* and those of a portfolio of stocks with low *BtM*. Again, the formation and rebalancing of each of these two portfolios is less than trivial, but you don't have to worry about it. In Ken French's web page you'll find annual returns for the *HML* portfolio from 1927 on. The fourth column of Table 8.1 displays these returns for the 1994–2003 period. Note that, on average *since 1927*, cheap (value) stocks outperformed expensive (growth) stocks by almost 4.5 percentage points a year.

We have already discussed the estimation of *MRP* in detail in the previous chapter (and briefly at the beginning of this chapter), so one final quick comment now. The returns of this portfolio available from Ken French's web page are calculated a bit differently from how we discussed it (and from standard practice). Nothing you should worry about from a practical point of view. The second column of Table 8.1 displays the annual returns of the *MRP* portfolio for the 1994–2003 period, and the (arithmetic and geometric) average *since 1927*.

The three betas we need to implement the three-factor model are estimated jointly by running a time-series regression between the risk premium of stock i, $RP_i = R_i - R_f$, and the three portfolios that capture the market, size, and value premiums (*MRP*, *SMB*, and *HML*), that is,

$$R_{it} - R_{ft} = \beta_0 + \beta_1 \cdot MRP_t + \beta_2 \cdot SMB_t + \beta_3 \cdot HML_t + u_t \qquad (8.4)$$

where $\beta_0, \beta_1, \beta_2$, and β_3 are coefficients to be estimated, u is an error term, and t indexes time. Note that β_1 is the usual beta with respect to the market, β_2 is the size beta (β_i^S), and β_3 is the value beta (β_i^V).

This regression is typically estimated using monthly returns during a five-year period. Monthly returns for the *MRP*, *SMB*, and *HML* portfolios are available from Ken French's web page. It is not unusual in practice to run this regression with the returns of stock i (R_{it}) as the dependent variable, instead of with the risk premium of stock i as in equation (8.4). In theory, the estimates of the betas should be the same either way. In practice, however, because R_f varies a bit over time, the two sets of estimates may be slightly different.

The three-factor model: Application

Let's now put everything together and estimate required returns on equity from the three-factor model. And let's do it, as in the previous chapter, for the 30 stocks of the Dow. For the risk-free rate we'll use, also as in the previous chapter, the yield on the 10-year US Treasury note, which at the end of 2003 was 4.3%.

To estimate *MRP*, we'll depart slightly from the last chapter. Instead of using a market risk premium of 5.5% as we did before, we'll now use 6.4%, which is the (geometric) average *MRP* since 1927 as calculated by Fama and French (see the last line of Table 8.1). To estimate *SMB* and *HML* we'll also use the portfolios calculated by Fama and French. And as the last line of Table 8.1 shows, from 1927 on, the (geometric) average *SMB* and *HML* are 2.9% and 3.4%, respectively.

We then have all the estimates *common to all stocks* that we need to implement the three-factor model. In other words, we will estimate required returns from the expression

$$E(R_i) = 0.043 + 0.064 \cdot \beta_i + 0.029 \cdot \beta_i^S + 0.034 \cdot \beta_i^V \qquad (8.5)$$

Note that equation (8.5) is the same as (8.3) but with specific estimates for R_f, MRP, SMB, and HML. All we need now to use this model, then, are estimates for the three betas of any of stock of our interest.

We'll estimate the three betas for each of the 30 stocks of the Dow using equation (8.4), five years of monthly returns (January 1999–December 2003), and the three portfolios provided by Fama and French. These betas are shown in the second, third, and fourth columns of Table 8.2.

TABLE 8.2

Company	β_i	β_i^S	β_i^V	CAPM (%)	3FM (%)	Diff (%)
3M	0.6	−0.2	0.2	8.2	8.3	0.1
Alcoa	1.8	0.1	0.4	15.8	17.5	1.7
Altria	0.3	0.0	0.6	6.3	8.3	2.0
American Express	1.2	−0.7	0.2	11.8	10.6	−1.2
American Intl.	0.8	−0.9	0.1	9.7	7.3	−2.4
Boeing	0.8	0.1	0.7	9.1	11.5	2.4
Caterpillar	1.1	−0.4	0.7	11.2	12.3	1.2
Citigroup	1.4	−0.5	0.3	13.4	13.1	−0.3
Coca-Cola	0.3	−0.1	0.4	6.3	7.3	1.0
DuPont	1.0	−0.4	0.3	10.5	10.2	−0.4
Exxon Mobil	0.4	−0.1	0.3	7.1	7.8	0.8
General Electric	1.1	−0.7	−0.2	11.1	8.3	−2.9
General Motors	1.3	0.0	0.5	12.6	14.5	1.9
Hewlett-Packard	1.7	1.0	0.0	15.0	17.9	2.9
Home Depot	1.3	0.0	−0.1	12.9	12.6	−0.3
Honeywell	1.4	−0.5	0.7	13.1	13.9	0.8
Intel	2.0	0.3	0.2	16.8	18.3	1.5
IBM	1.4	0.3	0.6	13.3	16.0	2.8
Johnson & Johnson	0.3	−0.7	0.0	6.0	4.0	−2.0
JP Morgan Chase	1.8	0.0	0.6	15.6	17.5	1.9
McDonald's	0.8	−0.4	0.3	9.1	9.1	0.0
Merck	0.3	−1.2	0.1	6.5	3.4	−3.1
Microsoft	1.5	0.1	−0.2	14.2	13.9	−0.3
Pfizer	0.4	−0.7	0.1	6.7	4.9	−1.8
Procter & Gamble	−0.1	−0.1	0.1	3.7	3.9	0.1
SBC Comm.	0.8	−0.6	0.5	9.7	9.5	−0.2
United Tech.	1.1	−0.3	0.2	11.1	10.8	−0.4
Verizon	1.0	−0.6	0.4	10.5	10.2	−0.3
Wal-Mart	0.7	−0.6	−0.1	9.0	7.1	−2.0
Walt Disney	1.0	0.0	0.4	11.0	12.5	1.6
Average	**1.0**	**−0.3**	**0.3**	**10.6%**	**10.7%**	**0.2%**

Note from the outset that although the monthly *MRP* we used to estimate betas in this chapter is different from the monthly *MRP* we used in the previous chapter, the betas with respect to the market risk premium (β_i) are virtually identical. (Compare, company by company, the betas in the second column of Table 8.2 with those in the second and fifth columns of Table 7.3.)

The fifth column from Table 8.2 shows the required return on equity estimated from the CAPM using only the first two terms of the right-hand side of equation (8.5), that is, $E(R_i) = 0.043 + 0.064 \cdot \beta_i$. If we compare, company by company, the required returns on equity from the CAPM shown in Tables 8.2 and 7.3, the difference between them is not substantial. In fact, the average difference across all 30 companies of 0.9% (10.6% in this chapter versus 9.7% in the previous chapter) follows almost exclusively from the higher *MRP* we're using in this chapter (6.4% here versus 5.5% in the previous chapter).

The sixth column of Table 8.2 shows the required return on equity of the 30 companies of the Dow estimated with the three-factor model using equation (7.5). Note that, company by company, the difference between these numbers and those generated by the CAPM is in general not large. In fact, as the last column shows, *on average*, both models yield almost exactly the same required return on equity (10.6% the CAPM and 10.7% the three-factor model). Note, however, that positive and negative differences tend to cancel out in the average. Still, even if we take the average of the *absolute value* of the differences, we find that it is 1.3%.

Could this explain, at least partially, the popularity of the CAPM? Note that the CAPM is widely taught in business schools, is easy to understand, and easy to implement. Most alternative models are rarely taught at business schools, are more demanding in terms of data collection, their intuition is not always clear, and they are more difficult to implement. Is the additional trouble worth the extra cost of implementation? Well, if the differences in required returns between the CAPM and alternative models are around 1%, probably not. After all, that is usually quite a bit less than the difference between using a short-term and a long-term risk-free rate when we implement the CAPM.

The big picture

The CAPM makes the strong statement that the only variable that should have an impact on the required or expected return of a stock is the stock's beta. However, evidence both from the US and from international markets seems to quite clearly show that size and value do matter. That is, small stocks tend to outperform large stocks, and stocks with high book-to-market ratios tend to outperform those with low book-to-market ratios.

The three-factor model is the main contender of the CAPM and its popularity has been increasing steadily. It accounts for both the size premium and the value premium, besides the market premium already incorporated into the CAPM. But the jury is still out on whether the required returns estimated out of this model are substantially different from those estimated out of the CAPM.

Excel section

As we mentioned in the Excel section of the previous chapter, we discuss how to run regressions in Excel in Chapter 30 and there is no need to do it again here. However, in the same way that in the previous chapter we discussed a shortcut to estimate the slope of a regression with one explanatory variable using the 'linest' command, we discuss a similar shortcut here to estimate the slopes of a regression with several explanatory variables.

Suppose you have a series of ten observations on a dependent variable in cells A1:A10. Suppose, also, that you have two series of ten observations, each on one of two independent variables in cells B1:B10 and C1:C10. Then,

- To estimate the two slope coefficients, one for each of the two independent variables, select the cells B11:C11, type '=linest(A1:A10, B1:C10)' and then hit 'Ctrl+Shift+Enter' *simultaneously*.

It is very important that you note the following: Excel will display the beta coefficients *in reverse order*! Instead of displaying the slope coefficients in the same order as that of the independent variables (which would imply that each beta is displayed below the last observation of its respective variable), the coefficients are displayed the other way around. Don't ask . . . Just make sure that when you read the coefficients you remember that instead of finding β_1 in B11 and β_2 in C11, you will find β_1 in C11 and β_2 in B11. More generally, if you have n independent variables and follow a procedure similar to the one described above, you will *not* find the slope coefficients listed as β_1, β_2 . . . β_{n1}, β_n but as β_n, β_{n-1} . . . β_2, β_1.

Challenge section

1 Consider the returns of Abbott Laboratories and Merrill Lynch (ML) between 1994 and 2003 displayed in Table 8.3. This table also shows, for the same period of time, the yield on the ten-year US Treasury note and the returns of the MRP, SMB, and HML portfolios discussed in this chapter.

  (a) Calculate the risk premium for Abbott and Merrill Lynch by subtracting from the returns of each company the risk-free rate (the yield on the ten-year Treasury notes).

  (b) Using equation (8.4), estimate jointly the beta, size beta, and value beta of both companies.

TABLE 8.3

Year	Abbott (%)	ML (%)	10-yr yield (%)	MRP (%)	SMB (%)	HML (%)
1994	13.0	−12.9	7.8	−4.1	0.4	−0.1
1995	30.5	45.7	5.6	31.0	−6.9	−3.5
1996	24.6	62.8	6.4	16.3	−1.9	0.2
1997	31.4	81.4	5.7	26.1	−3.7	11.1
1998	51.8	−7.4	4.6	19.4	−23.3	−15.0
1999	−24.8	26.6	6.4	20.2	11.7	−39.4
2000	35.8	65.5	5.1	−16.7	−5.7	21.4
2001	17.1	−22.7	5.0	−14.8	28.4	27.3
2002	−26.7	−26.0	3.8	−22.9	4.4	3.7
2003	19.3	56.8	4.3	30.7	28.1	15.1

2 In order to calculate required returns on equity, use the same inputs discussed before in this chapter, that is, a risk-free rate of 4.3% (the yield on the ten-year US Treasury note at the end of 2003), MRP = 6.4%, SMB = 2.9%, and HML = 3.4%.

  (a) Start by using the first two terms of equation (8.5), $E(R_i) = 0.043 + 0.064 \cdot \beta_i$, and estimate the required return on equity of both companies from the CAPM.

  (b) Then use the whole equation (8.5) and estimate the required return on equity of both companies with the three-factor model.

  (c) Finally compare, company by company, the required return on equity estimated from both models. Are they substantially different?

9

RISK IV: DOWNSIDE RISK

Did we ask what is risk?

Problems with the standard deviation

One step in the right direction

The semideviation

A brief digression on the semideviation

The VaR

The big picture

Excel section

Challenge section

There is little controversy about how to measure returns. When it comes down to assessing risk, however, views on how to measure it differ widely. But one thing is for certain: although investors associate risk with negative outcomes, the widely accepted and widely used risk measures we discussed so far don't. In this chapter we'll discuss a relatively new but increasingly accepted way of assessing risk that aims to capture only the impact of those negative outcomes.

Did we ask what is risk?

We sure did. Twice in fact. And we gave two different answers. First we argued that when we consider an asset in isolation we can think of risk in terms of volatility, measured by the standard deviation of returns. Later we argued that when the asset is part of a diversified portfolio, the unsystematic risk gets diversified away and the systematic risk that remains is measured by beta (which captures the contribution of the asset to the risk of the portfolio, or the asset's sensitivity to fluctuations in the market).

Now, if you really think about it, there's something inherently wrong with the standard deviation as a measure of risk. Consider an asset with a mean annual return of 10%, and assume that as time goes by this asset delivers returns of 20%, 45%, and 30%. Would that make you unhappy? Would you view this asset as risky because it tends to deviate *above* its mean? Certainly not. And yet, each of these deviations above the mean contributes to increasing the standard deviation.

Note that the standard deviation treats an x% fluctuation above and below the mean in the same way; that is, in both cases this measure of risk increases by the same amount. But investors obviously don't feel the same way about these two fluctuations. They usually consider deviations above the mean as good and those below the mean as bad. Shouldn't then a good measure of risk capture this asymmetry? (There is no special reason for which deviations should be measured with respect to the mean. In fact, different investors may be interested in measuring deviations with respect to different parameters. More on this below.)

There exist several measures of risk that isolate and measure the downside of assets. In this chapter we'll focus on two: one is the counterpart of the standard deviation but in a downside risk framework; the other is a measure of the worst expected outcome under some specified conditions. But before we get into details, let's think a bit harder about what's wrong with the standard deviation, perhaps the most widely accepted measure of risk.

Problems with the standard deviation

Take a look at Table 9.1, which in the second column displays the annual returns (*R*) of Oracle between 1994 and 2003. As the next-to-last row shows, the arithmetic mean annual return (*AM*) during this period was a healthy 46%. And as your eyes can tell you without resorting to any measure of risk, Oracle treated its shareholders to quite a rocky ride.

TABLE 9.1

Year	R (%)	R–AM (%)	(R – AM)²	Min(R – AM, 0) (%)	{Min(R – AM, 0)}²
1994	53.5	7.4	0.0055	0.0	0.0000
1995	44.0	–2.0	0.0004	–2.0	0.0004
1996	47.8	1.7	0.0003	0.0	0.0000
1997	–19.8	–65.9	0.4341	–65.9	0.4341
1998	93.3	47.2	0.2231	0.0	0.0000
1999	289.8	243.7	5.9398	0.0	0.0000
2000	3.7	–42.3	0.1790	–42.3	0.1790
2001	–52.5	–98.5	0.9708	–98.5	0.9708
2002	–21.8	–67.8	0.4603	–67.8	0.4603
2003	22.5	–23.5	0.0554	–23.5	0.0554
Average 46.0%			0.8269		0.2100
Square Root			90.9%		45.8%

We know how to easily calculate a standard deviation of returns in Excel, but let's take the long road here. The third column of the table displays the difference between each annual return and the mean annual return, for example 7.4% = 53.5% – 46.0%. The fourth column displays the square of these numbers, for example 0.0055 = 0.074². The average of these squared deviations from the mean is the variance (0.8269). And the square root of the variance is the standard deviation of returns; in this case, 90.9%. Note that this standard deviation is over four times higher than the historical standard deviation of the S&P500 (around 20%), which would make Oracle a very risky stock. Right?

Not so fast. Take a look at the numbers in the fourth column. All those numbers are positive, which means that each and every one of these observations adds to the standard deviation. In other words, every annual return, regardless of sign or magnitude increases this widely accepted measure of risk (unless it is exactly equal to the mean). In fact, the largest number in this fourth column (the one that contributes to increasing the standard deviation the most) is that for 1999 when Oracle delivered a return of almost 290%. Now, if you had held Oracle during 1999, by the end of the year would you be happy or unhappy? Would you count this performance *against* Oracle as the standard deviation does?

One step in the right direction

Tweaking the standard deviation so that it accounts only for deviations below the mean return is not difficult. The fifth column of Table 9.1 shows the lower of each return minus the mean return or 0. In other words, if a return is higher than the mean (and therefore the difference between the former and the latter is positive), the column shows a 0; if, on the other hand, the return is lower than the mean (and therefore the difference between the former and the latter is negative), the column shows the difference between the two.

In 1994, Oracle delivered a 53.5% return, which is higher than the mean return of 46%; therefore the fifth column shows a 0. In 1995, however, Oracle delivered a 44.0% return, which is 2 percentage points lower than the mean return of 46%; therefore, the fifth column shows the shortfall of –2%. If you compare the third and the fifth columns you will notice that when a return is lower than the mean both columns show the same number. When a return is higher than the mean, however, the third column shows the difference between these two numbers and the fifth column shows a 0. Finally, note that this fifth column shows only negative numbers and zeros but no positive numbers.

The last column of Table 9.1 shows the square of the numbers in the fifth column. As the next-to-last row shows, the average of these numbers is 0.2100, and, as the last row shows, the square root of this number is 45.8%. What does this number indicate? It has a simple and intuitive interpretation: it measures volatility but only *below* the mean. This obviously looks like a step in the right direction. We don't 'punish' Oracle for its deviations above the mean; we do it only when it deviates below this parameter.

Now, is there anything special about the mean return? Isn't it possible that some investors would be interested in measuring volatility below the return of the market? Or volatility below the risk-free rate? Or volatility below 0? Or, more generally, volatility below *any* given number that they may consider relevant?

The semideviation

That is exactly what one of the two measures of risk we'll discuss in this chapter intends to capture. The **downside standard deviation of returns** *with respect to a benchmark return* **B** **(SSD_B)** is formally defined as

$$SSD_B = \sqrt{(1/T) \cdot \sum_{t=1}^{T} \{\text{Min}[(R_t - B), 0]\}^2} \qquad (9.1)$$

where B is *any* benchmark return relevant to an investor, T is the number of observations, and t indexes time. Although it lends itself to some ambiguity, equation (9.1) is, for the sake of simplicity, usually referred to as the **semideviation of returns**, which is the name we'll use from now on.

Let's think a bit about equation (9.1), which is really not as complicated as it seems to be. It requires us to do the following. (1) In every period we calculate the difference between the return for the period and the benchmark return B; (2) in every period we take the lower of the return minus B or 0; (3) in every period we square the numbers in the previous step; (4) then we take the average of all the numbers in the previous step; and (5) we finally take the square root of the number in the previous step.

Take a look at Table 9.2, where we consider again the returns of Oracle during the 1994–2003 period, as well as three different benchmark returns. The third column performs the five steps outlined above and does so with respect to a benchmark equal to the mean return of 46%. (This column is identical to the last column of Table 9.1.) The fourth column does the same with respect to a benchmark equal to a risk-free rate (R_f) of 5%. And the last column does the same with respect to a benchmark of 0%. Finally, the last row shows the semideviation with respect to the three benchmarks.

How should we interpret these numbers? Each semideviation measures volatility below its respective benchmark. Note that, because the risk-free rate of 5% is below Oracle's mean return of 46%, we would obviously expect (and find) less volatility below the risk-free rate. Similarly, there is even less volatility below 0.

Now, if you're finding that a volatility of 21.5% below a risk-free rate of 5% (or a volatility of 19% below 0 for that matter) does not spark your intuition, you're not alone. That's why the semideviation is best used in two contexts: one is in relation to the standard deviation and the other is in relation to the semideviation of other assets.

TABLE 9.2

Year	R (%)	$\{Min(R - AM, 0)\}^2$	$\{Min(R - R_f, 0)\}^2$	$\{Min(R - 0, 0)\}^2$
1994	53.5	0.0000	0.0000	0.0000
1995	44.0	0.0004	0.0000	0.0000
1996	47.8	0.0000	0.0000	0.0000
1997	−19.8	0.4341	0.0617	0.0393
1998	93.3	0.0000	0.0000	0.0000
1999	289.8	0.0000	0.0000	0.0000
2000	3.7	0.1790	0.0002	0.0000
2001	−52.5	0.9708	0.3304	0.2754
2002	−21.8	0.4603	0.0718	0.0475
2003	22.5	0.0554	0.0000	0.0000
Average	46.0%	0.2100	0.0464	0.0362
Square root		45.8%	21.5%	19.0%

Take a look at Table 9.3, which shows the semideviations with respect to the arithmetic mean of each stock (SSD_{AM}), with respect to a risk-free rate of 5% (SSD_{Rf}), and with respect to 0 (SSD_0) for both Oracle and Microsoft during the 1994–2003 period. The semideviations for Oracle are the same as those in Table 9.2. The mean return of Microsoft during this period (not reported in the table) was 39.8%.

TABLE 9.3

Company	SD (%)	SSD_{AM} (%)	SSD_{Rf} (%0	SSD_0 (%)
Oracle	90.9	45.8	21.5	19.0
Microsoft	49.8	39.3	23.1	21.1

Note that, although Oracle is far riskier than Microsoft as measured by their standard deviations, their semideviations tell a different story. First, note that although the volatility of Oracle below its mean is about a half of its volatility (0.458/0.909 = 50.4%), the same ratio for Microsoft is almost 80% (0.393/0.498 = 78.9%). In other words, given the volatility of each stock, much more of that volatility is below the mean in the case of Microsoft than in the case of Oracle.

Of course, it is still the case that the semideviation of Oracle is larger than that of Microsoft. But recall that the mean return of Oracle (46%) is also higher than that of Microsoft (39.8%). In fact, it's perhaps more telling to compare semideviations with respect to the same benchmark for both stocks. If we compare, for example, the semideviations of Oracle and Microsoft below the same risk-free rate of 5%, we find that the downside volatility is higher in the case of Microsoft (23.1% versus 21.5%). And if we do the same comparison but with respect to 0, we also find that Microsoft exhibits higher downside volatility (21.1% versus 19.0%).

A brief digression on the semideviation

It should be clear from our previous discussion that a key advantage of the semideviation over the standard deviation is that it considers only the downside volatility that investors view as harmful. Volatility above the mean, which investors view as desirable, does not increase the semideviation but does increase the standard deviation. Note also that, in this framework, volatility is no longer *necessarily* bad. In fact, volatility below the benchmark is bad, but volatility above the benchmark is good. Doesn't this make sense?

In addition, the semideviation can be calculated with respect to any benchmark, not just with respect to the mean. This implies that different investors using different benchmarks may perceive the same asset as more or less risky depending on the benchmark they use. And, of course, different investors do have different benchmarks; after all, not all of them invest for the same reasons or have the same goals. Again, doesn't this make sense?

We mentioned above that calling semideviation the downside standard deviation of returns may be a bit ambiguous. The reason is, as you probably suspected, that the word 'semideviation' indicates volatility on only one side of the benchmark but does not explicitly indicate which side (above or below). However, it is usually implicit in the normal use of the word 'semideviation' that the deviations considered are *below* the benchmark.

Having said that, note that we can also calculate the *upside* standard deviation of returns, which measures volatility *above* the benchmark B. The steps needed to calculate this magnitude are identical to those outlined above for the semideviation except that in the second step we now need to take the *higher* of the return minus B or 0. (Formally, we need to replace the 'Min' in equation (9.1) by a 'Max.') Try calculating the upside standard deviation of returns with respect to the mean, the risk-free rate, and 0 using the returns of Oracle in Table 9.2, and you should find that these are 75.8%, 97.4%, and 100.1%, respectively.

If you compare these three numbers with the semideviations reported in Table 9.2, you'll notice that, for all three benchmarks, the upside semideviations are higher. This indicates that there is more volatility above than below each of these benchmarks or, similarly, that Oracle is more likely to deliver returns above the benchmarks than below them. The fact that there is more volatility above than below the mean, in particular, indicates that the distribution of Oracle's returns exhibits positive skewness, a characteristic that investors find desirable. (The concept of skewness is discussed in Chapter 29.)

Finally, although equation (9.1) may seem complicated, calculating a semideviation in Excel is just a tiny bit more complicated than calculating a standard deviation. As we'll see at the end of the chapter, the semideviation can be calculated in Excel in just one cell.

The VaR

It's often important for investors or companies to have an idea of how bad adverse outcomes can really be. To answer this question, JP Morgan introduced in 1994 a measure called Value at Risk (VaR), which basically yields the worst expected outcome over a given time horizon for a given confidence level. (Don't panic, we'll explain.)

In order to calculate a VaR, two parameters have to be chosen. The first is a time interval, which can be any that is relevant for an investor or company. A bank, for example, may want to know its worst expected outcome on a daily basis in order to set appropriate capital requirements; a long-term investor, on the other hand, may be interested in the worst expected outcome on an annual or a five-year basis. The second choice is the confidence level (c), which will indirectly determine the probability that the outcome is worse than the calculated VaR (as we'll see shortly). The most typical confidence levels are $c = 95\%$ and $c = 99\%$.

Take a look at Exhibit 9.1, which depicts the probability distribution of a random variable X, which we could think of as returns, revenues, profits, or any other variable of our interest. Let's assume that the variable is measured on a daily basis (the time interval), and let's choose a 95% confidence level (hence, $c = 95\%$). There are two identical ways of thinking about the VaR in this context. We could define it as the worst expected outcome, over one day, at a 95% confidence level. Or, perhaps more telling, we could say that *a daily outcome worse than the VaR will occur with a probability of 5%.*

As Exhibit 9.1 shows, the VaR is a number on the horizontal axis, and is measured in the same units as the variable of interest. If returns are measured in percentages, then the VaR will be measured in percentages; if revenues or profits are measured in dollars, then the VaR will be measured in dollars; and so forth. Note, also, that having chosen a confidence level c, $(1 - c)\%$ of the area of the distribution will be *to the left* of the VaR.

EXHIBIT 9.1
VaR

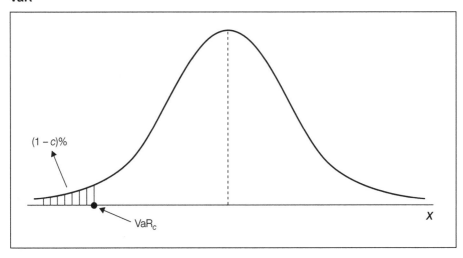

Formally, the **value at risk (VaR)** is defined as

$$\text{VaR}_c = x \quad \text{such that} \quad P(X'' \, x) = 1 - c \tag{9.2}$$

In other words, this expression says that the VaR is a number x such that the probability that the variable X takes a value lower than or equal to x is equal to $1–c$, where c is the chosen confidence level.

The calculation of the VaR is not necessarily trivial. As you can see from Exhibit 9.1, it implies the calculation of a number that leaves $(1 - c)\%$ of the distribution to its left. This, in turn, implies that we first need to characterize the distribution, and then calculate this probability (therefore having to calculate an integral, as discussed in Chapters 28 and 29). But don't throw your arms in despair just yet. If the variable X follows a normal distribution, then calculation of the VaR is very simple indeed. In fact, under normality, the VaR is defined as

$$\text{VaR}_c = AM - z \cdot SD \tag{9.3}$$

where *AM* and *SD* denote the (arithmetic) mean and standard deviation of the underlying distribution, and z is a number that comes from the standard normal distribution (discussed in Chapter 28). For the most widely used confidence levels, 95% and 99%, z takes a value of –1.64 and –2.33, respectively.

Take a look at Table 9.4, which reports the mean monthly return and monthly standard deviation of four markets between January 1994 and December 2003. The distribution of monthly returns of these four markets is approximately normal, so the assumption that sustains equation (9.3) approximately holds.

TABLE 9.4

	France (%)	Italy (%)	Japan (%)	UK (%)
AM	0.9	1.0	0.0	0.7
SD	5.6	6.7	6.0	4.1
VaR$_{95}$	–8.3	–10.0	–9.8	–6.0
VaR$_{99}$	–12.2	–14.7	–13.9	–8.9

Recall that before calculating the VaR we need to select a time horizon and a confidence level. Let's select then a monthly time interval (to make it consistent with the frequency of the returns in Table 9.4), and a confidence level of 95%. Let's also consider the French market, which between 1994 and 2003 delivered a mean monthly return of 0.9% with a standard deviation of 5.6%. The 95% VaR then is simply calculated as $0.09 - 1.64 \cdot 0.056 = -8.3\%$. In other words, the worst expected outcome in the French market over one month at a confidence level of 95% is –8.3%. Or, perhaps clearer, in the French market the probability of a monthly *loss* higher than 8.3% is 5%.

What if we change the significance level to 99%? Well, the probability distribution of returns doesn't change, so the mean and standard deviation remain the same. The only change in equation (9.3) is the value of z, which will now be –2.33. Therefore, the 99% VaR for the French market is calculated as $0.09 - 2.33 \cdot 0.056 = -12.2\%$. In other words, in the French market the probability of a monthly *loss* higher than 12.2% is 1%. Note, obviously, that the higher the confidence level, the lower the VaR. Or, put differently, the lower the VaR, the more unlikely it becomes that scenarios worse than the VaR materialize.

Following the same steps you can calculate the rest of the VaRs displayed in Table 9.4. Note that, from these four markets, the worst expected losses are in Italy. Not surprisingly, in fact, Italy has the largest monthly semideviation of these four markets (4.6%, not reported in the table).

One final comment. Note that normality is an assumption that may or may not apply to the variable of our interest. That's why it is important to test whether or not the distribution for which we need to calculate the VaR is normal. (The distribution of returns of Oracle, for example, is nowhere close to normal.) If it is not, then the calculation of the VaR is more complicated than indicated by equation (9.3). The idea of the VaR remains the same regardless of the underlying distribution, that is, we're looking for a number that leaves $(1 - c)\%$ of the area under the distribution to its left. But its actual calculation may change substantially depending on the type of distribution of the relevant asset.

The big picture

Most investors associate risk with negative outcomes. However, one of the most widely used definitions of risk, the standard deviation, does not. Downside risk is an increasingly popular alternative to traditional notions of risk. It captures the downside that investors want to avoid and not the upside that investors want to be exposed to.

The semideviation defines risk as volatility below a benchmark. This benchmark is determined by each individual investor or company, which adds to the plausibility of this measure of risk. The semideviation also highlights the fact that not all volatility is bad; only volatility below the benchmark. The VaR, on the other hand, provides investors with an idea of how bad adverse scenarios can be. It is easy to interpret, useful, and widely used in banks and financial institutions.

Excel section

The semideviation can be calculated in Excel in more than way. We'll focus here on two ways, emphasizing the first, which is the easier of the two (it takes just one cell). Let's introduce a command that simply counts the number of observations in a series. Suppose you have a series of returns in cells A1:A10.

▪ To count the number of observations in the series simply type '=count(A1:A10)' in cell A11 and then hit 'Enter.'

In order to calculate the semideviation, let's assume that we have entered the 'count' command in cell A11, where we therefore have the number of observations in the series (ten in our case). Let's also assume that in cell A12 we have entered the 'average' command to calculate the mean return of the series.

■ To calculate a semideviation with respect to the mean type '**=sqrt (sumproduct(A1:A10–A12, A1:A10–A12, n(A1:A10<A12))/A11)**' in cell A13 and then hit 'Ctrl+Shift+Enter' *simultaneously*.

A few comments about this calculation. First, the expression above is an array and it requires that we hit 'Ctrl+Shift+Enter' simultaneously rather than 'Enter.' Second, the 'sumproduct' command basically enables us to multiply, period by period, one variable by another and then to add the products. In our case, it actually multiplies a variable (each return minus the mean return) by itself and then adds the products. The 'n' command checks, period by period, whether the return is lower than the mean. If it is, then it instructs 'sumproduct' to multiply the difference between the two by itself; if it is not, then it instructs 'sumproduct' to return a 0 for that period. (If you don't want to bother with the details of the 'sumproduct' and 'n' commands, you can simply use the expression above to get the semideviation.)

There is a longer road to the calculation of the semideviation, which is basically the way in which the semideviations in Table 9.2 were calculated. This longer road makes use of the 'if' command. More precisely, you can do the following:

■ Type '**=if(A1<A\$12, (A1–A\$12)^2, 0)**' in cell B1 and then hit 'Enter.'
■ Then copy all the way down to cells B2 through B10.
■ Type '**=average(B1:B10)**' in cell B11.
■ And finally type '**=sqrt(B11)**' in cell B12.

Challenge section

1 Consider the annual returns of the Chinese and the Korean markets (both summarized by the MSCI indices, in dollars, and accounting for both capital gains and dividends) during the years 1994 and 2003 displayed in Table 9.4. Then,

(a) Calculate the (arithmetic) mean and standard deviation of both markets.

(b) Calculate the semideviation with respect to the mean return of both markets.

(c) Calculate the semideviation with respect to a risk-free rate of 5% of both markets.

(d) Calculate the semideviation with respect to 0 of both markets.

(e) Which market is riskier? Why? (Be careful. This question can be assessed from several different points of view. Try to be as thorough as possible.)

TABLE 9.5

Year	China (%)	Korea (%)
1994	−46.4	23.7
1995	−21.1	−3.3
1996	37.5	−38.1
1997	−25.3	−66.7
1998	−42.4	141.1
1999	13.3	92.4
2000	−30.5	−49.6
2001	−24.7	48.7
2002	−14.0	8.6
2003	87.6	35.9

2 Given the returns of the Chinese and the Korean markets in Table 9.4, calculate the VaR of both markets for confidence levels of 95% and 99%. What do you make out of your findings?

10

RISK AND RETURN IV:
RISK-ADJUSTED RETURNS

Returns and good luck

Returns and risk taking

An example

The Jensen index

The Treynor index

The Sharpe ratio

The RAP

The Sortino ratio

A few final thoughts

The big picture

Excel section

Challenge section

We rank assets all the time. We rank stocks, funds, countries, you name it. Problem is, most of the time we do it the wrong way. Investors focus way too often on past returns. And even if these are representative of expected returns (and many times they are not), what about risk? Just about every model or relationship in finance is based on a careful balance between risk and return. And that of course also applies to the ranking of assets, which is the issue we address in this chapter. We'll discuss different ways of ranking assets taking into account both their risk and their return or, more concisely, their *risk-adjusted* performance.

Returns and good luck

It happens all the time. You open a financial newspaper or magazine and there you have it, a ranking of mutual funds based on their performance. And how is performance measured? Simply by last year's (or worse, last quarter's) returns. Actually, it gets even worse. Investors tend to pour their money into the funds at the top and withdraw it from the funds at the bottom. That flies in the face of just about everything we know in finance.

It is of course important to assess the returns delivered by different funds, but it's just as important to assess the impact of luck and risk. In fact, a careful analysis must disentangle the impact of three different factors on returns: luck, risk taking, and ability. Let's consider them one at a time. (The discussion that follows, and this chapter in general, is focused on mutual funds, but you should have little trouble generalizing the discussion to assess the performance of any type of asset.)

Suppose you walk into a casino, head straight to the roulette, bet on 17 . . . and win! Would you conclude that you know how to play roulette? What if for the first time in your life you bet on a horse (the black one that looks good) and win? Would you conclude that you know about horses? You probably answered no both times. Why, then, would many investors conclude that the top-performer in a list of funds ranked by last year's return is the best fund, or that its manager is the most competent? Isn't it possible that the fund manager just got lucky with a few stock picks?

Of course it is. The bottom line is that there's very little we can say about a fund by observing its return performance over one year. Or, put differently, by observing only one year of returns, we can't rule out the impact of luck on performance. In fact, we can only do it by assessing performance over long periods of time. That's why rankings based on three-year returns and five-year returns are more useful, although longer periods would be even better. In short, the longer the evaluation period, the lower the influence of luck on performance.

And yet, even if we could safely establish that luck is not the reason for which a fund delivered the best return performance, we could still not conclude that this fund is the best, or that its manager is the most competent. In order to make an apples-to-apples comparison, we would first need to account for the impact of one other factor, and that is, precisely, the key issue we discuss in this chapter.

Returns and risk taking

It is a cornerstone result in finance that, in the long term, higher risk pays off with a higher return. This suggests another reason for which a fund may end up at the top of a ranking based on long-term returns: it may simply be a very risky fund. In other words, top-performing managers may be doing something that we could perfectly do ourselves: exposing their portfolios to high risk in order to earn a high return.

The risk–return trade-off is open to all participants in the market, and there is no reason to give credit to a manager for playing a game we could play ourselves. A manager that delivers high returns simply by exposing investors to a high level of risk is adding little or no value. In other words, a proper ranking of performance would need to remove from returns the impact of luck *and* the impact of risk taking. We can take care of the former by evaluating performance on the basis of long-term returns. And we can take care of the latter by assessing *risk-adjusted* (return) performance with the measures we discuss below.

So, suppose we make a ranking of funds based on their long-term, risk-adjusted performance. Can we now trust that the top-performing funds are the best, or that their managers are the most competent? The short answer is yes. Having accounted for the impact of luck and risk taking on returns, what remains is performance due to superior information or skill. And putting our money in the top-performing funds of such ranking is a smarter move than betting on 17 or on that black horse.

An example

Take a look at Table 10.1, which displays annual summary statistics for the returns of six Fidelity funds and the S&P500 (S&P) for the ten-year period

1994–2003. The summary statistics are the mean return (*AM*), the standard deviation (*SD*), the beta with respect to the S&P, and the semideviation with respect to a risk-free rate of 5% (*SSD*). The funds are the Fidelity New Millennium (FNM), Fidelity Value (FV), Fidelity Low Priced Stocks (FLPS), Fidelity Select Defense and Aerospace (FSDA), Fidelity Real Estate Investment (FREI), and Fidelity Select Technology (FST).

TABLE 10.1

	FNM	FV	FLPS	FSDA	FREI	FST	S&P
AM	23.3%	12.7%	16.9%	16.5%	13.1%	24.6%	13.0%
SD	28.9%	16.3%	13.1%	17.6%	12.4%	37.1%	15.8%
Beta	1.3	0.8	0.6	0.8	0.2	1.8	1.0
SSD	26.8%	20.4%	18.1%	21.0%	18.2%	33.1%	20.8%

Note that there is wide variability in both the return and the risk of these funds. The ten-year period for which we're calculating these summary statistics seems to be long enough to rule out the impact of luck on returns. As for risk, note that we're assessing it in three different ways: through total risk (*SD*), systematic risk (beta), and downside risk (*SSD*). Note also that, if we were to rank these funds on the basis of their return performance, FST would be at the top and FV at the bottom. Should we then put our money in FST?

Not so fast. Although we're assessing returns over a ten-year period and we can therefore virtually rule out the impact of luck, we still have not adjusted the return of these funds by their risk. And there are, in fact, different ways of doing so, the most relevant of which we discuss below.

The Jensen index

Our first measure of risk-adjusted returns is based on a simple comparison between *observed* returns and *expected* (or required) returns. Obviously, we would rate favorably any fund that performs above our expectation, and negatively any fund that performs below it. The expectation can be thought of as the required compensation for bearing the risk of the fund and it can be estimated with more than one model. The obvious candidate, however, is the CAPM (discussed in detail in Chapter 7), the most widely used pricing model.

Then, for any fund i, the **Jensen index (J_i)** is given by

$$J_i = R_i - (R_f + MRP \cdot \beta_i) = \alpha_i \qquad (10.1)$$

where R_i is the observed return of fund i, R_f is the risk-free rate, MRP is the market risk premium, and β_i is the beta of fund i with respect to the market. Note that equation (10.1) is often referred to as *Jensen's alpha* or simply *alpha* (α_i). Note, also, that the expression in parenthesis is the equation for the CAPM; this implies that we calculate required returns based on the fund's risk as measured by its beta.

The interpretation of the Jensen index is straightforward. A positive alpha indicates risk-adjusted performance above our required compensation for risk, and a negative alpha indicates the opposite. Furthermore, the larger the alpha, the better the fund's risk-adjusted performance. An alternative way of thinking about the Jensen index is as a measure of risk-adjusted performance relative to a passive (buy-and-hold) strategy of investing in the market. Therefore, a positive alpha indicates risk-adjusted performance above the passive strategy; a negative alpha indicates the opposite; and the larger the alpha, the better the fund.

Let's apply this measure to the funds in Table 10.1. Let's assume a risk-free rate of 5%, and a market risk premium equal to the difference between the 13% mean return of the S&P in the table and the 5% risk-free rate (that is, 8%). Consider the FNM fund, which delivered a mean annual return of 23.3%. Given its beta of 1.3, the required return on this fund is 15.7% = 0.05 + 0.08 · 1.3. And, given its observed return and required return, its alpha is 7.6% = 23.3% – 15.7%, which indicates that this fund performed 7.6 percentage points above the required compensation for its risk (and above the risk-adjusted performance of the market, which is, by definition, 0). In fact, as the second row of Table 10.2 shows, the FNM fund has the largest alpha and is therefore the top *risk-adjusted* performer.

TABLE 10.2

	FNM	FV	FLPS	FSDA	FREI	FST	S&P
Jensen	7.6%	1.7%	6.9%	5.2%	6.2%	5.4%	0.0%
Treynor	13.8	10.3	19.1	14.7	34.4	11.1	8.0
Sharpe	63.4	47.5	90.4	65.4	65.4	52.9	51.0
RAP	15.0%	12.5%	19.3%	15.3%	15.3%	13.3%	13.0%
Sortino	68.5	37.9	65.4	54.7	44.3	59.2	38.7

Take a closer look at the second row of Table 10.2 and compare it with the second row of Table 10.1. Note that the best-performing fund in terms of returns (FST) is not the best-performing fund in terms of risk-adjusted returns (FNM), and the worst-performing fund in terms of returns (FV) is not the worst-performing investment in terms of risk-adjusted returns. (In the latter case, the FV fund outperforms, on a risk-adjusted basis, an investment in the market.)

The FST fund, for example, delivered mean annual returns of 24.6%, much higher than those of the FSDA fund (16.5%). But that is an 'unfair' comparison. FST has a much higher beta than FSDA (1.8 versus 0.8) and therefore a much higher required return (19.2% versus 11.3%). On a risk-adjusted basis, FST did outperform FSDA but only very slightly (5.4% versus 5.2%). In short, a proper ranking of funds should consider *both* the return delivered by the funds *and* the risk borne by investors.

Note, finally, that the funds we're dealing with performed well in the sense that they all delivered a return higher than required as compensation for their risk. Although it is not the case among our funds, at least during the time period we're evaluating them, it is perfectly possible that a fund or an asset has a negative alpha. (You'll find one in the Challenge Section.)

The Treynor index

The Jensen index is a widely used measure for assessing the risk-adjusted performance of funds but it's not free from problems. To illustrate this, consider two funds, A and B, with required returns of 10% and 40%. Assume that over a ten-year period the observed mean returns of A and B were 15% and 45%, which would yield an alpha of 5% in both cases. According to the Jensen index, then, the (risk-adjusted) performance of these two funds has been the same. But are they equally attractive to investors?

Not really. Think about it this way. Both A and B outperformed their required return by 5 percentage points. In the case of A, 5 points is 50% of its required return (5%/10%), but in the case of B, 5 points is just 12.5% of its required return (5%/40%). Which fund would you choose?

Exactly. The problem with the Jensen index is that it doesn't capture appropriately performance *per unit of risk* (or per unit of required return). Compare, for example, the FSDA and FST funds, which have betas of 0.8 and 1.8, required returns of 11.3% and 19.2%, and alphas of 5.2% and 5.4%. Therefore, the risk-adjusted performance of FST is 0.2% better than that of FSDA. But would you really pick FST over FSDA? Does a superior performance of 0.2% a year make up for an increase in risk (beta) from 0.8 to 1.8? Or, put differently, does an outperformance of 5.4% over a required return of 19.2% look better than one of 5.2% over a required return of 11.3%?

You see the problem with the Jensen index. It is certainly an improvement over assessing funds solely on the basis of their returns, but it could also be improved upon. In fact, that is just what our next measure of risk-adjusted returns does. For any fund i, the **Treynor index (T_i)** is given by

$$T_i = \frac{R_i - R_f}{\beta_i} \qquad\qquad (10.2)$$

and measures excess returns (that is, returns in excess of the risk-free rate) per unit of risk (beta). For the sake of clarity, this expression is often multiplied by 100.

A couple of comments about this index before we go back to our example. First, unlike the Jensen index, which produces a number expressed in percentages and easy to grasp, the Treynor index produces a number with little intuition (unless you consider excess returns per unit of beta risk an intuitive definition!). Second, given its lack of intuitive interpretation, the Treynor index is used only as a tool to assess *relative* performance; that is, if given two funds A and B it is the case that $T_A > T_B$, the risk-adjusted performance of fund A is better than that of fund B.

Let's now go back to the FSDA and FST funds. The first has a Treynor index of $100 \cdot (0.165 - 0.05)/0.8 = 14.7$ and the second one of $100 \cdot (0.246 - 0.05)/1.8 = 11.1$. These two numbers have, as we have just argued, little intuitive meaning but put together indicate that, contrary to the result we arrived at in the previous section, FSDA outperforms FST in terms of risk-adjusted returns. To be sure, it will not always be the case that rankings of funds based on the Jensen index and the Treynor index will differ but, when they do, the latter provides the more reliable ranking. Let's see why.

At the beginning of this section we argued that the Jensen index does not capture appropriately returns per unit of risk. Another way of making the same point is to say that the Jensen index ignores the impact of leverage on performance. Take a look at Exhibit 10.1, which depicts the FSDA and FST funds as well as the securities market line (SML), which indicates required or expected returns according to the CAPM. Note that the Jensen index is measured as the vertical distance between each fund and the SML. As we had seen before, this index is 5.2% for FSDA and 5.4% for FST.

EXHIBIT 10.1
Jensen index v. Treynor index

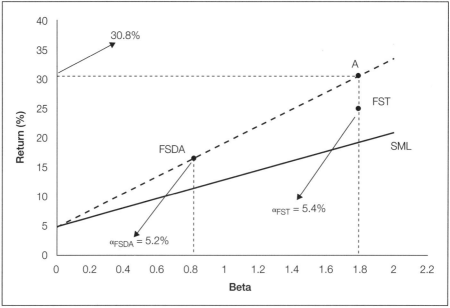

Now, here's something we could do: we could borrow money at the risk-free rate, invest that money plus our initial capital in the FSDA fund (this is of course what leverage is all about), and end up with portfolio A. By construction, portfolio A has the same risk as the FST fund (a beta of 1.8), but the interesting point is that it also has a higher return (30.8%). So, by leveraging our position in FSDA, we end up with a two-asset portfolio (a long position in the FSDA fund and a short position in the risk-free rate) that outperforms FST on a risk-adjusted basis. In short, FSDA provides better risk-adjusted returns than FST.

Three final points. Note, first, that graphically the Treynor index of a fund is represented by the slope of a line connecting the risk-free rate and the fund, just like the dotted line that connects the 5% risk-free rate and the FSDA fund in Exhibit 10.1. Second, note that as the Treynor indices in Table 10.2 show, although FSDA outperforms FST, it is itself outperformed by the FREI and FLPS funds. And third, note that the rankings based on the Jensen and Treynor indices differ. Whenever this is the case, given the problem with the Jensen index discussed above, the rank based on the Treynor index is more reliable. (Still, don't count out the Jensen index which, despite its flaw, is widely used in practice.)

The Sharpe ratio

The Treynor index adjusts returns by risk as measured by beta. This may be appropriate for investors who are diversified *across funds*; that is, for those who spread their capital over several funds. However, many investors diversify *across stocks* by putting their money into just one or two funds. Some investors, for example, buy the Fidelity Magellan fund or the Vanguard 500 Index fund as a way to diversify broadly across US stocks.

In these cases, the systematic risk of a fund does not get diversified away and beta ceases to be the appropriate measure of risk. In other words, investors that concentrate their holdings into just one or two funds bear the *total* risk of the fund (rather than just its systematic risk), which as we know is measured by the standard deviation of returns. That is, precisely, the insight of our third measure of risk-adjusted returns.

For any fund i, the **Sharpe ratio (S_i)** is given by

$$S_i = \frac{R_i - R_f}{SD_i} \qquad (10.3)$$

where SD_i is the standard deviation of fund i. As equation (10.3) clearly shows, the Sharpe ratio measures excess returns per unit of risk, the latter measured by the standard deviation of returns. For the sake of clarity, this expression is often multiplied by 100.

Note that, just like the Treynor index, the Sharpe ratio yields a number with little intuition (excess returns per unit of total risk). For this reason, the Sharpe ratio is also used only as a tool to assess *relative* performance; that is, if given two funds A and B it is the case that $S_A > S_B$, the risk-adjusted performance of fund A is better than that of fund B.

The calculation of Sharpe ratios, as equation (10.3) suggests, is very simple. The FLPS fund, for example, has a Sharpe ratio of $100 \cdot (0.169 - 0.05)/0.131 =$ 90.4 and is, according to this measure, the top performer on a risk-adjusted basis. Note that a ranking of our six funds based on Sharpe ratios is different from a ranking based on either the Jensen index or the Treynor index. This should not be entirely surprising. These last two indices measure risk with beta and the Sharpe ratio with the standard deviation of returns. In other words, if we change the definition of risk, we're likely to change the ranking of funds.

Very often you will find that summary information about funds includes at least their mean return, volatility measured by the standard deviation, and the

Sharpe ratio. The reason that the Sharpe ratio is more widely used than the Treynor index is simple. The intention of most ranks is to assess the performance of each individual fund in isolation, from where the emphasis on total risk follows directly.

Finally, note that the Treynor index and the Sharpe ratio do not always rank funds in different order. There are at least two circumstances in which the two ranks concur. First, when for any given set of funds differences in systematic risk are roughly proportional to differences in total risk. And second, when the funds evaluated are all broadly diversified.

The RAP

The Sharpe ratio is, without a doubt, one of the most widely used tools to assess the risk-adjusted performance of funds. However, as we have discussed, it has one little problem it shares with the Treynor index: the number it yields has little intuitive interpretation. This motivated Nobel-prize winning economist Franco Modigliani and his granddaughter Leah Modigliani (from Morgan Stanley) to develop the RAP, a measure that preserves the attractive characteristics of the Sharpe ratio but at the same time has a more intuitive interpretation.

For any fund i, its **risk-adjusted performance (RAP_i)** is given by

$$RAP_i = R_f + (R_i - R_f) \cdot (SD_M/SD_i) = R_f + (SD_M \cdot S_i) \qquad (10.4)$$

where SD_M is the standard deviation of returns of the market portfolio. The idea behind the RAP is to adjust the return of each fund in such a way that funds that are riskier than the market are 'punished' with a decrease in their mean return, and those that are less risky than the market are 'rewarded' with an increase in their mean return. Not very clear? Let's look at the numbers.

Let's compare the FLPS fund, which has a mean return of 16.9% and a volatility of 13.1%, with the FNM fund, which has a mean return of 23.3% and a volatility of 28.9%. Note that given the volatility of the market (15.8%), FLPS is less risky than the market and FNM is more risky. Note, also, that a simple comparison of mean returns would indicate that FNM is much more attractive than FLPS, given that it delivered a substantially higher mean return (6.4 percentage points). But we know by now that there's more to a proper comparison than just that. Let's then look at the RAPs.

The RAP of the FLPS fund is equal to

$$0.05 + (0.169 - 0.05) \cdot (0.158/0.131) = 19.3\%$$

and that of the FNM fund is equal to

$$0.05 + (0.233 - 0.05) \cdot (0.158/0.289) = 15\%$$

This indicates that FLPS outperforms FNM on the basis of risk-adjusted returns. But the RAP numbers provide some further intuition. The RAP of FLPS (19.3%) indicates that after rewarding this fund for being less volatile than the market, its mean return increases from 16.9% to 19.3%. The RAP of the FNM fund (15.0%), on the other hand, indicates that after punishing this fund for being more volatile than the market, its mean return decreases from 23.3% to 15.0%. The 4.3 percentage points difference in the RAPs, then, is a pure difference in risk-adjusted returns.

The reward and punishment imposed by the RAP on mean returns seeks to avoid a comparison between apples and oranges. Funds of different risk are not directly comparable. But once funds are punished and rewarded for being more or less volatile than the market, then they are made comparable among themselves *and* comparable to the market. In other words, if we compare the returns of different funds we compare apples and oranges, but if we compare the RAPs of different funds we compare apples and apples. *And* we compare them in percentages, which are easier to grasp than ratios with little intuitive meaning.

Note that the RAPs in Table 10.2 indicate that all funds outperformed the market on a risk-adjusted basis. (By definition, the market's RAP is equal to its mean return, 13% in our case.) Note, also, that a ranking of funds by their RAPs and another by their Sharpe ratios are identical. This follows directly from the second equality in (10.4), which shows that the RAP is simply a monotonic transformation of the Sharpe ratio. This is just a fancy way of saying that if we multiply Sharpe ratios by a positive number (in our case, the standard deviation of the market) and then add another number (in our case, the risk-free rate), then the relative ordering of the funds *must* be the same as that produced by the Sharpe ratios.

In sum, the RAP measures risk with the standard deviation of returns just like the Sharpe ratio; it preserves the rankings produced by the Sharpe ratio; but it's expressed in percentages and therefore has a more intuitive interpretation than the Sharpe ratio.

The Sortino ratio

Our last measure of risk-adjusted returns is very similar to the Treynor ratio and the Sharpe ratio but uses a different definition of risk. In this case, risk is measured by the semideviation (or downside standard deviation of returns). Downside risk in general and the semideviation in particular are discussed in Chapter 9 and, as argued there, both are becoming increasingly popular among practitioners.

For any fund i, the **Sortino ratio (N_i)** is given by

$$N_i = \frac{R_i - B}{SDD_{Bi}} \qquad (10.5)$$

where B is a benchmark return and SDD_{Bi} is the semideviation of fund i with respect to the benchmark B. Essentially, the Sortino ratio adjusts the returns of the fund in excess of any benchmark B relevant for the investor by the volatility of the fund *below* that benchmark. Note that, again only for the sake of clarity, equation (10.5) is often multiplied by 100.

As equation (10.5) shows, calculating Sortino ratios is very simple. Considering a benchmark return equal to the risk-free rate ($B = R_f$), the Sortino ratio of the FNM fund is equal to $68.5 = 100 \cdot (0.233 - 0.05)/0.268$. As Table 10.2 shows, FNM is the best-performing fund according to this measure. This table also shows that the ranking of funds on the basis of their Sortino ratios is different from the rankings based on our previous measures of risk-adjusted returns. Again, this should not be surprising. Although the numerators of the Treynor index, the Sharpe ratio, and the Sortino ratio are the same (in this last case because we chose a benchmark equal to the risk-free rate), their denominators (that is, their definition of risk) are all different.

Finally, note that one of the appealing characteristics of the Sortino ratio is that it can be tailored to any benchmark return B that is relevant to each individual investor. Once this benchmark is chosen by the investor, *both* excess returns and downside volatility are calculated with respect to that benchmark.

A few final thoughts

Not all the rankings of funds in the financial press are flawed. In fact, some take steps to account for the two main factors we discussed in this chapter. In order to account for the impact of luck, besides the one-year return, most rankings also provide three-year and five-year returns. And, in order to account for risk, most rankings group funds into 'styles' (such as growth, value, small cap, large cap) with the idea that although risk is quite different *across* styles, it is not so different *within* each style. Having said that, the risk of different funds within a style may in fact vary substantially and the best way to account for this variation is to compare them on the basis of risk-adjusted returns.

Morningstar, the best-known fund-rating company, has popularized the use of the 3×3 style box with three styles at the top (value, core, and growth) and three styles on the side (large cap, mid cap, and small cap). This yields a square with nine boxes, each box representing a different style. Funds are then allocated to the boxes and evaluated with respect to their peers. A fund that invests in technology stocks and another that invests in utilities have little in common. They would therefore be placed in different boxes and evaluated in relation to their respective peers. However, note that although comparing the returns of these two funds would in fact be pointless (just as comparing apples with oranges), comparing their risk-adjusted returns would be entirely appropriate and, at the end of the day, is the correct comparison to make.

Finally, a brief reference to the widely used and abused expression 'beating the market.' Hopefully by now you have realized that this expression is largely pointless. Beating the market last year means little because maybe we just got lucky. And beating the market in the long term is always possible if we're willing to take more risk than that of the market. A rightful claim to beating the market can only be made on the basis of long-term, risk-adjusted returns; that is quite different from the context in which this expression is typically used. In sum, next time you hear someone bragging that last year he beat the market, you now have the tools to perhaps prove him wrong – and at the same time become the most boring person in the party.

The big picture

Investment opportunities should not be ranked on the basis of their returns. A proper ranking must take into account both the risk and the return of the relevant assets or, more precisely, their risk-adjusted returns. In fact, a proper ranking must disentangle the impact on returns of luck, risk taking, and ability. The impact of luck can be removed by assessing returns over long periods of time. The impact of risk can be assessed with the methods discussed in this chapter.

There exist several ways of adjusting returns by risk, largely depending on the relevant definition of risk. These different methods may yield substantially different rankings of assets, which reinforce both the ambiguity and the importance of the concept of risk. Be that as it may, it is clear that the only proper way of ranking assets is on the basis of their long-term, risk-adjusted returns.

Excel section

There is no new Excel material in this chapter.

Challenge section

1 Consider the annual summary statistics for the returns of the G-7 countries and the world market for the ten-year period 1994–2003 reported in Table 10.3. The summary statistics include the mean return (*AM*), standard deviation (*SD*), beta with respect to the world market, and semideviation with respect to a risk-free rate of 5% (*SSD*). As a first step, rank all countries by their mean return. Which is the best-performing country? And the worst?

TABLE 10.3

	Canada	France	Germany	Italy	Japan	UK	US	World
AM	13.6%	11.0%	10.6%	12.3%	1.9%	9.1%	13.3%	8.7%
SD	19.7%	19.4%	23.0%	23.4%	20.7%	14.2%	15.9%	14.8%
Beta	1.1	1.1	1.2	0.9	0.9	0.8	1.0	1.0
SSD	23.3%	23.1%	25.7%	25.1%	25.9%	20.4%	20.9%	20.9%

2 Now calculate risk-adjusted returns and rerank these countries. More precisely:
   (a) Calculate the Jensen index for all countries and the world market, and rank all countries (and the world market) according to this measure.
   (b) Do the same for the Treynor index.
   (c) Do the same for the Sharpe ratio.

(d)   Do the same for the RAP.

(e)   Do the same for the Sortino ratio.

3 Do the rankings based on different measures of risk-adjusted returns concur? Why?

4 After having ranked these seven countries on the basis of different measures of risk-adjusted returns, in which one country would you invest? Why?

11

RISK AND RETURN V: OPTIMAL PORTFOLIOS

Investors' goals

Inputs and output

Minimizing risk

Minimizing risk subject to a target return

Maximizing expected returns subject to a target level of risk

The optimal portfolio: Maximizing risk-adjusted returns

Restrictions

The big picture

Excel section

Challenge section

I n Chapter 4 we discussed how to calculate the risk and return of a portfolio. In this chapter we'll discuss how to obtain optimal portfolios. More precisely, we'll see how to minimize risk; how to minimize risk for any desired level of return; how to maximize expected return for any target level of risk; and how to maximize risk-adjusted returns. And we'll discuss in detail how to do all this in Excel. (Before reading this chapter, it is essential that you become familiar with all the concepts discussed in Chapter 4. It is also essential that you both read the Excel section and work out the problems in the Challenge section.)

Investors' goals

We all invest for different reasons and we may all have different goals. Some people save for retirement, others to go to college, some to eventually buy a home, others attempt to become rich quickly. The goals are endless, and yet we can group most of the different reasons for investing into four main goals, all of which we'll discuss below.

Each of these goals can be stated formally as a mathematical problem. And in all these cases, investors face some restrictions (sometimes given, sometimes self-imposed) that must also be incorporated into the mathematical problem. Although all these problems are different, they do, however, share some common characteristics.

First, all problems have the final goal of either maximizing or minimizing some target magnitude, generally called the objective function. Second, the maximization or minimization of the objective function is subject to at least one restriction, and often to more than one. Third, the common restriction to all problems is to invest all the capital that has been allocated to the portfolio. This means that optimization problems do not determine how much capital to invest; rather, *given* the capital to be invested, they determine how to optimally allocate it among the assets considered.

So, what are the four major problems? Investors are usually interested in (1) minimizing the risk of their portfolio; or (2) minimizing the risk of their portfolio subject to a target return; or (3) maximizing the expected return of their portfolio subject to a target level of risk; or, the ultimate goal, (4) maximizing risk-adjusted returns.

We'll discuss all these problems below, but a bit of notation first. We'll call E_p and SD_p the expected return and risk of a portfolio, respectively. We'll call R_f the risk-free rate. And we'll call x_i the proportion of the portfolio invested in asset i, that is, the amount of money invested in asset i divided by the amount of money invested in the portfolio. Finally, as discussed in Chapter 4, the expected return and risk of a portfolio are respectively given by

$$E_p = x_1 \cdot E(R_1) + x_2 \cdot E(R_2) + \ldots + x_n \cdot E(R_n) \tag{11.1}$$

$$SD_p = \left\{ \sum_{i=1}^{n} \sum_{j=1}^{n} x_i \cdot x_j \cdot Cov_{ij} \right\}^{1/2} \tag{11.2}$$

where $E(R_i)$ denotes the expected return on asset i, Cov_{ij} denotes the covariance between assets i and j, and n is the number of assets in the portfolio.

Inputs and output

All optimization problems require some inputs in order to yield an output. What are the inputs and output in our problems? The inputs consist of expected returns, variances (or standard deviations), and covariances (or correlations). More precisely, for each asset we need to input its expected return, its variance, and its covariances to the rest of the assets in the portfolio. For a portfolio of n assets, this implies n expected returns, n variances and $(n^2 - n)/2$ covariances. (Recall that $Cov_{ij} = Cov_{ji}$.)

How to estimate these parameters, however, is controversial. We could base our estimates on historical (ex-post) returns or on forward-looking (ex-ante) returns. The main problem with historical estimates is that means, variances, and covariances tend to change over time and their past values may or may not reflect their *expected* values, which are the ones we really need for portfolio optimization. The problem with forward-looking estimates, on the other hand, is how to estimate them properly without resorting to historical data, or how to adjust the historical estimates to reflect changing expectations.

The output of all these problems is a set of weights x_1^*, x_2^* ... x_n^* that achieve the goal stated in the objective function subject to the restrictions of the problem. (In finance and economics the '*' symbol is typically used to denote optimality.) Having obtained these optimal weights, we can then plug them back into the objective function in order to determine its optimal value.

Minimizing risk

Let's start with the simplest of all problems, which consists of finding the combination of assets that yields the portfolio with the lowest possible risk. Formally, this problem is stated as

$$\text{Min}_{x_1 \cdot x_2 \cdot \ldots \cdot x_n} SD_p = \left\{ \sum_{i=1}^{n} \sum_{j=1}^{n} x_i \cdot x_j \cdot Cov_{ij} \right\}^{1/2}$$

$$\text{Subject to} \quad \rightarrow x_1 + x_2 + \ldots + x_n = 1$$

The first line states the goal, which is to minimize the risk of the portfolio as measured by its standard deviation of returns. The second line is the 'allocation restriction' that we mentioned above, which states that, given the capital to be invested in the portfolio, we need to find how to optimally allocate it among all the assets considered.

The solution to this problem is a set of weights x_1^*, x_2^* ... x_n^* that determines the portfolio with the lowest risk (measured by its standard deviation of returns). We can then plug these optimal weights (together with the inputs of the problem) into equations (11.1) and (11.2) to determine the expected return and risk of this portfolio which, as discussed in Chapter 4, is called the *minimum variance portfolio* (MVP).

Minimizing risk subject to a target return

Investors often have a target return they want to achieve, and they obviously want to achieve it bearing the lowest possible risk. Formally, this problem can be stated as

$$\text{Min}_{x_1 \cdot x_2 \cdot \ldots \cdot x_n} SD_p = \left\{ \sum_{i=1}^{n} \sum_{j=1}^{n} x_i \cdot x_j \cdot Cov_{ij} \right\}^{1/2}$$

$$\text{Subject to} \quad \rightarrow E_p = x_1 \cdot E(R_1) + x_2 \cdot E(R_2) + \ldots + x_n \cdot E(R_n) = E^T$$
$$\rightarrow x_1 + x_2 + \ldots + x_n = 1$$

The first line states the goal, which is (as in the previous problem) to find the portfolio with the lowest risk. The second line states the restriction that the portfolio must have an expected return of E^T (the target return). And the third line is the allocation restriction we already discussed.

The solution to this problem is a set of weights x_1^*, x_2^* ... x_n^* that determines the portfolio with an expected return E^T that has the lowest risk. We can then plug these optimal weights (together with the inputs of the problem) into equation (11.2) to determine the risk of this portfolio. (Its expected return is predetermined in the first constraint and is equal to E^T.)

Maximizing expected returns subject to a target level of risk

Some investors may have a maximum level of risk they are willing to bear, and want to find the portfolio that yields the highest expected return for that level of risk. Formally, this problem can be stated as

$$\text{Max}_{x_1 \cdot x_2 \cdot \ldots \cdot x_n} \quad E_p = x_1 \cdot E(R_1) + x_2 \cdot E(R_2) + \ldots + x_n \cdot E(R_n)$$

$$\text{Subject to} \quad \rightarrow \quad E_p = \left\{ \sum_{i=1}^{n} \sum_{j=1}^{n} x_i \cdot x_j \cdot Cov_{ij} \right\}^{1/2} = SD^T$$

$$\rightarrow x_1 + x_2 + \ldots + x_n = 1$$

The first line states the goal, which is to find the portfolio with the highest expected return. The second line states the restriction that the portfolio must have a target level of risk of SD^T. And the third line is the allocation restriction.

The solution to this problem is a set of weights x_1^*, x_2^* ... x_n^* that determines the portfolio with a risk of SD^T that has the highest expected return. We can then plug these optimal weights (together with the inputs of the problem) into equation (11.1) to determine the expected return of this portfolio. (Its risk is predetermined in the first constraint and is equal to SD^T.)

The optimal portfolio: Maximizing risk-adjusted returns

All the previous problems state different goals (and restrictions) that investors may have. However, finance theory suggests that the ultimate goal of a rational investor should be to find the portfolio that optimally balances risk and return.

In other words, the ultimate goal of the rational investor is unequivocal: *to maximize risk-adjusted returns.*

The issue of risk-adjusted returns is explored in detail in the previous chapter. For our current purposes, it suffices to highlight two issues. First, that the 'best' portfolio is *not* the one that maximizes the expected return. If that were the case, we'd put all our money in the *one* asset with the highest expected return. But that is not what we usually do. We care also about risk and therefore we diversify. In other words, we care both about returns and sleeping soundly at night too.

Second, although there are many ways of defining risk-adjusted returns (as discussed in the previous chapter), perhaps the most widely used definition is the relatively simple **Sharpe ratio (S_p)** which is given by

$$S_p = \frac{E_p - R_f}{SD_p} \qquad\qquad (11.3)$$

Note that an increase in the expected return of the portfolio or a decrease in its risk will increase the Sharpe ratio.

We can now restate the goal of maximizing risk-adjusted returns as finding the portfolio that maximizes the Sharpe ratio. Formally,

$$\operatorname*{Max}_{x_1 \cdot x_2 \cdot \ldots \cdot x_n} S_p = \frac{E_p - R_f}{SD_p} = \frac{x_1 \cdot E(R_1) + \ldots + x_n \cdot E(R_n) - R_f}{\left\{ \sum_{i=1}^{n} \sum_{j=1}^{n} x_i \cdot x_j \cdot Cov_{ij} \right\}^{1/2}}$$

$$\text{Subject to} \quad x_1 + x_2 + \ldots + x_n = 1$$

The first line states the goal, which is to find the portfolio with the highest Sharpe ratio, and the second line is the allocation restriction. The solution to this problem is a set of weights $x_1^*, x_2^* \ldots x_n^*$ that determines the portfolio with the highest risk-adjusted return. We can then plug these optimal weights (together with the inputs of the problem) into equations (11.1), (11.2), and (11.3) to determine the expected return, risk, and Sharpe ratio of this portfolio.

Restrictions

Finally, a quick comment on the restrictions of all the problems we discussed. Besides the allocation restriction (and the other two we considered), we can add to these problems as many constraints as necessary. We could, for example, restrict short-selling by adding the restriction

$$x_1 \geq 0, x_2 \geq 0 \ldots x_n \geq 0$$

Or we could limit ourselves to invest not more than 20% of the capital in the portfolio in any single asset by adding the restriction

$$x_1 \text{''} \ 0.20, x_2 \text{''} \ 0.20 \ldots x_n \text{''} \ 0.20$$

The possibilities are, of course, endless. The portfolio-optimization program in Excel discussed below can solve all the problems we discussed above and handle as many restrictions as necessary.

The big picture

The optimization of portfolios cannot be implemented without the aid of spreadsheets or specialized software packages. Even when considering just a few assets, the problems are usually too daunting to solve by hand. All programs used to optimize portfolios, however, require the same inputs, which basically consist of expected returns, variances or standard deviations, and covariances or correlations. Given those inputs, the program will provide as output the optimal weights, as well as the risk and return of the optimal portfolio.

Some investors may want to minimize risk. Others may want to minimize risk subject to a target return. Others may want to maximize returns subject to a target level of risk. And all of them want, at the end of the day, to maximize risk-adjusted returns. The Excel program discussed below will help you to solve all these problems.

Excel section

We'll discuss in this section a rather simple Excel program to optimize portfolios. The discussion is based on a four-asset portfolio but you should have little trouble in adapting the program to any number of assets. It is also based on the problem of maximizing risk-adjusted returns, but once again you should have little trouble in adapting the program to solve the problems in the other sections of the chapter. In fact, in the Challenge section you will be asked to do both things.

The program makes use of the Solver in Excel, which means that it finds numerical (rather than analytical) solutions. Far from being a weakness, this makes it easy handle as many restrictions as desired by simply making slight changes in the Solver dialogue box.

The program basically works in three steps. First, we input the required parameters (a risk-free rate, expected returns, standard deviations, and covariances); then, we make some calculations based on those inputs; and finally we use the Solver to find the optimal solution. The output of the program consists of the set of optimal weights and the risk, return, and Sharpe ratio of the optimal portfolio.

TABLE 11.1

	A	B	C	D	E	F	G	H	I
1									
2		A portfolio-optimization program in Excel							
3		Chapter 11							
4									
5									
6									
7									
8		Rf						Weights	
9									
10			1	2	3	4			
11		ERs							
12									
13		SDs							
14								Ep	
15		Covs							
16									
17								SDp	
18									
19									
20		Weights						Sp	
21		Sum							
22									
23		ER Vector							
24									
25		SD Matrix							
26									
27									
28									
29									

Take a look at Table 11.1, which contains the set-up of the model. The cells shaded in light gray are the ones in which we'll input the parameters; the cells shaded in darker gray are the ones in which we'll perform some calculations. This is, step-by-step, what we need to do to find an optimal portfolio using this program:

- Inputs:
  - Enter the *risk-free rate* in cell C8.
  - Enter the *expected returns* in cells C11:F11.
  - Enter the *standard deviations* in cells C13:F13.
  - Enter the *covariances* in cells C15:F18.
  - Enter the *weights* (25% in our case) to initialize the Solver in cells C20:F20.
- Calculations:
  - Enter '=**sum(C20:F20)**' in cell F21.
  - Block cells H9:H12, enter '=**transpose(C20:F20)**' and hit 'Ctrl+Shift+Enter' *simultaneously*.
  - Enter '=**C20*C11**' in cell C23 and copy this expression to cells D23:F23.
  - Enter '=**sum(C23:F23)**' in cell H15.
  - Enter '=**C$20*C15*$H9**' in cell C25, copy this expression to cells D25:F25, and then copy the range C25:F25 to the range C26:F28.
  - Enter '=**sqrt(sum(C25:F28))**' in cell H18 and hit 'Ctrl+Shift+Enter' *simultaneously*.
  - Enter '= **(H15-C8)/H18**' in H21.
- Solver:
  - Target Cell: H21
  - Equal to: Max
  - By Changing Cells: C20:F20
  - Subject to Constraints: F21=1

That's it! Not too bad, is it? Before you rush to implement this program, however, let's highlight a few things. The program requires us to calculate all the necessary inputs beforehand. In other words, before initializing the program, we need to have numbers for the risk-free rate, the expected returns, the standard deviations, and all covariances. That means that first we have to calculate these parameters from the relevant data (or come up with our own forward-looking best guesses), and only then move on to work with the program.

In order to start looking for the optimal solution Solver needs to be initialized with a set of arbitrary weights. The actual value of these weights is largely irrelevant as long as they add up to 1. A good rule-of-thumb for the initial values is to enter weights equal to $1/n$ (where n is the number of assets in the portfolio) in all the relevant cells. In other words, we initialize Solver by giving it the values of an equally weighted portfolio (that is, weights of 50% in the two-asset portfolio, 25% in the four-asset portfolio, 20% in the five-asset portfolio, and so on).

The calculations we're required to perform, and the commands we're required to use, are all very simple. When transposing the weights (second step in the required calculations) and calculating the risk of the portfolio (sixth step), you must remember to hit 'Ctrl+Shift+Enter' simultaneously. This is because both these calculations are arrays and that's just the way they're entered into Excel.

To activate the Solver we simply go to the 'Tools' menu and select 'Solver' from the choices. When in the Solver's dialogue box, the target cell we enter is the one with the value of the Sharpe ratio, and we ask Solver to maximize this value. The cells that Solver will adjust in order to find the portfolio with the highest Sharpe ratio are the portfolio weights, taking into account the constraint that these weights add up to 1. In order to input this restriction, we first need to click 'Add' in 'Subject to Constraints,' then fill the three required boxes (the cell reference, the sign, and the numerical value), and click 'OK.' Once we're done with these steps, we click 'Solve' and then (when asked whether we want to keep the solution) 'OK.'

Finally, adding more constraints when necessary is very easy. If we wanted to restrict short-selling (that is, if we wanted Solver to restrict the solution to only positive weights), for example, all we need to do is, in the Solver's dialogue box, click 'Add' in 'Subject to Constraints' and enter '**C20:F20**' in 'Cell Reference,' select '>=' in the choice of signs, enter '0' in 'Constraint,' and finally hit 'OK' and 'Solve.' If we wanted instead to restrict the weights to being no larger than 20%, we would click 'Add' in 'Subject to Constraints' and enter '**C20:F20**' in 'Cell Reference,' select '<=' in the choice of signs, enter '0.2' in 'Constraint,' and finally hit 'OK' and 'Solve.'

If the whole thing looks a little messy, don't worry; this is a typical case of 'easier done than said.' Once you run the program a couple of times, you will see that you can obtain solutions very quickly and effectively. That's why the one below is a Challenge section that you can't skip. Get to work on it then!

Challenge section

1 Consider Table 11.2, which contains annual summary statistics for four emerging markets, Argentina, Brazil, Chile, and Mexico (all summarized by MSCI indices, in dollars, and accounting for both capital gains and dividends) between 1988 and 2003. Panel A reports the mean return (AM), standard deviation (SD), maximum return, and minimum return; panel B reports the variances and covariances.

TABLE 11.2

| | Panel A | | | |
	Argentina (%)	Brazil (%)	Chile (%)	Mexico (%)
AM	40.9	33.6	25.1	31.3
SD	105.1	62.0	38.9	46.9
Maximum	405.0	172.2	116.1	126.0
Minimum	-50.5	-61.6	-28.5	-40.6

| | Panel B | | | |
	Argentina	Brazil	Chile	Mexico
Argentina	1.1039	0.5186	0.3240	0.3557
Brazil	0.5186	0.3850	0.1943	0.1673
Chile	0.3240	0.1943	0.1515	0.1291
Mexico	0.3557	0.1673	0.1291	0.2203

Using the portfolio-optimization program discussed in the Excel section, and a risk-free rate of 5%, for each of the questions below find the set of optimal weights, as well as the expected return, risk, and Sharpe ratio of the optimal portfolio. (*Note*: It is implicit in all questions that the restriction $x_1 + x_2 + x_3 + x_4 = 1$ must apply.)

(a) Find the portfolio with the highest risk-adjusted return.

(b) Find the portfolio with the highest risk-adjusted return, subject to the restriction that no short-selling is allowed (that is, restricting all weights to be positive).

(c) Find the portfolio with the highest risk-adjusted return, subject to the restrictions of no short-selling and that no asset can take more than 30% of the money invested in the portfolio (that is, restricting all weights to be no larger than 30%).

(d) Find the minimum variance portfolio (MVP).

(e) Find the portfolio with the lowest risk given a target return of 30%.

(f) Find the portfolio with the highest expected return given a target risk (standard deviation) of 40%.

2 Go back to panel A of Table 5.2 containing the annual returns of Disney and Microsoft between 1994 and 2003 and calculate the relevant covariance. Then, using the portfolio-optimization program discussed in the Excel section, and a risk-free rate of 5%, for each of the questions below find the set of optimal weights and the expected return, risk, and Sharpe ratio of the optimal portfolio. (*Note*: It is implicit in all questions that the restriction $x_1 + x_2 = 1$ must apply.)

(a) Find the minimum variance portfolio (MVP).

(b) Find the portfolio with the lowest risk given a target return of 15%.

(c) Find the portfolio with the highest expected return given a target risk of 26%.

(d) Find the portfolio with the highest risk-adjusted return.

12

RISK AND RETURN VI:
THE LONG RUN

What is this all about?

Long-term returns

Long-term risk: Volatility

Long-term risk: Shortfall probability

Time diversification and mean reversion

Forecasting target returns

The big picture

Excel section

Challenge section

Finally we come to the end of the first part. But we can't really finish without having at least a brief discussion about the long run. You see, it turns out that the investment horizon is a critical variable when making investment decisions, and although financial advisors do factor it carefully into their advice, most books ignore it almost completely. This one won't.

What is this all about?

Answer, fast, which asset is riskier, stocks or bonds? If you're like most people, the first answer that came to mind was stocks. But why? Probably for two reasons. Most investors tend to read a lot more about the stock market than about the bond market, and therefore are more aware of the jumps and volatility in the former than in the latter. In addition, and perhaps more importantly, risk is often thought of as the volatility of annual returns. In the US, the annual standard deviation of the stock market is around 20% and that of the bond market around 10%; hence, the usual perception of relative risk.

There are, however, at least three problems with this perception. First, as we'll discuss below, there are two different ways of defining long-term volatility, and they give contradicting results. Second, as we have discussed in previous chapters, volatility is not the only way of assessing risk, and again different risk measures may yield contradicting results. And third, as we'll see, for long investment horizons the data tells a different story.

Long-term returns

Let's get this straight: in the long term, the compounding power of stocks *trounces* the compounding power of bonds. There you have it. There is really no question about it. Want some evidence? In his fantastic book *Stocks for the Long Run* (3rd edn, 2002, McGraw-Hill), Jeremy Siegel reports that $1 invested in the US stock market in 1802 would have turned into $8.8 *million* by the end of 2001. In comparison, the same dollar invested in bonds would have turned into $13,975. Now, *that* is a difference!

Take a look at Table 12.1, which displays arithmetic (*AM*) and geometric (*GM*) mean annual returns, in both nominal and real terms, for 16 countries and the world market during the period 1900–2000. Real returns are nominal returns net of inflation and capture changes in purchasing power.

TABLE 12.1

Country	Stocks				Bonds			
	Nominal		Real		Nominal		Real	
	GM (%)	AM (%)	GM (%)	AM (%)	GM (%)	AM (%)	GM (%)	AM (%)
Australia	11.9	13.3	7.5	9.0	5.2	5.8	1.1	1.9
Belgium	8.2	10.5	2.5	4.8	5.1	5.6	−0.4	0.3
Canada	9.7	11.0	6.4	7.7	5.0	5.4	1.8	2.4
Denmark	8.9	10.7	4.6	6.2	6.8	7.3	2.5	3.3
France	12.1	14.5	3.8	6.3	6.8	7.1	−1.0	0.1
Germany	9.7	15.2	3.6	8.8	2.8	4.7	−2.2	0.3
Ireland	9.5	11.5	4.8	7.0	6.0	6.7	1.5	2.4
Italy	12.0	16.1	2.7	6.8	6.7	7.0	−2.2	−0.8
Japan	12.5	15.9	4.5	9.3	5.9	6.9	−1.6	1.3
Netherlands	9.0	11.0	5.8	7.7	4.1	4.4	1.1	1.5
S. Africa	12.0	14.2	6.8	9.1	6.3	6.7	1.4	1.9
Spain	10.0	12.1	3.6	5.8	7.5	7.9	1.2	1.9
Sweden	11.6	13.9	7.6	9.9	6.2	6.6	2.4	3.1
Switzerland	7.6	9.3	5.0	6.9	5.1	5.2	2.8	3.1
UK	10.1	11.9	5.8	7.6	5.4	6.1	1.3	2.3
US	10.1	12.0	6.7	8.7	4.8	5.1	1.6	2.1
World	9.2	10.4	5.8	7.2	4.4	4.7	1.2	1.7
Average	10.3%	12.7%	5.1%	7.6%	5.6%	6.2%	0.7%	1.7%

Source: Adapted from *Triumph of the Optimists: 101 Years of Global Investment Returns*, by Elroy Dimson, Paul Marsh, and Mike Staunton. Princeton University Press, New Jersey, 2002

The evidence is shockingly clear: the mean return of stocks, geometric and arithmetic, nominal and real, is higher than the mean return of bonds in *every* country and in most cases by a substantial margin. The difference between the compounding power of both assets can be viewed from different angles but here's an interesting one. Take a look at the last line, which shows averages across the 16 countries, and note that the mean annual compound real return of stocks is 5.1% and that of bonds 0.7%. These figures imply that by investing in stocks purchasing power would double in just under 14 years. In bonds? It would take only 98.5 years.

Long-term risk: Volatility

However impressive the differential compounding power of stocks and bonds may be, unfortunately none of us have a 200-year investment horizon. In fact, for most investors the long run is a 30-year period at most, and often much shorter than that. Whatever the length of the investment horizon, though, the interesting question is, how does risk evolve with it. In other words, how does risk evolve as the holding period increases from 1, to 5, to 10, to 30, or to any number of years?

To be sure, this question doesn't have an undisputed answer. As a matter of fact, its answer is very controversial. Even if we agreed that the proper way to capture risk is with the standard deviation of returns (and that's a big if), the controversy would not end there. To see why, take a look at Table 12.2, which is based on an asset with a standard deviation of annual returns of 17%, roughly equal to the annual standard deviation of the US stock market between 1871 and 2003. How should we assess risk for, say, five-year holding periods? There are at least two ways: one is with the *cumulative* standard deviation and the other with the *annualized* standard deviation. Let's focus on the former first.

TABLE 12.2

Holding period (Years)	Annual %	Cumulative %	Annualized %	$P(R < 0\%)$ %	$P(R < 3\%)$ %	$P(R < 5\%)$ %
1	17.0	17.0	17.0	30.6	37.0	41.3
5	17.0	38.0	7.6	12.9	22.9	31.2
10	17.0	53.8	5.4	5.5	14.7	24.4
15	17.0	65.8	4.4	2.5	9.9	19.8
20	17.0	76.0	3.8	1.2	6.9	16.4
30	17.0	93.1	3.1	0.3	3.4	11.5
100	17.0	170.0	1.7	0.0	0.0	1.4

The cumulative standard deviation

Recall how we calculate a standard deviation of annual returns. As discussed in detail in Chapter 3, all we need to do is to calculate annual returns over the relevant time period and then calculate the standard deviation of those returns. If we did that for the (nominal) annual returns of the US market between 1871 and 2003, we would obtain roughly 17%. This suggests one way of calculating the cumulative standard deviation of five-year returns: calculate returns for every five-year period between 1871 and 2003, and then calculate the standard deviation of those five-year returns.

Actually, there's a shortcut. (This shortcut requires the assumption of independent returns, which basically means that returns are uncorrelated over time.) For any holding period or investment horizon T, we can calculate the **cumulative standard deviation of returns (CSD)** simply as

$$CSD = SD \cdot \sqrt{T} \qquad\qquad (12.1)$$

where SD denotes the *annual* standard deviation of returns. For example, the cumulative standard deviation of five-year returns is $0.17 \cdot (5)^{1/2} = 38.0\%$, as shown in the third column of Table 12.2.

Now, as is obvious from equation (12.1) and the third column of Table 12.2, the longer the holding period T, the larger the cumulative standard deviation. This is the intuition. If we consider a sample of daily returns and calculate its mean and standard deviation, both numbers would be fairly small, largely because daily returns are fairly small. If we do the same for monthly returns, then both the mean and the standard deviation would be larger, simply because monthly returns are larger than daily returns. If we do the same for annual returns, then both the mean and the standard deviation would be larger, simply because annual returns are larger than daily and monthly returns. If we do the same for five-year returns . . . Get the picture?

As we increase the length of the period for which we calculate returns, the returns themselves increase and so do their mean and standard deviation. Therefore, as we increase the holding period from 1 to 5, to 10, to 20, or more years, risk (measured by the *cumulative* standard deviation) also increases. Or, viewed from another angle, swings in the capital invested on any asset would typically be larger over 20 years than over 10 years, over 10 years than over 5 years, over 5 years than over 1 year, and so forth. This is, in short, the intuition behind the cumulative standard deviation as a measure of long-term risk.

The annualized standard deviation

That sounds like a plausible story, doesn't it? Great. Now let's change it! Exhibit 12.1 is based on (nominal) returns for the US stock market between 1871 and 2003. Each bar shows the maximum and minimum return that could have been obtained during each holding period considered. To illustrate, if we consider every one-year return between 1871 and 2003, in the best year we would have obtained 56% and in the worst we would have lost 42.5%. If we consider every five-year holding period instead, in the best we would have obtained a 28.6% *mean annual compound* return (that's 28.6% on top of 28.6%, on top of 28.6%, on top of 28.6%, on top of 28.6%), and in the worst we would have lost money at a *mean annual compound* rate of 11.1% (that's –11.1%, on top of –11.1%, and so on).

EXHIBIT 12.1
Holding-period returns: Best v. worst

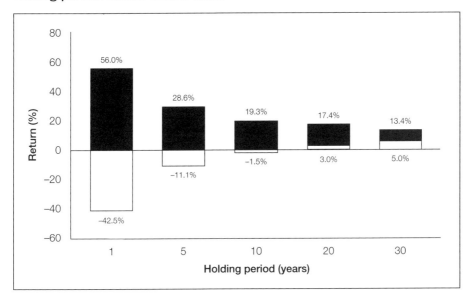

Can you see the pattern in the picture? The spread between the best and the worst in one-year holding periods is very large; in any given year, just about anything can happen. But as we increase the holding period to five years, the spread between the best five-year mean return and the worst five-year mean return decreases substantially. If we increase the holding period to ten years, the spread decreases even more. Essentially, what the picture shows is that as we increase the holding period, the mean annual compound return tends to converge to its long-term average (9%).

This intuition can be formally captured by the **annualized standard deviation of returns (ASD)**, which is given by

$$ASD = \frac{SD}{\sqrt{T}}$$ (12.2)

where again *SD* denotes the *annual* standard deviation of returns and *T* the holding period. For example, the annualized standard deviation of five-year returns is $0.17/(5)^{1/2} = 7.6\%$, as shown in the fourth column of Table 12.2.

Note that, as is obvious from equation (12.2) and the fourth column of Table 12.2, as the investment horizon increases, risk (measured by the *annualized* standard deviation) *decreases*. Or, put differently, the longer the holding period, the lower the dispersion around the long-term mean annual compound return. (Incidentally, note from Exhibit 12.1 that the mean annual compound return of the *worst* 20-year and 30-year holding periods in the US were 3% and 5%, respectively, both positive and higher than inflation.)

There you have it. Two plausible stories that yield opposite results. Perhaps you can now see why this is a controversial issue. But we won't leave it just like that. We'll look at this issue from yet another angle, and perhaps a clearer picture will emerge.

Long-term risk: Shortfall probability

When investing in any asset, an investor may be interested to know how likely is the asset to underperform a given benchmark. The investor, for example, may be interested to know how likely is the asset to deliver negative returns, or returns below inflation, or returns below a risk-free asset, or below any other benchmark he may consider relevant. This likelihood is usually known as the *shortfall probability*; that is, the probability that an asset falls short of a benchmark return. The interesting question is how this shortfall probability evolves as the holding period increases.

Take a look at the last three columns of Table 12.2, which display the shortfall probabilities of the US stock market with respect to 0%, to an annual rate of inflation of 3%, and to an annual risk-free rate of 5%. We'll discuss how to calculate these numbers later in the chapter; for now, just focus on the numbers themselves.

Note that all these probabilities decrease steadily as we increase the holding period. There is roughly a 31% probability of obtaining a negative return in any given year, but the chances of obtaining a negative mean annual compound return over ten years are less than 6%. Similarly, although the probability of obtaining less than the mean annual rate of inflation (3%) is 37% in any given year, the probability of obtaining less than a mean annual compound return of 3% over 20 years falls to under 7%. Finally, although there is roughly a 41%

probability of obtaining less than the mean annual risk-free rate (5%) in any given year, the probability of obtaining less than a mean annual compound return of 5% over 30 years falls to under 12%. The message is clear: whatever the benchmark, the probability of falling short of it decreases steadily as we increase the investment horizon. (For this statement to be strictly true, the benchmark must be lower than the asset's mean compound return.)

The previous numbers are estimations based on the distribution of US (nominal) stock returns between 1871 and 2003. But the historical data itself has an interesting story to tell. Take a look at Exhibit 12.2, based on data discussed in *Stocks for the Long Run*, which shows the proportion of periods in which stocks underperformed bonds during the years 1871 to 2001. If we consider all the one-year periods between 1871 and 2001, stocks underperformed bonds in basically four periods out of ten. Perhaps you consider this number surprisingly high, but remember that the annual volatility of stocks is roughly twice as high as that of bonds. And note that this exhibit is based on whether one asset outperformed the other, but not by how much. In other words, if stocks outperformed bonds by 20% in any given period, and bonds outperformed stocks by 1% in the next period, this exhibit would count one win for each asset.

EXHIBIT 12.2
Shortfall probability

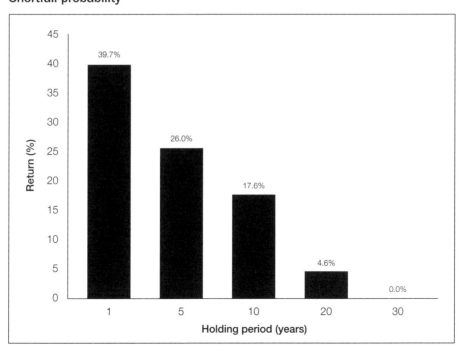

Now look at what happens as the holding period increases. If we consider five-year investment horizons, stocks underperformed bonds in only one period out of four; in ten-year holding periods, in less than one period out of five; in 20-year holding periods, in less than one period out of twenty. And in 30-year periods? Surprise! There has been *no* 30-year period in the (1871–2003) history of the US markets in which stocks underperformed bonds.

Now, of course some investors can theorize and forecast probabilities as much as they'd like. But it should still be rather comforting for most stock investors to know that in 30-year periods stocks *never* underperformed bonds, and that even in 20-year periods such underperformance occurred in less than one period out of twenty.

Time diversification and mean reversion

The idea behind the annualized standard deviation as a measure of long-term risk is that, as the investment horizon increases, the dispersion around the long-term mean compound return decreases. In other words, the longer the holding period, the more likely an asset is to deliver its long-term mean compound return. The idea behind the shortfall probability as a measure of long-term risk, in turn, is that, as long as the benchmark is lower than the asset's long-term mean compound return, the longer the investment horizon, the less likely the asset is to underperform the benchmark.

Putting these two ideas together and comparing two assets, one riskier than the other, it follows that, the longer the holding period, the more likely the riskier asset is to outperform the less-risky asset. For example, if we compare stocks and bonds, these arguments would suggest that, the longer the holding period, the more likely stocks are to outperform bonds. The evidence in Exhibit 12.2 seems to confirm that this is indeed the case.

These arguments are part of the hotly debated issue of *time diversification*, in which most practitioners believe and some (but certainly not all) academics don't. Although this concept can be defined in many ways, all of them suggest that as the investment horizon increases, the probability that a riskier asset outperforms a less risky asset also increases. Note that this definition implies that the shortfall probability (the probability that the riskier asset delivers a return below that of the less risky asset) decreases as the holding period increases. It also implies that the longer the holding period, the more likely it becomes that above-average returns offset below-average returns (and that the asset delivers its long-term mean compound return).

Many theoretical arguments can be (and have been) made against time diversification. However, even those who don't believe in this idea agree that, under *mean reversion*, time diversification indeed holds. What is, then, mean reversion? It is simply the tendency of an asset to revert to its long-term trend. Flip a coin a few times, and the proportion of heads can be way off from the expected 50%. But keep flipping the coin, and the larger the number of flips, the more that the proportion of heads will approach 50%. Or spin a roulette a few times, and the proportion of 17s can be way off from its expected proportion of 1/37. But spin the roulette one million times and the proportion of 17s will be quite close to 1/37. Mean reversion is, in fact, as simple as that.

Whether or not there is mean reversion in returns is at the end of the day an empirical question, so let's look at some evidence. Exhibit 12.3 shows the path followed by a $100 investment in the US stock market at the end of 1870 and compounded at the market's annual real returns through the end of 2003. The straight line is simply a trend increasing constantly at the market's long-term mean annual compound real return of 6.8%. As the graph clearly shows, periods of above-average returns tend to be followed by periods of below-average returns (and all along returns fluctuate rather closely around their long-term trend). This is exactly what mean reversion is all about.

Note that, during the years 1995 to 1999, the market delivered returns way above its long-term mean annual compound return. Mean reversion would not

EXHIBIT 12.3
Shortfall probability

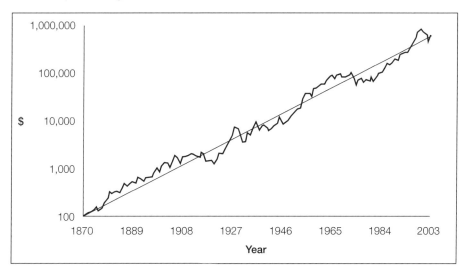

Year

predict when, but it would predict that a correction was only a matter of time. Sure enough, during the years 2000 to 2002, the market delivered returns way below its long-term mean annual compound return. Interestingly, note that by the end of 1999, after five consecutive years of far above-average returns, the market was way above its long-term trend. The three following years of far below-average returns took the market below its long-term trend.

Forecasting target returns

We'll conclude our discussion of long-term risk and return with a simple tool designed to answer a question financial advisors face repeatedly. Given an asset, a target return, and a holding period, how likely is the asset to deliver at least the target return in the planned investment horizon? (In what follows we'll use the concepts of simple and continuously compounded returns, as well as normal and lognormal distributions. If you're not clear about the difference between these two types of returns and distributions, you may want to read Chapters 1, 28, and 29 before proceeding.)

Let's start with a bit of notation. Let's call AM and SD the (arithmetic) mean and standard deviation of a series of continuously compounded returns (r), and let's assume that these returns follow a normal distribution. This implies that simple returns (R) follow a lognormal distribution. Then, the probability of obtaining *at least* a mean annual compound return of R^* over T years follows from a two-step procedure:

■ Calculate

$$z^* = \frac{\ln(1 + R^*) - AM}{SD/\sqrt{T}} \tag{12.3}$$

■ Calculate

$$P(R \geq R^*) = P(z \geq z^*)$$

This procedure basically transforms the lognormal variable $1 + R$ into a standard normal variable z, with the purpose of bypassing the lognormal distribution and calculating probabilities out of the more widely used standard normal distribution. As the second step indicates, once we find the probability that $z \geq z^*$, $P(z \geq z^*)$, then we have also found the probability that $R \geq R^*$, $P(R \geq R^*)$. Note that we're actually interested in the probability of obtaining target *simple* returns. However, as argued in Chapters 2 and 29, continuously compounded returns are sometimes a necessary intermediate tool, and that is exactly the way in which we're using them here.

Let's focus again on the history of the US stock market between the years 1871 and 2003. The distribution of annual continuously compounded returns has an arithmetic mean of 8.6% and a standard deviation of 16.8%. (This last number is the one that we rounded to 17% in Table 12.2. And the tool we're now discussing is the one that generated all the shortfall probabilities, for a mean return of 8.6%.) The distribution of annual simple returns, on the other hand, has an arithmetic mean of 10.5%, a geometric mean of 9.0%, and a standard deviation of 17.8%. What is the probability, then, that the market returns 5% next year?

That's simple. Using equation (12.3) we get

$$z^* = \frac{\ln(1.05) - 0.086}{0.168/1^{1/2}} = -0.22$$

and the area *above* this number under the standard normal distribution is 0.588. In other words, there is a 58.8% probability that the market returns at least 5% next year. What about a mean compound return of 5% over the next 30 years? Again, using equation (12.3) we get

$$z^* = \frac{\ln(1.05) - 0.086}{0.168/30^{1/2}} = -1.22$$

and the area above this number under the standard normal distribution is 0.889. In other words, the probability that the market returns at least a mean compound return of 5% over 30 years is 88.9%. Finally, what about the probability that the market returns 20% next year and over the next 20 years? Try that one yourself, and you should find that these probabilities are 28.3% and 0.5%.

We could go on, but let's take a shortcut. Take a look at Table 12.3, which displays the probabilities that the US market delivers several target returns (vertically aligned) over several holding periods (horizontally aligned). It is important to note that these targets are not cumulative returns but mean *annual* compound returns. That's why in equation (12.3) we have annual magnitudes in the numerator, and the *annualized* standard deviation in the denominator.

Take a good look at the numbers in the table, think about them, and draw your own conclusions. But note at least two things. First, that for any target return below 9% (the long-term mean annual compound return), as the holding period increases, the probability of obtaining at least the target return also increases. And second, that, for any target return above 9%, the probability of obtaining at least the target return decreases as the holding period increases. Taken together, these points reinforce the argument that, as the investment horizon increases, the mean annual compound delivered by the market tends to converge to its long-term mean annual compound return.

TABLE 12.3

Target return	1 yr (%)	5 yr (%)	10 yr (%)	15 yr (%)	20 yr (%)	25 yr (%)	30 yr (%)
				Holding period			
–5%	79.4	96.7	99.5	99.9	100.0	100.0	100.0
0%	69.6	87.5	94.8	97.7	98.9	99.5	99.8
5%	58.8	69.1	75.9	80.6	84.0	86.7	88.9
10%	47.8	45.1	43.1	41.6	40.3	39.2	38.2
12%	43.5	35.8	30.4	26.5	23.4	20.8	18.7
14%	39.4	27.4	19.8	15.0	11.5	9.0	7.1
16%	35.5	20.3	12.0	7.5	4.8	3.1	2.1
18%	31.8	14.5	6.7	3.3	1.7	0.9	0.5
20%	28.3	10.0	3.5	1.3	0.5	0.2	0.1
25%	20.7	3.4	0.5	0.1	0.0	0.0	0.0
30%	14.6	0.9	0.0	0.0	0.0	0.0	0.0

Tables such as 12.3 are extremely useful for making investment decisions and are widely used by financial advisors. The two-step procedure that generates it, in turn, is very versatile and can be used to answer many interesting financial questions, some of which you will find in the Challenge section.

The big picture

The relationship between risk, return, and the investment horizon is extremely important for investors and has received wide attention from both academics and practitioners. There is little question that, in the very long term, the compounding power of stocks is vastly higher than that of bonds. There is also little question that, in the short term, stocks are more volatile than bonds. The controversy is, precisely, about how does the relative risk of stocks and bonds evolves as the investment horizon increases.

The empirical evidence seems to support the benefits of time diversification. In the US, it clearly shows that as the holding period increases, the proportion of periods in which stocks underperformed bonds decreases. It also shows the existence of mean reversion, implying that as the holding period increases, the mean compound return of stocks converges towards its long-term historical average (6.8% in real terms). All in all, the evidence does seem to indicate that in the long term stocks seem to be a much better bet than bonds (this statement being more true the longer the investment horizon).

Financial advisors clearly factor time diversification into their advice, recommending larger exposure to stocks the longer the investment horizon of the client. Even simple rules-of-thumb for wealth allocation such as $x_S = 100 -$ Age, where x_S is the proportion of wealth invested in stocks, are clearly based on the idea of time diversification.

And yet, the issue remains extremely controversial, perhaps for no other reason than that risk is so hard to define or is perceived so differently across investors. That has led many to abandon the idea of finding a universal definition of risk and to emphasize instead that risk, like beauty, may be in the eye of the beholder.

Excel section

Calculating probabilities out of the normal and lognormal distributions is simple in Excel. However, because we discuss this issue in some detail in Chapters 28 and 29, we'll cover only the essentials here. Consider a variable z that follows a standard normal distribution (which, by definition, has a mean of 0 and a standard deviation of 1). Then,

■ To calculate the probability that z takes a value larger than or equal to z_0, simply type '=1–normsdist(z_0)' and hit 'Enter.' (Note that you don't have to type z_0 but *the actual value* of this magnitude.)

Excel also easily calculates probabilities straight out of the lognormal distribution, but there's a quirk: You need to input the parameters of the associated *normal* distribution. To illustrate, suppose that continuously compounded returns (r) follow a normal distribution with mean *AM* and standard deviation *SD*, which implies that simple returns (R) follow a lognormal distribution. Although we are interested in forecasting the probability of obtaining target *simple* returns, Excel requires you to input the mean and standard deviation of the distribution of *continuously compounded* returns. Don't ask . . . Just do the following:

- To calculate the probability that R takes a value larger than or equal to R_0, type '**=1–lognormdist(1+R_0, AM, SD)**' and hit 'Enter.' (Note, first, that you don't have to type $1+R_0$, AM, and SD but *the actual values* of these magnitudes; and, second, that AM and SD refer to the distribution of continuously compounded returns.)

If you want to use this function to calculate tables such as Table 12.3, it is important to keep in mind that the target return should be a mean *annual* compound (simple) return; AM should be the arithmetic mean of *annual* (continuously compounded) returns; and SD should be the *annualized* standard deviation of (continuously compounded) returns, calculated as the standard deviation of annual (continuously compounded) returns divided by the square root of the number of years. (Yes, do read this paragraph slowly again.)

Challenge section

1 Between 1970 and 2003, the distribution of annual continuously compounded returns of the European market had an arithmetic mean return of 10.9% with a standard deviation of 17.0%. The distribution of annual simple returns, on the other hand, had an arithmetic mean return of 13.4%, a geometric mean return of 11.5%, and a standard deviation of 17.0%. Fill a table similar in structure to Table 12.3, with the probabilities that the European market delivers different target returns over different investment horizons. Then think about the following:
   (a) What happens to the estimated probabilities for a one-year holding period as the target return increases?
   (b) What happens to the estimated probabilities for a ten-year holding period as the target return increases?
   (c) What happens to the estimated probabilities for a target return of 10% as the holding period increases?
   (d) What happens to the estimated probabilities for a target return of 14% as the holding period increases?

2 Consider an initial investment of $1,000 and investment horizons of 1, 5, 10, 15, 20, 25, and 30 years. Then calculate:

(a) The probability of turning the initial $1,000 into at least $1,500.

(b) The amount of money such that the probability of obtaining at least that amount is 50%.

part II:

VALUATION

13

STOCKS I: THE DIVIDEND DISCOUNT MODEL

First things first

Discounted cash flow models

The dividend discount model: Theory

The dividend discount model: Versions

The dividend discount model: An example

The big picture

Excel section

Challenge section

There exist many models of equity valuation, some based on discounted cash flow and others based on multiples. Many academics and practitioners portray the dividend discount model as the simplest of the discounted cash flow models. That's a big mistake. If you learn one thing from this chapter, let it be this: the dividend discount model is deceptively simple, it can easily be misused, and its proper implementation is much more difficult than is usually believed.

First things first

There are three important distinctions to keep in mind when discussing valuation. Two are specific to equity valuation, the first a distinction between fundamental analysis and technical analysis, and the second between absolute valuation and relative valuation. The third is more general, applying to the valuation of all assets, and is a distinction between price and value.

Fundamental analysis refers to a valuation technique that focuses on the drivers of a company's value. It involves the analysis of the company's financial statements, financial ratios, market, competitors, and many other factors in order to determine its value. Technical analysis, on the other hand, largely focuses on the trading history of a stock. It does not really attempt to value a company; rather, it involves the extrapolation of trends and patterns from past prices in order to extract clues as to how the price may behave in the future.

Models of equity valuation can be grouped into two types. Models of *absolute* (or *intrinsic*) *valuation* estimate the value of a company on the basis of its own fundamentals; models of *relative valuation* assess it in relation to the value of comparable companies. The former estimate value by discounting expected cash flows at a rate that reflects their risk; the latter do it by comparing ratios usually called multiples. Both types of models belong to the category of fundamental (as opposed to technical) analysis.

The dividend discount model (DDM), the weighted-average cost of capital (WACC) model, the adjusted present value (APV) model, and the flows-to-equity (FTE) model are all discounted cash flow (DCF) models. Price-to-earnings (P/E) ratios, price-to-book (P/B) ratios, price-to-cash flow (P/CF), and price-to-dividend (P/D) ratios are some of the most widely used multiples in relative valuation.

Finally, it is important to keep in mind a critical distinction between *price* and *value*. The former simply indicates the number of dollars an investor has to pay for a share of a company, just like the number of dollars we pay for a dinner or an airplane ticket. The latter is much more subtle. In a way, it is the number of dollars an investor *should* pay for a share of a company. This means that given the fundamentals of the company and what it is expected to deliver, there is an appropriate price to pay for its shares. This appropriate price, which may or may not be equal to the market price, is called 'value' or 'intrinsic value.'

Note that *all* pricing models yield an estimate of intrinsic value, that is, they all yield the price investors *should* pay for a company or one of its shares. In fact, the whole concept of market efficiency is based on whether market prices appropriately reflect intrinsic values; the more this is the case, the more efficient markets are.

Discounted cash flow models

All DCF models are based on the calculation of a present value (discussed in Chapter 21). The various versions of this model differ in the type of cash flows discounted and therefore in the discount rate. Other than that, all DCF models require the analyst to estimate expected cash flows and the appropriate rate at which they should be discounted.

In this chapter we'll deal with dividends, the 'simplest' of all cash flows. Perhaps one reason for which the DDM is considered the simplest of all DCF models is because dividends are observed directly but other types of cash flows have to be calculated from financial statements. This obviously applies to the past values of these magnitudes. Looking forward, all three magnitudes need to be forecasted and it's not at all clear that forecasting dividends is any easier than forecasting other types of cash flow.

The underlying idea behind the discount rate is that it should capture the risk of the cash flows discounted. That's why DCF models that differ in their definition of cash flow also differ in their discount rate. Some DCF models discount cash flows at the cost of equity whereas some others do it at the cost of capital. The discount rate for the DDM we discuss in this chapter is the former.

Finally, in the typical implementation of DCF models, analysts make some assumptions about the expected growth rate of the cash flows to be discounted. These assumptions may range all the way from constant growth to two or more stages of growth. It is also typical for analysts to estimate a terminal value; this is the last cash flow to be discounted and attempts to summarize in a single number all the cash flows from that point on. The two most widely used alternatives for estimating the terminal value are a *growing perpetuity* (an infinite sequence of cash flows growing at a constant rate) or a *multiple* of some fundamental variable (such as earnings or cash flow).

The dividend discount model: Theory

The underlying idea of the DDM is both very simple and very plausible: an investor should pay for a share of a company the present value of all the cash flows he expects to receive from the share. And what does an investor pocket from a share? Dividends (if the company pays them) for as long as he holds the stock, and a final cash flow given by the price at which the investor expects to sell the share. It can't really get much simpler than that, and that's one of the reasons why, mistakenly, the DDM is sold as a 'simple' model. However, as we'll discuss below, the devil is in the detail.

But let's leave the devil for later. The formal expression of the DDM is given by

$$
p_0 = \frac{E(D_1)}{(1+R)} + \frac{E(D_2)}{(1+R)^2} + \frac{E(D_3)}{(1+R)^3} + \ldots + \frac{E(D_T) + E(p_T)}{(1+R)^T} \quad (13.1)
$$

where p_0 denotes the intrinsic value of (or, misusing the word, the price an investor *should* pay for) a share of the company, $E(D_t)$ the expected dividend per share in period t, $E(p_T)$ the expected share price at time T, R the discount rate, and T the number of periods for which dividends are forecast.

Note that the cash flows we're discounting, dividends, end up in the pocket of shareholders, who are then the ones bearing their risk. The discount rate must then reflect the return shareholders require from holding the shares of the company. This required return on equity, sometimes also called the cost of equity, can be estimated with many models, the most popular of which is the capital asset pricing model, CAPM (discussed in Chapter 7). Therefore, the discount rate is usually estimated as $R = R_f + MRP \cdot \beta$, where R_f, MRP, and β denote the risk-free rate, the market risk premium, and the company's beta, respectively.

It is possible, though in no way essential, to forecast $E(p_T)$ as a function of the dividends expected to be received from time T on, that is, $E(p_T) = f\{E(D_{T+1}), E(D_{T+2}), E(D_{T+3}) \ldots\}$. In that case, equation (13.1) turns into the present value of an infinite sequence of dividends. That is,

$$
p_0 = \frac{E(D_1)}{(1+R)} + \frac{E(D_2)}{(1+R)^2} + \frac{E(D_3)}{(1+R)^3} + \ldots + \frac{E(D_T)}{(1+R)^T}
$$
$$
+ \frac{E(D_{T+1})}{(1+R)^{T+1}} + \frac{E(D_{T+2})}{(1+R)^{T+2}} + \ldots \quad (13.2)
$$

You may find the idea of an 'infinite' sequence of dividends a bit hard to grasp. But although no investor is going to hold a share 'for ever,' the life of the company is in principle unlimited. If it makes your life easier, just think of equation (13.2) as the present value of a 'very long' sequence of dividends. You can even drive this thought home by noting that dividends that are very far away add very little to p_0.

The dividend discount model: Versions

The DDM is not used in practice as stated in equation (13.2). Its usual implementation imposes some structure on the expected growth of dividends, with different assumptions generating different versions of the DDM. It is important to keep in mind that an assumption about the way dividends are expected to evolve is a statement about the company's expected dividend policy. This policy, in turn, depends not only on the expected profitability of the company but also on the existence of alternative uses for the company's profits (investment opportunities). This is one of the reasons that, however simple some versions of the DDM may look, its proper implementation is far from trivial. Again, the devil is in the detail.

No growth

The simplest assumption we could make about expected dividends is that they will remain constant at the level of the last dividend paid by the company (D_0), that is, $E(D_1) = E(D_2) = E(D_3) = \ldots = D_0$. Substituting this stream of dividends into (13.2) we get

$$p_0 = \frac{D_0}{(1 + R)} + \frac{D_0}{(1 + R)^2} + \frac{D_0}{(1 + R)^3} + \ldots = \frac{D_0}{R} \tag{13.3}$$

Now, if you've never dealt with this model before or are not a bit trained in math, the second equality may surprise you. But it is indeed the case that if we discount an infinite sequence of a constant magnitude (D_0 in our case), then the sum of the infinite terms collapses into the constant magnitude divided by the discount rate. Mathematically, this is called a *perpetuity*. Whether or not it makes for a good pricing model we'll discuss later.

Constant growth

A second possibility is to assume that dividends will grow at a constant rate g beginning from the last dividend paid by the company, that is, $E(D_1) = D_0 \cdot (1 + g)$, $E(D_2) = D_0 \cdot (1 + g)^2$, $E(D_3) = D_0 \cdot (1+g)^3$, and so on. Substituting this stream of dividends into equation (13.2) we get

$$p_0 = \frac{D_0 \cdot (1 + g)}{(1 + R)} + \frac{D_0 \cdot (1 + g)^2}{(1 + R)^2} + \frac{D_0 \cdot (1 + g)^3}{(1 + R)^3} + \ldots = \frac{D_0 \cdot (1 + g)}{R - g}$$

(13.4)

Again, if you haven't dealt with this model before or are not a bit trained in math the second equality may surprise you. But again it is the case that an infinite sum of terms collapses into something relatively simple. Mathematically, this is called a *growing perpetuity* and holds as long as $R > g$.

Whether the assumption that dividends will grow at a constant rate in perpetuity is a plausible one we'll discuss later. At this point, it's important to note that this assumption shouldn't be thought of as implying that dividends are expected to grow *exactly* at the rate g; that would be naive. Rather, g should be though of as an *average* growth rate of dividends. That is, in some periods dividends may grow at more than g% and in some others at less than g%, but on average we do expect them to grow at g%.

Two stages of growth

A third possibility is to assume that dividends will grow at a rate g_1 over the first T periods, and at the rate g_2 from that point on, usually (but not necessarily always) with $g_1 > g_2$. Imposing this assumption on equation (13.2) we get the rather-scary expression

$$p_0 = \frac{D_0 \cdot (1 + g_1)}{(1 + R)} + \frac{D_0 \cdot (1 + g_1)^2}{(1 + R)^2} + \ldots + \frac{D_0 \cdot (1 + g_1)^T}{(1 + R)^T} + \frac{\dfrac{\{D_0 \cdot (1 + g_1)^T\} \cdot (1 + g_2)}{R - g_2}}{(1 + R)^T}$$

(13.5)

Let's think about equation (13.5) a bit. The first T terms of the right-hand side simply show a sequence of dividends growing at the rate g_1 during T

periods. The numerator of the last term is the terminal value and therefore an estimate of the stock price at time T. Note that this numerator is basically the same as equation (13.4) but set at time T rather than at time 0: if dividends grow at the rate g_1 over T periods, the dividend in period T will be $D_0 \cdot (1 + g_1)^T$; and if beginning from that level dividends grow at g_2 from that point on (in perpetuity), then at time T the stock price should be

$$\frac{\{D_0 \cdot (1 + g_1)^T\} \cdot (1 + g_2)}{R - g_2}$$

The denominator of the last term is simply the discount factor for a cash flow expected at the end of period T.

The first growth rate (g_1) is usually thought of as a period of fast growth in dividends; the second (g_2) as the growth in dividends after the company matures. The number of periods for which dividends are expected to grow at g_1 (T) in principle depends on each individual company, its stage of growth, and its dividend policy. However, in practice, $T = 5$ and $T = 10$ are popular choices (perhaps for no particularly good reason).

Other possibilities

Analysts might consider it appropriate for a company at some point in time to model three or even more stages of growth in dividends. Or they may consider one or more stages of growth in dividends and a terminal price estimated with a multiple. The possibilities are, of course, endless.

The dividend discount model: An example

In 2003, General Electric (GE) delivered a profit of $15 billion on revenues of $133 billion. Its market cap at the end of the year was $312 billion and its stock price $30.98. Its earnings per share (EPS) and dividends per share (DPS) were $1.49 and $0.76, respectively, giving it a price to earnings (P/E) ratio of 21 and a healthy dividend payout ratio (DPR) of 51%. How much *should* an investor have paid for a share of GE at that time? This is the question we'll attempt to answer using the DDM. (Throughout our analysis we'll assume that we're valuing GE at the end of the year 2003.)

Before we get to the numbers bear this in mind: our goal here is to go over different versions of the DDM and briefly discuss their pros and cons, *not* to make a strong statement about GE's intrinsic value. This implies that we'll be making different assumptions about how dividends are expected to grow over time, effectively making an 'if–then' analysis (*if* the dividends evolve this way, *then* the price should be that). This is obviously *not* the way analysts implement the DDM (or any other model). Analysts derive their estimates from what they consider their most plausible scenario, perhaps complementing it with some sensitivity analysis, but they do not go over widely different scenarios as we'll do here for illustrative purposes.

It's also important to keep in mind that it's fundamentally wrong to make a set of assumptions, get an estimate of intrinsic value, compare that with the market price, and determine from the comparison whether *our assumptions* are right. That defeats the very purpose of the analysis. Stock pricing is about coming up with what we believe is a plausible set of assumptions, getting an estimate of intrinsic value that follows from those assumptions, and then deciding whether to buy, hold, or sell based on the comparison between our estimate of intrinsic value and the market price. *Never* compare an estimate of intrinsic value to a market price to assess the plausibility of your assumptions; always use assumptions that you believe to be plausible to start with.

The discount rate

As discussed above, the discount rate for the DDM is the required return on equity and is typically estimated with the CAPM. At year-end 2003 the yield on ten-year notes was 4.3% and GE's beta was 1.1. For the market risk premium we can use the popular estimate of 5.5% (see Chapter 7). Putting these three numbers together we get a cost of equity for GE of $0.043 + 0.055 \cdot 1.1 = 10.4\%$. That will be our discount rate.

No growth

Let's start by assuming that our best estimate of GE's expected dividends is that they will remain constant at the level of the last dividend paid by the company ($0.76). According to equation (13.3), then, our best estimate of GE's intrinsic value would be $0.76/0.104 = 7.3. The calculation is trivial, but is this version of the DDM plausible?

Not really. Note that a constant nominal dividend implies that the real dividend will eventually be 0, that is, owing to inflation, the dividend will gradually lose purchasing power. That doesn't sound like a plausible dividend policy for a company to follow. Constant nominal dividends may be plausible for a few years, but not in the long term.

Unsurprisingly, then, our estimate of GE's intrinsic value is much lower than its price. Given that GE has a long history of increasing its dividend (by roughly 13% a year over the past 20 years), the market is plausibly factoring some growth in dividends into GE's price. In short, because our assumption is not very plausible, neither is our estimate of intrinsic value.

Constant growth

Let's now assume a more plausible dividend policy for GE. Let's assume that we expect the company to keep the purchasing power of its dividend constant over time. If we expect inflation to run at an average of 3% a year (the historical annual rate), and GE to increase its annual dividend at that rate in the long term, then according to equation (13.4), our best estimate of GE's intrinsic value would be $0.76 · (1.03)/(0.104 − 0.03) = $10.7. If we believe our assumption of 3% constant growth in dividends, then we should also believe that GE should be trading at $10.7 and therefore that at $31 it's overpriced.

What if we expected GE to increase its dividend at the rate of 6% in the long term instead? Then according to equation (13.4), GE's intrinsic value would be $0.76 · (1.06)/(0.104 − 0.06) = $18.5, and we would still conclude that GE is overpriced. Note that under both assumptions our estimate of intrinsic value is much lower than the market price. Should we then conclude that the market is expecting a much higher *long-term* growth in dividends?

Hard to believe. The reason is that the constant-growth model makes an assumption about the *long-term* growth of dividends. In the long term, the growth in dividends, the growth in earnings, and the growth of the company's value must align. In addition, this rate of growth cannot outpace the growth of the overall economy, simply because the growth of a component factor cannot for ever outpace that of the aggregate.

Historically, the US economy has grown at an annual rate of roughly 6% (3% in real terms plus 3% inflation). That becomes an upper boundary for any plausible estimate of the *long-term* growth of dividends. In other words, whenever we use the constant-growth model, or any model in which the terminal value is expressed as a growing perpetuity, it is simply not plausible to assume a long-term growth beyond, roughly, 6%. Other economies may of course have different long-term rates of growth, but it would be hard to make a plausible case for rates much higher than 6% or so.

Two stages of growth

The main problem with the constant-growth model is its lack of flexibility. Perhaps we plausibly expect GE to increase its dividend at a much higher rate than 6% in the short term, but we cannot accommodate that in the constant growth model. The extra flexibility of the two-stage model then becomes valuable.

At the end of 2003, analysts expected GE to increase its EPS at the annual rate of 10% for the following five years. Let's then assume that dividends will grow at the same 10% rate during those five years. And let's also assume that from that point on dividends will grow at a long-term rate of 6% a year. According to equation (13.4) then, our best estimate of GE's intrinsic value would be

$$p_0 = \frac{\$0.76 \cdot (1.10)}{(1.104)} + \ldots + \frac{\$0.76 \cdot (1.10)^5}{(1.104)^5} + \frac{\dfrac{\{\$0.76 \cdot (1.10)^5\} \cdot (1.06)}{0.104 - 0.06}}{(1.104)^5} = \$22.0$$

Note that, if we believe our assumptions, given its price of $31, GE at $22 is overpriced. Note, also, that our assumptions lead us to a terminal price of $29.8, whose present value is roughly $18. Therefore, some 80% of our estimated value of $22 comes from the terminal value. Although this proportion is unusually high, it's not uncommon for a terminal value to be around 50–60% of the estimated intrinsic value. This fact makes sensitivity analysis on the terminal value a critical part of any valuation.

Terminal value as a multiple

Finally, let's consider a DDM in which we model the terminal value as a multiple (rather than as a growing perpetuity). Let's assume, first, that over the next five years dividends will grow at the annual rate of 13%, that is, the rate at which they've been growing over the past 20 years. Let's also assume that over the next five years EPS will grow at the 10% annual rate expected by analysts; that would imply EPS of $2.40 = ($1.49) \cdot (1.10^5)$ five years down the road. Finally, let's assume that at that point in time GE's P/E ratio remains at its current 21, which would give us a terminal value of $50.4 = (21) \cdot ($2.40)$. According to equation (13.1), then, our estimate of intrinsic value would be

$$p_0 = \frac{\$0.76 \cdot (1.13)}{(1.104)} + \ldots + \frac{\$0.76 \cdot (1.13)^5}{(1.104)^5} + \frac{(21) \cdot (\$2.40)}{(1.104)^5} = \$34.9$$

Although we're assuming now a faster short-term growth in dividends than we did in our previous case (13% now and 10% before), most of the difference between the current estimate and the previous one comes from the terminal value ($50.4 now and $29.8 before). Note that, in this case, the present value of the terminal value accounts for roughly 60% of our estimated intrinsic value of $34.9. Note, finally, that if we believe our assumptions, we should conclude that, at $31, GE is a good buying opportunity.

The big picture

At this point you may be wondering, 'So, where's the devil?' No part of our discussion appears to pose any great challenge, and you may be tempted to join the camp of those who argue that the DDM is a very simple model. That would be a mistake.

Recall the 'if–then' nature of our analysis. What we largely did was to make different assumptions and come up with the intrinsic values that followed from those assumptions. That is of course not difficult to do. *The problem is, precisely, how to come up with a set of plausible assumptions to estimate the expected dividends*.

Note that for the DDM to yield a precise estimate of intrinsic value, *everything* that is relevant for the valuation of the company must be summarized in a sequence of dividends. Managerial strategies, the evolution of the competitive landscape, expected innovations in technology, possible changes in management . . . you name it. That and much more must *all* come down to one or two numbers that summarize the expected growth in dividends. Do you think that's an easy task?

In addition, the constant-growth DDM almost invariably yields an estimate of intrinsic value below the market price; most times, in fact, way below. The same goes for the two-stage DDM with a growing perpetuity as a terminal value. And this problem is especially severe in companies that have low dividend payout ratios (DPRs). Does the market consistently overprice these companies or is the DDM inappropriate in these cases?

The 6% limit in the long-term growth of dividends is part of the problem, but assuming a faster growth in the long term makes little sense. Sure, we could model long stages of high growth in dividends and then a terminal value expressed as a growing perpetuity. But that of course begs the question of how many stages, how long each stage should be, and at what rate dividends should grow. Throwing some numbers into a formula and coming up with a number is not difficult; doing that and at the same time making sense is.

In short, the DDM is a model with impeccable logic behind it for a share of a company pay the present value of the cash flows you expect to pocket from it. But it's implementation is much more difficult than a few simple formulas may suggest. That is perhaps one of the reasons why, however plausible the DDM may be, the WACC model discussed in the next chapter is far more widely used.

Excel section

There is no new Excel material in this chapter.

Challenge section

1   In 2003, Coca-Cola delivered a profit of $4.3 billion on revenues of $21 billion. Its market cap at the end of the year was $124 billion and its stock price $50.75. Its EPS and DPS were $1.77 and $0.88, respectively, giving it a P/E ratio of almost 29 and a DPR of almost 50%. At the end of 2003, Coca-Cola's beta was a very low 0.3 and the yield on ten-year notes stood at 4.3%. (For an estimate of the market risk premium you may use 5.5%, as we've done in the text for the analysis of GE.)

   (a)   Estimate the appropriate discount rate for the DDM. Does it look high? Low? Why?

   (b)   If you expect Coca-Cola's dividends to remain at their level of $0.88 in perpetuity, how much would you pay for a share of this company?

   (c)   How much would you pay if you expect Coca-Cola's dividends to grow at 3% in the long term? How much if you expect dividends to grow at 4% in the long term?

   (d)   How much would you pay if you expect Coca-Cola's dividends to grow at 10% a year over the next five years, and at 4% a year from that point on?

2 Assume that Coca-Cola will grow its dividend at 10% a year over the next five years. Assume, also, that five years down the road Coca-Cola's P/E will remain at its current 29, and that its EPS will grow over the next five years at the 10% annual rate expected by analysts. How much would you then pay for a share of Coca-Cola?

14

STOCKS II: THE WACC MODEL

Earnings and cash flow

Cash flow and cash flow

Valuation with the WACC model: Overview

Valuation with the WACC model: An example

The big picture

Excel section

Challenge section

There is little question that the technically correct way of valuing a company is with the discounted cash flow (DCF) model. As we discussed in the previous chapter, this model has many variations depending on the definition of cash flow and the discount rate used. In this chapter we'll discuss the weighted-average cost of capital (WACC) model, the most widely used version of the DCF model.

Earnings and cash flow

It is often said that earnings are an opinion and cash flows are a fact. And it is largely true. As a matter of fact, the accounting scandals of the past few years did nothing but reinforce this idea. Regardless of what accountants report, at the end of the day investors care about the ability of companies to generate cash. And that is the ultimate goal of all DCF models: to forecast the generation of cash, to account for the risk of that cash, and to bring both together into the estimation of an intrinsic value.

But before we go any further, a fair warning. We'll be giving names to several concepts, and you may have seen the same or similar concepts named differently elsewhere. In fact, it would be surprising if you had not. Accountants agree on names just as much as traders do on whether the market will be up or down tomorrow. That's one reason for trying to keep the discussion down to the essentials.

Let's start by considering Table 14.1. The left column shows a simplified income statement. Beginning from the revenues generated by the company, we subtract all operating costs (cost of goods sold; selling, general, and administrative expenses; and so on), depreciation and amortization, the interest expense (if any), and taxes to arrive at the company's net income. That is what accountants usually refer to as the company's earnings.

TABLE 14.1

Revenue	**Net income**
– Operating costs	+ Depreciation and amortization
– Depreciation and amortization	– Net capital expense
= Earnings before interest and taxes (EBIT)	– Increase in net working capital
– Interest	= **Equity Free Cash Flow (EFCF)**
= Earnings before taxes	+ After-tax interest
– Taxes	= **Capital free cash flow (CFCF)**
= **Net income**	

However, there are many reasons why this net income is not a proper measure of cash generation. Recall, first, that depreciation and amortization are non-cash charges, that is, they reduce earnings but do not affect cash flows. Recall, also, that the net income does not reflect changes in working capital or in fixed capital, both of which do affect cash flows.

In order to properly account for the inflows and outflows of cash, we start by adding back to the net income the non-cash charge of depreciation and amortization. Then we subtract the net capital *expense*, which is the difference between investments on and sales of fixed assets. And then we subtract the *increase* in net working capital, which consists of the cash contribution to the day-to-day operations of the company. The end result of this is what we'll call the **equity free cash flow (EFCF)**, also called *free cash flow to equity* or *levered free cash flow*, which is given by

$$\text{EFCF} = \text{Net income} + \text{Depreciation and amortization} - \text{Net capital expense} \\ - \text{Increase in net working capital} \qquad (14.1)$$

Finally, if we add the after-tax interest payments we get the **capital free cash flow (CFCF)**, also called *free cash flow to the firm* or *unlevered free cash flow*, which is given by

$$\text{CFCF} = \text{Net income} + \text{Depreciation and amortization} - \text{Net capital expense} \\ - \text{Increase in net working capital} + \text{After-tax interest} \qquad (14.2)$$

Cash flow and cash flow

Let's think a bit about these two definitions of cash flow. We can think of the EFCF as the cash available to the shareholders of a company. More precisely, this is the cash available to the shareholders after the company has paid interest to the debt holders and taken care of fixed capital and working capital requirements. We can also think of the EFCF as the highest dividend the company could afford to pay with the cash generated in any given period.

The CFCF, on the other hand, is the cash available to *all* the providers of capital after taking into account fixed capital and working capital requirements. In our somewhat-simplified discussion, this is the cash available to shareholders and debt holders. If the company had raised capital through additional sources of financing, such as preferred stock, then the CFCF would also include the cash available to preferred shareholders (in which case we would have to add a line between EFCF and CFCF in Table 14.1 with the preferred dividends). Note, then, that the main difference between CFCF and EFCF arises from claims to cash from non-equity holders.

There is another way of thinking of the difference between CFCF and EFCF and it is related to the impact of leverage on cash flows. The argument, in a nutshell, is this: the EFCF depends on the company's capital structure (that is, on its combination of debt and equity) whereas the CFCF does not. To see this, take a look at Table 14.2, which displays the calculation of the EFCF and the CFCF for a company under three different capital structures. This company borrows at 5% and pays taxes at the corporate tax rate of 35%.

TABLE 14.2

	0% Debt $	20% Debt $	40% Debt $
Debt	0	2,000	4,000
Equity	10,000	8,000	6,000
Capital	10,000	10,000	10,000
	Income Statement		
	$	$	$
Revenues	10,000	10,000	10,000
Operating costs	–6,000	–6,000	–6,000
Depreciation	–1,000	–1,000	–1,000
EBIT	3,000	3,000	3,000
Interest	0	–100	–200
Earnings before taxes	3,000	2,900	2,800
Taxes	–1,050	–1,015	–980
Net Income	1,950	1,885	1,820
	FCF calculation		
	$	$	$
Net income	1,950	1,885	1,820
Depreciation	1,000	1,000	1,000
Net capital expense	–1,000	–1,000	–1,000
Increase in NWC	–500	–500	–500
EFCF	**1,450**	**1,385**	**1,320**
After-tax interest	0	65	130
CFCF	**1,450**	**1,450**	**1,450**

Note that the more the company borrows, the higher the interest expense, and the lower that both the net income and the EFCF are. (In this example, the only difference between net income and EFCF stems from the $500 increase in net working capital, because depreciation and the net capital expense cancel each other out.) But note that the decrease in both net income and EFCF is *not* equal to the full amount of the interest payment; rather, it is equal to the *after-tax* interest payment, which accounts for the tax shield provided by debt. This after-tax payment is calculated simply as $(1 - t_c) \cdot$ (Interest), where t_c is the corporate tax rate.

Finally, the last line shows that the CFCF, the cash available to *all* the providers of capital, remains unchanged in the presence of leverage. Therefore, we can think of the CFCF as the free cash flow delivered by the company independently from its capital structure, or, alternatively, as the free cash flow of the unlevered company.

Valuation with the WACC model: Overview

As we discussed in the previous chapter, the underlying idea behind all DCF models is to discount cash flows at a rate consistent with their risk, which means that given the definition of cash flow the appropriate discount rate follows. The dividend discount model (DDM) we discussed in the previous chapter discounts expected dividends at the cost of equity. The WACC model we discuss in this chapter discounts expected *capital free cash flows* at the *cost of capital* (or, more precisely, at the weighted-average cost of capital, which is where the name of this method comes from).

Formally, the WACC model can be expressed as

$$V = \frac{E(CFCF_1)}{(1 + R_{WACC})} + \frac{E(CFCF_2)}{(1 + R_{WACC})^2} + \cdots + \frac{E(CFCF_T) + TV}{(1 + R_{WACC})^T} \qquad (14.3)$$

where V denotes the value of the company, $E(CFCF_t)$ the expected capital free cash flow in period t, TV a terminal value, R_{WACC} the (weighted-average) cost of capital, and T the number of periods for which cash flows are forecasted. The cost of capital, in turn, is given by

$$R_{WACC} = (1 - t_c) \cdot x_D \cdot R_D + x_E \cdot R_E \qquad (14.4)$$

where R_D and R_E denote the required return on debt and the required return on equity, x_D and x_E denote the proportions of debt and equity (measured at market value) in the company's capital structure, and t_c denotes the corporate tax rate. The debt considered for the estimation of the cost of capital is interest-bearing (usually long-term) debt. Both the CAPM (the model most widely used to estimate the required return on equity) and the cost of capital are discussed in more detail in Chapter 7.

Before we apply this model to the valuation of a company, several issues are worth discussing. First, the terminal value (*TV*) is the last cash flow to be discounted and attempts to summarize in a single number all the cash flows from that point on. It can be estimated in different ways, although a growing perpetuity or a multiple of some fundamental variable are the two most widely used alternatives.

Second, the standard implementation of the WACC model consists of estimating one or more short-term rates of growth for the cash flows as well as a terminal value. Although short-term growth rates can be as high as it may be plausible to assume given the characteristics of the company, if the terminal value is estimated as a growing perpetuity the '6% restriction' applies. That is, in the long term, it doesn't make sense to assume a rate of growth in cash flows beyond the growth rate of the overall economy.

Third, it is essential to note that equation (14.3) does not yield the value of the company's equity but the value of the *equity plus debt*. Note that the CFCFs we're discounting are those to be distributed to shareholders *and* debt holders; therefore, the present value we're calculating is that of equity *and* debt. The important implication of this fact is that after arriving at an estimate of the value of the *company* using equation (14.3), in order to estimate the value of the company's *equity* we need to subtract the market value of long-term debt outstanding. (If you buy a house valued at $100,000 for which the owner has a mortgage and still owes $40,000, you would only pay $60,000. The remaining $40,000 is the debt you will be assuming.)

Finally, although the DDM is typically used in a way that yields the value of a company's *share*, the WACC model is typically used in a way that yields the value of the company's *equity*. Therefore, in order to estimate the intrinsic value of an individual share, we need to divide the resulting value of the equity by the number of shares outstanding.

Valuation with the WACC model: An example

In 2003, Dell delivered a profit of $2.6 billion on revenues of $41.4 billion. On January 30, 2004, when Dell's fiscal year 2003 concluded, the company's market cap was $85.5 billion and its stock price $33.44. At the same time, Dell's earnings per share (EPS) and price/earnings (P/E) ratio were $1.01 and 33, respectively. Our goal is to use the WACC model to assess the value of Dell at the end of January 2004.

Before we get to the numbers, bear this in mind: our goal is to illustrate the use of the WACC model, not to make a strong statement about Dell's intrinsic value. For the latter we would have to think long and hard about the most appropriate assumptions for the analysis. The assumptions we'll discuss below are plausible, but not necessarily those that a more thorough analysis of the company would yield. Having said that, take a look at the most relevant items of Dell's balance sheet, income statement, and cash flow statement for fiscal year 2003, displayed in Table 14.3.

TABLE 14.3

Balance sheet ($m)		Income statement ($m)	
Cash and equivalents	4,317	Revenue	41,444
Other current assets	6,316	Cost of goods sold	−33,629
Total current assets	10,633	Selling, general, and administrative	−3,544
Net fixed assets	1,517	R&D	−464
Other non-current assets	7,161	Depreciation and amortization	−263
Total assets	**19,311**	EBIT	3,544
Accounts payable	7,316	Net interest	180
Other current liabilities	3,580	Earnings before taxes	3,724
Total current liabilities	10,896	Taxes	−1,079
Long-term debt	505	**Net Income**	**2,645**
Other non-current liabilities	1,630		
Total liabilities	13,031	**Cash flow statement (excerpt, $m)**	
Equity	6,280	Net capital expense	−329
Total liabilities and equity	**19,311**	Change in net working capital	−872
		Other	−110

Free cash flow estimation

Our first step is to estimate Dell's CFCF based on the company's financial statements. The calculation and final result are displayed in Table 14.4, where all numbers are in millions.

TABLE 14.4

	$m
Net income	2,645
+ Depreciation and amortization	263
– Net capital expense	–329
– Increase in net working capital	872
– Other	–110
EFCF	3,341
+ After-tax interest	10
CFCF	**3,351**

A few things are worth mentioning. First, Dell actually *decreased* its working capital by $872 million, which has a *positive* impact on its CFCF. Second, the 'Other' item consists of several adjustments (such as exchange rate effects) that had a negative impact on Dell's cash flow. Third, of the positive $180 million of *net* interest in Dell's income statement, $14 million were interest payments. Therefore, the after-tax interest payment is $(1 - 0.29) \cdot (\$14m) = \$9.94m \approx$ $10m. (For a variety of reasons, Dell pays taxes at the rate of 29%, lower than the statutory rate of 35%.)

We now have to make some assumptions about how the CFCFs are going to evolve over time. Let's assume first that over the next five years (2004 to 2008), Dell's CFCFs will increase at the annual rate of 17%; this is actually the rate at which analysts expect Dell to increase its earnings during the same period. Let's also assume that over the following five years (2009 to 2013), Dell's CFCFs will slow down and increase at the annual rate of 10%. And let's finally assume that, from that point on, Dell's CFCFs will grow along with the economy at the annual rate of 6%. The expected CFCFs that follow from these assumptions are displayed in Table 14.5.

TABLE 14.5

Year	CFCF ($)	Year	CFCF ($)
2004	3,921	2010	8,890
2005	4,587	2011	9,779
2006	5,367	2012	10,756
2007	6,279	2013	11,832
2008	7,347	TV	161,956
2009	8,081		

Note that the last number in the table, roughly $162 billion, is the terminal value (*TV*) and is calculated as the present value of CFCFs growing at 6% in perpetuity from 2013 on. (If you have read the previous chapter, after estimating Dell's cost of capital below, you should have no difficulty in calculating this number yourself.)

Cost of capital estimation

Having an estimate of the expected CFCFs we now have to estimate the discount rate that captures their risk, that is, Dell's cost of capital. All the magnitudes relevant for its calculation are displayed in Table 14.6.

TABLE 14.6

(Long-term) debt		Equity	
6.55% Fixed-rate senior notes		**CAPM-related magnitudes**	
Book value	$200m	Risk-free rate	4.1%
Interest rate	6.55%	Market risk premium	5.5%
Market value	$227.6m	Beta:	1.8
Yield	3.50%		
Due	April 15, 2008	**Other equity-related magnitudes**	
7.10% Fixed-rate senior debentures		Stock price	$33.44
Book value	$300m	Shares outstanding	2,556,000
Interest rate	7.10%	Market value	$85.5bn
Market value	$358.1m		
Yield:	5.77%		
Due:	April 15, 2028		

Let's start with the debt. Dell has two types of interest-bearing (long-term) debt relevant for the calculation of the cost of capital; their book value, market value, interest rate, yield, and maturity date are all displayed in Table 14.6. Note that both bonds have a yield lower than their respective interest rate. (The difference between these two concepts is discussed in Chapter 18.) The total amount of long-term debt at market value is $585.7 million. We can estimate the required return on debt (R_D) as the weighted average of the return required on these two types of debt. That is,

$$R_D = (\$227.6\text{m}/\$585.7\text{m}) \cdot (0.0350) + (\$358.1\text{m}/\$585.7\text{m}) \cdot (0.0577) = 4.9\%$$

Now to the required return on equity, which we can estimate with the CAPM. Given the 4.1% yield on ten-year US Treasury notes, the historical market risk premium of 5.5%, and the beta of 1.8, Dell's required return on equity (R_E) is

$$R_E = (0.041) + (0.055) \cdot (1.8) = 13.8\% \, .$$

Finally, we need to calculate the proportions of debt and equity at market value. The total amount of long-term debt is $585.7 million. Given Dell's share price of $33.44 and the 2,556,000 shares outstanding, the market value of equity is $85,472.6 million. Therefore, the total amount of capital is equal to $86,058.3 million. The proportions of debt and equity follow directly and are calculated as $585.7m/$86,058.3m = 0.7% and $85,472.6m/$86,058.3m = 99.3%. Essentially, Dell is an unlevered company fully financed by equity.

Putting together the required returns on debt and equity, the proportions of debt and equity, and Dell's corporate tax rate (29%), we get that the company's cost of capital is

$$R_{WACC} = (1 - 0.29) \cdot (0.007) \cdot (0.049) + (0.993) \cdot (0.138) = 13.7\%$$

Discounting the CFCFs in Table 14.5 at this cost of capital, we get

$$V = \frac{\$3{,}921\text{m}}{(1.0137)} + \frac{\$4{,}587\text{m}}{(1.0137)^2} + \ldots + \frac{\$11{,}832\text{m} + \$161{,}956\text{m}}{(1.0137)^{10}} = \$80{,}399.6\text{m}$$

Recall, however, that this is the value of *both* Dell's equity and debt. Therefore, to get an estimate of the value of Dell's equity, we need to subtract from this figure the market value of long-term debt. After doing so, we get $80,399.6m – $585.7m = $79,813.9m.

Finally, dividing this number by the number of shares outstanding we get $79,813.9m/2,556m = $31.2. If we believe our assumptions, then, we should conclude that at $33.44 Dell is slightly overpriced. (However, note that Dell's EPS between 1994 and 2003 grew at an annual rate of over 47%. Perhaps the market is reasonably expecting from Dell a higher short-term growth than we assumed. Again, you should interpret our valuation more as an illustration of the WACC model than as a strong statement on Dell's valuation.)

The big picture

The WACC model is the most widely used version of the DCF model, and for good reason. Unlike the DDM, the WACC model enables analysts to perform a detailed analysis and prediction of different components of a company's financial statements, and to assess their impact on both free cash flows and intrinsic value. In this regard, spreadsheets have become an inseparable component of valuation with the WACC model.

All versions of the DCF model discount cash flows at a rate that appropriately captures their risk. The WACC model, in particular, discounts CFCFs at the cost of capital. It therefore yields the value of the whole company, not just the value of the equity. This means that the market value of the claims of non-equity holders must be subtracted from the present value of CFCFs in order to find the intrinsic value of the company's equity.

Although, in theory, all versions of the DCF model should yield the same value of a company's equity, in practice there are situations in which implementing one version is easier than implementing some other. That's why it pays to discuss two other versions of the DCF model, and that is exactly what we'll do in the next chapter.

Excel section

There is no new Excel material in this chapter.

Challenge section

1 In 2003, Oracle delivered a profit of $2.7 billion on revenues of $10.2 billion. On May 30, 2004, when Oracles's fiscal year 2003 concluded, the company's market cap was $58.9 billion and its stock price $11.40. At the same time, Oracle's earnings per share (EPS) and price/earnings (P/E) ratio were $0.50 and 23, respectively. Tables 14.7 and 14.8 display information relevant for the valuation of Oracle at the end of May 2004.

TABLE 14.7

Balance Sheet ($m)		Income statement ($m)	
Cash and equivalents	4,138	Revenue	10,156
Other current assets	7,198	Cost of goods sold	–2,083
Total current assets	11,336	Selling, general, and administrative	–3,975
Net fixed assets	1,068	Depreciation and amortization	–234
Other non-current assets	359	EBIT	3,864
Total assets	12,763	Interest income	102
Accounts payable	191	Interest expense	21
Other current liabilities	4,081	Earnings before taxes	3,945
Total current liabilities	4,272	Taxes	–1,264
Long-term debt	163	Net Income	2,681
Other non-current liabilities	333	Cash flow statement (excerpt, $m)	
Total liabilities	4,768	Net capital expense	–189
Equity	7,995	Change in net working capital	–60
Total liabilities and equity	12,763	Other	–202

TABLE 14.8

(Long-term) debt		Equity	
6.91% Senior notes		CAPM-related magnitudes	
Book value	$163m	Risk-free rate:	4.7%
Interest rate	6.91%	Market risk premium:	5.5%
Market value	$165.5m	Beta:	1.7
Yield	3.66%		
Due:	February 2007	Other equity-related magnitudes	
		Stock Price	$11.40
		Shares outstanding	5,171,000
		Market value	$58.9bn

Using the information provided in Tables 14.7 and 14.8, and a corporate tax rate of 35%, calculate Oracle's EFCF and CFCF for the fiscal year 2003. (Note that during fiscal year 2003 Oracle *decreased* its net working capital by $60 million.)

2 Assuming that Oracles's CFCF will increase at the annual rate of 10% over the next five years, at the annual rate of 8% over the following five years, and at 6% a year from that point on, calculate Oracle's expected CFCFs.

3 Using the information in Table 14.8, calculate Oracle's cost of capital.

4 Using the WACC model, estimate the intrinsic value of a share of Oracle.

5 Given your estimate and the market price, what would be your advice on Oracle stock? To buy? To sell? To hold?

15

STOCKS III: OTHER DCF MODELS

The FTE model

Valuation with the FTE model: An example

The APV model

Valuation with the APV model: An example

Additional issues

The big picture

Excel section

Challenge section

In theory, given the company and the point in time, all discounted cash flow (DCF) models should yield the same intrinsic value. In practice, however, that is frequently not the case. And implementing one version of the DCF model is often easier than implementing another. That's why in this chapter we'll discuss the flows-to-equity (FTE) and the adjusted present value (APV) models, two versions of the DCF model that, although less widely used than the WACC model, may be easier to apply in some circumstances. (In order to fully understand the issues discussed in this chapter it is essential that you're familiar with the issues discussed in Chapter 14.)

The FTE model

You may recall from our discussion in the previous chapter that the weighted-average cost of capital (WACC) model discounts capital free cash flows at the cost of capital. The present value calculated is therefore the intrinsic value of debt and equity. This implies that in order to find the value of the company's equity, we need to subtract from the present value calculated the market value of long-term debt.

The flows-to-equity (FTE) model is simpler than the WACC model on two counts. First, it estimates the value of the equity directly, so there is no need for the additional step of subtracting the long-term debt. Second, the discount rate is easier to estimate simply because it is just one component of the company's cost of capital.

Before we formally define the FTE model it is important to recall the difference between the *equity* free cash flow (EFCF), which is given by

$$\text{EFCF} = \text{Net income} + \text{Depreciation and amortization} - \text{Net capital expense} - \text{Increase in net working capital}, \tag{15.1}$$

and the *capital* free cash flow (CFCF), which is given by

$$\text{CFCF} = \text{Net income} + \text{Depreciation and amortization} - \text{Net capital expense} - \text{Increase in net working capital} + \text{After-tax interest} \tag{15.2}$$

As you may recall from the previous chapter, the former is the cash available to shareholders after the company has paid interest to debt holders and made the necessary investments in fixed assets and working capital. The latter, on the other hand, is the cash available to all the providers of capital, again after the company has made the necessary investments in fixed assets and working capital. You may also recall that the CFCF, unlike the EFCF, is independent of the company's capital structure.

Note that EFCFs belong to shareholders, who are the ones bearing the risk. The appropriate discount rate for these cash flows, then, is the required return on the company's equity. Therefore, the FTE model discounts EFCFs at the cost of equity and can be formally expressed as

$$E = \frac{E(EFCF_1)}{(1 + R_E)} + \frac{E(EFCF_2)}{(1 + R_E)^2} + \cdots + \frac{E(EFCF_T) + TV}{(1 + R_E)^T} \qquad (15.3)$$

where E denotes the value of the company's equity, $E(EFCF_t)$ the expected equity free cash flow in period t, R_E the required return on equity, TV the terminal value, and T the number of periods for which cash flows are forecasted. The required return on equity, sometimes called the cost of equity, is usually (but not exclusively) estimated with the CAPM (discussed at length in Chapter 7).

As we discussed in the previous chapter, the terminal value can be estimated in different ways, the two most widely used alternatives being a growing perpetuity or a multiple of some fundamental variable. In the first case, it is important to keep in mind that it is not plausible to assume a long-term growth rate larger than that of the economy, which limits the long-term growth of cash flows to not more than 6% or so a year.

Note that in the way it is usually implemented, the FTE model yields the value of the company's equity. Therefore, in order to estimate the intrinsic value of a share, the estimate resulting from equation (15.3) must be divided by the number of shares outstanding.

Valuation with the FTE model: An example

Let's apply the FTE model to the valuation of Dell at the beginning of the year 2004 using all the information we discussed in the previous chapter. Recall that in the year 2003, Dell delivered a profit of $2.6 billion on revenues of $41.4

billion. On January 30, 2004, when Dell's fiscal year 2003 concluded, the company's market cap was $85.5 billion and its stock price $33.44. At the same time, Dell's earnings per share (EPS) and price/earnings (P/E) ratio were $1.01 and 33, respectively.

In Table 14.4 of the previous chapter we had estimated that Dell delivered an EFCF of $3,341 million in fiscal year 2003. Let's assume that over the next five years (2004 to 2008) Dell's EFCFs will increase at the annual rate of 17%, which is the rate at which analysts expect the company to increase its earnings during the same period. Let's also assume that over the following five years (2009 to 2013) Dell's EFCFs will slow down and increase at the annual rate of 10%. And let's finally assume that, from that point on, Dell's EFCFs will grow along with the economy at the annual rate of 6%. (As you may have noticed, these are the same assumptions we made for the expected growth of the CFCFs in the previous chapter.) The expected EFCFs that follow from these assumptions are displayed in Table 15.1.

TABLE 15.1

Year	EFCF ($m)	Year	EFCF ($m)
2004	3,909	2010	8,863
2005	4,573	2011	9,750
2006	5,351	2012	10,724
2007	6,261	2013	11,797
2008	7,325	TV	160,021
2009	8,057		

Note that the last number in the table, roughly $160 billion, is the terminal value and is calculated as the present value of EFCFs growing at 6% in perpetuity from 2013 on. Importantly, note also that these EFCFs are very similar to the CFCFs displayed in Table 14.5 simply because Dell is a company almost fully financed by equity. This means that its interest payments are very small, and therefore so is the difference between CFCFs and EFCFs.

Using the CAPM, we estimated in the previous chapter that Dell's cost of equity was 13.8%. Therefore, putting together this discount rate with the expected EFCFs in Table 15.1, we can obtain the intrinsic value of Dell's equity at the end of January 2004, which was

$$E = \frac{\$3{,}909\text{m}}{(1.0138)} + \frac{\$4{,}573\text{m}}{(1.0138)^2} + \ldots + \frac{\$11{,}797\text{m} + \$160{,}021\text{m}}{(1.0138)^{10}} = \$79{,}367.8\text{m}$$

Finally, dividing this number by the number of shares outstanding (2,556 million), we get an intrinsic value per share of $79,367.8m/2,556m = $31.1.

Note that this number is virtually identical to the one we obtained in the previous chapter using the WACC model ($31.2). Although it is tempting to conclude that this virtual equality follows exclusively from theoretical reasons (that is, because if consistently implemented the WACC model and the FTE model *must* yield the same result), in this case it also follows from the fact that Dell is a company almost fully financed by equity. As a consequence, EFCFs are very similar to CFCFs, and the cost of equity is very similar to the cost of capital.

The APV model

The last DCF model we'll discuss, the adjusted present value (APV) model, attempts to separate two sources of value: one that stems from the cash flows of the unlevered company and another that stems from the net impact on debt. Formally, the APV model is expressed as

$$V = \frac{E(CFCF_1)}{(1 + R_U)} + \ldots + \frac{E(CFCF_T) + TV_E}{(1 + R_U)^T} + \text{PV (Net benefits of debt)} \tag{15.4}$$

where V denotes the value of the company, $E(CFCF_t)$ the expected capital free cash flow in period t, R_U the required return on unlevered equity (defined below), TV_E the terminal value of equity, and T the number of periods for which cash flows are forecasted.

In principle, the last term of the right-hand side takes into account the present value of the *net* benefits of debt, that is, it considers both the positive *and* the negative impact of debt on the company's value. However, in practice, the APV is typically used in a way in which *only the benefits* of debt are taken into account (more on this below). In that case, the APV model can be expressed as

$$V = \frac{E(CFCF_1)}{(1 + R_U)} + \ldots + \frac{E(CFCF_T) + TV_E}{(1 + R_U)^T} + \frac{t_c \cdot I \cdot D_0}{(1 + I)} + \ldots + \frac{t_c \cdot I \cdot D_{T-1} + TV_D}{(1 + I)} \tag{15.5}$$

where t_c denotes the corporate tax rate, D_t the (interest-bearing) debt in period t, I the interest rate paid on the debt, and TV_D the terminal value of debt. If it is reasonable to assume that the amount of debt will remain constant over time at a level D, then equation (15.5) simplifies to

$$V = \frac{E(CFCF_1)}{(1 + R_U)} + \ldots + \frac{E(CFCF_T) + TV_E}{(1 + R_U)^T} + t_c \cdot D \qquad (15.6)$$

Let's think a bit about equation (15.5) first. The first half of the right-hand side is the present value of the expected CFCFs discounted at the unlevered cost of equity. We can think of this present value as the value of the unlevered company; that is, the value of the company if it was fully financed by equity. This present value captures the company's ability to generate cash from its business activity, independently from the impact of debt on its value.

The second half of the right-hand side, in turn, represents the present value of the tax shields generated by the interest payments on the debt. Each annual tax shield is given by $t_c \cdot I \cdot D_t$ and their discount rate is given by the interest rate paid on the debt. (This is actually a bit controversial, but we'll pass up on this rather technical controversy.) The terminal value of the debt (TV_D) is given by the present value of tax shields from period T on.

Essentially, then, the APV model estimates the value of the unlevered company and adds to it the benefits of debt measured by the present value of the tax shields it provides. Equation (15.6) expresses the same idea as (15.5) but under the assumption that the amount of debt remains constant at a level D. In that case, the tax shields become a perpetuity and its present value can be calculated as $t_c \cdot I \cdot D/I = t_c \cdot D$.

Finally, the APV model estimates (just like the WACC model) the value of both equity *and* debt. Therefore, in order to estimate the value of the company's equity, we need to subtract from the value calculated from either equation (15.5) or (15.6) the market value of outstanding long-term debt. If, in addition, we want to estimate the intrinsic value of a share, we need to divide the resulting equity value by the number of shares outstanding.

The required return on unlevered equity

The (systematic) risk of any company can be thought of as the sum of two components: business risk and financial risk. The former is inherent to the industry in which the company operates and related to its business activity;

the latter stems from leverage and is increasing in the company's level of indebtness.

The betas we observe (which we usually estimate by running a regression between the returns of the company and those of the market) are *levered* betas, that is, they reflect both the company's business risk *and* financial risk. However, under some assumptions (which we won't get into), we can strip from this beta the financial risk and obtain an unlevered beta that reflects only business risk. More precisely, the relationship between the unlevered beta (β_U) and the levered beta (β_L) is given by

$$\beta_U = \frac{\beta_L}{1 + (1 - t_c) \cdot (D/E)} \tag{15.7}$$

where D/E is the company's (long-term) debt/equity ratio measured at market value. Note that because the denominator of this equation is larger than or equal to 1, then the unlevered beta is always lower than or equal to the levered beta. (Only when the company is unlevered will these two betas be equal.) This makes intuitive sense because the levered beta reflects both business and financial risk whereas the unlevered beta reflects only business risk.

Having obtained a company's unlevered beta, to estimate its required return on unlevered equity (or cost of unlevered equity) all we need to do is to input the value of β_U in the expression for the capital asset pricing model (CAPM). Therefore, the required return on unlevered equity (R_U) can be calculated as

$$R_U = R_f + MRP \cdot \beta_U \tag{15.8}$$

where R_f and MRP denote the risk-free rate and the market risk premium.

Valuation with the APV model: An example

We'll illustrate the application of the APV model going back once again to Dell at the beginning of the year 2004. We'll base our estimation on equation (15.6), therefore assuming that we expect Dell to keep its current level of long-term debt constant over time. According to this expression, we need to estimate Dell's expected CFCFs, a terminal value for unlevered equity, the required return on unlevered equity, and the present value of the debt tax shields.

For the expected CFCFs we'll go back to those estimated in the previous chapter and displayed on Table 14.5. As you may recall, those forecasts assumed a growth of 17% a year over the first five years, 10% a year over the following five years, and 6% a year from that point on.

In order to calculate Dell's required return on unlevered equity, we start by computing its unlevered beta, for which we need Dell's (long-term) debt/equity ratio. This can be easily calculated by dividing the market value of long-term debt by the market value of equity, in which case we obtain $D/E = \$585.7m/\$85,472.6m = 0.01$. Therefore, Dell's unlevered beta is equal to

$$\beta_U = \frac{1.8}{1 + (1 - 0.29) \cdot (0.01)} = 1.8$$

Actually, using one more decimal, Dell's levered beta is 1.77 and its unlevered beta 1.76, just a tiny bit lower. This is due to the fact that Dell is virtually unlevered, and therefore its levered beta and unlevered beta are virtually identical.

Using the same risk-free rate (4.1%) and market risk premium (5.5%) we used in the previous chapter, Dell's required return on unlevered equity is therefore given by $0.041 + (0.055) \cdot (1.8) = 13.8\%$. Again, given that Dell is almost fully financed by equity, it should come as no surprise that this number is the same as the required return on equity we calculated before. (Actually, using one more decimal we would obtain a required return on levered equity of 13.81% and a required return on unlevered equity of 13.77%, again both virtually identical to each other.)

In order to calculate the present value of the debt tax shields we need the rate at which Dell pays corporate taxes (29%) and the book value of its long-term debt ($505m, as shown in Table 14.3). Note that in this case we don't use the market value but the *book* value of debt. This is because interest is paid on the book (and not on the market) value of debt outstanding. Putting all these numbers together, we get

$$V = \frac{\$3,921m}{(1.138)} + \ldots + \frac{\$11,832m + \$161,469m}{(1.138)^{10}} + (0.29) \cdot (\$505m) = \$80,280.3m$$

Recall, however, that this is the value of the equity *and* debt. Therefore, subtracting from this value the market value of outstanding long-term debt we get the value of Dell's equity, which is given by $\$80,280.3m - \$585.7m = \$79,694.6m$. Finally, dividing this number by the number of shares outstanding we get $\$79,694.6m/2,556m = \$31.2$.

Again, it is tempting to conclude that all three DCF models yield the same intrinsic value due to theoretical reasons. However, it is again important to keep in mind that because Dell is almost fully financed by equity, then EFCFs are very similar to CFCFs; the cost of capital, cost of equity, and cost of unlevered equity are all very similar to each other; and the present value of the tax shields is very small.

Additional issues

Let's conclude this chapter with a few comments and remarks on all the DCF models we discussed. We'll focus first on comparisons across models, and then on a couple of issues specific to the APV model and the WACC model.

Consistency across models

We have argued before, and reiterate now, that all DCF models (DDM, WACC, FTE, and APV), if consistently applied, should yield the exact same value of a company's equity. This is a theoretical equivalence that we won't prove. But, however different the cash flows and discount rates across models may seem to be, it is indeed the case that all these models should yield the same intrinsic value.

If we compare the WACC and the APV models, for example, it is not too difficult to see intuitively why they should yield the same intrinsic value. The APV model discounts CFCFs at the cost of unlevered equity, and adds to that the benefit of using debt. The WACC model also discounts CFCFs, but instead of considering the benefit of debt in a separate term, it accounts for it by lowering the discount rate. (The cost of capital is always lower than or equal to the cost of unlevered equity.) In other words, the APV model accounts for the benefit of debt through and additional term and the WACC model does it by lowering the discount rate.

The WACC and the FTE models, however, seem to be quite different. Both discount different free cash flows at different discount rates. However, the only difference between them rests (again) in how they deal with the impact of debt. The WACC model does it by lowering the discount rate, as we have just discussed. The FTE model, in turn, does it by lowering the cash flows (EFCFs are always lower than or equal to CFCFs) and increasing the discount rate (the cost of equity is always higher than or equal to the cost of capital).

Finally, both the FTE and the DDM models use the same discount rate (the cost of equity) but discount different cash flows. The obvious condition under which these two models yield the same intrinsic value of equity is that dividends equal the EFCFs. However, there is a second (and more subtle) condition under which the equality between these models holds: when the excess free cash flows (the difference between EFCFs and dividends) are invested in projects with zero net present value.

When to use each model

The reasons for choosing to implement one model over another can only be practical. Again, in theory, all models should yield the same result when the relevant assumptions are consistently applied.

Suppose that a company's debt *ratio* is expected to be constant over time. In other words, assume that the company intends to maintain a constant capital structure, therefore fixing the *proportions* of debt and equity. In this case, the WACC and the FTE models are easier to implement than the APV model. This is because when the proportions of debt and equity are constant over time, so are both the cost of equity and the cost of capital, and therefore the discount rates of the WACC and the FTE models. (This argument assumes that the business risk of the company will remain constant over time, a plausible assumption in most cases.)

Consider now a company that plans to maintain the *level* of debt constant over time. In this case, the proportions of debt and equity may change over time, and so can the cost of equity and the cost of capital. Note, however, that no discount rate in any DCF model we have considered has a subscript t, that is, we have never assumed a time-varying discount rate. It is of course possible to do so, though rarely done in practice simply because the calculations become quite a bit more complicated. (With a time-varying discount rate we can no longer raise the quantities one plus the discount rate to increasing powers as the periods go by. The proper discount rate for a cash flow ten years down the road, for example, is equal to the product of one plus the discount rate in each year of the ten years.)

When a company plans to maintain a constant level of debt, then, the APV model becomes easier to apply for two reasons. First, because the cost of unlevered equity is independent of the company's capital structure and therefore constant over time; and second, because the impact of debt can easily be calculated as the product of the corporate tax rate and the constant level of debt. (This argument again assumes that the business risk of the company will remain constant over time.)

In short, if the *proportions* of debt and equity are expected to remain constant over time, then the WACC and the FTE models are the easier to implement. If, on the other hand, the *level* of debt is expected to be constant over time, then the APV model is the easier to implement.

A practical limitation of the APV model

Equation (15.4) shows that the APV model adds to the value of the unlevered company the *net* impact of debt. However, in practice, it is almost always the case that only the benefits of debt (basically the present value of the tax shields) are explicitly considered.

This is unfortunate for several reasons but one of them is obvious. If we take equations (15.5) and (15.6) at face value, both of which incorporate only the benefits of debt, the APV model is implicitly saying that the higher the amount of debt, the higher the value of the company. This obviously doesn't make a lot of sense. Increasing the level of debt reduces the cost of capital (and increases the value of the company) only up to a point; beyond that point, the opposite is the case. Debt, like many other things, is beneficial in prudent amounts but detrimental in excessive amounts. Unfortunately, the usual implementation of the APV model ignores this obvious fact.

Market value weights and target weights

It may sound strange that in order to estimate the intrinsic value of a company's equity with the WACC model we have to use the market value of the company's equity. Recall that this is what we do when calculating the weights (x_D and x_E) of the cost of capital. It sounds like a contradiction to first rely on market prices to estimate the cost of capital, and then to use this magnitude to estimate the company's intrinsic value, thus somehow neglecting the market price.

There is indeed a bit of a circularity problem in the standard application of the WACC model. Essentially, we use the market value of equity in order to come up with our estimate of the intrinsic value of equity. This issue gets very technical very quickly so let's just make one point. The best way around this circularity is to use *target* values for the proportions of debt and equity. The idea behind this argument is that we should first figure out what is the company's optimal capital structure, and then use the proportions of debt and equity in that capital structure for the estimation of both the cost of capital and the intrinsic value of equity.

The big picture

The FTE model and the APV model are two variations of the DCF model. The former yields directly the value of equity, whereas the latter yields the value of the company. The former is preferred when the proportions of debt and equity are expected to be constant over time, whereas the latter is preferred when the level of debt is expected to be constant over time.

All DCF models require the analyst to estimate free cash flows and the proper discount rate to discount them. The FTE model discounts EFCFs at the cost of equity; the APV model discounts CFCFs at the cost of unlevered equity and then adds the benefit of debt. In theory, both models yield the same value; in practice, this is only the case when the relevant assumptions are applied consistently, which is not always easy to do.

Excel section

There is no new Excel material in this chapter.

Challenge section

1 Consider all the information about Oracle provided in the Challenge section of the previous chapter and estimate the intrinsic value of a share of Oracle using the FTE model.
2 Using the same information, estimate the intrinsic value of a share of Oracle using the APV model.
3 Are the estimates that follow from these two models similar? Why? Are they in turn similar to the value you estimated using the WACC model in the previous chapter? Why?

16

STOCKS IV: REVERSE VALUATION

What is this all about?

A simple example

A more realistic set-up

Yahoo!

A few comments

The big picture

Excel section

Challenge section

All discounted cash flow (DCF) models require the analyst to forecast expected cash flows and to estimate their proper discount rate. Estimating cash flows, however, is a mix of art and science (with a fair share of sorcery). But there is a way around. We can reverse engineer market prices to infer the market's expected growth rate of cash flows. We can then evaluate the plausibility of the expectations and finally pass judgment on the stock's valuation. Read on; it's less difficult than it sounds.

What is this all about?

The idea behind reverse valuation is to expose the assumptions implicitly built into stock prices in order to evaluate their plausibility. The technique basically goes like this: 'If this and that happen, then this stock is fairly valued at current market prices. Now, are this and that likely to happen?'

Essentially, reverse valuation is a type of 'if–then' analysis. That is, *if* some conditions are met, *then* the company is fairly valued at current prices. Or, put differently, reverse valuation is a technique that enables us to compare the things that *must* happen for the stock to be fairly valued at current prices with the things that *are likely* to happen.

Reverse valuation requires us to start with a model. Given the model, some of its inputs, and market prices, we solve for one of the variables that summarizes the market's expectations. We then compare what the market is expecting with what we believe the company can reasonably be expected to deliver. If what the market is expecting is above what we believe the company can deliver, then we should conclude that the stock is overvalued; if the opposite is the case, then we should conclude that the stock is undervalued.

A simple example

Consider a company that has just delivered free cash flows of $10 million. The company has no debt and its cost of equity (and cost of capital) is 12%. The expected annual growth of free cash flows over the long term is 5%. We could then use the constant-growth version of a DCF model in order to estimate the intrinsic value of this company. More precisely, we could use the model

$$E = \frac{FCF_0 \cdot (1 + g)}{R - g} \tag{16.1}$$

where E denotes the company's equity, FCF_0 the observed free cash flow, g the expected long-term growth rate of cash flows, and R the discount rate. Using (16.1) and the assumptions above it's trivial to determine that the intrinsic value of this company is $E = (\$10m) \cdot (1.05)/(0.12 - 0.05) = \$150m$.

Nothing new here. We just put together expected cash flows and their discount rate within an analytical framework and determined the company's intrinsic value. That is the standard way of applying the DCF model, in which we input all the terms of the right-hand side in order to solve for the variable on the left-hand side.

Note that the previous analysis requires us to form an expectation of the rate at which the free cash flows will grow. Most of the time, though, properly determining one or more expected growth rates of cash flows is far from trivial. That's where the mix of art, science, and sorcery comes in. And that is, precisely, where reverse valuation becomes helpful.

Suppose we observe that the company we've been discussing has a market capitalization of $270 million. An interesting question we may ask, then, is the following. At what annual rate do its free cash flows need to grow in the long term for this company to be fairly valued at $270 million?

Formally, the answer to this question can be found by solving for g from the expression

$$\$270m = \frac{\$10m \cdot (1 + g)}{0.12 - g} \tag{16.2}$$

where we input the *observed* market valuation on the left-hand side, and we have the unknown on the right-hand side. In this case, solving for g analytically is simple. Alternatively, we could find a numerical solution by using the Solver in Excel. Either way, we should find that the g that solves equation (16.2) is 8%. Paraphrasing our statement above, then, we could now say: *if* this company grows its free cash flows at the annual rate of 8% in the long term, *then* it is fairly valued at $270 million.

But solving equation (16.2) doesn't mean we're done. Having found that g is equal to 8% is just *the beginning* of the analysis. In fact, we have only found the condition that sustains the market valuation. In other words, if this company is valued at $270 million, then the market must be expecting an annual long-term growth of free cash flows of 8%. And now comes the hard part: is this a plausible expectation? Are free cash flows likely to grow at that rate? At a higher rate? At a lower rate? Only by answering these questions we can finally determine whether the company is properly valued.

It is essential to note that reverse valuation does not say that the company *will* grow its free cash flows at the annual rate of 8%. Reverse valuation says that *if* the company grows its free cash flows at the annual rate of 8%, *then* it is fairly valued at $270 million. The difference is subtle but critical. Remember, reverse valuation is an 'if–then' analysis.

Note, also, that reverse valuation basically involves two steps. In the first we find the expectations factored into the market valuation; in the second we determine the plausibility of those expectations. The first step is largely mathematical; it is in the second step where the analyst's skill comes in.

Incidentally, it should be clear by now where the name 'reverse valuation' comes from. We're reverse engineering the market price in order to solve for one of the components that determines it. Note that we're not solving (as usual) for the variable on the left-hand side of the equation; rather, we're solving for one of the components of the right-hand side.

A more realistic set-up

The constant-growth model we have just used to illustrate the essence of reverse valuation is not very widely used in practice. As we discussed in Chapter 13, this model gives no flexibility to accommodate different stages of growth. A more widely used alternative is the two-stage model, in which we forecast cash flows for the first T periods and then add a terminal value that summarizes the cash flows from that point on.

The two-stage version of a DCF model with a terminal value expressed as a growing perpetuity can be written as

$$E = \frac{FCF_0 \cdot (1 + g_1)}{(1 + R)} + \ldots + \frac{FCF_0 \cdot (1 + g_1)^T}{(1 + R)^T} + \frac{\dfrac{\{FCF_0 \cdot (1 + g_1)^T\} \cdot (1 + g_2)}{R - g_2}}{(1 + R)^T}$$

(16.3)

where g_1 is the expected growth rate of free cash flows during the first T periods and g_2 the expected growth rate of free cash flows from period T on. A standard DCF analysis would require the analyst to come up with estimates for all terms on the right-hand side in order to obtain the left-hand side (the intrinsic value of the company's equity).

A reverse valuation analysis, in turn, would require the analyst to calculate the last free cash flow generated by the company (FCF_0), to estimate the proper discount rate (R) and the long-term growth of cash flows (g_2), and to observe the current market value of the company (E). The unknown in equation (16.2), then, would be g_1, that is, the expected annual growth rate of free cash flows over the first T periods.

Let's go back to our hypothetical company that has just delivered free cash flows of $10 million, is unlevered, has a cost of equity of 12%, and a market value of $270 million. Let's assume now that its free cash flows from year 5 on are expected to grow at the annual rate of 5%. We can then ask: at what annual rate would its free cash flows need to grow over the next five years for this company to be fairly valued at $270 million?

Formally, the answer to this question can be found by solving for g_1 from the expression

$$\$270\text{m} = \frac{\$10\text{m} \cdot (1 + g_1)}{(1.12)} + \ldots + \frac{\$10\text{m} \cdot (1 + g_1)^5}{(1.12)^5} + \frac{\dfrac{\{\$10\text{m} \cdot (1 + g_1)^5\} \cdot (1.05)}{0.12 - 0.05}}{(1.12)^5}$$

$$(16.4)$$

Obviously, solving for g_1 now is a lot more complicated than solving for g in equation (16.2). Still, the Solver in Excel can find a numerical solution for this equation in the blink of an eye, which in this case is $g_1 = 19.7\%$. So, *if* this company grows its free cash flows over the next five years at 19.7% a year, and at 5% a year from that point on, *then* it is fairly valued at $270 million.

Note that this more realistic set-up comes at a price: it is now mathematically more difficult to uncover the market's expectations (that is, solving for g_1). But it is still the case that the critical part of the analysis is to evaluate the plausibility of the solution, that is, to determine whether the company can plausibly be expected to grow its free cash flows at the annual rate of 19.7%.

Yahoo!

On April 12, 1996, Yahoo! traded publicly for the first time. At the end of its first day of trading, Yahoo! closed at a (split-adjusted) price of $1.39. As shown in panel A of Exhibit 16.1, between then and January 3, 2000, its all-time high, Yahoo!'s stock price increased by 8,505%, closing the day at $118.75. It was all downhill from there. Between then and December 31, 2003, Yahoo!'s stock price fell by 81%, closing the year 2003 at $22.51. Panel B of Exhibit 16.1 displays the performance of Yahoo! between its first day of trading and the end of 2003.

EXHIBIT 16.1
Yahoo!'s stock price

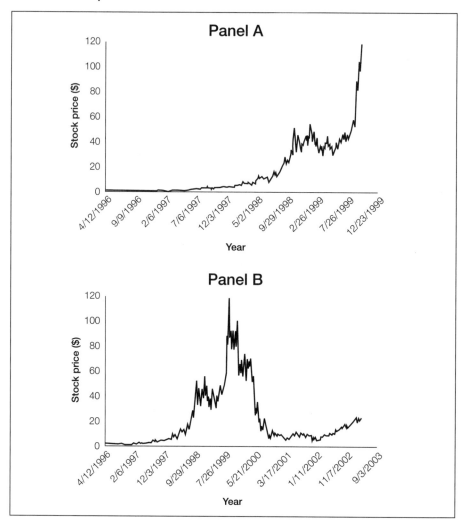

Let's apply reverse valuation to Yahoo! at the end of 1999, just one day before its all-time high. Table 16.1 shows the calculation of the company's free cash flow for the year 1999. Because Yahoo! was at the time fully financed by equity, its capital free cash flow (CFCF) is equal to its equity free cash flow (EFCF), and its cost of capital is equal to its cost of equity. As the exhibit shows, during the year 1999 Yahoo generated a free cash flow of $166.8 million and its cost of equity was 25.5%.

TABLE 16.1

Free cash flow estimation ($m)		Cost of capital estimation	
Net income	61.1	Risk-free rate (%)	6.5
+ Depreciation and amortization	42.3	Market risk premium (%)	5.5
− Net capital expense	−49.5	Beta	3.4
− Increase in net working capital	59.2	Cost of equity = Cost of capital (%)	25.5
+ Other	53.6		
EFCF = CFCF	166.8		

The market capitalization of Yahoo! at the end of 1999 (just one day before its all-time high) was $115,267.7 million, or over $115 billion. However outrageous that number may look nowadays, many (if not most) investors at the time seemed to feel comfortable about that valuation. Reverse valuation enables us to pose the critical question: at what rate would Yahoo!'s free cash flows need to grow to justify such valuation?

To answer this question, let's use a two-stage DCF model, and let's assume a long-term growth of cash flows of 5% after ten years of rapid growth. The more precise question then becomes: *at what rate would Yahoo!'s free cash flows need to grow between the years 2000 and 2009 to justify a market capitalization of $115,267.7 million?*

Formally, the answer to this question can be found by solving for g_1 from the expression

$$\$115{,}267.7m = \frac{\$166.8m \cdot (1+g_1)}{(1.255)} + \ldots + \frac{\$166.8m \cdot (1+g_1)^{10}}{(1.255)^{10}} + \frac{\dfrac{\{\$166.8m \cdot (1+g_1)^{10}\} \cdot (1.05)}{0.255 - 0.05}}{(1.255)^{10}}$$

$$(16.5)$$

This expression may be too difficult to solve analytically, but using the Solver in Excel we can quickly find that $g_1 = 95.5\%$. So, *if* Yahoo!'s free cash flows grow at the annual rate of 95.5% a year between 2000 and 2009, and at 5% a year from that point on, *then* Yahoo! is properly valued at $115.3 billion. (You may now laugh at this number, but at the beginning of 2000 most investors would have probably nodded in agreement.)

This, of course, should not be the end but the beginning of the analysis. Now we would have to get into the hard part, that is, assessing whether or not that growth expectation built into the market price is realistic. In other words, in order to justify its market valuation, Yahoo!'s free cash flows would need to grow at the annual rate of 95.5% between 2000 and 2009 (and at 5% from 2009 on). But is Yahoo! likely to deliver such growth? Is the growth likely to be lower? Or perhaps even higher?

As usual, our goal is to illustrate the use of a technique rather than passing judgment on the valuation of a company. But still, let's push the analysis a bit further. In order to evaluate the plausibility of the growth rate embedded in the price, we would first need to find the conditions that would make this growth possible, and then to evaluate the plausibility of such conditions. Note that this implies that we would first determine the condition that sustains the market valuation; to evaluate the plausibility of that condition we would find the conditions that make the first condition plausible; and then we would evaluate the plausibility of this second set of conditions. Good analysts would go through as many rounds of conditions and plausibility of conditions as necessary until they could reliably answer the relevant questions.

Having established that Yahoo! needs to grow its free cash flows at the annual rate of 95.5% a year between 2000 and 2009 (and at 5% a year from 2009 on), we should ask what are the conditions that would make this growth possible. We may find, for example, that if Yahoo!'s advertising revenues grow at the annual rate of $x\%$ between 2000 and 2009, then an annual growth of free cash flows of 95.5% during the same period is plausible. The question would then become whether we can plausibly expect Yahoo! to increase its advertising revenues at $x\%$ a year during the 2000–09 period.

We could go on, but by now you have surely got the picture. Reverse valuation pushes us to go through as many rounds of conditions–plausibility as necessary until we can ultimately and reliably answer whether or not the expectation that sustains the market valuation is plausible.

A few comments

It may be useful to conclude this discussion with a few caveats and comments. First, note that reverse valuation requires us to use a specific valuation model. If we choose a model that is not appropriate for the situation at hand, the results from a reverse valuation analysis will be misleading. Often, for example, using a constant-growth version of a DCF model for a growth company will lead us to conclude that the company is overvalued. However, this may simply follow from the model's inability to accommodate high growth in the short term.

Second, the solution of a reverse-valuation problem depends on the rest of the values we input in the model. Therefore, if we input implausible estimates for the discount rate or the long-term growth rate of free cash flows, so the short-term growth of cash flows in the model will also be implausible. The solution of a reverse-valuation problem will also be affected by the length of the short term, that is, whether the growth of cash flows we solve for applies to the first five, ten, or any other number of years.

Third, reverse valuation does not spare us completely from having to estimate expected cash flows. In order to evaluate the plausibility of the growth of cash flows expected by the market we need to have a good idea of what the company can deliver. It may actually be easier to assess the plausibility of a given rate of growth than estimating it. But reverse valuation does not imply that we don't have to deal with expected cash flows at all.

Finally, reverse valuation is more general than we're discussing here. This technique may also be used, for example, to infer the discount rate (cost of equity or cost of capital) that sustains a market valuation. In this case, we would need to input short-term and long-term growth rates of cash flows, and the current market valuation, in order to solve for the discount rate.

The big picture

The main obstacle to a proper implementation of DCF models is forecasting the expected cash flows correctly. This is, as mentioned above, a mix of art, science, and sorcery. But there is no way around. If we want to value companies using a DCF model, we need to both forecast expected cash flows and assess their risk.

But, actually, there is a way around. The idea behind reverse valuation is to expose the conditions that sustain a market valuation and to evaluate the plausibility of those conditions. This technique pushes the analyst to evaluate as many rounds of conditions and plausibility of conditions as necessary until he can reliably answer whether or not the assumptions built into the market valuation are plausible.

It may have been close to impossible to forecast the growth of Internet companies such as Yahoo! by the end of the 1990s. However, exposing that the market was basically expecting Yahoo! to double its cash flows year after year, for ten years in a row, would probably have led many investors to question the valuation of this company. And that is exactly the type of situation in which reverse valuation is particularly useful.

Excel section

There is no new Excel material in this chapter. The use of the Solver is discussed in the Excel section of Chapter 11.

Challenge section

1 Let's use reverse valuation to assess the value of Yahoo! just one year after we did in the text. During the year 2000, Yahoo! generated free cash flows of $394.4 million. At the end of that year, Yahoo! remained unlevered and therefore equity free cash flows were the same as capital free cash flows. Yahoo!'s cost of equity (and cost of capital) had decreased a little, from 25.5% at the end of 1999 to 24.6% at the end of 2000, largely due to a decrease in interest rates. Yahoo!'s market cap, in turn, had fallen substantially, from $115,267.7 million at the end of 1999 to $16,884.9 million at the end of 2000, a fall of roughly 85%. Assuming a long-term growth of free cash flows of 5%, at what annual rate would Yahoo!'s free cash flows need to grow over the years 2001 to 2010 to justify its market valuation?

2 Using the information provided in the previous question, but now assuming a long-term growth of free cash flows of 6%, at what annual rate would Yahoo's free cash flows need to grow over the years 2001 to 2005 to justify its market valuation?

17

STOCKS V: RELATIVE VALUATION

Definition and problems

Multiples

Benchmarks: Basics

Benchmarks: A few comments

The second problem

The PEG ratio

The big picture

Excel section

Challenge section

instein taught us that everything is relative. Perhaps that's the reason why analysts widely use tools of relative valuation. This type of analysis, based on ratios usually referred to as multiples, is often misinterpreted as being a simple comparison between two numbers. Far from that being the case, relative valuation can be just as complicated as absolute valuation. Read on and you'll see why.

Definition and problems

In their most general definition, relative valuation models assess the value of a company relative to a benchmark. The implementation of these models basically involves three steps: first, comparing a ratio to a benchmark; second, determining the reasons why the ratio and the benchmark may differ; and third, making an assessment on the stock's valuation relative to the benchmark.

An analyst using relative valuation has two critical problems to deal with: (1) determining the appropriate benchmark of comparison; and (2) determining why the ratio and the benchmark may differ. In order to understand these two problems and how they fit into the whole valuation process, we first need to consider the most widely used ratios and benchmarks.

Multiples

Most of the ratios used in relative valuation, usually called *multiples*, consist of a share price divided by a fundamental variable expressed on a per-share basis. Price-to-earnings (P/E) ratios, price-to-book (P/B) ratios, price-to-cash flow (P/CF) ratios, price-to-sales (P/S) ratios, and price-to-dividend (P/D) ratios are some of the most widely used. Table 17.1 reports these ratios for several companies in the pharmaceutical industry at the end of the year 2003. (We'll discuss g_{+5} and PEG later.)

These ratios are called multiples simply because they express the number of dollars that investors must pay per dollar of the fundamental variable. Abbott's P/E of 25, for example, indicates that investors have to pay \$25 per \$1 of the company's earnings per share; Abbott's P/CF of 16, in turn, indicates that investors have to pay \$16 per \$1 of the company's cash flow per share. All these multiples mean very little when considered in isolation; they provide useful information only when compared with something else.

There is little to discuss about the numerator of all these multiples; it is simply the current market price of a share. The denominator, however, can be

TABLE 17.1

Company	P/E	P/B	P/CF	P/S	P/D	g_{+5}	PEG
Abbott	24.9	5.2	16.1	3.5	44.5	12.0%	2.1
Amgen	36.6	3.6	26.6	10.0	n/a	20.0%	1.8
AstraZeneca	27.2	6.2	19.7	4.4	62.0	10.0%	2.7
BASF	30.1	1.6	7.3	0.8	35.1	6.0%	5.0
Baxter	20.1	5.6	9.7	2.1	52.6	10.0%	2.0
Bayer	n/a	1.4	6.7	0.7	29.1	9.5%	n/a
Bristol-Myers Squibb	18.0	5.7	16.4	2.7	25.5	-0.5%	n/a
Eli Lilly	29.7	8.1	21.4	6.0	52.5	12.3%	2.4
GlaxoSmithKline	18.4	15.7	14.6	3.8	34.8	6.5%	2.8
Johnson & Johnson	21.5	5.8	16.8	3.7	55.5	12.0%	1.8
Merck	15.2	6.6	13.1	4.6	31.6	3.0%	5.1
Novartis	22.6	3.7	18.4	4.6	64.6	12.4%	1.8
Pfizer	65.4	4.1	20.8	5.7	58.9	11.0%	5.9
Sanofi-Aventis	22.5	7.2	19.2	5.8	77.0	10.5%	2.1
Schering-Plough	n/a	3.5	28.0	3.1	30.5	22.5%	n/a
Wyeth	27.6	6.1	23.1	3.6	46.1	9.0%	3.1

tricky. Take, for example, the widely used P/E ratio. Those earnings per share can be observed or expected, the former usually being those that the company delivered over the past four quarters, and the latter those that the company is expected to deliver over the next four quarters. (P/E ratios based on the former are usually called *trailing* P/Es and those based on the latter *forward* P/Es.)

In addition, when determining the company's earnings, some analysts use net income as stated in the income statement whereas others subtract one-time charges. And when valuing companies from different countries, different accounting standards make the comparison of earnings and P/E ratios even more complicated. (It's not unusual to read about companies that earn billions of dollars under European accounting standards and at the same time *lose* billions of dollars under American accounting standards.)

Much the same can be said about other multiples. The definitions of book value and cash flow may also differ across analysts, and so will the multiples they estimate. Pick a company, go to three different websites, and you will most likely find differences in the respective P/Es, P/Bs, and P/CFs they report. (In this regard, price-to-dividend ratios and price-to-sales ratios are much less subject to differences across analysts.) In short, when using relative valuation, it's always important to know precisely how the multiples are defined.

Benchmarks: Basics

Consider the P/E ratio of Eli Lilly at the end of 2003 displayed in Table 17.1. Sure, we can immediately see that an investor who buys shares of Eli Lilly is paying about $30 per $1 of the company's earnings per share (EPS). But in terms of valuation, what does that mean? Is Eli Lilly stock cheap, expensive, or fairly valued?

Considering only the P/E ratio, we just can't tell. That's why this and other multiples are tools of *relative* valuation; because we need to evaluate this information *in relation to* something else. Which begs the question: in relation to what? This is, precisely, where the issue of benchmarks comes in.

One (rather narrow) possibility is to benchmark Eli Lilly against some other pharmaceutical company. For example, we might say that Eli Lilly (P/E = 30) is expensive relative to Merck (P/E = 15) and cheap relative to Amgen (P/E = 37). But be careful! We'll get back to this issue below, but this is a *simplistic* (rather than a simple) analysis. If all it takes to value a company is to say that 30 is lower than 37 but higher than 15, then we'd all be analysts. Relative valuation is a lot more complicated than that.

For now, let's retake our discussion of possible benchmarks against which to compare Eli Lilly's P/E in order to assess the current value of this stock. There are in fact, three standard benchmarks, two of which are widely used. We will refer to one as a *temporal* benchmark and to the other as a *cross-sectional* benchmark. The third, which we'll call a *theoretical* benchmark, is less widely used.

A *temporal* benchmark seeks to assess the current value of a company relative to its historical valuation. This benchmark, calculated simply as the average multiple of the company over the previous several years, is then compared with the company's current multiple. To illustrate, over the past 15 years, Eli Lilly's P/E averaged 28. Therefore, given its current P/E of 30, the company does not seem to be much more expensive than it has been in the past.

A *cross-sectional* benchmark seeks to assess the current value of a company relative to the current value of 'comparable' companies. (For the time being, let's say that a comparable company is one that's in the same industry as the company of our interest. It's actually a bit more complicated than that, but we'll get back to this issue below.) This benchmark, calculated simply as the average current multiple of companies in the same industry as the company of our interest, is then compared with the company's current multiple. To illustrate, the average current P/E of the pharmaceutical companies in Table 17.1 (not including Eli Lilly) is 27. Therefore, given its current P/E of 30, Eli Lilly seems to be priced a bit above its peers. (Again, it does not follow from this comparison that Eli Lilly is overvalued. That's the simplistic analysis we mentioned before. There may be good reasons for Eli Lilly to be valued higher than its competitors.)

Finally, a *theoretical* benchmark seeks to assess the current value of a company relative to its intrinsic or fair value, that is, the value the company should have given its fundamentals. In this case, we would first need to determine the relevant fundamentals, then estimate a (regression) model that relates the selected multiple to the relevant fundamentals, and then estimate the proper benchmark on the basis of this model.

Suppose we believe that P/E ratios are largely determined by the growth of EPS, dividend payout ratios, and risk. That's our model. We would then collect information on all these variables for several companies (and perhaps also over time) and run a regression. We would then use this regression model to estimate the P/E ratio that the company of our interest *should* have. And finally we would compare this number with the company's current P/E.

Benchmarks: A few comments

Relative valuation with a temporal benchmark implicitly states that if the fundamentals of a company or market haven't changed over time, neither should their valuation. When you hear that the US market may be overvalued because its current P/E ratio is around 20 but historically it's been around 15, you're hearing an argument based on relative valuation with a temporal benchmark. (Again, concluding that the market is overvalued based on a comparison between these two numbers is a simplistic analysis.)

When performing this type of analysis, it's important to assess whether we're comparing apples with apples. It may well be the case that a company today has little to do with what the company has been in the past, and therefore comparing current and historical multiples makes little sense. Think of European telecommunication companies, for example, that until a few years ago were protected monopolies in one line of business and nowadays are companies competing in several lines of business in a market with no legal barriers to entry. By the same token, those who disregard comparisons between the market's current P/E and its historical average argue that the market has changed so much that the comparison is pointless.

How many years should we go back to estimate the historical average? Hard to say, but here's where the analyst's skill comes in. Ideally, we should go back enough years to obtain an average that is not heavily influenced by a few good or bad years. But at the same time we shouldn't go so far back that the average is mostly made up of years in which the company was very different from what it is now. That's a tricky trade-off.

Relative valuation with a cross-sectional benchmark implicitly states that comparable companies should have similar valuations. This of course makes sense, as long as we can properly define a comparable company. Essentially, for the purpose of valuation, comparable companies are those that have similar cash flows, growth prospects, and risk. In practice, however, the shortcut is to use companies in the same industry, although often it is the case that these companies don't have the same cash flows, growth prospects or risk. As Table 17.1 shows, the expected annual growth in EPS over the 2004–08 period (g_{+5}) is far from similar across these pharmaceutical companies.

Also, when performing this cross-sectional analysis, it's important to assess whether the whole industry is overvalued or undervalued. Think, for example, of internet companies during the 1995–99 period. Had we performed a comparison between some internet company and the industry, we would have found that the company may have been a bit more or less expensive than the industry. And yet, that naive analysis would have missed the fact that *the whole industry* was at the time grossly overvalued.

Finally, to briefly illustrate the use of a theoretical benchmark, consider the simplest possible framework, the sometimes-called Fed Stock Valuation Model (FSVM), which compares the earnings yield (E/P) of the S&P500 with the yield on ten-year US Treasury notes (y). This model states that the P/E ratio of the S&P500 *should* be equal to $1/y$, the latter being the proper (theoretical) benchmark. According to this model, then, we should compare the market's current P/E to the current $1/y$ in order to determine whether the market is overvalued or undervalued.

It's important to note that using one of these three benchmarks does not preclude the use of the other two. Quite the contrary: a thorough analysis should include all three or at least both temporal and cross-sectional benchmarks. It's also important to note that we shouldn't always expect all three comparisons (or even two) to point in the same direction. It's not unusual to find, for example, that a company may be expensive relative to its historical performance but cheap relative to its peers.

The second problem

We mentioned above that an analyst using relative valuation has two critical problems to deal with, namely, the choice of the appropriate benchmark and the determination of the reasons for which a multiple and the selected benchmark may differ. We have just discussed the first problem and by now you probably agree that it's not trivial. The second problem is even more difficult.

Let's go back to comparing Eli Lilly (P/E = 30) with Merck (P/E = 15). A naive analysis would simply compare these two numbers and conclude that Eli Lilly is expensive relative to Merck. Now, how much would you pay an analyst to make this comparison for you? Right, nothing, because there is no insight gained from this comparison. Putting these two numbers together should be *the beginning*, not the end of the analysis.

The next obvious step is to ask why. That is, to ask whether there's any reason why Eli Lilly *should* be more expensive than Merck. It is at this point that the analyst adds value by looking into the fundamentals of both companies and assessing whether these fundamentals justify the difference in valuation revealed by the multiples. If they do, then there is no trading opportunity; that is, although these two companies belong to the same industry but have a different valuation, both still are properly priced. If they do not, then there may be a trading opportunity. In the situation we're discussing, given that the cross-sectional P/E is 27, perhaps we should (short-) sell Eli Lilly and buy Merck. That is, again, *if* the fundamentals cannot explain the difference in valuation.

If we compare a company with a temporal or cross-sectional benchmark, the steps to follow are basically the same. In the first case we would ask whether the current fundamentals of the company grant a different valuation from the company's historical valuation. In the second case, we would ask whether the current fundamentals justify a valuation different from that of other companies in the industry.

Now you can see why relative valuation is only *seemingly* simple. Assessing the fundamentals that may explain differences in valuations is not at all simple and requires the same skills necessary for implementing a proper DCF valuation. So, far from being a simple comparison of two numbers (a multiple and a benchmark), relative valuation is a tool that uses this comparison as *the starting point* of the inquiry.

At this point you may be wondering which are the fundamentals that determine differences in valuation. That is of course the million dollar question. It is also the point at which the analyst adds value by using his skill and knowledge to determine the three or four fundamentals that may explain the observed differences between a multiple and a benchmark. Some fundamentals, such as growth and risk, immediately come to mind; others may depend on the multiple used in the analysis or on the type of company considered.

To illustrate, consider the P/E ratio, which can be written as

$$P/E = \frac{DPR \cdot (1 + g)}{(R - g)} \tag{17.1}$$

where DPR denotes the dividend payout ratio (the ratio between dividend and earnings), g the expected growth in EPS, and R risk (or, more precisely in this case, the company's required return on equity). This expression shows that differences in P/E ratios could be explained by differences in dividend payout ratios, growth, or risk.

Having detected a difference between the P/E ratios of two companies, or between the P/E ratio of a company and its historical or cross-sectional benchmark, an analyst would attempt to justify such difference in terms of differential payout policies, expected growth, or risk. That analysis would not necessarily exhaust all the possible sources of differences in valuation, but in the case of P/E ratios, they are the obvious starting point of the search.

Determining how much more growth a company would need to show in order to justify a given difference in P/Es, or how much less risky it should be, is again not easy. And it's here again where the analyst's skill and knowledge come into play. Of all the possible adjustments that P/Es can be subject to, the adjustment by growth is both the best known and the most widely used.

The PEG ratio

Let's go back once again to Eli Lilly and Merck. The first, with a P/E ratio of almost 30, seems to be substantially more expensive than Merck, with a P/E ratio of just above 15. But it should be clear by now that rushing to conclude that Merck is a better buy would be premature. The question we should ask right away is whether this difference in valuation can be explained by differences in fundamentals.

Equation (17.1) shows that differences in P/E may be explained by differences in growth. Now, as can be seen in Table 17.1, the expected annual growth in EPS over the years 2004 to 2008 is much higher for Eli Lilly (12.3%)

than for Merck (3%). Can we then really say that Eli Lilly is more expensive than Merck? We can answer this question with the help of the PEG ratio, which is a P/E ratio adjusted by growth.

Formally, the PEG ratio is defined as

$$PEG = \frac{P/E}{g} \tag{17.2}$$

where g denotes the expected growth in EPS. As it often happens with ratios, the definition is not clear cut. Besides the different possibilities for the P/E in the numerator (discussed above), the expected growth in EPS may be for the next four quarters, for the next year, or annual for the next five years. Again, when dealing with ratios you'd better make sure you know the exact definition of their components.

Note that when comparing companies on the basis of their PEGs, the lower, the better: that is, a lower PEG indicates either a less expensive valuation or a higher expected growth (or both). Note also that, as equation (17.2) shows, calculating PEG ratios is trivial. The PEG ratios for Eli Lilly and Merck are given by 29.7/12.3 = 2.4 for the former and 15.2/3 = 5.1 for the latter. In other words, once we adjust the P/Es by their differential expected growth, Eli Lilly is actually *cheaper* than Merck.

This is, precisely, the insight provided by the PEG. It shows that differences in P/Es may be reflecting differences in expected growth. In our case, Eli Lilly is more expensive than Merck because the market is expecting the annual growth of the former to be about four times higher than that of the latter. So, after adjusting for this differential growth, Eli Lilly is actually cheaper than Merck. (A thorough analysis, however, would not end here; it would go on to look at other fundamentals that may explain the differences in P/Es.) PEG ratios for the pharmaceutical companies in Table 17.1 are reported in the last column.

Some analysts look for GARP (growth at a reasonable price) in stocks with PEGs lower than 1, that is, in stocks whose P/E is lower than the expected annual growth rate in the company's earnings. This rule was made popular by Peter Lynch, the venerable former manager of the Fidelity Magellan fund. However, though its use is quite widespread, it has little or no support from theory.

The big picture

Relative valuation seeks to value companies and markets relative to some benchmark. This tool should be thought of not as a substitute but as a *complement* of absolute or intrinsic valuation. In fact, a thorough analysis should involve both multiples and DCF analysis.

Relative valuation is only seemingly simple. Far from being a comparison between two numbers, such comparison is only the beginning of a proper analysis. Selecting the appropriate benchmark, and determining the factors that may explain the difference between a multiple and a benchmark are no trivial tasks. In fact, a proper analysis of relative valuation is not necessarily less difficult than a proper DCF valuation.

Excel section

There is no new Excel material in this chapter.

Challenge section

1 Assess the valuation of Pfizer relative to Eli Lilly and Merck. How do they compare on the basis of their P/Es, P/Bs, P/CFs, P/Ss, and P/Ds? Do all the comparisons point in the same direction? What do you make of these comparisons?

2 Over the past 16 years, Pfizer's P/E ratio averaged approximately 36. Given its current P/E ratio of over 65, can you safely conclude that Pfizer is overvalued on a historical basis?

3 The average current P/E ratio of the pharmaceutical companies in Table 17.1 (not including Pfizer) is 24. Given its current P/E ratio of over 65, can you safely conclude that Pfizer is overvalued relative to its peers?

4 Consider the PEG ratio of Pfizer in Table 17.1 (5.9) and compare it with that of Eli Lilly and Merck. Once P/E ratios are adjusted by growth, is Pfizer still expensive relative to these two peers?

18

BONDS I: PRICES AND YIELDS

The basics

Bond pricing

Prices, interest rates, and discount rates

The yield to maturity

The effective yield to maturity

The big picture

Excel section

Challenge section

Some think that bonds are boring, others that their returns are too low, and others that they're for wimps. But bonds are an asset class that financial markets could hardly survive without. In this and the next two chapters we'll cover the basics to understand their risk and return characteristics, as well as many of those things you probably always wanted to know about bonds but were afraid to ask.

The basics

A bond is just a loan in which the issuer is the borrower and the investor the lender. The *maturity date* is the time at which the bond expires and the issuer returns the amount borrowed, called the *principal* or *face value*. Between the time when the bond is issued and the maturity date most bonds make periodic interest payments based on the bond's *interest rate* (also called the *coupon*), which is expressed as a percentage of the bond's face value. All the relevant terms of the loan agreement between the borrower and the lender are contained in a contract called the bond's *indenture*.

To illustrate, consider a ten-year bond with a face value of $1,000 and an interest rate of 10%. The holder of this bond will receive $100 in annual interest payments during nine years, and the final interest payment ($100) plus the principal ($1,000) in the tenth year. Because most bonds pay interest semi-annually, the buyer of this bond would actually receive two interest payments of $50 a year rather than $100 a year all at once.

Bonds can be *floated* (that is, issued) by governments, states, municipalities, and corporations, among others. In fact, just about anybody can issue a bond. Rock and roll stars David Bowie and Michael Jackson, for example, have issued bonds, the former in 1997 and the latter in 1998. (And at good rates too! David Bowie raised $55 million with a ten-year bond issued with an interest rate of 7.9%, just 1.5% more than the US government was paying at the time. Michael Jackson's bonds, however, are currently in default.)

Not all bonds have a fixed interest rate. *Floating-rate bonds* have an interest rate that is adjusted over time (usually semiannually) and is usually linked to the rate of some benchmark bond (such as a government bond). Also, not all bonds have a fixed principal. *Inflation-protected bonds* (such as Treasury Inflation-Protected Securities, or TIPS), for example, have a principal that is adjusted periodically (usually semiannually) by inflation. This implies that although the interest rate of these bonds is fixed, their interest payments are not because the principal on which they are calculated changes over time.

Depending on their maturity, US government bonds are classified into *bills*, maturing in one year or less; *notes*, maturing in two to ten years; and *bonds*, maturing in more than ten years. US corporate bonds, in turn, are classified into *short term*, maturing between one and five years; *medium* (or *intermediate*) *term*, maturing between six and twelve years; and *long term*, maturing in more than twelve years.

Secured bonds are those backed by assets pledged by the issuer. Should the issuer not meet its obligations, the collateral can be liquidated and the proceeds distributed among the debt holders. *Unsecured bonds* (also called *debentures*), in turn, are backed only by the good name of the issuer, which means that there are no assets to liquidate if the issuer does not meet its obligations.

Bearer bonds are those belonging to whoever holds them. They are traded without any record of ownership, and have coupons that must be clipped and sent to the issuer in order to receive the scheduled payments. *Registered bonds*, on the other hand, are those belonging to the registered holder. The issuer keeps a record of ownership and automatically sends the scheduled payments.

Convertible bonds are issued by corporations and can be converted into a specified number of shares in the company at certain times during the bond's life. The terms of the conversion (basically the number of shares per bond and the time at which the exchange can be made) are specified in the bond's indenture. Given that this option is valuable for investors, these bonds pay a lower interest rate than similar bonds without a conversion option.

Callable bonds are those that the issuer can call (that is, buy back) before maturity. The terms of the call provision (basically when the bonds can be called and at what price) are specified in the bond's indenture. In general, the call provision does not apply to the first few years of the bond's life; during this time the bond is said to be *call protected*. Given that this option is valuable for issuers (because they exercise it only when they can replace outstanding bonds by new bonds with a lower interest rate), these bonds pay a higher interest rate than similar bonds without the call option.

Consols are bonds that make interest payments for ever but never return the principal. They never mature and therefore have an infinite life. The Bank of England issued consols in the eighteenth century and they are still traded nowadays; the US government issued consols to finance the construction of the Panama Canal but eventually retired them. *Zero-coupon bonds* (or *zeros*), in contrast, don't make any interest payments and only return the principal. Curiously, taxes have to be paid on the annual interest accrued (but not paid!) by these bonds. All US Treasury bills are zero-coupon bonds.

Bond pricing

It is important to note from the outset that price and face value are different concepts. The face value or principal we already discussed, and it's the amount the issuer promises to pay to the bondholder on the maturity date. The *price*, on the other hand, is the number of dollars an investor has to pay to buy the bond. For reasons we'll explore below, most of the time these two magnitudes differ.

In fact, although the price of a bond fluctuates almost continuously, its face value remains constant. (This is true for most, but not all, bonds. As mentioned above, the face value of inflation-protected bonds is indexed to inflation.) A bond with a fixed face value of $1,000 may sell in the market for $900, $1,100, or any other price (including $1,000). It may also sell at one price at 10.30 am and at a different price at 10.31 am.

When the bond's price is higher than its face value, the bond is said to sell *at a premium*. Conversely, when the bond's price is lower than its face value, the bond is said to sell *at a discount*. Finally, when the price and face value are the same the bond is said to sell *at par*.

Let's first consider a coupon bond; that is, one that makes periodic interest payments and has a maturity date. Its pricing is actually fairly straightforward, involving the calculation of a present value. Formally, the intrinsic value of this bond (p_0) is given by

$$p_0 = \frac{C}{(1+R)} + \frac{C}{(1+R)^2} + \ldots + \frac{C+FV}{(1+R)^T} \tag{18.1}$$

where C denotes the bond's coupon payment, FV the bond's face value, R the discount rate (or required return on the bond), and T the number of periods until maturity. Note that this is the price an investor *should* pay for a bond, which may or may not be equal to the bond's current market price. (The critical difference between price and intrinsic value is discussed in Chapter 13.)

Equation (18.1) is the calculation of a present value, and can also be thought of as a discounted cash flow (DCF) calculation. Note that it involves discounting the cash flows the bondholder will receive from the bond (that is, the coupons and the principal) at a rate consistent with their risk. (Yes, bonds *are* risky and we'll explore the sources of risk in the next chapter.) Perhaps the main difference between stock and bond valuation, in this regard, is that the bond's cash flows are not expected but (at least contractually) certain. That is, the issuer commits to make specific payments at specific points in time.

As an example, let's consider again the ten-year bond with a face value of $1,000 and an interest rate of 10%. This means that the holder of this bond will receive $100 in annual interest payments during nine years, and the final interest payment ($100) plus the principal ($1,000) in the tenth year. Let's assume that the proper discount rate for this bond is 12%. (We'll discuss shortly why the discount rate and the interest rate may differ.) Then, the intrinsic value of this bond is

$$p_0 = \frac{\$100}{(1.12)} + \frac{\$100}{(1.12)^2} + \ldots + \frac{\$100 + \$1,000}{(1.12)^{10}} = \$887.0$$

Note, first, that if the bond is trading at this price (that is, if the market price properly reflects the bond's intrinsic value), although the bond's face value is $1,000, its price is $887, that is, price and face value differ. Note, also, that although the bond's interest rate is 10%, its required return (or discount rate) is 12%. We'll discuss this below. For the time being, keep in mind that a bond's price and face value can be (usually are) different, and so can be (again, usually are) the bond's interest rate and required return.

Zero-coupon bonds

There is little mystery in the pricing of zero-coupon bonds. They deliver only one cash flow, at maturity, and make no interest payments before that date. Therefore, the intrinsic value of a zero is given by

$$p_0 = \frac{FV}{(1 + R)^T} \tag{18.2}$$

For example, a five-year zero with a face value of $1,000 and a discount rate of 8% should be priced at

$$p_0 = \frac{\$1,000}{(1.08)^5} = \$680.6$$

Note that these bonds *must* sell at a discount. In other words, if a bondholder expects to receive $1,000 T years down the road and no interest payments before that date, the only way to obtain a positive return from this bond (if held until maturity) is to pay today less than $1,000.

Consols

There is again little mystery in the pricing of these bonds. Formally, a consol is a perpetuity (briefly discussed in Chapter 13) and therefore its intrinsic value is given by

$$p_0 = \frac{C}{(1+R)} + \frac{C}{(1+R)^2} + \frac{C}{(1+R)^3} + \ldots = \frac{C}{R} \tag{18.3}$$

For example, an 8% consol (thus making perpetual annual payments of $80) with a discount rate of 6% should be priced at $80/0.06 = $1,333.3.

Prices, interest rates, and discount rates

It should be clear by now that the price and the face value of a bond are different concepts, and that they can also be numerically different. The three bonds we discussed in the previous section had a face value of $1,000 but they all had prices different from this face value. However, if you are unfamiliar with bonds, the difference between the interest rate and the discount rate of these bonds may be less clear. As you may have noticed, these two numbers are not equal to each other in any of the three bonds we discussed. Let's see why.

The interest rate or coupon of a bond plays only one role: determining the amount of the periodic coupon payment. As we discussed above, in most cases this rate is fixed throughout the life of the bond. What is the discount rate then? It is the return *required* by investors as a compensation for bearing the risk of a bond. And it's not difficult to see why it may differ from the bond's interest rate.

Consider an airline that two years ago issued a five-year bond with a 10% interest rate, which was the return investors required as a compensation for the risk of this bond at that time. By now, two years after the bond was issued, many things could have changed. The general economic situation, the airline industry, and the company itself may all be in a vastly different shape. Would you, as an investor, then require the same return from this bond as you did two years ago?

Obviously not. If the economy, the airline industry, and the airline itself are in worse shape, you'd require a higher return to compensate you for the higher risk; if the opposite is the case, then you'd require a lower return. Another way to say the same thing is that, as the risk of the bond increases, your willingness to pay for it decreases; and as its risk decreases, your willingness to pay for it increases.

Let's go back to our ten-year bond with a face value of $1,000 and an interest rate of 10%. As we saw above, if investors required an annual return of 12%, this bond should trade at $887. If, for example, the economic outlook improves and investors required an annual return of 11% instead, then this bond should trade at

$$p_0 = \frac{\$100}{(1.11)} + \frac{\$100}{(1.11)^2} + \ldots + \frac{\$100 + \$1,000}{(1.11)^{10}} = \$941.1$$

If, on the other hand, the outlook for the airline industry worsens and investors required an annual return of 13%, then this bond should trade at

$$p_0 = \frac{\$100}{(1.13)} + \frac{\$100}{(1.13)^2} + \ldots + \frac{\$100 + \$1,000}{(1.13)^{10}} = \$837.2$$

It should come as no surprise that, given fixed cash flows, if the discount rate increases the bond price falls, and if the discount rate falls the bond price increases. In other words, *there is an inverse relationship between bond prices and required returns (or discount rates).* And this should also come as no surprise: with everything else equal, an increase in risk must be compensated with a higher return, which is obtained when current prices fall.

In short, then, the face value and interest rate of most bonds are set when they're issued and remain fixed throughout the bond's life. Their price and required return (or discount rate), in turn, fluctuate almost continuously.

The yield to maturity

Take another look at equations (18.1) to (18.3), or at those in which we calculated intrinsic values in the previous sections. They all have at least one thing in common: the 'causality' runs from the right-hand side to the left-hand side. That is, if we input the bond's promised cash flows and discount rate, we obtain the bond's intrinsic value as a result.

But what if instead of estimating a bond's intrinsic value we want to calculate the bond's *return* instead? We could calculate it in more than one way, but by far the most widely used magnitude is the bond's **yield to maturity (y)**, which formally solves from the expression

$$p_M = \frac{C}{(1+y)} + \frac{C}{(1+y)^2} + \ldots + \frac{C+FV}{(1+y)^T} \tag{18.4}$$

where p_M denotes the bond's current market price.

Now, you may be wondering what's the difference between (18.4) and (18.1). Have we only changed the notation of the price and the discount rate? No. The change is more fundamental than that and it goes back to the 'causality' mentioned above. In equation (18.1) we input the bond's promised cash flows and discount rate and find the bond's intrinsic value as a result. In (18.4), however, we input the bond's promised cash flows *and current market price*, and *solve for the discount rate*, that is, for the yield to maturity.

Before we define this concept more precisely, let's go back once again to our ten-year bond with a face value of $1,000 and an interest rate of 10%, and let's suppose that it's currently trading at $950. Then, this bond's yield to maturity solves from the expression

$$\$950 = \frac{\$100}{(1+y)} + \frac{\$100}{(1+y)^2} + \ldots + \frac{\$100 + \$1,000}{(1+y)^{10}}$$

and is equal to 10.8%. Let's think about this a bit.

First, what exactly is 10.8%? It is the *compound annual return* we get from buying this bond *at $950* and holding it *until maturity*. It is important to note that the return that we get depends on how much we pay for the bond. In other words, different prices will determine different returns. It is also important to note that this is the return we'll obtain *only* if we hold the bond until maturity. If we buy a ten-year bond but sell it after one year, our return doesn't have to be anywhere close to the yield to maturity.

Second, note that a bond's yield to maturity is identical to what in project evaluation we refer to as a project's internal rate of return (discussed in Chapter 21). In fact, we could perfectly define the yield to maturity as a bond's internal rate of return. Third, from a mathematical point of view, the calculation of a bond's yield to maturity is much more complicated than the estimation of a bond's intrinsic value. Still, as usual, Excel delivers in the blink of an eye.

Fourth, the yield to maturity implicitly assumes that all cash flows are reinvested at this rate. This may or may not be possible (usually it's not), which gives way to the so-called reinvestment risk. We discuss this issue in the next chapter, so for the time being let's say that in order to obtain the return stated in the yield to maturity, we must reinvest all interest payments at exactly this rate.

Fifth, the yield to maturity is, by far, the magnitude most widely used to describe a bond's return; in fact, you will find it next to every bond in the financial pages. This yield to maturity is also the number we use as the required return on debt for the calculation of the cost of capital (discussed in Chapter 7).

Sixth, if markets do a good job at pricing bonds, then higher yields always reflect higher risk. This implies that (again, *if* bonds are properly priced in the market) the yield to maturity provides information not only about the return of a bond *but also about its risk*. In other words, if we compare two bonds with different yields, the one with the higher yield not only offers a higher return but also exposes the investor to a higher risk.

Finally, it is important not to confuse the yield to maturity with the *current yield*. The latter is simply calculated as the coupon payment divided by the current market price, that is, C/p_M. (This magnitude is similar to the dividend yield of a stock, which is calculated as the annual dividend divided by the current market price.) The current yield of our ten-year bond with a face value of $1,000 and a market price of $950, is $100/$950 = 10.5\%$ (different from the yield to maturity of 10.8%). This number is a quick calculation of the annual cash flow received as a percentage of the market price, but it's not nearly as widely used as the yield to maturity to characterize the return of a bond.

The effective yield to maturity

Most bonds make semiannual interest payments. When this is the case, the calculation of a bond's intrinsic value and yield to maturity are slightly different from that discussed above. Let's start with the intrinsic value, which with semiannual coupon payments is calculated as

$$p_0 = \frac{C/2}{(1 + R/2)} + \frac{C/2}{(1 + R/2)^2} + \cdots + \frac{C/2 + FV}{(1 + R/2)^{2T}} \tag{18.5}$$

Comparing equation (18.5) with (18.1), it's easy to see that the adjustments are straightforward: we halve the coupon; we halve the discount rate; and we double the number of periods. To illustrate this, if our ten-year bond with a face value of $1,000, an interest rate of 10%, and a discount rate of 12% paid interest semiannually (instead of annually as we have assumed so far), its intrinsic value should be

$$p_0 = \frac{\$50}{(1.06)} + \frac{\$50}{(1.06)^2} + \ldots + \frac{\$50 + \$1,000}{(1.06)^{20}} = \$885.3$$

The calculation of the yield would require a similar adjustment. Formally, the yield to maturity of a bond that makes semiannual interest payments solves from the expression

$$p_M = \frac{C/2}{(1 + y/2)} + \frac{C/2}{(1 + y/2)^2} + \ldots + \frac{C/2 + FV}{(1 + y/2)^{2T}} \tag{18.6}$$

where it's important to keep in mind that p_M, the current market price, is an input (just as C, FV, and T) and that we're solving for y.

Comparing (18.6) and (18.4) it's easy to see that the adjustments are again straightforward: we halve the coupon; we halve the yield; and we double the number of periods. Just to bow to the way Excel calculates yields (more on this in Excel section), let's rewrite equation (18.6) as

$$p_M = \frac{C/2}{(1 + SAy)} + \frac{C/2}{(1 + SAy)^2} + \ldots + \frac{C/2 + FV}{(1 + SAy)^{2T}} \tag{18.7}$$

where $SAy = y/2$ denotes the semiannual yield to maturity. This is simply to underscore that when dealing with semiannual coupons, Excel solves for a semiannual yield.

Let's go back once again to our ten-year bond with a face value of $1,000 and an interest rate of 10%. Let's assume that this bond now makes semiannual interest payments and that it is currently trading at $950. In that case, its yield to maturity solves from the expression

$$\$950 = \frac{\$50}{(1 + SAy)} + \frac{\$50}{(1 + SAy)^2} + \ldots + \frac{\$50 + \$1,000}{(1 + SAy)^{20}}$$

and is equal to 5.4%.

Note, again, that this is a semiannual yield but we're still interested in an annual magnitude. What is usually referred to as the *annual yield to maturity* is simply twice the semiannual yield; in our case, it would be $2 \cdot 0.054 = 10.8\%$. However, this yield would ignore the impact of compounding.

Note that with semiannual interest payments, the $50 we get half way into the year earns interest on interest. (This is a bit tricky. Here again is where the assumption implicit in the calculation of the yield to maturity, that all cash flows are reinvested at this yield, comes in.) In order to take into account the impact of compounding, we need to calculate the **effective annual yield to maturity (Ey)**, which is given by

$$Ey = \left(1 + \frac{y}{2}\right)^2 - 1 = (1 + SAy)^2 - 1 \qquad (18.8)$$

In our case, then, $Ey = (1 + 0.054)^2 - 1 = 11.1\%$. Note that this effective yield is higher than the annual yield we calculated before (10.8%). This is *always* the case, simply because the effective yield takes into account the impact of compounding that the annual yield ignores.

The big picture

Bonds are an essential asset class. They may receive less attention than stocks in the financial press, but they provide issuers with a critical source of financing, and investors with a relatively predictable source of income. Federal, state, and local governments, as well as corporations, could hardly do without them.

The price of a bond is given by the present value of the interest payments and principal it promises to deliver, discounted at a rate that reflects its risk. A bond's return, in turn, is most properly summarized by its yield to maturity. In most cases, although the face value and interest rate are fixed throughout the bond's life, its price and yield to maturity fluctuate almost continuously.

If markets price bonds efficiently, the yield to maturity not only summarizes their return but also their risk, that is, bonds with different yields are also bonds of different risk. Yes, bonds can be risky, and that is precisely what we discuss in the next chapter.

Excel section

Calculating intrinsic values and yields to maturity is easy in Excel, as long as you're aware of a few little quirks. Let's suppose you have ten semiannual coupon payments in cells A2 through A11, the last being the semiannual coupon plus the principal. (Leave cell A1 empty for now.) Then,

- To calculate the bond's intrinsic value, you type '=**NPV(DR, A2:A11)**' where DR is a numerical value for the (semiannual) discount rate, and then hit 'Enter.' (Note that what Excel calls NPV is really a *present value*, which is what you need to calculate an intrinsic value.)

There is actually an easier way to calculate intrinsic values (or, misusing the word, prices) and that is by using the 'price' function. The advantage of this alternative is that you don't have to lay out the bond's cash flows in order to calculate its price. You do, however, have to input some relevant information. Suppose you input the date for which you want to calculate the price in cell B1; the maturity date in cell B2; the annual coupon rate in cell B3; the annual discount rate in cell B4; 100 in cell B5; and the number of coupon payments per year in cell B6. Then,

- To calculate the bond's intrinsic value, you type '=**price(B1, B2, B3, B4, B5, B6)**' and then hit 'Enter.'

A couple of comments are in order. First, Excel requires you to enter both the day of evaluation and the maturity date. This can be a nuisance if you want to calculate the price of some hypothetical bond for which you care about its maturity but not about specific dates. There's an easy way around, though. If you want to price a, say, five-year bond, enter '1/1/2000' as the date of evaluation and '1/1/2005' as the maturity date. Excel will then interpret that this bond is five years away from maturity. More generally, if you don't care about specific dates, you can always 'fool' Excel by entering any two dates that are as far apart as the time to maturity of your bond.

Second, you enter the '100' in B5 because Excel calculates a price for each $100 of face value. For this reason also, if you want to calculate the price of a bond with a face value of $1,000, you must multiply the value resulting from the 'price' function by 10.

In order to calculate a (semiannual) yield to maturity, you need to input the bond's current market price. In fact, you need to input *minus* the market price. Once you do that in cell A1,

- To calculate the *semiannual* yield to maturity, you type '**=IRR(A1:A11)**' and then hit 'Enter.'

Recall, however, that this is a semiannual yield. If you want to calculate the annual yield, you multiply the previous result by 2; and if you want to calculate the effective annual yield, you can use equation (18.8).

Again, there's an easier way to calculate yields to maturity that has the advantage that you don't have to lay out the bond's cash flows. But again, you still have to input some relevant information. Suppose you have the date in which you want to calculate the price in cell C1; the maturity date in cell C2; the annual coupon rate in cell C3; the bond price in cell C4; 100 in cell C5; and the number of coupon payments per year in cell C6. Then,

- To calculate the *annual* yield to maturity, you type '**=yield(C1, C2, C3, C4, C5, C6)**' and then hit 'Enter.'

A couple of comments are again in order. First, Excel calculates the yield for each $100 of face value. This means that if your bond has a face value of $1,000, you must enter one-tenth of its price (or its price divided by 10). Second, Excel asks you to input the date of the evaluation and the maturity date, but if you don't care about specific dates, you can again 'fool' Excel by entering any two dates that are as far apart as the time to maturity of your bond. Finally, note that Excel gives you the annual yield. Therefore, to calculate the effective annual yield, you can use equation (18.8).

Challenge section

1 Let's consider the four bonds for which data is displayed in Table 18.1. The first is a US Treasury note and the other three are corporate bonds from Berkshire Hathaway (BH), Motorola, and Delta Airlines. We will consider these four bonds at somewhat different points in time so that all of them are six years away from maturity.

▶

TABLE 18.1

	US Treasury	BH	Motorola	Delta
Face value	$1,000	$1,000	$1,000	$1,000
Annual coupon	5.75%	4.2%	7.625%	7.92%
Maturity	Aug. 15, 2010	Dec. 15, 2010	Nov. 15, 2010	Nov. 18, 2010
You are	Aug. 15, 2004	Dec. 15, 2004	Nov. 15, 2004	Nov. 18, 2004
Periodic payment	Semiannual	Semiannual	Semiannual	Semiannual
SADR-1	2.0%	2.5%	3.0%	3.5%
SADR-2	3.0%	3.5%	4.0%	4.5%
Actual price	$1,112.7	$1,000.5	$1,164.1	$722.9

(a) Calculate the price of each bond assuming that you are at the dates indicated in the 'You are' row, and using the semiannual discount rates displayed in the 'SADR-1' row.

(b) Recalculate the price of each bond assuming that you are at the dates indicated in the 'You are' row, but now using the semiannual discount rates displayed in the 'SADR-2' row.

(c) How does the price of each bond react to the increase in its discount rate? Why?

2 Calculate the semiannual yield to maturity of each bond in Table 18.1 assuming that you are at the date indicated in the 'You are' row and given the price indicated in the 'Actual price' row. Then calculate both the annual yield and the effective annual yield of each bond. Are these last two yields different for each bond? Why?

19

BONDS II: DEFAULT RISK AND MARKET RISK

Sources of risk

Yield to maturity: The hidden catch

Default risk

Market risk

The big picture

Excel section

Challenge section

t may come as a surprise to some but yes, bonds are risky, and yes, money can be lost by investing in bonds. The sources of risk are many and varied but we'll focus here on the main two, default risk and market risk. (In order to understand this chapter, it is essential that you are familiar with the concepts discussed in the previous chapter.)

Sources of risk

Suppose we buy a corporate bond that matures in five years but that we intend to hold for only one year. What can go wrong? What are the sources of risk we face? Can we actually *lose* money? In a nutshell, many things can go wrong, because bonds are risky in more than one way, and yes, we can lose money by investing in this or in any other bond. Just to drive this point home, note that even investors in 'super-safe' US Treasury bonds can lose money. Long-term Treasuries delivered *negative* returns of 9% in 1999, 1% in 1996, and 8% in 1994.

The first and obvious source of risk is that the company defaults on its payments. Let's say the company goes bankrupt; not only does it not make the coupon payment we expected for the year we hold the bond but nor will it make any other payment in the future (coupons or principal). Well, that's too bad. We just suffered a 100% loss on our investment. We'll discuss this possibility in more detail below, but for the time being let's call this *default risk*, that is, the uncertainty about whether the company will make the bond's promised payments.

But things don't have to get that bad for us to lose money on our bond. Let's assume that the company does not default. And let's assume that during the year we hold the bond the general level of interest rates goes up (which, as we discussed in the previous chapter, will push bond prices down). Our bond will then suffer a capital loss. And if this capital loss is larger than the coupon payment, we would lose money on our bond. We'll also discuss this possibility in more detail below, but for the time being let's call this *market risk* or *interest rate risk*, that is, the uncertainty about the price at which we'll sell a bond (or the uncertainty about whether we'll suffer a capital loss).

What else can go wrong? Well, in some cases it may not be easier to find a buyer for our bond. If we buy a government bond from a developed country, or a corporate bond from a solid corporation, selling the bond should not be a problem. Those bonds change hands very frequently and buyers and sellers are always easy to find. However, many bonds trade infrequently, buyers and sellers may be scarce, and finding a buyer may not be trivial. Let's call this *liquidity risk*, that is, the uncertainty about our ability to quickly find a buyer for our bond.

Now, to focus on two other sources of risk, let's assume that instead of holding our bond for just one year we'll hold it until maturity (five years down the road). Let's also assume that the issuer is a blue-chip company, and therefore neither default risk nor liquidity risk is an issue. And let's finally assume that the bond's yield to maturity is 4%. What if in a completely unexpected way inflation increases substantially and runs over the next five years at the annual rate of 5%? Well, that's too bad, because we're only earning 4%. Although the 4% return is certain, it is also certain that our nominal return will not keep up with inflation, and that we'll suffer a loss in real terms. Let's call this *inflation risk*; that is, the uncertainty about whether the return we lock into by holding a bond until maturity will keep up with inflation.

Finally, recall that the calculation of the yield to maturity implicitly assumes that the cash flows generated by the bond are reinvested at that rate. (We'll discuss an example in the next section.) However, that may or may not be possible. Let's call this *reinvestment risk*, that is, the uncertainty about the rate at which we'll be able to reinvest the coupon payments made by the bond.

In short, then, bonds are far from risk-free. Their sources of risk are many and varied, and those we just discussed are not an exhaustive list. Before we go deeper into the two most relevant types of risk, default risk and market risk, let's briefly discuss the reinvestment assumption implicitly built into the calculation of the yield to maturity.

Yield to maturity: The hidden catch

Let's consider a five-year bond with a face value of $1,000, a 6% coupon, and a current price of $920. Just to simplify it, let's assume that this bond makes annual (rather than the usual semiannual) coupon payments, which means that at the end of each of the first four years we'll receive $60, and at the end of the fifth and final year we'll receive $1,060. You know by now how to calculate yields to maturity, so if you run the calculation you should find that it is 8.0%.

We argued before that this 8% yield hides an implicit reinvestment assumption. What does that mean? Let's think about it this way. Let's say we get the first coupon payment of $60 at the end of the first year, and that we put it in the bank at 8% a year over four years. Then, by the time the bond matures, the $60 will have turned into $60 · $(1.08)^4 = \$81.6$.

Let's do something similar for the rest of the coupon payments. When we receive the second $60 two years down the road, we put it in the bank at 8% a year over three years, which by the time the bond matures will have turned into

$60 \cdot (1.08)^3 = \$75.6$. When we receive the third $60 we put it in the bank at 8% a year over two years, which will turn into $70.0 by the time the bond matures. And when we get the fourth $60 we put it in the bank at 8% for one year, which will turn into $64.8 by the time the bond matures. Finally, five years down the road, we'll receive $1,060 which is the last coupon payment plus the principal.

So, what should we get in five years' time? We should get the sum of all the cash flows calculated above, that is, $81.6 + $75.6 + $70.0 + $64.8 + $1,060 = $1,352. And here comes the clincher. Remember the bond's price of $920? Well, what would we get five years down the road if we deposited $920 in the bank at the annual rate of 8%? Surprise! We'd get exactly $1,352! In other words, in order to turn $920 into $1,352 by investing at the annual rate of 8% over five years, *we must reinvest at 8% all the interest payments made by the investment.*

Problem is, this is unlikely to be possible. First, if our investment is small the coupon payment may not be large enough to buy another bond, even if we could find one that has the same yield as the one we already have. Second, finding a bond of similar quality to the one we already have, and which also pays the same yield, is less than trivial (even if we're investing in government bonds), particularly when we have to do it year after year. And third, even if we could get around the previous two problems (that is, we do find another bond of similar risk and same yield, and our coupon payment is large enough to buy it), once the new bond makes a coupon payment, we'd have the same problems all over again.

All this in no way means that the yield to maturity is a flawed measure of a bond's return. In fact, the calculation of the internal rate of return of an investment project has the same built-in reinvestment assumption, and yet this tool is routinely used by corporations to evaluate projects. But it's always important to know the limitations of, and the hidden assumptions behind, widely used financial tools. (Chapter 21 discusses in some detail the internal rate of return as a tool for project evaluation.)

Default risk

Not all bond issuers are equally likely to fulfill their promises. Governments of developed countries and blue-chip companies are virtually certain to honor their obligations to bondholders; governments of emerging markets or less-established companies not necessarily are. The government of Argentina, for example, defaulted on over $80 billion of debt in December 2001 (the largest sovereign default in history). The job of rating agencies is, precisely, to assess the likelihood of such events.

The two largest rating agencies are Standard & Poor's (S&P) and Moody's. These agencies provide investors with ratings that indicate the likelihood of default. The rating system used by S&P, as well as the meaning of each rating, is shown in Table 19.1, which also shows the equivalent rating by Moody's.

TABLE 19.1

S&P[a]	Description	Moody's
AAA	An obligation rated 'AAA' has the highest rating assigned by S&P. The obligor's capacity to meet its financial commitment on the obligation is extremely strong.	Aaa
AA	An obligation rated 'AA' differs from the highest rated obligations only in small degree. The obligor's capacity to meet its financial commitment on the obligation is very strong.	Aa
A	An obligation rated 'A' is somewhat more susceptible to the adverse effects of changes in circumstances and economic conditions than obligations in higher rated categories. However, the obligor's capacity to meet its financial commitment on the obligation is still strong.	A
BBB	An obligation rated 'BBB' exhibits adequate protection parameters. However, adverse economic conditions or changing circumstances are more likely to lead to a weakened capacity of the obligor to meet its financial commitment on the obligation.	Baa
BB	An obligation rated 'BB' is less vulnerable to nonpayment than other speculative issues. However, it faces major ongoing uncertainties or exposure to adverse business, financial, or economic conditions which could lead to the obligor's inadequate capacity to meet its financial commitment on the obligation.	Ba
B	An obligation rated 'B' is more vulnerable to nonpayment than obligations rated 'BB', but the obligor currently has the capacity to meet its financial commitment on the obligation. Adverse business, financial, or economic conditions will likely impair the obligor's capacity or willingness to meet its financial commitment on the obligation.	B
CCC	An obligation rated 'CCC' is currently vulnerable to nonpayment, and is dependent upon favorable business, financial, and economic conditions for the obligor to meet its financial commitment on the obligation. In the event of adverse business, financial, or economic conditions, the obligor is not likely to have the capacity to meet its financial commitment on the obligation.	Caa
CC	An obligation rated 'CC' is currently highly vulnerable to nonpayment.	Ca
C	A subordinated debt or preferred stock obligation rated 'C' is currently highly vulnerable to nonpayment. The 'C' rating may be used to cover a situation where a bankruptcy petition has been filed or similar action taken, but payments on this obligation are being continued. A 'C' also will be assigned to a preferred stock issue in arrears on dividends or sinking fund payments, but that is currently paying.	C
D	An obligation rated 'D' is in payment default. The 'D' rating category is used when payments on an obligation are not made on the date due even if the applicable grace period has not expired, unless S&P believes that such payments will be made during such grace period. The 'D' rating will also be used upon the filing of a bankruptcy petition or the taking of a similar action if payments on an obligation are jeopardized.	

[a] The ratings from AA to CCC may be modified by the addition of a plus or minus sign to show relative standing within the major rating categories.

Source: Standard & Poor's

Bonds rated AAA, AA, A, and BBB are called *investment grade* bonds and are very unlikely to default. Bonds rated BB and below are called *high-yield* (or *junk*) bonds and are speculative in the sense that, although they offer high yields, they also have a relatively high probability of default. (In fact, some organizations such as pension funds are prohibited from buying bonds of quality lower than investment grade.) Companies that achieve investment grade status, then, have a substantially lower cost of debt (and cost of capital) than companies that do not.

Rating agencies are usually criticized for being slow to downgrade issuers whose fundamentals deteriorate rapidly. Many times, in fact, rating agencies have downgraded companies or governments to junk status *after* critical situations became public news. During the Southeast Asian crisis of 1997, for example, rating agencies were widely criticized for downgrading countries long after markets were trading their bonds at yields consistent with a much lower rating than the countries had at the time. More recently, although Enron filed for bankruptcy on December 2, 2001 (the second largest corporate bankruptcy in US history), S&P downgraded the company to junk status only four days earlier, on November 28.

In the long term, however, credit ratings are highly reliable; that is, they do predict accurately the probability of default. Table 19.2 displays 'mortality rates' between the years 1971 and 2003. The figures show the proportion of US companies that defaulted five and ten years after being rated. As the table clearly shows, the lower the rating (and therefore the riskier the company), the higher the mortality rate, that is, the higher the proportion of companies that did default.

TABLE 19.2

S&P rating	5 Years (%)	10 Years (%)
AAA	0.03	0.03
AA	0.50	0.55
A	0.28	0.82
BBB	7.64	9.63
BB	12.17	19.69
B	28.32	37.26
CCC	47.30	58.63

Source: Adapted from Edward Altman and Gonzalo Fanjul, 'Defaults and returns in the high yield bond market: the year 2003 in review and market outlook,' Working Paper, 2004

This being the case, it should come as no surprise that, the lower the rating, the more issuers have to pay in order to convince investors to buy their bonds. In other words, the lower the rating, the higher the risk, and the higher the yield. Table 19.3 shows the bond yields of several companies in different rating categories at the end of 2003, as well as the yield of a US Treasury note with similar maturity. (All bonds mature between August and October 2009.)

TABLE 19.3

Bond	S&P rating	Yield (%)	Spread (%)
US Treasury	n/a	3.39	n/a
General Electric	AAA	3.94	0.55
Procter & Gamble	AA	3.99	0.60
Transcanada Pipe	A	4.27	0.88
Safeway	BBB	4.49	1.10
MGM Mirage	BB	5.43	2.04
Continental Airlines	B	11.93	8.54
Sbarro	CCC	16.87	13.48

As the table clearly shows, yields increase as the credit rating worsens. The last column shows the spread over US Treasury notes, a magnitude that is often thought of as reflecting expectations about the economy. When the economy is expected to grow at a fast pace, spreads tend to tighten reflecting a lower probability of corporate default. Conversely, and for the opposite reason, when the economy is expected to be sluggish spreads tend to widen. (The same goes for emerging market bonds, whose spreads over Treasuries tend to tighten or widen depending on the good or bad growth prospects of these economies.)

In short, then, rating agencies assess the fundamentals of issuers and assign a rating on their bonds. These ratings accurately predict the long-term probability of default, and therefore investors require a higher yield the lower the rating of the issuer. Finally, issuers that qualify for investment grade status enjoy a cost of debt (and cost of capital) substantially lower than those that do not.

Market risk

Investors who buy government bonds (from developed markets) are virtually free from both default risk and liquidity risk. However, they are still subject to both inflation risk and reinvestment risk, as well as the market risk that is the focus of this section.

It should be clear from the discussion in the previous chapter that a bond's discount rate and its price move in opposite directions. It should also be clear that discount rates may change because of changing expectations about the performance of the issuer and that of the overall economy.

Let's consider a five-year bond and a ten-year bond, both with a face value of $1,000, a 10% coupon, and a discount rate of 10%. It is straightforward to calculate that both bonds should sell for $1,000 (that is, they should sell at par). The relevant question for us now is what happens to the price of these bonds if the general level of interest rates (and therefore the discount rate of both bonds) increases by, say, 1 percentage point. We know that the price of both bonds should fall, but the question is by how much.

Again, by now we know how to perform the relevant calculations. It is easy to determine that given an 11% discount rate, the five-year bond should trade at $963 and the ten-year bond at $941.1. Note, then, that the bond with the longer maturity falls more (5.9%) than the one with shorter maturity does (3.7%).

What if the general level of interest rates (and therefore the discount rate of both bonds) were to fall by, say, 1 percentage point? Then, given a 9% discount rate, the five-year bond should trade at $1,038.9 and the ten-year bond at $1,064.2. Note, then, that the bond with the longer maturity rises more (6.4%) than the one with shorter maturity does (3.9%).

What this simple example shows is that, everything else being equal, given two bonds of different maturity, the one with the longer maturity will be more sensitive to changes in interest rates. In other words, the longer a bond's maturity, the more its price will be affected by changes in discount rates (or, similarly, the higher its price volatility).

Just to drive this point home, Exhibit 19.1 shows the prices of 30 different bonds (all with a face value of $1,000, a coupon of 10%, and maturities between 1 and 30 years) at discount rates (DR) of 9%, 10%, and 11%. As is clear from the exhibit, the longer a bond's maturity, the larger the change in price (both upwards and downwards) for any given change in discount rates. Or, in other words, *the longer the maturity, the higher a bond's market risk.*

The intuition behind this result is rather straightforward. The longer we are locked into a contract that pays 10% when the market's interest rate is only 9%, the more we stand to gain. Conversely, the longer we are locked into a contract that pays 10% when the market's interest rate is 11%, the more we stand to lose. Therefore, the longer a bond's maturity, the more we stand to gain *and* lose when interest rates change and we remain locked into the bond's interest rate.

It is important to note that this result applies only when we hold other things constant. In other words, given the face value, the coupon, and the discount rate,

EXHIBIT 19.1
Market risk

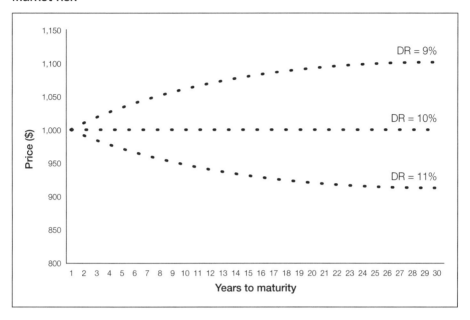

the longer a bond's maturity, then the higher its market risk. Or, put differently, if we compare two bonds with the same face value, coupon, and discount rate, but with different maturity, the one with the longer maturity *must* have a higher market risk. However, if we compare two bonds with different maturity, but also with different coupon and/or discount rate, it does *not necessarily* follow that the one with the longer maturity will have the higher market risk.

Price volatility is also related to the magnitude of the coupons. In fact, everything else being equal, *the larger the coupon, the lower a bond's market risk*. Table 19.4 shows five bonds with different coupons but the same $1,000 face value and five-year maturity, as well as their price at a discount rate (DR) of 5%. (Assume, for simplicity, that all bonds make annual coupon payments.) Because all bonds have different initial prices, it makes sense to think of price volatility as the *percentage* (rather than the absolute) change in prices.

When the discount rate falls to 4%, the price of the bonds with 2% coupon and 10% coupon increase by 4.7% and 4.2%, respectively. Similarly, when the discount rate falls from 5% to 3%, the price of the bonds with a 2% coupon and 10% coupon increase by 9.7% and 8.6%, respectively. And, as the last two rows of the table show, when the discount rate increases from 5% to 6% and 7%, the price of the bonds with lower coupons falls by more than that of the bonds with larger coupons.

TABLE 19.4

	2% Coupon	4% Coupon	6% Coupon	8% Coupon	10% Coupon
3% DR	9.7%	9.3%	9.0%	8.8%	8.6%
4% DR	4.7%	4.5%	4.4%	4.3%	4.2%
5% DR	$870.1	$956.7	$1,043.3	$1,129.9	$1,216.5
6% DR	−4.4%	−4.3%	−4.1%	−4.0%	−3.9%
7% DR	−8.6%	−8.3%	−8.1%	−7.9%	−7.7%

Finally, price volatility is also related to the magnitude of the yield (or discount rate). In fact, everything else equal, *the higher the yield, the lower a bond's market risk*. Table 19.5 shows five bonds with different yields but the same $1,000 face value and five-year maturity, as well as their price at their initial yields. (Assume, again for simplicity, that all bonds make annual coupon payments.) Because all bonds have different initial prices, it makes sense again to think of price volatility as the percentage (rather than the absolute) change in prices.

When all yields fall by half a percentage point (because, for example, inflationary expectations for the economy fall by that amount), the price of the bonds with 3% yield and 15% yield increase by 2.1% and 1.8%, respectively. Similarly, when all yields fall by one percentage point, the price of the bonds with 3% yield and 15% yield increase by 4.3% and 3.6%, respectively. And, as the last two rows of the table indicate, when all yields increase by half a percentage point and one percentage point, the price of the bonds with lower yields falls by more than that of the bonds with higher yields.

TABLE 19.5

	3% Yield	6% Yield	9% Yield	12% Yield	15% Yield
Yield − 1%	4.3%	4.1%	3.9%	3.8%	3.6%
Yield − 0.5%	2.1%	2.0%	1.9%	1.9%	1.8%
Yield	$1,320.6	$1,168.5	$1,038.9	$927.9	$832.4
Yield + 0.5%	−2.1%	−2.0%	−1.9%	−1.8%	−1.8%
Yield + 1%	−4.0%	−3.9%	−3.7%	−3.6%	−3.5%

In short, then, bond prices react to changes in discount rates and expose investors to price volatility. This market (or interest rate) risk is the main source of risk of default-free government bonds, and more generally a critical source of risk of all bonds. Holding other things constant, this market risk is increasing in a bond's maturity, decreasing in a bond's coupon, and decreasing in a bond's yield.

The big picture

Bonds, like just about all financial assets, are risky. Their sources of risk are many and varied and, as long as markets price bonds properly, higher levels of risk translate into higher bond yields. Liquidity risk, inflation risk, and reinvestment risk are important but not very easy to quantify. Default risk and market risk, on the other hand, are the two main drivers of differences in yields and are more easily quantifiable.

Default risk is related to the uncertainty about whether the issuer will make the bond's promised payments. It is assessed by rating agencies and captured in credit ratings, which are widely used and highly reliable in the long term. Investment grade bonds are very safe and a timely payment of their promised cash flows is virtually certain. High-yield bonds, on the other hand, are much more likely to default and therefore compensate investors with higher yields. Market (or interest rate) risk is related to price volatility and, therefore, to uncertainty about future bond prices. This market risk increases with a bond's maturity, decreases with its coupon, and decreases with its yield.

Excel section

There is no new Excel material in this chapter.

Challenge section

1 Let's go back to the same four bonds we considered in the Challenge section of the previous chapter, namely, a US Treasury note, and corporate bonds from Berkshire Hathaway (BH), Motorola, and Delta Airlines. Relevant information about these bonds is displayed in Table 19.6.

TABLE 19.6

	US Treasury	BH	Motorola	Delta
Face value	$1,000	$1,000	$1,000	$1,000
Annual coupon	5.75%	4.2%	7.625%	7.92%
S&P rating	n/a	AAA	BBB	B–
Maturity	Aug. 15, 2010	Dec. 15, 2010	Nov. 15, 2010	Nov. 18, 2010
You are	Aug. 15, 2004	Dec. 15, 2004	Nov. 15, 2004	Nov. 18, 2004
Periodic payment	Semiannual	Semiannual	Semiannual	Semiannual
SADR-1	2.0%	2.5%	3.0%	3.5%
SADR-2	3.0%	3.5%	4.0%	4.5%
SADR-3	1.0%	1.5%	2.0%	2.5%

(a) Calculate the price of each bond assuming that you are at the dates indicated in the 'You are' row, and using the semiannual discount rates displayed in the 'SADR-1' row. This is our base case.

(b) Calculate the price of each bond assuming that you are at the dates indicated in the 'You are' row, and using the semiannual discount rates displayed in the 'SADR-2' row.

(c) Calculate the price of each bond assuming that you are at the dates indicated in the 'You are' row, and using the semiannual discount rates displayed in the 'SADR-3' row.

2 Consider the percentage change in the price of each bond in Table 19.6 when discount rates change from those in the base case ('SADR-1' row) to those in the 'SADR-2' and 'SADR-3' rows. Which of the four bonds is the most sensitive to changes in interest rates? Which is the least sensitive? Why?

3 Are default risk and market risk positively correlated in the sense that bonds that have a higher default risk also have a higher market risk? Why?

20

BONDS III: DURATION AND CONVEXITY

Maturity reconsidered

Duration: An example

Determinants of duration

Modified duration

Convexity

Applications

The big picture

Excel section

Challenge section

At this point we know how to price bonds and how to assess their default risk and market risk. The former is actually evaluated by rating agencies and summarized in credit ratings. The latter can be assessed with two critical tools widely used by bond managers, duration and convexity, both of which we discuss in this chapter.

Maturity reconsidered

We discussed in the previous chapter that one of the most important sources of a bond's risk is its market risk, or price volatility. We also discussed that, holding other things constant, this price volatility is increasing in a bond's maturity. However, when bond traders think about the volatility of a bond, they hardly ever relate it to its maturity; almost invariably they relate it to its duration. Is there any relationship, then, between maturity and duration? There sure is.

The lifetime of a bond is given by its maturity, which is the number of years until the bond returns the principal. However, this is not a good measure of a bond's *effective* lifetime. To see why, compare a five-year zero with a five-year bond with a 10% coupon, both with a face value of $1,000. Although we have to wait five years to get a cash flow from the first bond, by the end of the fourth year the second bond will have paid almost 27% (=$400/$1,500) of the total cash flows it will deliver. In fact, note that with this second bond we receive its cash flows, on average, after three years, that is, $(1 + 2 + 3 + 4 + 5)/5 = 3$.

Three years, however, is not a good measure of the second bond's effective maturity. The reason is that we receive a much larger cash flow in the fifth year ($1,100) than in any of the previous years ($100). Should we then give a larger weight to five years than to any other time to receive cash flows? Yes. Should we then assign these weights according to the cash flows paid by the bond? No.

The reason is that if we do so we would give the same weight to both one year and two years because in both cases we receive $100. However, $100 after one year is more valuable than $100 after two years. Which suggests the best way to assign weights to each time to receive cash flows: we should weight them by *the present value* of the cash flows to be received.

A bond's *duration*, then, is the weighted-average time to receive a bond's cash flows, with the weights being the present value of each cash flow relative to the bond's price. Do I hear you saying . . . *what?!*

Duration: An example

Let's go again, this time step by step. It's actually less difficult than it sounds. Let's go back to our five-year bond with a face value of $1,000 and a 10% coupon. Assuming, for simplicity, annual coupon payments, this bond pays $100 at the end of each of the first four years and $1,100 at the end of the fifth year. What is this bond's duration?

Take a look at Table 20.1. The first column shows the times to receive cash flows (t) measured in years and ranging from 1 to 5. The second column shows the actual cash flows (CF) paid by the bond, as well as its price at a discount rate of 8%. The third column shows the present value of each cash flow (PVCF), again discounted at 8%; the sum of these present values is, of course, equal to the bond's price. The fourth column shows the present value of each cash flow relative to the bond's price (RPVCF); these weights should obviously add to 1. The last column shows the product between the first and the fourth columns ($t \cdot$ RPVCF), that is, each time to receive cash flows multiplied by the relative present value of each cash flow. The sum of these numbers (4.2) is, finally, the duration of our bond.

TABLE 20.1

t	CF ($)	PVCF ($)	RPVCF (%)	$t \cdot$ RPVCF
1	100	92.6	8.6	0.09
2	100	85.7	7.9	0.16
3	100	79.4	7.4	0.22
4	100	73.5	6.8	0.27
5	1,100	748.6	69.3	3.47
Price	$1,079.9			
Sum		$1,079.9	100.0%	4.20

Let's think about this a bit. If we buy a five-year zero, we have to wait five years to get a cash flow. In this case, the maturity of the zero is a good measure of its effective lifetime simply because the time to receive the final cash flow (five years) has a weight of 1. In fact, rather unsurprisingly, the duration and maturity of zero-coupon bonds always coincide.

If we buy our five-year coupon bond instead, we receive a $100 cash flow at the end of each of the first four years, and a much larger cash flow ($1,100) at maturity. Because we don't have to wait the whole lifetime of the bond to get some its cash flows, then its duration is lower than its maturity. In fact, *duration is lower than maturity for all coupon bonds*, simply because these bonds pay out some cash flows before they mature. In the case of our bond, 4.2 years indicates the (weighted-) average maturity of the bond's cash flows.

Note that the first $100 'mature' after one year; the second $100 after two years; the third $100 after three years; the fourth $100 after four years; and the final $1,100 after five years. We already know why we shouldn't calculate the average maturity of these cash flows simply as (1 + 2 + 3 + 4 + 5)/5. And we also know that we should weight each of these 'maturities' by the relative present value of each cash flow. If we take into account both the average maturity *and* the appropriate weights, then we get the duration of 4.2 years.

Formally, a bond's **duration (D)** is given by

$$D = \left(\frac{1}{p_0}\right) \cdot \left(\frac{1 \cdot CF_1}{(1+R)} + \frac{2 \cdot CF_2}{(1+R)^2} + \ldots + \frac{T \cdot CF_T}{(1+R)^T}\right) \qquad (20.1)$$

where T denotes the time to maturity, CF_t the cash flow paid by the bond at the end of period t, R the discount rate (or yield to maturity), and p_0 the bond's current market price. Applying equation (20.1) to our five-year coupon bond we get

$$D = \left(\frac{1}{\$1,079.9}\right) \cdot \left(\frac{1 \cdot \$100}{1.08} + \frac{2 \cdot \$100}{1.08^2} + \ldots + \frac{5 \cdot \$1,100}{1.08^5}\right) = 4.2 \text{ years}$$

which is of course the same result as we calculated in Table 20.1.

It should be clear by now what is the idea behind the concept of duration. It attempts to capture the effective maturity of a bond by taking into account not only the different times to receive the bond's cash flows but also the size of each cash flow relative to the bond's price. Or, put differently, it attempts to capture the weighted-average maturity of a bond's cash flows. The duration of our five-year coupon bond, 4.2 years, is lower than 5 years simply because the bond pays some cash flows before its maturity. And it's higher than 3 years simply because most of the bond's cash flows are paid at maturity.

Note that, as Table 20.1 shows, only 8.6% of the bond's price is recovered at the end of the first year, and 69.3% of the price is recovered at maturity. Note, also, that the first cash flow contributes very little to the bond's duration (9% of a year, or just over a month), whereas the last cash flow contributes almost 3.5 years to the bond's duration of 4.2 years.

Determinants of duration

We started this chapter arguing that when bond traders think about price volatility they usually relate it to a bond's duration. So at this point you may fairly ask what does duration have to do with price volatility or market risk? After all, our discussion so far seems to suggest that duration measures the effective maturity of a bond, taking into account both the timing of the bond's cash flows and their relative present value.

We argued in the previous chapter that, everything else being equal, market risk is directly related to a bond's maturity, and inversely related to its coupon and discount rate. Well, it turns out to be the case that a bond's duration is also directly related to its maturity and inversely related to its coupon and discount rate.

To illustrate, consider the four bonds in Table 20.2, the first of which is the five-year bond we've been discussing so far. Let's use this bond as a reference and ask what happens to its duration as we change, *one at a time*, its maturity (second bond), its coupon (third bond), and its discount rate (last bond).

TABLE 20.2

Face value	$1,000	$1,000	$1,000	$1,000
Maturity	5 years	6 years	5 years	5 years
Coupon	10%	10%	6%	10%
Coupon paid	Annually	Annually	Annually	Annually
Discount rate	8%	8%	8%	4%
Price	$1,079.9	$1,092.5	$920.1	$1,267.1
Duration	4.2 years	4.8 years	4.4 years	4.3 years

As Table 20.2 shows, holding everything else constant, if the bond's maturity increases, its duration also increases; if its coupon decreases, its duration increases; and if its discount rate decreases, its duration increases. Therefore, as we argued above, a bond's duration is directly related to its maturity and inversely related to its coupon and discount rate.

The direct relationship between duration and maturity should be obvious. After all, the former is just a more sophisticated way of thinking about the latter. The relationship between these two magnitudes, however, is not linear. Table 20.3 shows that, as the maturity of our five-year coupon bond increases, its duration also increases but at a lower rate. Note, for example, that when the bond's maturity increases by a factor of 10, from 5 years to 50 years, its duration only increases by a factor of just over 3, from 4.2 to 13.1.

TABLE 20.3

Maturity (years)	5	10	20	30	40	50
Duration (years)	4.2	7.0	10.2	11.8	12.6	13.1

The intuition behind this result is that, as maturity increases, later cash flows are discounted more heavily than earlier cash flows, that is, very distant cash flows have a very small present value. As a result, duration increases with maturity but at a lower rate. This is in fact the case for all coupon bonds. In the case of zeros, however, duration and maturity are always the same and therefore increase at the same rate. (In the case of deep-discount bonds the relationship is a bit more complicated. Duration increases with maturity but only up to a point, and then decreases from that point on.)

The inverse relationship between a bond's duration and its coupon is also intuitive. Larger coupon payments increase the percentage of cash flows received before maturity, which obviously decreases duration. Finally, the inverse relationship between a bond's duration and its discount rate is explained by the fact that, as the discount rate increases, the discount factor of later cash flows increases more than that of earlier cash flows.

Modified duration

You may still be wondering what does duration have to do with market risk or price volatility. But hey, we have given a few steps ahead! Among them, we established in the previous section that the same factors that affect market risk also affect duration, and that they do so in the same direction. That is, both market risk and duration increase as maturity increases, coupons decrease, and discount rates decrease. As a result, there is a direct relationship between a bond's duration and its market risk; that is, the larger a bond's duration, the higher its price volatility.

In fact, tweaking slightly the definition of duration we've been discussing (often referred to as *Macaulay*'s duration), we can obtain a measure of a bond's sensitivity to changes in interest rates. More precisely, a bond's **modified duration (D_M)** is given by

$$D_M = \frac{D}{(1 + R/n)} \tag{20.2}$$

where n is the number of coupon payments per year (hence, $n = 1$ for annual coupons and $n=2$ for semiannual coupons). This expression yields an approximation of the percentage change in a bond's price given a change in the bond's discount rate.

Let's go back to our five-year coupon bond which, as we already calculated, has a duration of 4.2 years. At a discount rate of 8%, the modified duration of this bond will be $D_M = 4.2/1.08 = 3.9$. What does this number indicate? It says that if the bond's discount rate were to change by 1%, then its price would change by 3.9% (obviously, in the opposite direction). Modified duration, then, is a measure of a bond's price sensitivity to changes in its discount rate, and therefore, a measure of a bond's market risk. So, finally, we have linked duration and market risk!

There is a little problem, though . . .

Convexity

Let's put it this way. We know that when the discount rate is 8% our five-year coupon bond should trade at $1,079.9. If the discount rate increases from 8% to 9%, the bond should then sell for $1,038.9 for a decrease of 3.8%. If, on the other hand, the discount rate falls from 8% to 7%, the bond should sell for $1,123.0 for an increase of 4.0%. Note that, in both cases, the percentage change in the bond's price is close, but not exactly equal, to the 3.9% change predicted by its modified duration of 3.9. That's why we said before that modified duration is an *approximation* to the sensitivity of a bond's price to changes in its discount rate.

How good is the approximation? That depends on two factors, the magnitude of the change in the discount rate and the so-called *convexity* of the bond. To understand this concept, let's first consider *small* changes in the discount rate. The second column of Table 20.4 shows the price of our five-year coupon bond at a discount rate of 8% and at other rates close to that number. The third column shows the percent changes in price with respect to the initial price of $1,079.9. The fourth column shows the prices implied (or predicted) by a duration of 3.9. And the final column shows the percentage change in the implied prices, again with respect to the initial price of $1,079.9. Note that the numbers in this last column are all calculated as the product between the modified duration (3.9) and the change in the discount rate; for example, $1.95\% = 3.9 \cdot (0.08 - 0.075) = 3.9 \cdot 0.005$.

TABLE 20.4

Discount rate (%)	Price ($)	% Change	Implied price ($)	% Change
7.5	1,101.1	1.97	1,100.9	1.95
7.6	1,096.8	1.57	1,096.7	1.56
7.7	1,092.6	1.18	1,092.5	1.17
7.8	1,088.3	0.78	1,088.3	0.78
7.9	1,084.1	0.39	1,084.1	0.39
8.0	1,079.9	n/a	1,079.9	n/a
8.1	1,075.7	-0.39	1,075.7	-0.39
8.2	1,071.5	-0.77	1,071.4	-0.78
8.3	1,067.3	-1.16	1,067.2	-1.17
8.4	1,063.2	-1.54	1,063.0	-1.56
8.5	1,059.1	-1.92	1,058.8	-1.95

The table clearly shows that the actual changes in price and those predicted by a modified duration of 3.9 are identical for small departures from 8%. As the change in the discount rate gets larger, the differences between these two percentage changes also get larger, although they remain negligible. In other words, for small changes in the discount rate, a bond's modified duration is a very good predictor of the expected change in the bond's price.

Exhibit 20.1, however, shows that as the changes in the discount rate get larger (still beginning from 8%), the approximation provided by modified duration worsens. The dotted line shows the actual prices at different discount rates, and the solid line the prices predicted by a modified duration of 3.9. Note that the predicted prices fall along a straight line whereas the actual prices fall along a *convex* line. In other words, modified duration predicts prices assuming a linear relationship between a bond's price and its discount rate, but the actual relationship between these two variables is convex.

Note that if the discount rate of our bond increased from 8% to 15%, the bond's price should fall by 22.9%; using modified duration, however, we would predict a fall of 27.2%. If, on the other hand, the discount rate of our bond fell from 8% to 1%, the bond's price should increase by 33.1%; using modified duration, however, we would predict an increase of 27.2%. In other words, as the picture makes clear, the larger the change in the discount rate, the larger the error we would make when predicting (changes in) prices using modified duration.

How large can these errors be? That depends on the convexity of the dotted line. That is, in fact, what the issue of convexity is all about: The more convex

EXHIBIT 20.1
Convexity

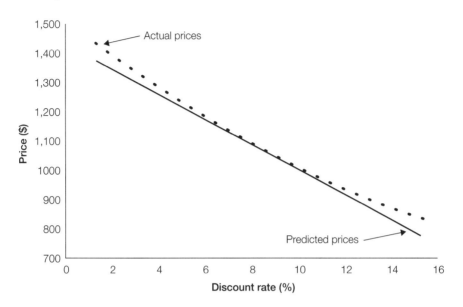

the line representing the relationship between actual prices and discount rates, the larger the differences between the actual prices and those predicted on the basis of modified duration. (Alternatively, convexity can be thought of as the sensitivity of a bond's duration to changes in its discount rate.)

It still remains the case, however, that for small changes in the discount rate, modified duration accurately predicts the change in price. Note that the straight line is tangent to the convex line at the initial discount rate of 8%. This implies that, at that point of intersection, the slope of both lines is the same. Mathematically speaking, then, modified duration provides an accurate prediction of the price change only for *very* small changes in the discount rate.

This is not, however, as limiting as it may sound. Note that, as Table 20.4 shows, even for changes as large as half a percentage point up or down, modified duration provides a very good approximation to the actual changes in price. Swings in interest rates as large or larger, needless to say, hardly ever happen over short periods of time. Note, also, that very large changes in interest rates, such as those swings of 7 percentage points (from 8% to 15%, or from 8% to 1%) discussed above are virtually unheard of and only occur over very long periods of time. For practical purposes, then, modified duration provides a good approximation to a bond's market risk.

Finally, if the accuracy of the predictions based on modified duration decreases with the convexity of the relationship between actual prices and discount rates, then you may be wondering what determines the degree of convexity. In a nutshell, a bond's convexity is increasing in its maturity (and duration) and decreasing in its coupon and discount rate. In other words, modified duration predicts better the market risk of bonds with shorter maturity, higher coupon, and higher discount rate.

Applications

Both duration and convexity are essential tools for managers of bond portfolios and are the heart of *immunization strategies*. These are strategies that seek to protect bond portfolios from their main source of risk, changes in interest rates, and can be divided into two categories: income immunization and price immunization.

Income immunizations strategies seek to ensure that a stream of assets is sufficient to meet a stream of liabilities; these strategies are largely based on duration. A pension fund, for example, has a predictable stream of liabilities and needs to invest its assets in such a way as to be able to meet future cash outflows. In response, bond managers typically seek to match the duration of assets and liabilities in order to minimize the probability of a shortfall.

Price immunization strategies, on the other hand, seek to ensure that the market value of assets exceeds that of liabilities by a specified amount; these strategies are largely based on convexity. Bond managers may seek to match the duration of assets and liabilities, and at the same time achieve a convexity of assets larger than that of liabilities. With this strategy, if interest rates increase, the value of the assets will increase by more than that of the liabilities; and if interest rates decrease, the value of the assets will decrease by less than that of the liabilities.

These tools can also be used to immunize a bond portfolio from the impact of changing interest rates. By setting the portfolio's duration equal to the investor's investment horizon, if interest rates increase, the capital loss on the value of the bonds is offset by the higher rate at which the bonds' cash flows will be reinvested. If, on the other hand, interest rates fall, the lower rate at which the bonds' cash flows will be reinvested is offset by the capital gain in the value of the bonds.

Finally, these tools can be used to either enhance or protect the value of a bond portfolio given an expected change in interest rates. If a bond manager expects interest rates to fall, he can increase the duration of his portfolio in order to leverage the expected capital gain. If, on the other hand, he expects interest rates to increase, he can reduce the duration of his portfolio in order to mitigate the impact of the expected capital loss.

The big picture

Duration and convexity are two critical concepts that every bond investor needs to understand. They are also widely used by bond managers in order to both protect and enhance the value of their portfolios.

The duration of a bond measures its effective maturity by taking into account both the timing of the bond's cash flows and their relative present value. A bond's modified duration, in turn, measures the sensitivity of the bond's price to changes in interest rates and is a tool widely used to assess a bond's market risk.

Modified duration, however, provides only an approximation to a bond's market risk. The accuracy of the approximation depends on two factors, the magnitude of the change in interest rates and the convexity of the relationship between the bond's price and its discount rate. For most practical purposes, the approximation is good enough and therefore modified duration is widely used to assess the price volatility of bonds.

Excel section

You already know how to calculate both bond prices and bond yields in Excel. Calculating a bond's duration is just as simple. Suppose you have the date in which you want to calculate the duration in cell A1; the maturity date in cell A2; the annual coupon rate in cell A3; the annual discount rate in cell A4; and the number of coupon payments per year in cell A5. Then,

■ To calculate the bond's duration, you type '=**duration(A1, A2, A3, A4, A5)**' and hit 'Enter.'

Note that Excel requires you to enter both the date in which you are making the calculation and the bond's maturity date. As we discussed in Chapter 18, if specific dates are irrelevant for your purpose, you can always enter any two dates just as far apart as the time to maturity of the bond you're dealing with.

Challenge section

1 Consider the same four bonds we considered in the Challenge Section of Chapters 18 and 19, namely, a US Treasury note, and corporate bonds from Berkshire Hathaway (BH), Motorola, and Delta Airlines. Relevant information about these bonds is displayed in Table 20.5.

TABLE 20.5

	US Treasury	BH	Motorola	Delta
Face value	$1,000	$1,000	$1,000	$1,000
Annual coupon	5.75%	4.2%	7.625%	7.92%
S&P rating	n/a	AAA	BBB	B–
Maturity	Aug. 15, 2010	Dec. 15, 2010	Nov. 15, 2010	Nov. 18, 2010
You are	Aug. 15, 2004	Dec. 15, 2004	Nov. 15, 2004	Nov. 18, 2004
Periodic payment	Semiannual	Semiannual	Semiannual	Semiannual
SADR-1	2.0%	2.5%	3.0%	3.5%
SADR-2	2.5%	3.0%	3.5%	4.0%
SADR-3	1.5%	2.0%	2.5%	3.0%

  (a) Calculate the price of each bond assuming that you are at the dates indicated in the 'You are' row, and using the semiannual discount rates displayed in the 'SADR-1' row. This is our base case.

  (b) Calculate the price of each bond assuming that you are at the dates indicated in the 'You are' row, and using the semiannual discount rates displayed in the 'SADR-2' row.

  (c) Calculate the price of each bond assuming that you are at the dates indicated in the 'You are' row, and using the semiannual discount rates displayed in the 'SADR-3' row.

2 Calculate the duration of each of the four bonds in the base case. (Recall that Excel requires you to input the *annual* discount rate, so make sure you remember to double the magnitudes in the 'SADR-1' row.) Are these durations longer or shorter than the 6-year maturity of these bonds? Why? Are these durations longer or shorter than the 3.5-year average maturity of these bonds calculated as $(1 + 2 + 3 + 4 + 5 + 6)/6$? Why?

3 Calculate the modified duration of each of the four bonds in the base case. What is the sensitivity of each bond with respect to changes in interest rates?

4 Calculate the percentage change in the price of each bond when discount rates change from those of the base case to those in the 'SADR-2' and 'SADR-3' rows. Are these changes in price similar to those predicted by the modified duration of each bond? Why?

part III:

OTHER IMPORTANT TOPICS

21

NPV AND IRR

Basic principles

Present value

Net present value

The internal rate of return

Applying NPV and IRR

Problems of the IRR approach

The big picture

Excel section

Challenge section

know, you do know and use NPV and IRR. But these two essential tools, as well as a few related ideas, are the backbone of many calculations in finance and just too important not to cover in any desktop companion. There are a few things worth reviewing and refreshing, and that's what we'll do in this chapter.

Basic principles

Let's start with three questions whose answers will lead us to three basic principles or ideas implicitly built into many financial tools and methods. First question: would you rather have $100 today or next year? No contest there, you prefer them today.

Inflation erodes the purchasing power of money. That's why we don't keep our money under the mattress but deposited in the bank, where we earn interest on the capital invested. The interest rate paid by the bank protects us against this loss of purchasing power. Which brings us to another way of seeing why we prefer the $100 today: because we can deposit it and start earning interest on that money immediately, which implies that a year from today we will be able to withdraw more than $100.

Second question: would you rather have $100 one year from now or two years from now? Again, no contest, you prefer the $100 one year from now. The reason is obvious and follows from the argument above. The more time passes by, the more purchasing power we lose. In other words, given the amount of money, the sooner we get it, the better.

Third and final question: would you rather have $100 for sure, or accept the outcome of the flip of a coin in which heads you get $200 and tails you get $0? This one depends on your degree of risk aversion, but most people will pocket the certain $100, though the expected value of the flip of the coin is also $100. (In fact, *all* risk-averse individuals should chose the certain $100. Risk-loving individuals would go for the coin toss, and risk-neutral individuals would be indifferent.) Just in case you're hesitating a bit on this one, change the $100 to $1 million and the $200 to $2 million. What would you choose now?

Now for the basic principles, which follow from the answers to the questions above. First, $1 today is worth more than $1 in the future. Second, $1 in the future is worth more than $1 in a more distant future. And third, both now and in the future, a certain $1 is worth more than an uncertain (or risky, or expected) $1. All basic common sense. And yet essential to understand the idea of present value, a central concept in finance.

Present value

The idea of discounting is central to many methods in finance. It follows from the fact that, as mentioned above, inflation erodes the purchasing power of money, which means that dollars received at different times in the future have different purchasing power. Therefore, adding dollars to be received one and two years away in the future is like adding apples and oranges.

In order to add apples and apples we need to turn the oranges into apples. That sounds somewhat impossible, but is more understandable when it comes to turning future dollars into current dollars. That's where *discounting*, a simple but powerful idea, comes in. The relevant question is, how much money should you ask for today (x) in order to be indifferent between receiving x today or $100 a year from now?

The answer, obviously, depends on the interest rate (I) you could earn in the bank. Given I, you would be indifferent between these two propositions when $x(1 + I) = \$100$, from which it follows that $x = \$100/(1+I)$. In other words, x is the *present value* of $100. If the interest rate were 5%, then you'd be indifferent between receiving $93.2 (= $100/1.05) today or $100 a year from today, simply because you could deposit the $93.2 at 5% and withdraw $100 one year down the road.

What about a two-year framework? That is, how much money should you ask for today (x) in order to be indifferent between receiving x today or $100 two years from now? Again very simple. You'd be indifferent between these two propositions when $x(1 + I)^2 = \$100$, from which it follows that $x = \$100/(1 + I)^2$. Again, x is the present value of $100. And if the interest rate were 5%, then you'd be indifferent between receiving $90.7 today or $100 two years from now, simply because you could deposit the $90.7 at 5% and withdraw $100 two years from today.

And how much money should you ask for today (x) in order to be indifferent between receiving x today or $100 one year from now *plus* $100 two years from now. You only need to add the present value of $100 one year from now and the present value of $100 two years from now, that is,

$$\$x = \frac{\$100}{(1 + I)} + \frac{\$100}{(1 + I)}$$

And with interest rates at 5% you should ask for $185.9.

We could go on but hopefully you have got the main two ideas by now. First, that the present value of $1 to be received T years from now is given by $x = \$1/(1+I)^T$. And second, that present values are additive. This is due to the fact that when we divide any amount to be received T years from now by $(1 + I)^T$ we're turning future dollars into current dollars (that is, oranges into apples).

One more thing. So far we haven't really dealt with risk. All those $100 we talked about were sure things, and that's why we've been discounting at a rate that is also risk free. When we deposit money in the bank, we know exactly how much we will be withdrawing T years down the road. (Well, in some countries people only *hope* they'll be able to withdraw that 'certain' amount . . .)

And yet, like we discussed above, you're not indifferent between $100 for sure and the 50/50 chance of $200 or $0 given a flip of a coin. Between those two, you prefer $100 for sure. Which is just another way of saying that, given a certain amount y to be received T years from now, and a lottery with an expected value of y also to be received T years from now, the present value of the lottery is lower than the present value of the certain amount. (Read this last sentence again and make sure you understand it.)

Note that, mathematically, this can only be the case if you discount the lottery at a rate higher than I. That is, $\$y/(1 + I)^T > \$y/(1 + DR)^T$ only if $DR < I$, where DR is a discount rate. The intuition here is clear: everything else equal, the riskier the proposition (or investment), the lower the value you place on it. Or, in other words, the riskier the proposition the higher the discount rate you apply to it.

So, finally, we arrive at one of the most useful and widely used expressions in finance. Given any investment expected to deliver the cash flows CF_1, CF_2 . . . CF_T in periods $1, 2 . . . T$, the **present value (PV)** of the investment is given by

$$PV = \frac{CF_1}{(1 + DR)} + \frac{CF_2}{(1 + DR)^2} + \ldots + \frac{CF_T}{(1 + DR)^T} \qquad (21.1)$$

where DR is a discount rate that captures the risk of the investment. Think of this discount rate as a hurdle rate, that is, the minimum acceptable return for a company to invest in a project or for an investor to put his money in an asset. (In a typical capital budgeting problem, this discount rate is usually a company's cost of capital. This magnitude, and more generally how to properly adjust for risk in the discount rate, are discussed in Chapter 7.)

Net present value

Going from present value to net present value is straightforward. The latter only 'nets' from the former the initial investment required to start a project. Therefore, the **net present value (NPV)** of an investment is given by

$$NPV = CF_0 + \frac{CF_1}{(1 + DR)} + \frac{CF_2}{(1 + DR)^2} + \cdots + \frac{CF_T}{(1 + DR)^T} \qquad (21.2)$$

Often, CF_0 is expressed as a strictly negative cash flow representing the amount of the upfront investment required to start the project. There are, however, projects in which the first cash flow can be positive (an example is considered below), so let's keep equation (21.2) as general as possible and assume that all cash flows can be either positive or negative.

Now, how do we decide whether or not to start a project by using the NPV approach? The rule is simple and you've surely seen it (and probably used it) many times before: calculate the NPV of an investment using the expression above, and then

- If NPV > 0   ⇒   Invest
- If NPV < 0   ⇒   Do not invest

The intuition is straightforward: a positive NPV indicates that the present value of the cash flows of the project outweighs the necessary investments; a negative NPV indicates the opposite.

If two competing (mutually exclusive) projects are evaluated, then the one with the higher NPV should be selected. That is, given any two competing projects i and j, calculate the NPV of both and then

- If $NPV_i > NPV_j$ ⇒   Invest in i
- If $NPV_i < NPV_j$ ⇒   Invest in j

Of course, the devil is in the detail. Throwing a bunch of numbers into a formula and coming up with another number is not difficult. The difficult part is to estimate correctly the cash flows to be generated by the project, and to capture the risk of those cash flows appropriately in the discount rate.

The internal rate of return

There exist many rules for project evaluation, many of which are so simplistic that we don't even bother to review them here. (Some of these include the payback period, the discounted payback period, and the average accounting return.) The main contender of the NPV approach is the **internal rate of return (IRR)**, which is formally defined as the discount rate that sets the NPV of a project equal to 0, that is,

$$NPV = CF_0 + \frac{CF_1}{(1 + IRR)} + \frac{CF_2}{(1 + IRR)^2} + \ldots + \frac{CF_T}{(1 + IRR)^T} = 0 \qquad (21.3)$$

Note that although it is not trivial to solve this expression for the IRR, Excel (and many other programs and even hand-held calculators) finds this number in the blink of an eye, as we will see at the end of the chapter. Note, also, that the IRR does not depend on market-determined parameters (such as the cost of capital); rather, it depends exclusively on the cash flows of the project considered.

How do we decide whether or not to start a project using the IRR approach? Again, the rule is simple and you've surely seen it (and probably used it) many times before. Calculate the IRR of project and then

- If IRR > DR ⇒ Invest
- If IRR < DR ⇒ Do not invest

The intuition of this rule is also straightforward. Recall that the discount rate is also the hurdle rate or the minimum acceptable return (and that in capital budgeting decisions this is usually the cost of capital). Then, the rule says that if the return of the project is higher than the hurdle rate we should invest in the project; otherwise, we should not.

Another way to see the intuition behind the IRR rule is the following. By definition, the IRR is the discount rate for which the NPV of a project is equal to 0. Then, any project with an IRR higher than the discount rate must have a positive NPV and should be accepted. Any project with an IRR lower than the discount rate, on the other hand, must have a negative NPV and should therefore be rejected. In other words, the two rules lead to the same decision. (But beware, this is not always true, as we will see below.)

Finally, if two competing (mutually exclusive) projects are evaluated, then the one with the higher IRR should be selected. That is, given any two projects i and j, calculate the IRR of both and then

- If $\text{IRR}_i > \text{IRR}_j$ ⇒ Invest in i
- If $\text{IRR}_i < \text{IRR}_j$ ⇒ Invest in j

Note, obviously, that for a company to invest at all, the higher of the two IRRs must be higher than the discount rate.

Applying NPV and IRR

Consider the projects in Table 21.1, all being evaluated by a company whose hurdle rate is 12%. You should have no difficulty in calculating the NPVs reported in the last line. According to the NPV rule, all projects but B are beneficial for the company, G being the most valuable project (the one with the highest NPV) and D the least valuable (the one with the lowest positive NPV). Project B has a negative NPV and is therefore detrimental for the company.

TABLE 21.1

Period	A ($)	B ($)	C ($)	C′ ($)	D ($)	E ($)	F ($)	G ($)
0	−100	100	−200	−100	−100	100	−100	−100
1	150	−150	280	130	260	−300	150	50
2					−165	250	25	150
NPV	$33.9	−$33.9	$50.0	$16.1	$0.6	$31.4	$53.9	$64.2
IRR	50.0%	50.0%	40.0%	30.0%	10.0%[a]	n/a	65.1%	50.0%

a Project D has another IRR equal to 50%.

Let's focus for a moment on project A, which has both a positive NPV ($33.9) and an IRR (50%) higher than the discount rate (12%). Therefore, the company should go for it. Exhibit 21.1 shows the relationship between NPV and IRR and drives home three points we made above. First, that whenever the IRR is higher than the discount rate, the NPV of the project is positive. (The opposite occurs when the IRR is lower than the discount rate.) Second, that the higher the IRR with respect to the discount rate, the higher the NPV of the project. (The lower the IRR with respect to the discount rate, on the other hand, the lower the NPV of the project.) And third, when the IRR is equal to the discount rate, the NPV of the project is 0.

EXHIBIT 21.1
NPV and IRR

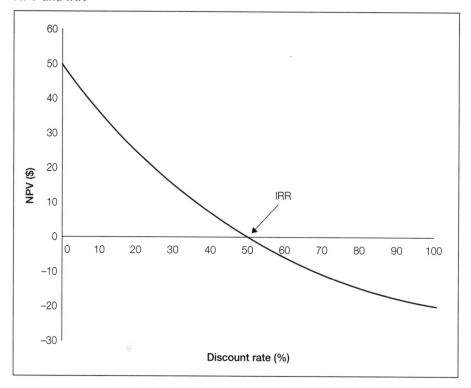

Now, before you get too excited with the consistency between the NPV and the IRR approaches, consider projects A and B in Table 21.1. The NPV rule would lead us to accept A and reject B, whereas the IRR rule would lead us to accept both. Not good. Now consider projects B and D. The NPV rule would lead us to accept D and reject B, whereas the IRR rule would lead us to do the opposite. Oh well, the consistency was fun while it lasted.

Problems of the IRR approach

What, then, should a company do in situations in which the NPV and the IRR criteria point in different directions? The answer is unequivocal: *follow the NPV approach*. This is due to some problems inherent in the IRR approach, which we will now discuss.

Multiple IRRs

Consider project D, which is depicted in panel A of Exhibit 21.2. As you can see, this project has two IRRs, 10% and 50%. If you're curious, this is due to the 'strange' pattern of cash flows, which goes from negative to positive and back to negative. These two changes in sign imply that there can be up to two IRRs. (In general, applying Descartes's rule, if a sequence of cash flows has n changes of sign, then the project could have up to n different IRRs.) These changes in sign are not uncommon among projects that require large subsequent investments after the start-up phase.

Note that the first IRR is lower than the hurdle rate and the second IRR higher than the hurdle rate. So what should a company do? Focus on the first IRR (10%) and reject the project, or focus on the second (50%) and accept the project? Actually, the IRR cannot be used in this or similar cases, and the decision of whether or not to go ahead with the project must be made with the NPV approach. (And because the NPV is positive, the company should accept the project.)

EXHIBIT 21.2
Problems of the IRR

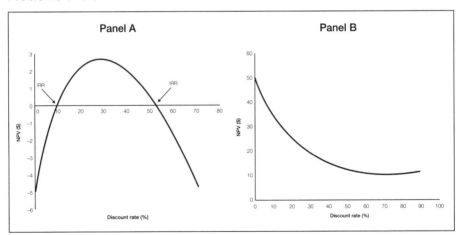

No IRR

Consider now project E, which has no IRR. As you can see in panel B of Exhibit 21.2, this is due to the fact that the project has a positive NPV for all discount rates. Again, the IRR approach cannot be used in this or similar cases, and the decision must be made with the NPV approach. (And given that the project has a positive NPV, the company should accept it.)

Lending versus borrowing

Consider and compare projects A and B. Note that B has a rather peculiar sequence of cash flows, beginning with an inflow and followed by an outflow. This is a bit unusual but not just hypothetical. In the typical executive education programs run by business schools, the participants pay in advance and the schools incur the costs of delivering the program at a later date.

Take project A first. Both approaches, NPV and IRR, point in the same direction and the company should accept the project. In the case of project B, however, the NPV approach suggests that the company should reject the project, but the IRR approach suggests the opposite. How can the NPV approach reject a project in which the IRR of 50% is so much higher than the hurdle rate of 12%?

Note that project A consists of an outflow followed by an inflow. If you think about it, this sounds similar to depositing money in a bank, with the negative cash flow being the deposit and the positive cash flow being the withdrawal. The difference is that in this case the company 'lends' the money to a project. In these cases, the higher the IRR (with respect to the discount rate), the better the project. After all, when we lend money, don't we want to receive the highest possible rate?

Now think about project B. Doesn't it sound like *borrowing* money from a bank, with the inflow coming first when the loan is received and the outflow coming later when the loan is repaid? Again, the difference is that the company is 'borrowing' money from a project. In these cases, the IRR rule must be reversed. A project must be accepted when the IRR is *lower* than the hurdle rate, and rejected when the IRR is *higher* than the discount rate. After all, when we borrow money, don't we want to pay the *lowest* possible rate?

Scale problems

Consider projects A and C and assume they are mutually exclusive, that is, if we invest in one, we cannot invest in the other. Based on their NPVs, the company should go for project C; based on their IRRs, however, the company should go for A. What is going on? What should the company do?

As we discussed above, when the NPV and the IRR approaches conflict, the company should base its decision on the NPV approach. In this case, that means going for project C. There are two ways of seeing why this is the right decision, both of them based on *incremental* cash flows, that is, the difference between the cash flows from project C compared with those of project A. This is exactly what 'project' C' shows.

First, note that the NPV of the incremental cash flows is positive. Given a discount rate of 12%, it pays to invest $100 more in project C (with respect to the investment in project A), in order to get an extra $130 (again, with respect to project A). Second, note that the incremental cash flows have an IRR of 30%, which given a hurdle rate of 12% would lead the company to (again) accept the project.

The 'problem' here is that the IRR is somewhat biased toward accepting projects with a small upfront investment because, the smaller the investment, the 'easier' it is to get a high return. Assuming a discount rate of 10%, which proposition would you choose: one in which I borrow $1 from you and return $2 in one year, or one in which I borrow $1 million from you and return $1.9 million in one year? The IRR of the first proposition is higher. Would you still choose it?

Timing problems

Consider now projects F and G. Note that we have a problem similar to the previous one, before, that is, the NPV criterion suggests that the company should accept project G, whereas the IRR criterion suggests that the company should accept project F. What is going on and what should the company do?

Take a look at Exhibit 21.3, which depicts the NPV of both projects at several discount rates. Note that, at 'low' discount rates project G is better, and at 'high' discount rates project F is better (at a discount rate of 25% both projects are equally profitable). This is not surprising. Project G delivers the high cash flows relatively late, and late cash flows are more valuable when the discount rate is low. (Note that at a discount rate of 0%, we'd be willing to pay the same for a cash flow today as for the same cash flow five years down the road. At a discount rate of 100%, however, the value we place on 'late' cash flows is far lower.)

This example shows that projects that deliver large cash flows relatively early in the project's life are more valuable when discount rates are high, and projects that deliver large cash flows relatively late in the project's life are more valuable when discount rates are low. However, *given* the discount rate, the NPV approach properly selects the right project. In our case, at a 12% discount rate, the company should select project G.

EXHIBIT 21.3
More problems of the IRR

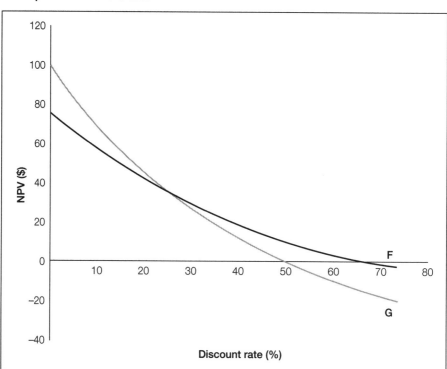

Time-varying discount rates

Finally, let's consider what happens if the appropriate discount rate for the project is expected to change substantially over time. This may happen when substantial changes are expected in either interest rates, or the company's capital structure (or some other variable that affects the risk of the company) over the project's life.

So, we have computed our IRR and now we need to compare it with a discount rate. But which one? The one expected for next year? The one for the year after? An average of the expected rates over the project's life? It's not at all clear. In other words, when discount rates change over time, the IRR approach loses its intuitive appeal.

The NPV approach, however, can still be applied, though not without an additional cost. Now we can no longer raise those $(1 + DR)$s to the power of 2, $3 \ldots T$, as the periods go by. If discount rates change over time, the discount factor for any period becomes the *product* of 1 plus the discount rate in each period, as equation (21.4) shows:

$$NPV = CF_0 + \frac{CF_1}{(1 + DR_1)} + \frac{CF_2}{(1 + DR_1) \cdot (1 + DR_2)} + \ldots + \frac{CF_T}{(1 + DR_1) \cdot \ldots \cdot (1 + DR_T)}$$

$$(21.4)$$

This expression is quite a bit more difficult to handle than equation (21.2). That's why, usually, companies do not use time-varying discount rates unless they expect a substantial change in this variable over the project's life. Having said that, spreadsheets have made the implementation of expressions like (21.4) a lot easier deal with.

The big picture

The preceding discussion about the problems of the IRR is not meant to put down this approach, which, truth to tell, many practitioners find valuable and use often. Note that it's the only alternative to the NPV approach that we have discussed. And that is because it's the only one that has some theoretical support *and* is widely used in practice. (But see also the real options approach discussed in the next chapter.)

But the IRR approach does have some problems and limitations, and practitioners must be aware of them. They also must be aware of its advantages, and one of them is *not* that this approach summarizes the project in a single number, which follows exclusively from the project's cash flows, and that is independent from market-determined discount rates. True, to calculate the IRR we don't need a market-determined parameter. But *to make an investment decision*, we do need a discount rate to compare with the IRR.

The NPV approach is the theoretically correct method to evaluate investment projects, perhaps properly complemented by the real options approach (discussed in the next chapter). The IRR may be a valuable tool, but like any other tool, handle it with care.

Excel section

Calculating NPVs and IRRs is very simple in Excel, though you must be aware of a few little quirks. Suppose you have a series of ten cash flows of a given project in cells B1 through B10, the first being a current (positive or negative but certain) cash flow, and the rest being the project's (positive or negative) expected cash flows. Suppose, also, that the proper discount rate for the project is in cell A1. Then you can do the following:

■ To calculate the project's NPV, you type '**=B1+NPV(A1, B2:B10)**' and hit 'Enter.'

■ To calculate the project's IRR, you type '**=IRR(B1:B10)**' and hit 'Enter.'

In the calculation of net present values, note that what Excel calls NPV is really a *present value* (no 'net'). This is so because Excel assumes that the first cash flow comes one year (or period) down the road. Therefore, if you have a current upfront investment to make (or current cash flow to receive), *you must add it* to the NPV calculation. That's exactly what the 'B1' in the calculation of the NPV above represents.

In the calculation of internal rates of return, note that Excel uses an iterative process that starts with a guess. Excel actually gives you the opportunity to make this guess yourself, but you may as well wave your hands at this opportunity. If you just type what is suggested above, Excel will make the guess itself. Having said that, note that in cases with multiple IRRs, Excel returns *just one* IRR. If you want to find out the others, the best strategy is the following. First, plot the NPV for many discount rates (like in Exhibit 21.1); then, visually determine the approximate values of the other IRRs; and finally, get Excel to calculate them, in each case making a guess close to the numbers that result from your visual inspection. In each of these cases, you should type '**=IRR(B1:B10, Guess)**', where 'Guess' is a numerical value equal to the approximate IRR from your visual inspection, and then hit 'Enter.'

Challenge section

1 Consider the projects in Table 21.2. The company that needs to evaluate them uses a discount rate of 10% in all its projects.
   (a) Compute the NPV of all projects.
   (b) Compute the IRR of all projects.

TABLE 21.2

Period	A	B	C	D	E
0	−100	−100	−100	100	−10
1	30	100	75	−15	4
2	30	100	75	−15	4
3	30	100	75	−15	3
4	30	75	75	−15	3
5	30	−300	−250	−15	3

2 Should the company go ahead with project A? Why?

3 Should the company go ahead with project B? Why? Do the NPV and IRR approaches lead the company to the same decision? Why?

4 Should the company go ahead with project C? Why? Do the NPV and IRR approaches lead the company to the same decision? Why?

5 If the company had to choose between projects A and E, which one should it choose? Why? Do the NPV and IRR approaches lead the company to the same decision? Why?

6 Go back to project E and consider it in isolation. Also, instead of a constant discount rate of 10%, assume that the company will gradually increase its leverage and therefore its discount rate. In fact, the company expects that over the next five years its discount rate will be $DR_1 = 20\%$, $DR_2 = 25\%$, $DR_3 = 30\%$, $DR_4 = 35\%$, and $DR_5 = 40\%$. Should the company go ahead with this project? Why? Do the NPV and IRR approaches lead the company to the same decision? Why?

22

REAL OPTIONS

A caveat

What's wrong with NPV?

What is a real option?

Types of real options

Valuation of real options

Problems in the valuation of real options

Misuses of real options

The big picture

Excel section

Challenge section

In the previous chapter we discussed the two traditional tools most widely used in project evaluation: net present value (NPV) and the internal rate of return (IRR). As we'll discuss in this chapter, however, NPV typically undervalues projects because it does not account for the value of flexibility. The real options approach we discuss in this chapter does and therefore enables companies to make better investment decisions. But, as we also discuss, this useful tool can easily be misused.

A caveat

The incorporation of real options into the evaluation of investment opportunities is a relatively new development. As we discuss below, it is both plausible and necessary to consider the value of real options embedded in projects in order to make correct investment decisions. Unfortunately, the actual implementation of this tool is far from trivial.

Companies that incorporate real options into their investment decisions must wrestle with two issues. First, the basics, that is, understanding the concept of a real option, the different types of options embedded in projects, the role they play in project evaluation, and the possible misuses of this tool. Second, the valuation of these options. This is a very technical topic (more for PhDs than for MBAs, so to speak) which requires not only a good grasp of option pricing theory but also knowledge of the twists and turns necessary to adapt this theory to the valuation of real options. Given our goals, we'll focus on the first issue.

What's wrong with NPV?

Think about the way companies typically make investment decisions. Given the project considered, a company forecasts its cash flows, then discounts the expected cash flows at a rate that reflects the risk of the project (or, more typically, at the company's cost of capital), and finally subtracts the value of the initial investment. If this NPV is positive, the company goes ahead with the project; if it is negative, the project is rejected. As we discussed in the previous chapter, an obstacle to the implementation of this tool is the correct estimation of cash flows and the proper assessment of their risk. And yet, that is not the only reason why NPV is a less than perfect tool for project evaluation.

To see why, think of a company considering a project to extract copper from a mine in a developing country. The company can buy the exclusive rights to exploit the mine during the next ten years for $5 million; after that time the rights will expire. The local government will buy all the copper extracted at an agreed price, which will remain fixed during the full ten years. This price is in local currency and the main source of uncertainty for the company is the exchange rate.

The developing country is currently negotiating a stand-by loan with the International Monetary Fund (IMF). If the negotiations are successful, stable economic conditions and fast growth will imply a strong local currency, in which case the project will deliver $30 million a year. If the negotiations fail, uncertainty and sluggish growth will imply a weak local currency, and the project will deliver only $10 million a year. As of today, the chances of successful negotiations are 50/50. The project requires an initial fixed investment on equipment of $150 million and the company's hurdle rate is 10%. Should the company invest in this project?

Well, we know by now how to estimate NPVs. Given that high and low cash flows are equally likely, the *expected* annual cash flow is $20 million during ten years, as shown in the second column of Table 22.1 (where all numbers are in millions). Discounting those expected cash flows at 10% we get a present value of $122.9 million, and subtracting the initial investment of $150 million we get an NPV of –$27.1 million. Therefore, the company should not buy the rights to extract copper from the mine.

TABLE 22.1

Year	Expected ($m)	Low ($m)	High ($m)	Low ($m)	High ($m)
0	−150	−150	−150		
1	20	10	30	−150	−150
2	20	10	30	10	30
3	20	10	30	10	30
4	20	10	30	10	30
5	20	10	30	10	30
6	20	10	30	10	30
7	20	10	30	10	30
8	20	10	30	10	30
9	20	10	30	10	30
10	20	10	30	10	30
NPV-0	−$27.1	−$88.6	$34.3		$10.4
NPV-1				−$92.4	$22.8

But wait a minute. The third column of Table 22.1 shows that with annual cash flows of $10 million, the NPV of the project is –$88.6 million. With annual cash flows of $30 million, however, the fourth column shows that its NPV is $34.3 million. (The –$27.1 million NPV of the project is obviously the equally weighted average of these two numbers.) Therefore, if the company could wait and get a better idea of the exchange rate prevailing during the life of the contract, it could make a much better investment decision. That is, it would invest in the project if the exchange rate is high and would not invest if the exchange rate is low.

The thing is, the company *can* wait. Let's assume the company buys the right to exploit the mine but doesn't make any investment during the first year. At the end of the year, when the country's negotiations with the IMF conclude, the company will have a much better idea of the economic outlook and therefore of the expected exchange rate. In that case, if the exchange rate is expected to be low, the company will refrain from investing in the mine. Note that, as the fifth column of Table 22.1 shows, investing $150 million at the end of the first year to get cash flows of $10 million during nine years has an NPV of –$92.4 million.

If, however, the exchange rate is expected to be high, the last column of the table shows that investing $150 million at the end of the first year to get annual cash flows of $30 million during nine years has an NPV of $22.8 million. But of course the relevant issue is, what should the company do *today*? Should it buy the rights for $5 million?

Well, if the negotiations with the IMF fail, which happens with a probability of 50%, the company will pass from this project, neither making the initial investment in equipment nor receiving any cash flows. If the negotiations succeed, which happens with a probability of 50%, the company will invest in a project with an NPV of $22.8 million *at the end of the first year*. Then, the expected value of this project *today* is given by

$$(0.5) \cdot \left(\frac{\$22.8m}{1.10} \right) + (0.5)(\$0m) = \$10.4m$$

and, therefore, it is worth paying $5 million for the rights to extract copper from the mine.

So, what is wrong with NPV? Simply that it fails to account for the value of flexibility. Note that a static NPV calculation based on expected cash flows leads the company to reject the mining project. However, this calculation ignores the fact that the company can choose to wait for one year until the main source of uncertainty disappears, and then decide whether it's worth investing $150 million to extract copper (which it would do only if the exchange rate is high). In other words, once the company takes into account the flexibility given by the option to delay the investment decision, it turns a project with a negative NPV into one with a positive NPV.

Note that the company can acquire the *right* (not the obligation) to exploit the copper mine. That flexibility to choose *whether* to exploit the mine is valuable, and yet that value is ignored by a static NPV analysis. In other words, the NPV approach fails to account for the value of the right to take certain actions and, as a result, it usually *undervalues* investment projects.

What is a real option?

You may have gotten the idea by now, but let's take a short walk before we run and first define a few important option-related terms. Regardless of whether they are financial or real, options can be classified into calls and puts. A *call* option gives its owner the right to buy the underlying asset at a fixed price at (or up until) a given point in time. A *put* option, on the other hand, gives its owner the right to sell the underlying asset at a fixed price at (or up until) a given point in time. In both cases the option holder has the right, not the obligation, to buy (in the case of calls) or sell (in the case of puts) the underlying asset.

The price at which the option holder can buy (in the case of calls) or sell (in the case of puts) the underlying asset is called the *exercise* (or *strike*) *price*. The last day in which the option can be exercised is called the *expiration date*. Depending on when calls and puts can be exercised, both can be either *American* options, which can be exercised at any time up to the expiration date, or *European* options, which can be exercised only on the expiration date. Finally, the underlying asset can be either financial, such as shares of stock, or real, such as an investment project.

A **real option**, then, is the *right* to take an action on a *non-financial asset* at a *given cost* during a *given period of time*. Several parts of this definition are important. First, a real option (like all options) gives a right, not an obligation, which means that the option can be exercised or simply discarded. In the example we discussed, the company can choose whether to extract copper from the mine and when to do so.

Second, the underlying asset of a real option is not financial, and the right is not to buy or sell the asset. Rather, these are options in the sense of choice, meaning that the owner can choose to take an action such as delaying, abandoning, expanding, or scaling back a project, to name but a few possible choices. In the example we have discussed, the company has the option to delay (up to ten years) the extraction of copper from the mine.

Third, exercising real *call* options is usually costly in the sense that the company has to pay to take the action contemplated in the option. In the example we discussed, the company can exercise the option to extract copper from the mine by investing $150 million. When exercising a *put* option, on the other hand, the company usually gets a benefit. A company that abandons a project can sell the remaining assets, and one that scales back a project can reallocate resources to more productive activities.

Finally, the right to take an action is usually limited to a specific period of time. In the example we discussed, the company has the option to delay the extraction of copper for up to ten years, after which period the right expires.

Types of real options

There are many types of real options, basically differing in the type of choice they provide the owner with. An *option to delay* gives its owner the right to delay taking an action. Technically, this option is an American call with the value of the underlying asset being the present value of the project and the exercise price being the initial investment required to start the project. In the example we have discussed, the rights to exploit the copper mine give the company the choice to begin extraction at any point in time during the length of the contract. This is valuable because the company can wait until uncertainty about the exchange rate resolves and then decide whether to invest.

An *option to expand* gives its owner the right to expand the scale of a project. Technically, this option is an American call with the value of the underlying asset being the present value of the project and the exercise price being the investment required to expand the project. Note that a project may be unattractive at a small scale but attractive at larger one, and yet the larger scale might make sense only under certain conditions. Setting up an institute for executive education may not be profitable at a small scale. However, a small-scale project may be valuable to test the demand for the institute's programs, and if this demand proves to be high, the institute could expand its scale and operate profitably. Alternatively, a pharmaceutical company can make a small investment in R&D for an AIDS vaccine. If the vaccine successfully clears the first tests, then the scale of the project can be enlarged for full-scale clinical trials.

An *option to abandon* gives its owner the right to abandon a project. Technically, this option is an American put with the underlying asset being the present value of the project and the exercise price being the liquidation value (if any). If the demand for executive education programs at the institute above proves to be disappointing, the institute could close and realize the liquidation value (such as, for example, selling the property where it operated). Alternatively, if the AIDS vaccine of the pharmaceutical company above fails any of the clinical trials, the operation could be shut down and its resources redeployed to other projects.

You can probably imagine many other types of real options, such as the option to scale back an operation, or to shut down and restart an operation. All of them are characterized by the fact that they provide the right but not the obligation to take an action; or, put differently, they provide *flexibility*. This flexibility is valuable and should be incorporated into the evaluation of projects, which is what the NPV approach fails to do. The devil, as usual, is in the detail.

Valuation of real options

Valuing financial options is no trivial matter, but valuing real options is even harder. Financial options are usually valued with the Black–Scholes model (discussed in Chapter 24), which is far from trivial. And yet, because the underlying asset (shares of stock) trades in a market and has observable prices, the inputs of this model are not hard to come by. What makes the valuation of real options particularly difficult is that these are options on a *non-traded* asset; therefore, the value and volatility of this asset are harder to determine.

Rather than attempting the daunting task of pricing a real option, we'll discuss the factors that affect its value and how they do so. The five factors we'll discuss are those necessary to price a financial option using the Black–Scholes model. These are the value of the underlying asset, the exercise price, the volatility in the value of the underlying asset, the time to expiration, and the risk-free rate.

In the case of financial options, the value of the underlying asset is the price of the stock on which the option is written. In the case of real options, the value of the underlying asset is given by the present value of a project's cash flows. The impact of this variable on the value of a real option depends on whether we are valuing a call or a put. In the case of a call, the higher the value of the asset, the higher the value of the real option; in the case of a put, the opposite is the case.

The exercise price also has a different impact on the value of a real option depending on whether we are valuing a call or a put. In the case of a call, the exercise price is the cost of the investment required to start or expand a project and is inversely related to the value of the real option. In the case of a put, the exercise price is the liquidation value of the project and is directly related to the value of the real option.

The value of a real (call and put) option is directly related to the volatility in the value of the underlying asset. It may sound strange that an increase in volatility makes an asset more (rather than less) valuable. However, note that the buyer of an option can never lose more than the price he paid for it. Therefore, given a limited downside, a higher volatility implies a higher probability that the value of the underlying asset will move in the direction favorable to the option holder.

The time to expiration is the period of time during which the owner of a real option can take an action on a project. The value of a real (call and put) option is directly related to the time to expiration. This is, again, because the loss of an option holder is limited to the price he paid for it. Therefore, given a limited downside, the longer the time to expiration, the more time the underlying asset has to move in the direction favorable to the option holder.

Finally, the risk-free rate mainly affects the present value of the exercise price and has a different impact on the value of real call and put options. In the case of a call, the higher the risk-free rate, the lower the present value of the exercise price, and the higher the value of the real option. In the case of a put, the opposite is the case.

Problems in the valuation of real options

As mentioned above, although valuing a financial option is not trivial, valuing a real option is even less so. To start with, the approach most widely followed to value a financial option, the Black–Scholes model, is far from appropriate to value real options. This model requires, for example, continuous (trading and) prices for the underlying asset. This requirement, largely fulfilled in the case of shares of stock, is hardly fulfilled in the case of investment projects.

Second, although the value of a financial option rests on a certain value for the underlying asset, the market price of a stock, the value of a real option rests on a value which is much more difficult to assess, the value of an investment project. This value, in fact, is not only more difficult to assess but also much more subjective. After all, different individuals evaluating the same investment opportunity can come up with very different assessments on the project's potential and the convenience to invest in it.

Third, although it is trivial to estimate the volatility in the returns of a stock, there is nothing trivial about estimating the volatility in the value of a project.

Because this value is not observed periodically and a history of its past values cannot be collected, calculating its volatility usually involves a rather wild guess. Often, the best course of action is to try to reduce the sources of uncertainty in the value of a project to one *tradable* factor, and then infer from the volatility of this factor the volatility in the value of the project. Needless to say, this requires a good mix of art, science, and sorcery.

Another possibility in order to assess the volatility in the value of a project is to outline some relevant scenarios, to assign a probability to each, and to estimate the expected cash flows in each. The standard deviation in the project's cash flow can then be estimated from these magnitudes. Again, this requires a good mix of art, science, and sorcery.

Fourth, although in the example we discussed above the company had a clear time frame to exercise its option (ten years), this is not always the case. Legal rights may have a very clear expiration date but not all the relevant rights are legal. A company assessing the value of an option to expand a project may find that it has no specific time limit in the right to do so. However, the entry of competitors, or the introduction of a new and better technology, may render this right worthless at *some* point in time in the future. This further complicates the valuation of a real option.

This short list is of course not exhaustive; there are many other complications that companies face when assessing the value of real options. But it should give an idea of why the task is far from trivial. The problem is the more uncertain the value of a real option, the more uncertain is the actual value of an investment opportunity. And it is for this reason, precisely, that real options can easily be misused.

Misuses of real options

The main danger of real options should be rather obvious at this point. Recall that a real option can only *add* to the NPV of a project. Recall, also, that the value of a real option is highly uncertain and may be subject to a wide variety of assessments. Then, as you have probably guessed, real options can be used by managers to justify investing in projects that a conventional NPV analysis would reject.

This is not necessarily wrong. The whole point of considering real options is to properly assess the value of investment projects. In many cases, these projects do come with valuable real options embedded, and in some cases the value of these options may turn a project with a negative NPV into one with a positive NPV. That was precisely the case in the example we discussed above, and (again) this is the whole point of considering real options.

But the potential for misuse is ample. This problem is particularly serious when the uncertainty about the value of the real option is high, and when the NPV of a project *without* incorporating the value of real options is close to 0. In the first case, a manager who wants to invest in a pet project will find it easier to justify the investment by adding to the project's negative NPV an arbitrarily high value of a real option. In the second case, even a low value of a real option may turn an unprofitable project into a profitable one. It is in these situations that real options may cease to be an asset and turn into a liability instead.

The big picture

The incorporation of real options into the evaluation of investment projects is a relatively new development. Many projects do come with options embedded and the rights they create to take future actions are valuable. The traditional and static NPV analysis ignores the value of this flexibility and, as a result, it typically undervalues investment opportunities.

However plausible the incorporation of real options into the evaluation of investment projects may be, the main problem lies in properly assessing the value of these options. Standard models for the valuation of financial options need to be twisted and turned in order to value real options. This usually creates high uncertainty about their actual value, which in turn lends itself to the potential misuse of this very useful tool. Real options, like most tools, must be handled with care.

Excel section

There is no new Excel material in this chapter.

Challenge section

1 Consider the same mining project we discussed above but with different numbers. Assume that the project will deliver $20 million a year if the exchange rate is low and $40 million a year if the exchange rate is high, in both cases during the ten years. Also assume that the initial investment required to start up the project is $200 million. Finally, keep the probability of successful and failed negotiations with the IMF at 50/50 and the price of the rights to extract copper from the mine at $5 million.

    (a) Calculate the project's NPV based on its *expected* cash flows. Should the company buy the rights for it?

    (b) Calculate the project's NPV based on its cash flows if the exchange rate is expected to be low. Should the company buy the rights for it?

    (c) Calculate the project's NPV based on its cash flows if the exchange rate is expected to be high. Should the company buy the rights for it?

2 Assume now that the company can delay for one year its decision on the project. In this case, the initial investment remains the same but the project will deliver cash flows for only nine years.

    (a) Calculate the project's NPV at the end of the first year based on its cash flows if the exchange rate is expected to be low.

    (b) Calculate the project's NPV at the end of the first year based on its cash flows if the exchange rate is expected to be high.

    (c) Should the company buy *today* the rights for the mining project? Why?

    (d) What is the value of the real option to delay embedded in this project?

23

CORPORATE VALUE CREATION

What should be the goal of management?

Accounting profits and economic profits

Residual income

Some evidence

EVA and MVA

Other measures of value creation

The big picture

Excel section

Challenge section

t is critical for corporations and shareholders to evaluate whether managers are creating or destroying value. And it is also important for managers because their compensation is usually tied to their performance. The problem is, there isn't an undisputed way to define value creation. In this chapter we discuss some definitions of this concept, paying special attention to residual income and its most well-known variation, EVA.

What should be the goal of management?

On the face of it, this is a very simple question. We could probably say that the goal of managers should be to make as much money as possible for the shareholders of the company. We'll paraphrase and define more precisely this goal below, but some would beg to disagree. They would claim that focusing *only* on shareholders is a very limited scope.

Managers, they would argue, should take into account the interest of *all* their constituencies, such as shareholders, employees, suppliers, and the local community, among others. This alternative point of view is often referred to as the stakeholder theory. In this view, managers are not supposed to focus narrowly only on the wellbeing of the company's shareholders but broadly on the wellbeing of all the company's stakeholders.

However interesting and important this debate may be, it is not the purpose of this chapter to address it. Rather, we'll focus on the goal of maximizing shareholder value and discuss different ways of defining this concept for two reasons. First, although there are several widely used tools to assess whether managers create shareholder value, there is no widely accepted way to assess (much less to quantify) whether they are creating stakeholder value. Second (and perhaps more arguably), it is difficult to see how managers can create shareholder value without taking care of the company's stakeholders. In other words, in the long term, a manager who creates shareholder value must be creating stakeholder value.

We'll take as given, then, that the goal of managers is to maximize shareholder value. And although this concept doesn't have an undisputed definition, we can safely agree that a manager who invests in projects with positive NPV creates value for shareholders. If, in addition, markets price securities properly, investing in projects with positive NPV should have a positive impact on the company's stock price. This is essentially the reason why value creation is usually associated with increases in a company's stock price.

Accounting profits and economic profits

Consider a company with $100 million in invested capital, $50 million in debt and $50 million in equity. Its cost of debt is 8%, its cost of equity 12%, and the corporate tax rate 35%. Its earnings before interest and taxes (EBIT) are $10 million. Is this company profitable?

Accountants define profit in a variety of ways. One measure of accounting profit is a company's *net income*, which in the case of our company is

	$m
EBIT	10.0
– Interest	4.0
Pretax income	6.0
– Taxes	2.1
Net income	**3.9**

From an accounting point of view, then, this company is profitable. But does it make enough profits to appropriately compensate its shareholders? Well, shareholders require a 12% return on $50 million of invested equity, so the company should make at least $6 million (= $0.12 \cdot \$50m$) in order to satisfy shareholders' demand for return. Therefore, being $2.1 million short of that target, the company is not profitable from an *economic* point of view.

Another accounting measure of profitability is a company's *net operating profit after taxes* (NOPAT), which in the case of our company is

	$m
EBIT	10.0
– Interest	4.0
Pretax income	6.0
– Taxes	2.1
Net income	3.9
+ After-tax interest	2.6
NOPAT	**6.5**

This NOPAT, which can also be calculated as EBIT after taxes ($\$10m \cdot 0.65 =$ $6.5m), can be thought of as the (accounting) profit the company would have made if it had no debt. Or, alternatively, as the (accounting) profit of the company independent from the composition of its capital. In other words,

NOPAT highlights the profitability of the capital invested regardless of who provided the capital. (It's easy to show that different capital structures would affect the company's net income but would leave NOPAT unaffected. Try!)

With a NOPAT of $6.5 million, the company is profitable from an accounting point of view. But does it make enough profits to appropriately compensate its capital providers? Not really. Given a cost of capital of 8.6% (= $0.65 \cdot 0.5 \cdot 0.08 + 0.5 \cdot 0.12$) and the $100 million in invested capital, the company should make at least $8.6 million. Therefore, being $2.1 million short of this target, the company is not profitable from an *economic* point of view.

Importantly, note that in both cases the company is $2.1 million short of appropriately compensating shareholders in the first case and capital providers in the second case. This is no coincidence. Note that debt holders receive interest payments based on their required return on debt, that is, debt holders are appropriately compensated for lending capital to the company. The $2.1 million shortage, then, affects only the company's shareholders.

This should not be entirely surprising. Debt holders have a fixed claim on the cash flows of the company, and this claim is satisfied by the interest payments of $4 million. Therefore, any shortage of cash after interest payments to debt holders and tax payments to the government is suffered by the residual claimants, that is, by the company's shareholders. (Conversely, if the company makes accounting profits larger than its cost of capital, the extra profits flow into the pockets of shareholders.)

In short, then, regardless of whether we look at our company exclusively from the point of view of shareholders, or that of all capital providers, we can safely say that the company is profitable from an accounting point of view but unprofitable from an economic point of view. Or, put differently, *this company did not create shareholder value*.

Residual income

The reason why net income cannot be considered a good measure of corporate performance should be clear by now. A positive net income may or may not compensate shareholders appropriately for investing their capital in the company. This is precisely where the measure of residual income comes in. Let's start by defining it.

Residual income (RI), sometimes called *economic profit*, can be defined as

$$RI = \text{Net income} - \text{Equity} \times \text{COE} \qquad (23.1)$$

where COE denotes the cost of equity; or, equivalently, as

$$RI = \text{NOPAT} - \text{Capital} \times \text{COC} \qquad (23.2)$$

where COC denotes the cost of capital, and capital is the sum of debt and equity both at book value. (More generally, a company's capital can be defined as the sum of all its sources of financing, thus including preferred stock, convertible debt, and other sources of capital.) The second term of the right-hand side of equation (23.1), Equity × COE, is usually called the *equity charge*; and the second term of the right-hand side of equation (23.2), Capital × COC, is usually called the *capital charge*.

Finally, if we define return on capital (ROC) as the ratio of NOPAT to capital (that is, ROC = NOPAT/Capital), then we can also define residual income as

$$RI = \text{Capital} \times (\text{ROC} - \text{COC}) \qquad (23.3)$$

Let's think a bit about the meaning of residual income. According to equation (23.1), residual income is what's left for shareholders *after* they have been appropriately compensated for providing the company with equity capital. Similarly, according to equation (23.2), residual income is what's left for shareholders *after* all capital providers have been appropriately compensated for providing the company with debt and equity. Note that, in both cases, we are defining an *economic* profit in the sense that we label a company profitable or unprofitable only if it generates accounting profits *in excess of* those required by the capital providers.

Here's another way of looking at this. Note that equation (23.1) subtracts from the company's net income the equity charge. Essentially, then, the company is being 'charged' for using equity at the return required by shareholders to 'lend' money to the company. Similarly, equation (23.2) subtracts from the company's

NOPAT the capital charge, indicating that the company is being 'charged' for using capital (debt and equity) at the average return required by the capital providers. Only after generating enough accounting profits to cover these charges a company is profitable from an economic point of view.

Equation (23.3) expresses the same idea in a different way. It says that residual income is created when the return on invested capital is larger than the cost of that capital. In other words, if the company manages to invest its capital in activities that generate a return higher than the cost of obtaining the capital, then it will create economic profits. Makes sense, doesn't it?

Well, if it does, then we can go one step further and say that

- **If RI > 0** ⇒ **The company *creates* shareholder value**
- **If RI < 0** ⇒ **The company *destroys* shareholder value**

Going back to our company in the previous section, note that its ROC is 6.5% (= $6.5m/$100m). Then, its residual income is given by

$$
\begin{aligned}
\text{RI} \quad &= \quad \$3.9m - \$50m \times 12.0\% \\
&= \quad \$6.5m - \$100m \times 8.6\% \\
&= \quad \$100m \times (6.5\% - 8.6\%) \\
&= \quad \textbf{-\$2.1m}
\end{aligned}
$$

As we discussed before, $2.1 million is how much the company is short from appropriately compensating its capital providers in general and its shareholders in particular. We can then safely say that, under this definition, this company *destroyed* shareholder value.

In short then, residual income measures the creation or destruction of value by subtracting from a company's accounting profits the profits required by the providers of capital. Therefore, a company creates value only when it makes accounting profits *in excess of* those required to compensate the capital providers, or, similarly, when it invests capital in activities whose return is larger than the cost of the capital invested.

Some evidence

It should be clear from the previous section that calculating residual income is fairly simple, consisting of magnitudes easy to either obtain or estimate. Using equation (23.3), Table 23.1 calculates the residual income of nine US industries and the market as a whole at the end of 2003. (These figures are based on information publicly available from Professor Aswath Damodaran's web page.) The second column displays returns on capital; the third costs of capital; the fourth the book value of the capital invested; and the last column the residual income.

TABLE 23.1

Industry	ROC (%)	COC (%)	Capital ($bn)	RI ($bn)
Banking	18.7	6.0	763.8	97.4
Biotechnology	6.6	10.6	26.9	−1.1
Hotel and gaming	10.8	7.2	86.4	3.1
Internet	1.2	18.6	4.9	−0.8
Securities brokerage	16.3	7.0	268.1	24.9
Semiconductors	16.5	17.7	104.5	−1.2
Telecom services	19.0	9.4	445.8	42.7
Tobacco	33.2	7.0	68.0	17.8
Wireless networking	5.2	12.9	14.9	−1.1
Market	11.9	7.8	10,821.9	437.6

The table shows that four industries (biotechnology, internet, semiconductors, and wireless networking) have a return on capital lower than their respective cost of capital, and, therefore, a negative residual income. Under this definition, then, we would say that these industries destroyed value during 2003. The other five industries, and the market as a whole, however, delivered positive residual income and, therefore, created value for their shareholders.

Note that value creation in this framework is a function of both the spread between the return on capital and the cost of capital and the capital invested. In other words, a large residual income may follow from little capital invested at a high spread, or from a lot of capital invested at a low spread. The tobacco industry, for example, has less capital invested than hotel and gaming but its spread is much higher and, therefore, its residual income is higher.

EVA and MVA

The concept of residual income is far from new. In fact, General Motors implemented a similar measure to evaluate its performance in the early 1920s.

However, the renewed interest in residual income follows from Stern Stewart Co.'s introduction of a variation of this concept in the early 1980s. Stern Stewart's trademarked variation of residual income is called **economic value added (EVA)** and is defined as

$$EVA = NOPAT^* - Capital^* \times COC \qquad (23.4)$$

where NOPAT* and Capital* denote *adjusted* NOPAT and *adjusted* capital, respectively. Just as was the case with residual income, in this framework a company is said to create value when its EVA is positive, and to destroy it when the opposite is the case.

What are the differences between residual income and EVA? At the end of the day, not very many. In fact, EVA is just a variation of residual income. Having said that, Stern Stewart emphasizes that in order to properly turn accounting profits into economic profits both the NOPAT and the capital need to go through several adjustments.

Which ones? Unfortunately, although Stern Stewart has identified over 100 possible adjustments, only a few of them are publicly known. This is, precisely, one of the trade secrets of the creators of EVA. A well-known adjustment, however, is the proper treatment of R&D. From an accounting point of view, R&D is an expense. From an economic point of view, R&D should be treated as a capital investment. This implies, first, that R&D is capitalized and amortized rather than expensed; and, second, that the accounting charge for R&D is added back to earnings for the calculation of the adjusted NOPAT.

Intimately associated with EVA is the concept of **market value added (MVA)**, which can be defined as

$$MVA = Market\ value\ of\ capital - Book\ value\ of\ capital \qquad (23.5)$$

Essentially, MVA is the difference between what capital providers have put into the company (and given up in the form of retained earnings) and what they can get from the company by selling their claims. Obviously, then, the larger this magnitude the better the *cumulative* performance of the company.

EVA can be thought of as a tool that serves the ultimate goal of maximizing a company's MVA. Formally, the link between these two magnitudes is given by the fact that MVA is the present value of expected EVAs (discounted at the company's cost of capital). Although this obviously implies a direct relationship between EVA and MVA, its creators emphasize that the *change* in EVA is more important than its actual level. This makes sense. Note that if a company is expected to generate a positive EVA but lower than in the past, then its MVA should be negatively affected. Similarly, if a company is expected to generate a negative EVA but less negative than in the past, its MVA should be positively affected.

Stern Stewart has made EVA the centerpiece of an integrated framework of performance evaluation and incentive compensation. It proposes to use EVA to measure value creation, take managerial decisions, motivate managers through compensation schemes, and (perhaps stretching the concept) changing the mindset of the whole corporation. It also publishes a well-known annual ranking of corporate value creators and destroyers in which companies are ranked on the basis of their MVAs.

Other measures of value creation

Many consulting companies offer different trademarked measures designed to assess corporate value creation and set executive compensation. These, plus some other non-commercial measures, form a crowded field of possible options for companies to choose from. We very briefly review three of them here.

Cash flow return on investment (CFROI), originally developed by Holt Associates (CSFB Holt since January 2002), is the internal rate of return of inflation-adjusted cash flows. In order to evaluate corporate performance, CFROI is compared with a company's *inflation-adjusted* (or real) cost of capital. If the former is larger than the latter, the company has created shareholder value; if the opposite is the case, the company has destroyed shareholder value.

Cash value added (CVA) is similar to EVA and also a measure of economic profits. It adjusts NOPAT by depreciation (adding back depreciation and subtracting *economic* depreciation) and then subtracts a capital charge. (The economic depreciation represents an annual amount invested in a sinking fund, earning the cost of capital and set aside to replace plant and equipment. Capital is measured as the full cash invested in the business.) In this framework, a positive CVA indicates that the company has created shareholder value; if the opposite is the case, the company has destroyed shareholder value.

Total shareholder return (TSR) is simply the sum of a stock's capital gain and dividend yield in any given period, just as the simple return we calculated in

Chapter 1. This return must then be compared with the stock's required return, calculated from a pricing model such as the CAPM (described in Chapter 7). If the total return is larger than the required return, then the company has created shareholder value; if the opposite is the case, the company has destroyed shareholder value.

These three measures far from exhaust the available possibilities. TBR (total business return), SVA (shareholder value added), and RAROC (risk-adjusted return on capital) are just three more among many other performance measures that companies can choose from.

The big picture

Managers create shareholder value when they invest in projects with positive NPV. No part of our discussion in this chapter contradicts this elementary statement. Our discussion focused on different ways of defining shareholder value. And although there is no undisputed way to define this concept, once a company decides to assess performance according to one particular measure, then executive compensation can be tied to that measure of performance.

The concept of residual income attempts to measure economic (as opposed to accounting) profits. This means that a company is profitable from an economic point of view only when accounting profits exceed the compensation required by capital providers. Or, put differently, a company creates shareholder value when its residual income is positive.

Several other measures of shareholder value exist. EVA, the best known and most widely used, is a modification of residual income that adjusts accounting profits and capital in order to better capture economic profitability. Other well-known measures of performance include CFROI, CVA, SVA, and RAROC.

Competition and shareholder activism are increasing around the world and there is increasing pressure on managers to create shareholder value. The challenge is not so much *what to do* to create this value (investing in projects with positive NPV would do); the real challenge is to implement a system *that gives managers the incentive* to make the right decisions and therefore create shareholder value.

Excel section

There is no new Excel material in this chapter.

Challenge section

1 Consider the return on capital (ROC), cost of capital (COC), and book value of capital for the year 2003 of the five industries displayed in Table 23.2. Calculate the NOPAT of each industry implied by the ROCs and capital levels in the table.

TABLE 23.2

Industry	ROC (%)	COC (%)	Capital ($bn)	NOPAT ($bn)	RI ($bn)
Cable TV	6.7	10.3	189.0		
Drugs	28.6	10.2	174.1		
Insurance (life)	51.3	8.4	126.7		
Insurance (property)	0.3	8.4	115.6		
Telecom equipment	4.6	14.2	39.8		

2 Calculate the residual income (RI) of each industry using equation (23.2) in the text.

3 Recalculate the residual income (RI) of each industry using equation (23.3) in the text. Are the RIs calculated the same (industry by industry) as those calculated in the previous question. Why?

4 Which industries created value during 2003? Which industries destroyed value during that year?

24

OPTIONS

The basics

Option valuation at expiration

Option valuation before expiration

The Black–Scholes model

Put–call parity

Why options?

The big picture

Excel section

Challenge section

The world of investing is certainly not limited to debt and equity. There are many other financial instruments investors can choose from, depending on their goals. One of them is options, which are both very useful and widely popular. In this chapter we'll discuss the basics of this financial instrument, including pricing and how they can be used to increase returns or limit losses.

The basics

We have already discussed real options, so in this chapter we'll focus on *financial* options. As the name suggests, in this case the underlying asset is not a project but a financial asset, such as shares of stock, stock indices, or currencies. We have also discussed the valuation of real options, which is based on well-established techniques for the valuation of financial options, such as the Black–Scholes model we discuss below.

We'll keep the discussion as general as possible. For that reason, we'll pass over issues that depend on the specific markets in which the options trade, such as possible expiration dates and exercise prices. Having said that, for ease of exposition we'll focus on options written on shares of stock with occasional references to other underlying assets. In any case, most of the issues we address are general and apply to all types of options.

Financial options can be classified into calls and puts. A *call option* gives its owner the right to buy the underlying asset at a fixed price at (or up until) a given point in time. A *put option*, on the other hand, gives its owner the right to sell the underlying asset at a fixed price at (or up until) a given point in time. In both cases the option holder has the right, not the obligation, to buy (in the case of calls) or sell (in the case of puts) the underlying asset.

The price at which the option holder can buy or sell the underlying asset is called the *exercise* (or *strike*) *price*. The last day on which the option can be exercised is called the *expiration date*. Depending on when calls and puts can be exercised, both can be either *American* options, which can be exercised anytime up to the expiration date, or *European* options, which can be exercised only on the expiration date.

At any time before expiration, a call option is *in the money* when the stock price is higher than the exercise price, and *out of the money* when the opposite is the case. A put option, on the other hand, is in the money when the stock price is lower than the exercise price and out of the money when the opposite is the case. Both calls and puts are *at the money* when the stock price and the exercise price coincide.

The price of an option is expressed on a per-share basis and is called the option *premium*. Because an option gives the right to buy or sell 100 shares of stock, a premium of $5 indicates that an investor must pay $500 to buy the option. Note that the premium is paid by the buyer and received by the seller, who is *not* the company behind the stock. Options are issued *by investors* not by companies.

Finally, note that although the option buyer has the right, not the obligation, to buy or sell the underlying asset, the seller does have the obligation, not the right, to buy or sell the asset. In other words, the buyer pays to acquire a right, and the seller is paid for committing to take an action (buying or selling the underlying asset) at some point in time in the future.

Option valuation at expiration

Let's consider a call option and a put option on shares of stock. Let's denote the current price of the stock with S, the exercise price of both options with X, the call premium with C, and the put premium with P. And let's assume that $X = 50. How valuable are these call and put options *on* the expiration date?

Well, that's not hard to figure out. The call option gives us the right to buy the stock at $50 a share so it will be valuable only if the stock trades for more than $50. If, on the expiration date, the stock is trading at $60 a share, we could exercise our right to buy shares at $50, sell them right away at $60, and pocket a profit of $10 a share (before transaction costs). Then, on the expiration date this call has a value of $1,000 (= $10 × 100 shares).

If, on the other hand, the stock is trading at $35 on the expiration date, then we would simply let the call expire without exercising it. No point exercising an option to buy shares at $50 when we can buy those same shares in the market at $35. Therefore, in this situation our call is worthless.

What about the put option? Equally simple. In this case we have the right to sell the stock at $50 a share, which will be valuable only if the stock trades for less than $50. If on the expiration date the stock is trading at $35 a share, we could buy shares in the market at that price and exercise right away our right to sell them at $50, for a profit of $15 a share (again, before transaction costs). Then, on the expiration date this put has a value of $1,500 (= $15 × 100 shares).

If, on the other hand, the stock is trading at $60, then we would simply let the put expire without exercising it. No point exercising an option to sell shares at $50 when we can sell those same shares in the market at $60. Therefore, in this case our put is worthless.

Just to formalize this a bit, we can say that on the expiration date a call option is worth the greater of $S - X$ and 0, and a put option is worth the greater of $X - S$ and 0. Expressed even more formally, on the expiration date,

$$C = \text{Max} (S - X, 0) \qquad (24.1)$$

and

$$P = \text{Max} (X - S, 0) \qquad (24.2)$$

It is obvious, then, that if we expect a company's stock price to rise we would buy a call (or sell a put), and if we expect its stock price to fall we would buy a put (or sell a call).

Option valuation before expiration

Calculating the value of an option on the expiration date is rather trivial, as we've just seen. The interesting (and far more complicated) issue, however, is to determine the value of an option anytime *before* the expiration date. Let's start with the variables that influence this value, which are five: the value of the underlying asset, the exercise price, the volatility in the value of the underlying asset, the time to expiration, and the risk-free rate.

We have already discussed the impact of the value of the underlying asset (the stock's price) and the exercise price on the value of calls and puts on the expiration date. And we know that the larger the difference between S and X, the more valuable will be the call on this date. For this reason, the higher S or the lower X at any time before expiration, the more likely that $S > X$ on the expiration date, and, therefore, the higher the value of the call.

It should be obvious that for a put the opposite is the case. Because on the expiration date a put is valuable only when $X > S$, then the higher X and the lower S anytime before expiration, the more likely that $X > S$ on the expiration date, and, therefore, the higher the value of the put.

The value of both calls and puts is directly related to the volatility in the value of the underlying asset (the stock). Although this may sound strange, note that the buyer of an option can never lose more than the premium he paid for it. This implies that the owner of a call has an unlimited upside (the higher $S - X$, the higher the value of the call) but a limited downside. Conversely, although the buyer of a put does not have an unlimited upside (on the expiration date he can never make more than X, which he would only when $S = 0$), he does benefit from large movements of S below X but still can't lose more that the option premium when S increases with respect to X. The combination of a substantial upside and a limited downside, then, makes volatility valuable for the owner of calls and puts.

The value of both calls and puts is also directly related to the time to expiration. This is the case, again, because the loss suffered by an option holder is limited to the price he paid for it. Therefore, given a limited downside, the longer the time to expiration, the more time the stock price has to move in the direction favorable to the option holder.

Finally, the risk-free rate mainly affects the present value of the exercise price and has a different impact on the value of calls and puts. Note that the option buyer pays the exercise price (if he exercises at all) on the expiration date, and that before expiration the present value of the exercise price decreases as the risk-free rate increases. (More intuitively, the ability to defer a payment is more valuable as the risk-free rate increases.) Therefore, the higher the risk-free rate, the higher the value of a call.

In the case of a put, the opposite is the case. The owner of a put will not receive the exercise price (if he exercises at all) until the expiration date, and the present value of the exercise price decreases as the risk-free rate increases. (Again more intuitively, having to wait for a payment is more costly as the risk-free rate increases.) Therefore, the higher the interest rate, the lower the value of a put.

Table 24.1 summarizes the impact of these five variables on the value of both calls and puts before expiration. Dividends also affect the value of options and we briefly refer to them later.

TABLE 24.1

Increase in . . .	Impact on C	Impact on P
Value of the underlying asset	Increases	Decreases
Exercise price	Decreases	Increases
Volatility in the value of underlying asset	Increases	Increases
Time to expiration	Increases	Increases
Risk-free rate	Increases	Decreases

It is important to note that between any point in time and the expiration date, the only variable that will not change for sure is the exercise price. For this reason, the fourth row of the table should be interpreted as saying that if we compare two calls (on the same stock) with different exercise prices, the one with the lower exercise price will be the more valuable. Conversely, if we compare two puts (on the same stock) with different exercise prices, the one with the higher exercise price will be the more valuable.

The Black–Scholes model

There is a good chance that, if you were unfamiliar with options, at this point you may be thinking that this stuff is not so hard after all. It's not too difficult to understand what an option is and how the relevant variables affect its value. Unfortunately, the fun ends (though some would say it actually begins!) when we try to figure out the option's value – not on the expiration date, and not whether it increases or decreases given a change in some variable, but a precise dollar value any time before the expiration date.

The most widely used framework to value options is the Black–Scholes model. This model, which comes down to a horrifying formula we'll discuss shortly, is based on several assumptions that are not relevant for our purposes except for two: that the option can be exercised only *on* the expiration date (hence, it values *European* options) and that the underlying stock pays no dividends. (Valuing options on dividend-paying stocks requires only a slight dividend yield adjustment to the expressions below.)

Without any further introduction, then, the value of a *call* option according to the **Black–Scholes model** is given by

$$C = S \cdot N(d_1) - X \cdot e^{-T \cdot R_f} \cdot N(d_2) \tag{24.3}$$

$$d_1 = \frac{\ln(S/X) + [R_f + (1/2) \cdot \sigma^2] \cdot T}{\sigma \cdot \sqrt{T}} \tag{24.4}$$

$$d_2 = d_1 - \sigma \cdot \sqrt{T} \tag{24.5}$$

where C denotes the value of the call, S the price of the underlying stock, X the exercise price, T the time to expiration (in years), R_f the (continuously compounded) annual risk-free rate, σ the annualized standard deviation of (continuously compounded) returns of the underlying stock, and $e = 2.71828$. The magnitudes $N(d_1)$ and $N(d_2)$ denote the probability that a variable following the standard normal distribution takes a value lower than or equal to d_1 and d_2, respectively. Still think that this stuff is not so hard?

A couple of points before using this model to value an option. First, don't try to make a lot of sense out of these three expressions; they're not really intuitive. (The model behind them is, but we'll wave our hands on that discussion.) Second, note that the value of a call option depends on the same five magnitudes we discussed before, that is, the stock price, the exercise price, the volatility in the stock price, the time to expiration, and the risk-free rate. And third, note that, however complicated the model may seem, it's not very demanding in terms of the inputs it requires.

Hands on now! Let's consider a call option with an exercise price of $30 and six months (half a year) away from expiration. The call is written on a stock that is currently trading at $35 a share and has a historical annual volatility (standard deviation) of 25%. The annual risk-free rate is 4%. How much should we pay for this call?

Again, do not look for much intuition behind this process. Better to start throwing numbers into the expressions above and see what we get. First step, then, let's calculate d_1 and d_2, which, using equations (24.4) and (24.5) are equal to

$$d_1 = \frac{\ln(\$35/\$30) + [0.04 + (1/2) \cdot (0.25)^2] \cdot 0.5}{0.25 \cdot \sqrt{0.5}} = 1.0735$$

$$d_2 = d_1 - \sigma \cdot \sqrt{t} = 1.0735 - 0.25 \cdot \sqrt{0.5} = 0.8968$$

What is the area under the standard normal distribution *below* these numbers? Using either a table of cutoff points (such as that at the end of Chapter 28) or the 'normsdist' command in Excel we find that $N(1.0735) = 0.8585$ and $N(0.8968) = 0.8151$. Finally, substituting these values into (24.3) we get

$$C = \$35 \cdot 0.8585 - \$30 \cdot e^{-(0.5 \cdot 0.04)} \cdot 0.8151 = \$6.1$$

In other words, then, a call option with an exercise price of $30, six months away from maturity, written on a stock with a historical annual volatility of 25% and currently trading at $35, when interest rates are at 4%, is worth $6.1. Note that this premium is higher than the difference between the current stock price and the exercise price ($5 = $35 − $30), indicating that investors find value in the upside potential of the stock.

Put–call parity

Are you wondering whether valuing a put is even more difficult than valuing a call? Fear not! In a way, valuing a put is less difficult, *if* the put is on a stock which also has a call with the same exercise price and time to maturity, *and* we have already valued the call. Under these conditions, the put and the call must be priced in such a way as to avoid arbitrage opportunities.

More precisely, given a call and a put with the same exercise price, the same time to maturity, and written on the same stock, arbitrage opportunities do not exist only if the call and the put meet the condition

$$C - P = S - X \cdot e^{-T \cdot R_j} \tag{24.6}$$

This relationship, called **put–call parity**, is one of the most important in option pricing. If it doesn't hold, arbitrage opportunities are available and implementing a trading strategy to exploit them is relatively simple. (If the right-hand side is larger than the left-hand side, we would buy the stock and the put and sell the call; if the opposite is the case, we would short-sell the stock, sell the put, and buy the call.)

In equilibrium, then, put–call parity must hold and the value of a put is obtained simply by rearranging terms in (24.6), that is,

$$P = C - S + X \cdot e^{-T \cdot R_j} \tag{24.7}$$

Returning to our example above, the value of a put with an exercise price of $30 and six months away from expiration (written on the same stock with an annual volatility of 25% and currently trading at $35, and with interest rates at 4%) would be equal to

$$P = \$6.1 - \$35 + \$30 \cdot e^{-(0.5 \cdot 0.04)} = \$0.5$$

Note, then, that investors seem to assign a very low probability to the stock price falling below $30 within the next six months. As a result, the right to sell the stock at $30 has very little value.

Having explored the pricing of both calls and puts, we can now confirm numerically the informal discussion above on valuation before expiration and the qualitative results in Table 24.1. Table 24.2 displays the value of the call and the put after changing, one at a time, the value of the five relevant parameters, each time beginning from the base case we discussed. The numbers in parentheses indicate the value of the parameters in this base case and their implied call and put premiums.

TABLE 24.2

| | S ($35) | | X ($30) | | σ (25%) | | T (0.50) | | R$_f$ (4%) | |
	$40.0	$30.0	$35.0	$25.0	35.0%	15.0%	1.00	0.25	6.0%	2.0%
Call ($6.1)	$10.7	$2.4	$2.8	$10.5	$6.7	$5.7	$7.2	$5.5	$6.3	$5.8
Put ($0.5)	$0.1	$1.8	$2.1	$0.0	$1.1	$0.1	$1.0	$0.2	$0.4	$0.5

To illustrate, beginning from the parameters of the base case, if the stock price increases from $35 to $40, the option premium increases from $6.1 to $10.7 and the put premium decreases from $0.5 to $0.1. If, on the other hand, the stock price falls from $35 to $30, the option premium decreases from $6.1 to $2.4 and the put premium increases from $0.5 to $1.8. This confirms the direct relationship between the price of a call and the stock price, and the indirect relationship between the price of a put and the stock price. Go over the rest of the numbers in the table and you will find that they confirm the qualitative results we anticipated in Table 24.1.

Why options?

There are many and varied reasons for buying and selling options. Of those, we'll briefly discuss here the two most important: gaining leverage and gaining protection. Interestingly, the former is implemented with the goal of increasing the risk (and as a result the expected reward) of a portfolio, and the latter with the goal of decreasing it.

Options magnify the risks and rewards of trading directly in stock due to the leverage they provide. Note that by investing in options an investor can control a large capital by investing only a small capital. In the example we've been discussing, an investment of $610 (the cost of buying the call) would enable an investor to control a capital of $3,500 (the market price of 100 shares).

What are the consequences of this leverage? Let's go back to our example and look at the bright side first. If the stock price increases from $35 to $40, an investor in the stock would obtain a 14.3% return; an investor in the call, however, would obtain a whopping 75.9% return (=$10.7/$6.1 − 1). This is what leverage is all about. But don't rush to call your broker to buy options just yet! Note that if the stock price falls from $35 to $30, the investor in the stock would lose 14.3%; the investor in the call, however, would lose 60.5% (=$2.4/$6.1 − 1). Leverage, then, is a double-edged sword; it amplifies *both* expected gains and expected losses.

This leverage is obviously not restricted to calls and can also be gained by buying puts. An investor who believes that a company's stock price will fall can profit by either short-selling the stock or buying a put. Going back to our example, if the stock price falls from $35 to $30 a short-seller would make a 14.3% return by short-selling at $35 and buying back at $30 to close the short position. By buying the put, however, this investor could have obtained a return of 273% (=$1.8/$0.5 − 1)!

But puts also are a double-edged sword. If against expectations the stock price rises to $40, the short-seller in the stock would lose 14.3%. The investor in the put, however, would lose 79.4% (=$0.1/$0.5 − 1). In short, then, although options amplify both the rewards and risks of investing directly in stock, investors who *hope* to leverage their gains find in options a useful tool.

The other good reason for buying options, we argued, is protection. Let's see how this would work. Consider an investor that, believing in an imminent rise, buys 100 shares in the stock we've been discussing at its current price of $35. And let's assume that, against his expectations, the stock takes a dive to $10, delivering a 71.4% capital loss. How could options have helped this investor?

Easy. At the same time he bought shares at $35 he could have also bought a put with an exercise price of $30. This way, he would have preserved all the upside, and at the same limited his downside (at a cost of $0.5 according to the Black–Scholes model). Note that, when the stock falls to $10, the investor could limit his loss by either exercising the put (selling his shares at $30 instead of at $10) or selling it (at $19.4 according to the Black–Scholes model).

Protection can of course be obtained not only with puts but also with calls. Let's assume now that another investor, believing in an imminent fall, short-sells 100 shares in the same stock we've been discussing at its current price of $35. What would happen if, against his expectations, the stock rises to $60? In this case the investor would suffer a 71.4% loss. (He pocketed $350 by short-selling

100 shares and now would have to spend $600 to buy them back to close the short position.) Would trading in options have helped this investor to limit his downside?

Absolutely. At the same time as he sold the 100 shares short at $35 he could have bought a call with an exercise price of $40 (at a cost of $1.0 according to the Black–Scholes model). By doing this, the investor could have preserved his upside if the stock falls, and at the same time protected his downside if it rises. Note that when the stock rises to $60, the investor could limit his loss by either exercising the call (buying back 100 shares at $40) or selling it (at $20.8 according to the Black–Scholes model).

Finally, there are good reasons for selling options too. The main difference with buying them is, of course, that an investor who buys an option has to pay for it, but one who sells an option is paid for it. In other words, an option writer (seller) is paid to bear the risk of committing to either buy or sell shares of stock at a predetermined price. If conditions move against the option writer, he will incur a loss for which, at least in principle, he has already been compensated by receiving an option premium.

The big picture

Investing in options is widely popular, and for good reasons. Compared with investing directly in the underlying stocks, options can be used to either magnify returns or limit risk. If that sounds too good to be true, it's not. Which doesn't mean that these benefits come at no cost. Options are bought for a price and the appropriate price is not trivial to estimate.

The framework most widely used to price options is the Black–Scholes model, which values them based on the price and volatility of the underlying stock, the exercise price and time to expiration of the option, and the risk-free rate. Interestingly, according to this model, volatility, which is harmful for investors in stock, is valuable for investors in options.

Options, however, are only one financial instrument of the many available to magnify returns or limit risk. Futures and forwards are also widely used for these purposes and we'll discuss them in the next chapter.

Excel section

There is no new Excel material in this chapter.

Challenge section

1 Consider a call option with an exercise price of $45 and nine months away from maturity. The call is written on a stock that is currently trading at $45 a share and has a historical annual volatility of 20%. The annual risk-free rate is 5%. How much would you pay for this call?

2 How much would you pay for a put option on the same stock, knowing that it has an exercise price of $45 and is nine months away from maturity?

3 Beginning from the numbers in the base case (those in the previous two questions and in parentheses in the table, except for the price of the call and the put that you must calculate yourself), recalculate the price of the call and the put for the parameters in Table 24.3.

TABLE 24.3

	S ($45)		X ($45)		σ (20%)		T (0.75)		R_f (5%)	
	$50.0	$40.0	$50.0	$40.0	25.0%	15.0%	1.00	0.50	6.0%	4.0%
Call (?)										
Put (?)										

4 Take a good look at all the numbers you calculated in the previous three questions. Do the qualitative relationships in Table 24.1 hold?

25

FUTURES AND FORWARDS

Basic definitions

Hedgers and speculators

Peculiarities of futures markets

Futures pricing

Some examples

Hedging with futures

Why hedging?

The big picture

Excel section

Challenge section

Derivatives are assets that derive their value from the value of some other underlying asset. Options, which we discussed in the previous chapter, are one example; futures and forwards, which we discuss in this chapter, are two others. These markets are complex and definitely not for inexperienced investors. Still, the essentials of how futures and forwards are priced, and how they can be used for hedging and speculating, are not difficult to understand. These are, precisely, the focus of this chapter.

Basic definitions

You've probably done it many times. You go into a store and that hot CD or book has already flown off the shelves. So what do you do? You order it, pay a small good-faith deposit, the seller promises to deliver the CD or book around a given date, at which time you pay the balance due and take the CD or book home. That is, more or less, what futures and forwards are all about.

More precisely, *futures* and *forwards* are contracts that specify an agreement to buy or sell a given quantity of an asset, at a given price, at a given point in time in the future. The asset can be real (commodities such as corn, cattle, coffee, or gold) or financial (such as currencies, bonds, or indices). In the case of commodities, the quality of the asset and the place of delivery are also specified in the contract; in the case of indices, which have no physical counterpart, the contract is settled in cash.

Futures and forwards differ from options in one critical aspect: options give their owners the *right* to buy or sell the underlying asset; futures and forwards, on the other hand, *obligate* the parties to buy or sell the underlying asset as specified in the contract. This does not imply, as we discuss below, that all transactions in these markets involve delivering an asset; in fact, the vast majority of transactions are offset before delivery.

Futures and forwards differ from each other in several aspects. Futures are standardized contracts specified by (and traded in) organized exchanges. They are highly liquid and enable traders to undo a position simply by making an offsetting transaction. Forwards, in turn, are contracts whose terms are set by agreement between the involved parties (usually financial institutions and corporations), that are traded in over-the-counter markets (basically a network of traders), and that can be undone only by consent between the involved parties. Therefore, although forwards are more flexible than futures regarding the specification of contract terms, they are also more difficult to undo.

Participants in these markets can take long or short positions. A party with a *long* position agrees to *receive* (buy) the underlying asset under the terms specified in the contract; a party with a *short* position, in turn, agrees to *deliver* (sell) the underlying asset under the terms specified in the contract. Delivering or taking delivery of an asset, however, are not the main reasons for participating in these markets. In fact, most participants do it with the goal of hedging or speculating.

Hedgers and speculators

There are two types of participants in futures and forwards markets: hedgers and speculators, who basically differ in their goals. *Hedgers* buy or sell contracts with the goal of protecting themselves from adverse movements in the price of an asset; *speculators* buy and sell contracts hoping to profit from short-term changes in prices. Hedgers, then, trade to reduce their risk; speculators hope to make a profit by exposing themselves to that risk.

Both hedgers and speculators can take long and short positions. Hedgers take long positions seeking protection from an increase in the price of an asset, and short positions seeking protection from a decrease in the price of an asset. An airline that buys oil (future or forward) contracts, for example, seeks protection against increases in the price of one of its most critical inputs; a farmer who sells corn (future or forward) contracts, for example, seeks protection against decreases in the price of the product he sells.

Speculators who take long positions expect the price of the underlying asset to increase; those who take short positions expect the price of the underlying asset to fall. In both cases, speculators do not seek to receive or deliver an asset. Rather, they only seek to exploit the inherent risk in futures and forward markets and profit from changes in prices.

In fact, as mentioned above, most of the transactions in futures and forwards markets are not made by parties interested in delivering or accepting delivery of an asset. Rather, the vast majority of positions are offset before delivery. All a party needs to do to close a long position in a contract is to take a short position of the same size in the same contract. Conversely, a party closes a short position in a contract simply by taking a long position of the same size in the same contract. In fact, even hedgers usually close their positions before delivery and then sell the underlying asset in the spot market (that is, the market for current delivery).

Peculiarities of futures markets

Futures markets are different from bond and stock markets in several aspects. We briefly discuss here two of these aspects: the existence of margins and the leverage inherent in futures transactions.

Individuals who want to operate with futures are required to open a *margin account*. These accounts require an *initial margin*, which is a minimum initial deposit required to operate in futures. The amount of the initial margin is set by the exchange, depends on the type of futures the individual intends to trade, and is a small percentage (usually around 5%) of the market value of that contract. It also varies depending on whether the account is opened by a hedger or a speculator; the latter is required to deposit a higher initial margin. In most cases, the cash in a margin account earns interest. Also, in most cases, individuals can deposit Treasury bills or stock instead of cash, but both are accepted at less than their face value.

Margin accounts have a *maintenance margin*, which is the minimum amount that must be kept in the account (usually around 75% of the initial margin). When the amount of cash in the account falls below this margin, even in the absence of any transaction, the individual gets a *margin call*, that is, a request to make a deposit in the account to bring it back to the initial (not to the maintenance) margin. If you're wondering why, in the absence of any transaction, the amount of money in a margin account may fall below the maintenance margin, or why it may fall at all, you're asking the right question.

Futures are *marked to market*, which means that daily gains and losses due to price fluctuations are credited or debited to the account. In other words, changes in the value of futures contracts are realized on a daily basis. (Forwards are not marked to market but settled in full at the end of their life.) The main reason for marking futures to market on a daily basis is to reduce the probability of default when the contract expires.

To illustrate, let's suppose we buy one June contract on the Dow Jones Industrial Average during the month of March, when this index is at 10,000. Futures on the Dow trade at 10 times the value of the index; therefore, the price of one contract would be $100,000. But we don't need that much money to trade in Dow futures; we'd only need to deposit an initial margin, which let's assume is 5% of the value of the contract ($5,000). What happens if by the end of the next day the Dow rises 2% to 10,200?

Well, the value of the contract will increase to $102,000 and therefore $2,000 would be credited to our account, for a closing balance of $7,000. We have made no transactions the day after opening the account and yet we have *realized* a $2,000 gain! Not bad. That's simply because our account has been marked to market.

But wait. What if the next day the Dow falls by 5% closing at 9,690? Well, the value of the contract will fall to $96,900 and therefore $5,100 (= $102,000 − $96,900) would be debited from our account, for a closing balance of $1,900. So, in this case, we made no transactions and still lost over $5,000. That *is* bad! But it's also the way futures markets work. Even worse, at this time we'd probably get a margin call from our broker asking us to deposit $3,100 to get our account back to the initial $5,000. This illustrates, briefly, the dynamics of margin accounts and the practice of marking to market.

Futures markets also exhibit another important characteristic, which is the leverage of the transactions. The investment of a small capital to control a much larger capital, which is what leverage is all about, increases both the return and the risk of investing in futures relative to investing directly in the underlying asset. This is not too different from the leverage provided by options (discussed in the previous chapter), but let's illustrate it by going back to the example we're discussing.

Let's compare two strategies, the first consisting of buying an index fund that mimics the behavior of the Dow, and the second investing in Dow futures. On the day the Dow rises 2%, our index fund would also rise 2%. However, we have seen that if we buy one futures contract on the Dow, on that same day we'd get a $2,000 deposit in our margin account, for a return of 40% (= $2,000/$5,000). That's quite a difference. Thumbs up to leverage!

But wait. Before you rush to call you broker to buy futures, consider what happens the next day. When the Dow goes down 5%, our index fund would also fall by that amount. But our margin account in the Dow futures, as we have seen, would be debited by $5,100, for a return of −72.9% (= −$5,100/$7,000). Big thumbs down to leverage! Still, that's what leverage is all about; it amplifies *both* the returns and the risk of investing in the underlying asset.

Futures pricing

The valuation of futures contracts is, from a technical point of view, slightly different from that of forward contracts. However, for most practical purposes, given the same asset and delivery date, it is safe to assume that the price of both contracts is the same. This price, as we'll discuss below, follows from the critical assumption of no arbitrage opportunities. (Just for the sake of convenience, the discussion below focuses on the valuation of futures although virtually the same arguments could be made for the valuation of forwards.)

The framework to value futures contracts is the cost-of-carry model, which links the futures price of an asset with the spot (or current) price of that asset. More precisely, the **cost-of-carry model** states that

$$F = S \cdot e^{(c-y) \cdot T} \tag{25.1}$$

where F and S denote the futures price and the spot price of the underlying asset, c and y the cost of carry and the convenience yield (both expressed as a proportion of the spot price), T the time to delivery (in years), and $e = 2.71828$. This model essentially says that the value of a futures contract is equal to the spot price of the underlying asset adjusted by the cost of carrying the asset for the relevant period of time. This requires some explanation.

Let's introduce, first, a relevant distinction between consumption assets (such as corn, oil, and coffee) and investment assets (such as gold, currencies, or stock). The former are held primarily for consumption purposes, the latter for investing purposes. This distinction is important because the type of asset underlying the futures contract determines both the cost of carry and the convenience yield. So, you may ask, what are these?

The *cost of carry* (c) is the cost of holding the asset for the relevant period of time. This cost may include financing costs, storage costs, insurance costs, and transportation costs, and obviously depends on the type of asset underlying the futures contract. For consumption assets such as corn or coffee, all these costs may be relevant; for investment assets such as stock or currencies, only the financing cost is relevant.

The *convenience yield* (y) is the benefit of holding the underlying asset, and arises because ownership of a physical asset may provide benefits not provided by a futures contract. Storing coffee enables Starbucks both to keep their coffee shops going and to prevent disruption in operations should coffee become scarce. This convenience yield depends on the market's expectations about the future availability of a commodity; the greater the probability of shortages, the larger the benefit of holding the physical asset, and the higher the convenience yield. (Although the convenience yield, strictly speaking, applies only to consumption assets, the income generated by some investment assets can be *thought of* as a convenience yield. More on this below.)

Note that in general the cost of carry is larger than the convenience yield (that is, $c > y$) and, therefore, $F > S$. This situation is usually referred to as *contango*. At times, however, when inventories of a physical asset are low and the probability of shortages is high, it may be the case that the convenience yield is high enough to offset the cost of carry (that is, $c < y$) and, therefore $F < S$. This situation is usually referred to as *backwardation*. Note, finally, that as time goes by, the futures price and the spot price tend to converge, until on the settlement date both magnitudes become the same.

A bit confused? That's OK, the examples below should clarify the idea behind the pricing model and the role its components play in the valuation of futures contracts on different assets.

Some examples

Let's start considering an investment asset, shares in a company, and let's assume that this company pays no dividends. Let's also assume that the stock currently trades at $50 a share and that the (continuously compounded) annual risk-free rate is running at 4%. What should be the price of a six-month futures contract to buy one of these shares?

Note, first, that because we're dealing with a futures contract on a share, there are no storage, insurance, or transportation costs; the cost of carry, then, is given only by the financing cost. Also, note that because the stock pays no dividends, there is no convenience yield. (If this is not entirely clear, don't worry, we'll get back to this below.) According to equation (25.1), then, the futures contract to buy one share in six months (half a year) should be valued at

$$F = \$50 \cdot e^{(0.04)\cdot 0.5} = \$51.0$$

But that is just throwing numbers into a formula. It is useful to think a bit why the futures *must* trade at this price.

Let's consider what would happen if the futures traded at $55. Well, in this case, clever as we are, we could borrow $50 for six months at the annual rate of 4%, buy one share, and take a short position in a futures contract (committing to deliver one share in six months in exchange for $55). What would happen at that time? We would use the share we bought to deliver the one we're committed to deliver, get $55 for this delivery, and use $51 (= $50 $\cdot$ $e^{0.04 \cdot 0.5}$) to pay back the loan. That would leave us with a *certain* profit of $4.

What if the futures traded at $45 instead? Well, in this case we could short sale one share and receive $50, invest that at the annual rate of 4% during six months, and take a long position in a futures contract (to take delivery of one share in six months in exchange for $45). What would happen at that time? We would get $51 (= $50 $\cdot$ $e^{0.04 \cdot 0.5}$) from our six-month investment at 4%, take delivery of the share and pay $45 for it, and use that share to cover the short position. That would leave us with a *certain* profit of $6.

Needless to say, we're not the only clever ones that can figure this out. The market is populated by thousands of clever investors looking for the tiniest of these opportunities, and therefore these arbitrage profits are not easy to find. That's why the futures contract *must* be priced at $51. Because if it's not, arbitrageurs would jump in, trade seeking to obtain arbitrage profits, and the resulting impact on prices would quickly eliminate the mispricing.

What would be different if the stock paid dividends? Simply that this dividend would be a benefit of holding the stock, and we can then think of the stock's dividend *yield* as the convenience yield in equation (25.1). Therefore, in the case of a dividend-paying stock, we have a cost of carry equal to the financing cost and a convenience yield equal to the stock's dividend yield. If the stock we've been discussing in this section had an annual (continuously compounded) dividend yield of 2%, then a futures contract to buy one share in six months should be valued at

$$F = \$50 \cdot e^{(0.04-0.02) \cdot 0.5} = \$50.5$$

Lastly, what about futures on consumption assets such as corn, coffee, or oil? Two main differences arise. First, besides financing costs, there would also be costs associated with storing and transporting the asset. In addition, if there is a risk that the asset can be damaged or spoiled, insurance costs would also add to the cost of carry. And second, for the reasons discussed above, all consumption assets have a positive convenience yield, that is, a benefit derived from having the physical asset readily available. In short, then, when valuing a futures contract on a consumption asset, we must take into account a cost of carry that is the sum of financing, storage, transportation, and insurance costs, as well as a positive convenience yield.

Hedging with futures

We have already discussed the fact that many participants in futures and forwards markets are hedgers who seek protection from changes in the price of an asset. We have also discussed long hedges which involve buying a futures contract seeking protection against price increases, and short hedges, which involve selling a futures contract seeking protection against price decreases. Positions that enable a hedger to completely eliminate the risk associated with price changes are called *perfect hedges* and are rare in practice.

Hedges can be static or dynamic. A *static hedge* is a position that is taken and left unchanged until the end of the hedge's life. A *dynamic hedge*, in turn, is a position that is taken and subsequently monitored and adjusted frequently. The discussion below involves a static hedge. (For ease of exposition, we'll ignore the daily settlement of futures contracts and treat them as forwards contracts. The loss of accuracy is not substantial and the essential points are more easily conveyed this way.)

Let's see how futures on the Dow can be used to hedge the risk of a portfolio. Let's assume we have a $2 million equity portfolio and we want to protect it for the next three months. Let's also assume that the (continuously compounded) annual risk-free rate is 4%, that the beta of our portfolio with respect to the Dow is 1, that the Dow has a (continuously compounded) annual dividend yield of 2%, and that it is now trading at 10,000.

Let's consider first what would happen to the unhedged portfolio if three months down the road the Dow closes down 5% at 9,500. Because the annual dividend yield of this index is 2%, the three-month dividend yield of 0.5% mitigates the loss and leaves it at 4.5%. And because our portfolio has a beta of 1 with respect to the Dow, it would also lose 4.5% and end up with $1,910,000, for a loss of $90,000. Using the same reasoning, we can easily determine that if, three months down the road, the Dow closes up 5% at 10,500, then our portfolio will end up with $2,110,000 (up 5.5%), for a gain of $110,000.

How can we use futures contracts on the Dow to reduce (at the limit, eliminate) the variability in the value of our portfolio? Note that because we have a long position in the equity portfolio, our hedge involves taking a *short* position on Dow futures. So the first thing we need to determine is how many contracts we need to sell. That's not hard. Because each futures contract on the Dow trades at 10 times the value of the index, and the index is trading at 10,000, each contract is worth $100,000. And because we need to hedge a $2 million portfolio, then we need to sell 20 contracts.

What is the fair value of a futures contract on the Dow? Using equation (25.1) we can easily determine that $F = \$10{,}000 \cdot e^{(0.04-0.02) \cdot 0.25} = \$10{,}050.1$, which means that three months down the road we'll be receiving $\$100{,}501.3$ (= $10 \cdot \$10{,}050.1$) for each of the 20 contracts we sell today.

What if the Dow closes at 9,500 then? Well, we know that in this case we'll suffer a loss of $\$90{,}000$ in our portfolio. But, at the same time, we'll gain $\$110{,}025.0$ from our short position in Dow futures. This is calculated as the difference between the price at which we'll deliver each contract in three months ($\$100{,}501.3$) and the actual value of each contract at the time ($\$95{,}000$), multiplied by the number of contracts we sold (20), that is, ($\$100{,}501.3 - \$95{,}000$) $\cdot$ (20). If we combine our loss on the portfolio with our gain in the Dow futures, then, we obtain a total gain of $\$20{,}025$.

Before we think a bit about this, let's consider what happens if the Dow closes at 10,500 instead. We know that in this case our portfolio will end up with a gain of $\$110{,}000$. But we'll lose on the futures this time. Note that we'll be receiving $\$100{,}501.3$ per contract delivered when the actual value of each contract will be $\$105{,}000$. Therefore, we'll lose $\$4{,}498.7$ per contract, for a total loss of $\$89{,}975$. If we now combine our gain on the portfolio with our loss in Dow futures, we obtain a total gain of . . . $\$20{,}025$!

Magic? Not really, it's called *hedging*. This is, in fact, what hedging is all about. We have formed a portfolio consisting of our equity portfolio and a short position in Dow futures, and the value of this portfolio is independent of the performance of the market or that of the stocks in the portfolio. This is exactly what hedgers seek to obtain by participating in the futures market. And of course they can protect not only the value of equity portfolios, but also the value of wheat, coffee, gold, oil, or currencies, to name but a few.

Note, importantly, that the $\$20{,}025$ we get regardless of the closing value of the Dow in three months is almost exactly what we would obtain by depositing $\$2$ million (the value of our equity portfolio) at the (continuously compounded) risk-free rate of 4% during three months ($\$20{,}100.3$). The only reason that these two numbers are not equal to each other is because we've been a bit sloppy with compounding. Had that not been the case, the total gain in our portfolio of equities and forwards would have been *exactly* equal to the gain from investing the value of our equity portfolio safely at the risk-free rate. In other words, because the hedge eliminated all risk, in equilibrium we must earn the risk-free rate.

Note, also, that we assumed that the beta of our portfolio with respect to the Dow is 1. What if this beta is anything but 1? In that case, the return on our portfolio would be calculated as $R_p = R_f + \beta \cdot (R_M - R_f)$, where R_p, R_f, and R_M denote the returns of our portfolio, the risk-free rate, and the returns of the market (the Dow in our case), respectively. In addition, the number of contracts to trade (N) would be given by $N = \beta \cdot (V_p/V_F)$, where V_p and V_F denote the value of our portfolio and the value of the stocks underlying one contract (10 times the value of the Dow in our case).

Table 25.1 displays the relevant numbers of the case we have discussed (second and third columns), as well as a similar case for a portfolio of the same value ($2 million) but with a beta of 1.5 with respect to the Dow (fourth and fifth columns). In the first column, 0 denotes the present time and 1 denotes the future time (three months down the road).

TABLE 25.1

	$\beta = 1$		$\beta = 1.5$	
S (0)	$10,000.0	$10,000.0	$10,000.0	$10,000.0
c	4.0%	4.0%	4.0%	4.0%
y	2.0%	2.0%	2.0%	2.0%
T	0.25	0.25	0.25	0.25
F (0)	$10,050.1	$10,050.1	$10,050.1	$10,050.1
Dow (0)	10,000	10,000	10,000	10,000
Dow (1)	9,500	10,500	9,500	10,500
R_M	-4.5%	5.5%	-4.5%	5.5%
Beta	1.0	1.0	1.5	1.5
Portfolio (0)	$2,000,000	$2,000,000	$2,000,000	$2,000,000
R_p	-4.5%	5.5%	-7.3%	7.8%
Portfolio (1)	$1,910,000.0	$2,110,000.0	$1,855,000.0	$2,155,000.0
Gain/Loss	-$90,000.0	$110,000.0	-$145,000.0	$155,000.0
F (0)	$10,050.1	$10,050.1	$10,050.1	$10,050.1
F (1) = S(1)	9,500	10,500	9,500	10,500
N	20	20	30	30
Gain/loss	$110,025.0	-$89,975.0	$165,037.6	-$134,962.4
Total gain/loss	$20,025.0	$20,025.0	$20,037.6	$20,037.6

Why hedging?

Perhaps you're wondering why would any investor bother hedging a portfolio if, at the end of the day, he would have faired just as well by selling the portfolio and investing the money safely at the risk-free rate. There are at least two reasons for doing so.

First, if an investor is confident in his portfolio but less so in the expected performance of the market, hedging would enable him to remove the risk arising from market swings and still remain exposed to the risk of the portfolio relative to the market. Second, if an investor is confident in his portfolio as a long-term investment but for some reason needs to protect it in the short term, hedging is quite likely to be better than selling the portfolio, investing its proceeds temporarily at the risk-free rate, and eventually buying back the portfolio, which would involve incurring high transactions costs.

Finally, recall that participants in futures markets hedge all sorts of assets, not just financial portfolios. Airlines hedge against increasing oil prices, farmers against falling corn prices, and exporters against falling local currencies, to name just a few. Hedging, in short, enables them to focus on their main business and avoid surprises from variables they can hardly control or predict.

The big picture

Futures and forwards may not be for the faint of heart. Although the essentials of these markets are not difficult to understand, hedging and speculating can be extremely complex. For this reason it should come as no surprise that the derivatives departments of investment banks are populated by PhDs in physics and mathematics rather than by MBAs! And yet, these markets play an essential role: they enable companies to focus on their core business without being distracted by the swings of variables they hardly control.

Futures and forwards are similar in some ways and different in others. Essentially, these markets enable hedgers to lock prices at which assets can be delivered in the future, enabling them to reduce uncertainty. And hedgers can do this only because speculators provide liquidity by exposing themselves to the risk of price fluctuations with the hope of making a profit. This is, in a nutshell, is what futures and forward markets are all about.

Excel section

There is no new Excel material in this chapter.

Challenge section

1 Consider the information in Table 25.2. The situation is similar to the one considered in the text, where we need to hedge the value of an equity portfolio using futures contracts on the Dow. Consider first the case in which the beta of a $4 million equity portfolio with respect to the Dow is 0.8 and calculate the value of all the relevant variables (the empty cells). Can you obtain a perfect hedge?

TABLE 25.2

	ß = 0.8		ß = 1.2	
S (0)	$10,000.0	$10,000.0	$10,000.0	$10,000.0
c	5.0%	5.0%	5.0%	5.0%
y	1.0%	1.0%	1.0%	1.0%
T	0.5	0.5	0.5	0.5
F (0)				
Dow (0)	10,000	10,000	10,000	10,000
Dow (1)	9,000	11,000	9,000	11,000
R_M				
Beta	0.8	0.8	1.2	1.2
Portfolio (0)	$4,000,000	$4,000,000	$4,000,000	$4,000,000
R_p				
Portfolio (1)				
Gain/loss				
F (0)				
F (1) = S(1)				
N				
Gain/loss				
Total gain/loss				

2 Consider the same $4 million equity portfolio but assume now that its beta with respect to the Dow is 1.2. Again, calculate the value of all the relevant variables (the empty cells). Can you obtain a perfect hedge in this case?

26

CURRENCIES

A word of caution

The exchange rate

The law of one price

Purchasing power parity

The Fisher effect

The international Fisher effect

Interest rate parity and forward parity

The big picture

Excel section

Challenge section

You're of course familiar with traveling, exchanging money, and exchange rates. You're also familiar with interest rates and inflation. And perhaps a bit less familiar with forward contracts. In this chapter we'll bring them all together and relate them to each other. And, in doing so, perhaps we'll understand a bit better the impact on all these variables of the international flows of capital, so widely discussed in financial newspapers.

A word of caution

The *international parity conditions* are a set of equilibrium relationships involving exchange rates, forward exchange rates, interest rates, and inflation rates that make up the backbone of international finance. These parity conditions hold under some assumptions that include no transactions cost (such as transportation costs), no barriers to trade (such as tariffs or quotas), and competitive markets. Not much like the world we know, to be sure.

We don't have to take these or any other assumptions at face value; they are merely useful devices to focus on the relevant insights provided by the parity conditions. And when the discussion grants it, we'll consider the impact of relaxing some of these assumptions. As usual, a solid theory plus a fair bit of common sense go a long way toward understanding reality.

The exchange rate

Most people like to travel, particularly when it's cheaper to go abroad than stay at home. And what determines whether nice hotels, good meals, and rental cars are cheaper at home or abroad? Many factors, including one that plays a central role in the discussion of this chapter: the exchange rate between currencies.

However familiar you might be with traveling, exchanging money, and exchange rates, before we go any further let's formally define this last concept. And we'll do it mostly for one reason: the exchange rate can be defined in two different ways, and *both* of them are widely used. This often is, needless to say, a source of confusion.

The exchange rate, which is simply the price of one currency in terms of another, can be defined as units of domestic currency per unit of foreign currency, or as units of foreign currency per unit of domestic currency. Throughout our discussion we'll use the former and therefore define the **nominal exchange rate (E)** as

$$E = \frac{\text{Units of domestic currency}}{\text{One unit of foreign currency}} \qquad (26.1)$$

Given this definition, when the euro was launched at the beginning of 1999, Americans would say that the exchange rate was (roughly) 1.15, meaning that they needed \$115 to buy €100. Europeans, in turn, would say that the exchange rate was (roughly) 0.87, meaning that for each €87 they took out of their pockets they could buy \$100.

The rate at which currencies can be exchanged changes over time. A *depreciation* of the local currency consists in a decrease in its purchasing power, which implies that more local currency is needed to buy the same amount of foreign currency. An *appreciation* of the local currency, in turn, consists in an increase in its purchasing power, which means that less local currency is needed to buy the same amount of foreign currency.

Given the way we have defined the exchange rate, then, a depreciation consists in an increase in the exchange rate, and an appreciation of a decrease in the exchange rate. To illustrate this, between the launch of the euro at the beginning of 1999 and the summer of 2001, the dollar appreciated with respect to the euro, going from 1.15 in January 1999 to 0.85 in July 2001. Between that time and the end of 2003, however, the dollar depreciated with respect to the euro, going from 0.85 in July 2001 to 1.20 in December 2003. These changes in the dollar/euro parity are shown in Table 26.1.

TABLE 26.1

January 1999		July 2001		December 2003
$E = \dfrac{\$1.15}{€1}$	Revaluation →	$E = \dfrac{\$0.85}{€1}$	Devaluation →	$E = \dfrac{\$1.20}{€1}$

Depreciations and appreciations of a currency obviously affect purchasing power. Even if the price of a sporty Mercedes had remained unchanged at, say, €50,000, Americans buying this car at the end of 2003 would have spent 41% more than those who bought it in the summer of 2001 (\$60,000 compared with \$42,500). Conversely, even if the daily rates of a nice hotel in Paris had remained unchanged at, say, €200, Americans traveling to Europe in the summer of 2001 would have spent 26% less than those traveling at the beginning of 1999 (\$170 compared with \$230).

Therefore, European goods become cheaper for Americans when the dollar appreciates, and more expensive when the dollar depreciates. In contrast, American goods become cheaper for Europeans when the dollar depreciates, and more expensive when the dollar appreciates.

The law of one price

No conscientious shopper would pay more for an item in one store if he can buy the same item at a cheaper price in another store. Unless, of course, it's too much trouble to get the item from the other store. If we replace the word 'store' by 'country' we get the law of one price, which states that when an identical item sold in two different countries is expressed in a common currency, its price should be the same.

Formally, the **law of one price (LOP)** states that

$$p_D = E \cdot p_F \tag{26.2}$$

where p_D and p_F denote the domestic and the foreign price of an item. For concreteness, from this point on we'll assume that the US is home and Europe is abroad, and, therefore, that domestic and foreign prices refer to American and European prices, respectively.

Consider a laptop that costs $1,000 in the US and €1,100 in Europe, and assume that the exchange rate is 0.909 dollars per euro. Americans could buy the laptop in the US for $1,000, or take the same $1,000, exchange them for €1,100, and buy the laptop in Europe. Similarly, Europeans could buy the laptop in Europe for €1,100, or take the same €1,100, exchange them for $1,000, and buy the laptop in the US. If the law of one price holds, then, Americans and Europeans are indifferent about where they buy the laptop.

What would happen if the laptop were priced at $1,000 in the US and at €1,300 in Europe? Simply that Europeans would be better off by exchanging €1,100 for $1,000 and buying the laptop in the US, thus saving €200. This would put upward pressure on the price of the laptop in the US, downward pressure on the price of the laptop in Europe, or downward pressure in the exchange rate. (As Europeans demand more dollars to buy laptops in the US the dollar will strengthen with respect to the euro and E will fall.) In symbols, if

$p_D < E \cdot p_F$, then p_D must rise, or p_F must fall, or E must fall until the equality in (26.2) is restored.

What would happen, in turn, if the laptop were priced at \$1,200 in the US and at €1,100 in Europe? In this case Americans would be better off by exchanging \$1,000 for €1,100 and buying the laptop in Europe, thus saving \$200. This would put upward pressure on the price of the laptop in Europe, downward pressure on the price of the laptop in the US, or upward pressure in the exchange rate. (As Americans demand more euros to buy laptops in Europe, the euro will strengthen with respect to the dollar and E will rise.) In symbols, then, if $p_D > E \cdot p_F$, then p_D must fall, or p_F must rise, or E must rise until the equality in (26.2) is restored.

As it has surely crossed your mind already, in reality things don't work out quite that way. We know that any given laptop is a lot cheaper in the US than in Europe. And here is, precisely, where some of those things we assumed away come in. For the law of one price to hold, transaction costs have to be zero, or at least very low. However, if Europeans want to take advantage of the price differential and order the laptop from the US, the shipping costs may (more than) offset the price differential. And, even if shipping costs were low, if Europeans try to buy the laptop in the US, they get a cute screen saying something like, "Sorry we don't ship this stuff to Europe but please buy on our site there." (Talk about price discrimination!).

There may also be other considerations that determine Europeans to buy at home if the price differential is not too large. Some consumers find that buying a laptop at home has the advantage that all programs come in the local language and the keyboard is set up according to local custom. In other words, the law of one price holds when transaction costs are zero (or very low) *and* the items are identical (or very similar). Besides, note that, although laptops can be bought at home or abroad, lunch at noon, heating for the bedroom, and the monthly fee for the gym are bought and consumed at home, that is, the law of one price applies only to *tradable* goods and services.

In short, then, although the law of one price may not be a very accurate description of relative prices across countries, it is still a useful tool to think about price differentials across countries. And, as we discuss below, in the *long run* and in terms of *changes* in prices and exchange rates, it actually does hold quite well empirically.

Purchasing power parity

When the law of one price is applied to aggregate price indices rather than to the price of an individual item, it receives the name of *absolute purchasing power parity*. This is not, however, the PPP that you may have heard so much about. Before we get to it, let's formally define **absolute purchasing power parity** as

$$P_D = E \cdot P_F \tag{26.3}$$

where P_D and P_F denote the domestic and foreign aggregate price indices. Think of them, for example, as consumer price indices.

As you can see from a straightforward comparison between equations (26.2) and (26.3), the only difference between the law of one price and absolute purchasing power parity is that the former refers to the price of an individual item and the latter to the aggregate price of a basket of goods and services. Intuitively, then, we can say that absolute purchasing power parity states that when the same basket of goods and services in two different countries is expressed in a common currency, its price should be the same. Or, put differently, one unit of a currency must have the same purchasing power across countries; one dollar, for example, should buy just as much as the euros that can be bought with that dollar.

Now for the PPP you probably have heard much about. Let's start with a formal definition. **Purchasing power parity (PPP)** is given by

$$\frac{E_1 - E_0}{E_0} = \frac{1 + \pi_D}{1 + \pi_F} - 1 \approx \pi_D - \pi_F \tag{26.4}$$

where E_0 and E_1 denote the exchange rate at the beginning and the end of a period, and π_D and π_F the domestic and foreign rates of inflation during the same period. The second equality is an approximation that works well when the rates of inflation are low.

PPP can be thought of as the dynamic version of absolute PPP. It states that when prices in one country increase at a faster rate than those in another country, the currency of the country with higher inflation must depreciate with respect to the currency of the country with lower inflation. This depreciation is just enough to offset the differential inflation so that the absolute PPP equilibrium is restored. And once this happens, both currencies will again have the same purchasing power in both countries.

Or think about it this way. If inflation in the US increases relative to that of Europe, American goods become relatively more expensive to Europeans; therefore, the dollar gets cheaper to offset the higher prices and make American goods just as desirable to Europeans as they were before. At the same time, European goods become relatively cheaper to Americans, but the more expensive euro just offsets the price differential; therefore, European goods are just as desirable to Americans as they were before.

Suppose we start from an absolute PPP equilibrium in which the dollar/euro exchange rate is 1.2, and over one year prices in the US increase by 10% and in Europe by 5%. According to equation (26.4), the absolute PPP equilibrium would be restored when the dollar depreciates 1.10/1.05 – 1 = 4.76% to 1.257. Let's make sure we understand why this must be the case.

Let's look at this situation from the point of view of Americans first. Prices in the US have increased by 10%; would it then be cheaper for Americans to shop in Europe given that prices there have increased only 5%? Not really. To shop in Europe, Americans need to exchange dollars for euros and euros have become 4.76% more expensive. Then, for Americans, the cost of shopping in Europe has increased by (1.05) · (1.0476) – 1 = 10.0%. In other words, Americans are indifferent whether they shop in the US or in Europe.

Let's look at the same situation from the point of view of Europeans now. Prices in the US have increased by 10%. At the same time, the euro/dollar exchange rate went from 0.833 (= 1/1.2) to 0.795 (= 1/1.257), decreasing by 4.55%. Then, for Europeans, the cost of shopping in the US has increased by (1.10) · (1 – 0.0455) – 1 = 5.0%. Therefore, Europeans are indifferent whether they shop in Europe or in the US.

Note, finally, that equation (26.4) can be used to calculate the *level* of the exchange rate consistent with PPP after an inflation differential distorts relative prices. By manipulating this expression a bit we get

$$E_1 = E_0 \cdot \left(\frac{1 + \pi_D}{1 + \pi_F} \right) \tag{26.5}$$

which is usually referred to as the *PPP exchange rate*. Applying (26.5) to the example we just discussed we'd get that the PPP dollar/euro exchange rate is equal to $E_1 = (1.2) \cdot (1.10/1.05) = 1.257$, which is of course the same number we calculated before.

As for empirical evidence, the consensus on PPP seems to be the following. Although short-term inflation differentials do not seem to explain variations in exchange rates well, in the long term the opposite is the case, that is, long-term variations in exchange rates are largely explained by inflation differentials. Or, put differently, in the long term, exchange rates do tend to revert to the levels predicted by PPP.

The Fisher effect

Let's say we put $100 safely in the bank at the annual rate of 4%. One year down the road we withdraw $104. Are we better off or worse off? Not so fast; it depends. Remember that the real reason for saving is to increase future *consumption*. And whether $104 in one year enables us to consume more or less than $100 today depends on the rate of inflation. If, during the year, we keep the money in the bank at 4% prices increase by 2%, our purchasing power would increase. If prices increase by 6% instead, our purchasing power would decrease.

Another way of saying the same thing is that what investors really care about is the rate at which they can exchange current consumption for future consumption, which is given by the *real* interest rate. The rate at which current dollars can be exchanged for future dollars, in turn, is given by the *nominal* interest rate. More formally, the **nominal interest rate (I)** is given by

$$I = (1 + i) \cdot (1 + \pi) - 1 \oplus i + \pi \qquad (26.6)$$

and, therefore, the **real interest rate (i)** is given by

$$i = \frac{1 + I}{1 + \pi} - 1 \approx I - \pi \qquad (26.7)$$

where, as before, π denotes the rate of inflation. Equation (26.6) is usually referred to as the **Fisher effect (FE)**. The second equalities in (26.6) and (26.7) are approximations that work well when the rates of interest and inflation are low.

Given that investors care about their purchasing power, which depends on the real return they obtain from their investments, equation (26.6) states that if inflationary expectations increase so will the demand for a nominal return in order to keep purchasing power constant. Equation (26.7), in turn, says that purchasing power depends on the difference between the nominal interest rate and the rate of inflation; if $I > \pi$, purchasing power increases, and if $I < \neq$, purchasing power decreases.

Note that when comparing returns across countries, the nominal interest rate is largely irrelevant. This is the case because a country may have a high nominal interest rate as well as a high rate of inflation, so there may be little to gain (or may be even something to lose) by chasing high nominal returns. Again, what investors really care about (and therefore compare) are *real* returns, and they're willing to jump from country to country to obtain the highest possible. As a result, differences in real returns are quickly eliminated and, in equilibrium, real returns across countries are all the same.

The international Fisher effect

The only way we'll get to the equilibrium we have just described is by moving money around from country to country until differences in real returns are eliminated. But we cannot take our money from one country to invest it in another without first exchanging one currency for another, which will affect exchange rates.

That brings us to the **international Fisher effect (IFE)**, which is given by

$$\frac{E_1 - E_0}{E_0} = \frac{1 + I_D}{1 + I_F} - 1 \approx I_D - I_F$$

(26.8)

where I_D and I_F denote the domestic and foreign nominal interest rates. The second equality is an approximation that works well when interest rates are low.

In other words, the international Fisher effect states that when (nominal) interest rates are higher in one country than in another, the currency of the country with the higher interest rate must depreciate with respect to the currency of the country with the lower interest rate. Or, put differently, differences in nominal interest rates are offset by changes in the exchange rate. Let's see why this must be the case.

Let's assume that nominal (annual) interest rates are 13% in the US and 8%

in Europe, and that the dollar/euro exchange rate is 1.2. According to equation (26.8), then, the dollar must depreciate with respect to the euro by 1.13/1.08 − 1 = 4.63% to 1.256. In this situation, Americans could invest $100 in the US at the annual rate of 13% and get $113 one year down the road. Alternatively, they could exchange $100 for €83.3 (at the current exchange rate of 1.2) invest them in Europe at the annual rate of 8%, get €90 in one year, convert them back into dollars at the rate of 1.256 dollars per euro, and end up with the exact same $113. In other words, Americans are indifferent between investing in the US or in Europe.

Let's look at it from the European point of view now. Europeans could invest €100 in Europe at the annual rate of 8% and get €108 one year down the road. Alternatively, they could exchange €100 for $120 (at the rate of 1.2 dollars per euro), invest them for a year at 13% in the US, get $135.6 in one year, convert them back to euros at the rate 0.796 euros per dollar (= 1/1.256), and end up with the exact same €108. In other words, Europeans are indifferent between investing in Europe or in the US

To formalize this example, note that manipulating equation (26.8) a bit we get

$$1 + I_D = (E_1/E_0) \cdot (1 + I_F)$$

In other words, the return from investing at home is equal to the return from investing abroad, the latter being the compound return of investing in a currency and investing at the foreign interest rate. And because investing at home and abroad yield the same return, the equilibrium is such that there is no incentive to keep moving money around.

Note, also, that if we combine equations (26.4) and (26.8) we get

$$\frac{1 + I_D}{1 + I_F} = \frac{1 + \pi_D}{1 + \pi_F} \approx I_D - I_F \approx \pi_D - \pi_F \tag{26.9}$$

which basically says that if one country has a rate of inflation higher than another, it must also offer higher interest rates to compensate investors for the faster loss of purchasing power. In short, then, in equilibrium differences in inflation are fully compensated by differences in interest rates.

Finally, reshuffling terms in equation (26.9) we get

$$\frac{1 + I_D}{1 + \pi_D} = \frac{1 + I_F}{1 + \pi_F} \approx i_D \approx i_F \qquad (26.10)$$

where i_D and i_F denote the domestic and foreign real interest rate, which formalizes a result we informally discussed before, that is, in equilibrium real interest rates across countries are all the same.

Interest rate parity and forward parity

A forward is a contract that specifies an agreement to buy or sell a given quantity of an asset, at a given price, at a given time in the future. For our current purposes, the relevant forward contract consists of an agreement to exchange a given amount of one currency for another, at a given exchange rate, at a given time in the future. (Futures and forwards are discussed in Chapter 25.)

The **interest rate parity (IRP)** states that

$$\frac{F - E_0}{E_0} = \frac{1 + I_D}{1 + I_F} - 1 \approx I_D - I_F \qquad (26.11)$$

where F is the forward exchange rate. The second equality is an approximation that works well when interest rates are low. Note that by manipulating equation (26.11) a bit we get

$$F = E_0 \cdot \frac{1 + I_D}{1 + I_F}$$

In other words, the forward exchange rate is the current exchange rate adjusted by the difference in interest rates. Or, put differently, the currency of a country with high interest rates is expected to depreciate with respect to the currency of a country with low interest rates, that is, interest rate differentials are fully offset by depreciations.

The IRP is an equilibrium condition in the sense that, if it doesn't hold, then arbitrage opportunities exist. To see this let's go back to the example we've been discussing in which nominal interest rates in the US and Europe are 13% and 8%, and the dollar/euro exchange rate is 1.2. Solving (26.11) for F, then, we get a one-year forward rate of 1.256, that is, the dollar is expected to depreciate by 4.63% with respect to the euro. Let's consider first what would happen if the forward rate were lower than stated by IRP. Let's assume that $F = 1.2$.

In this case, clever as we are, we could borrow €100 at the annual rate of 8%; turn them into $120 and lend them at 13%; and buy a forward to get €108 in one year in exchange for $129.6 (= €100/1.2). One year down the road we'd get $135.6 from our investment at 13%, use $129.6 to buy €108 under the forward contract, pay off the loan in euros (€108), and obtain a *riskless* profit of $6. Not bad, huh? How about doing the same with €100 *million*?

Let's consider now a forward rate higher than stated by IRP. Let's assume that $F = 1.4$. In this case we could borrow $100 at 13%; turn them into €83.3 and lend them at 8%; and buy a forward to get $113 in one year in exchange for €80.7 (= $113/1.4). One year down the road we'd get €90 from our investment at 8%, use €80.7 to buy $113 under the forward contract, pay off the loan in dollars ($113), and obtain a *riskless* profit of €9.3. Another round of trades we'd better make with $100 million!

You can see now why the futures *must* be priced at 1.256; any other value will give investors the opportunity to obtain riskless profits. But, as soon as they try to exploit this opportunity, their trading will push the futures price toward this equilibrium value.

Finally, the **forward parity (FP)** is given by

$$F = E_1^e \tag{26.12}$$

where E_1^e denotes the expected exchange rate at the end of a period. This parity condition simply states that forward rates are unbiased predictors of future exchange rates. Which is not to say, of course, that they are perfect (or even good) predictors. It simply says that, on average, forward rates do not systematically overestimate or underestimate future spot rates.

The big picture

The international parity conditions are a set of equilibrium relationships widely used to understand the linkages among interest rates, inflation rates, exchange rates, and forward exchange rates. We have already discussed each relationship separately; Exhibit 26.1 shows how they relate to each other.

Suppose that next year inflation in the US is expected to be 5% higher than in Europe. Then, according to PPP, the dollar should depreciate by roughly 5% against the euro, and according to the Fisher effect (FE) nominal interest rates in the US should be 5% higher than in Europe. According to interest rate parity (IRP), then, the one-year forward dollar/euro rate should be 5% higher than the dollar/euro spot rate, implying a 5% depreciation of the dollar against the euro; and given the forward parity (FP) this 5% depreciation gives an unbiased prediction of the dollar/euro spot rate one year down the road. Finally, the international Fisher effect (IFE) reaffirms that, with a 5% interest rate differential, the dollar is expected to depreciate 5% against the euro.

EXHIBIT 26.1
International parity conditions

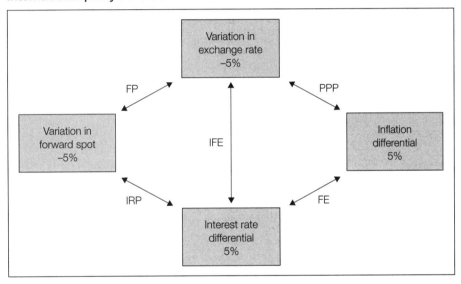

Excel section

There is no new Excel material in this chapter.

Challenge section

1 Consider a flat-screen TV that sells in the US for $5,000 and in Europe for €6,000 at a time when the dollar/euro exchange rate is 0.833.

(a) Is it cheaper for Americans to buy the TV in the US or in Europe? What about for Europeans?

(b) Suppose that, given the same exchange rate, the TV sold for $5,500 in the US and for €6,000 in Europe. Where would it be cheaper to buy the TV? Is this an absolute PPP equilibrium? Why?

(c) Suppose that, given the same exchange rate, the TV sold for $5,000 in the US and for €6,500 in Europe. Where would it be cheaper to buy the TV? Is this an absolute PPP equilibrium? Why?

2 Suppose we start from an absolute PPP equilibrium in which the dollar/euro exchange rate is 1.5, and that over the next year prices in the US are expected to increase by 6% and in Europe by 3%. Real interest rates across all countries are roughly 3%.

(a) What do you think will happen to the dollar/euro exchange rate?

(b) What do you think will happen to nominal interest rates in the US and in Europe?

(c) What do you think will happen to the dollar/euro one-year forward exchange rate?

(d) Are Americans better off investing $100 for one year in the US or in Europe?

(e) Are Europeans better off investing €100 for one year in Europe or in the US?

(f) What would you do if the one-year forward exchange rate were 1.5?

(g) What would you do if the one-year forward exchange rate were 1.6?

part IV:

STATISTICAL BACKGROUND

27

STATS I: SUMMARY STATISTICS

Random variables

Summarizing information

The mean

The median

The mode

The variance

The standard deviation

The covariance

The correlation coefficient

The big picture

Excel section

Challenge section

know, you are likely to hate stats. You are also likely to have had your share of it at school but barely remember that stuff. Well, the goal of this chapter is to get you back up to speed. We will not to go over any details, it's all very basic stuff. But a word of caution first: like any other tools in statistics or finance, the magnitudes below should be used with caution. They will hardly ever give us, by themselves, all the relevant information we need to make a decision. But they will help, so just read on.

Random variables

Finance and uncertainty are two concepts inevitably linked to each other. Just about all the variables we deal with in finance are characterized by our imperfect knowledge about their future values. In fact, all we usually know is some historical probability or likelihood of the different outcomes the variables can take.

This is one way of saying that in finance we deal with **random variables**, which are variables that take values determined by the outcome of a random process. They can be *discrete* or *continuous*, the former indicating that the variable can take a finite (or a countably infinite) number of values, and the latter indicating that the variable can take an infinite (not countable) number of values.

Consider the roll of a dice. It can only take 6 values (1 through 6), but we don't know beforehand which one will occur on any given roll. Or consider roulette, which can take 37 values (0 through 36) but again we don't know beforehand which one before spinning the wheel. Or consider the temperature, which can take an infinite number of values. Or consider the returns of a stock, which again can take an infinite number of values. All of these are random variables, the first two discrete and the last two continuous.

Note that the fact that the outcome of an process is uncertain doesn't mean that we're completely ignorant about it. When we role a dice we know beforehand the possible outcomes and their probabilities (1/6 for each of the six possible outcomes). When we spin a roulette wheel we also know both the possible outcomes and their probabilities (1/37 for each of the possible 37 numbers).

Much the same can be said about the temperature or the returns of a stock. We don't know the future with certainty, but past experience can help us assess the likelihood of the different values these variables can take. We have historical data on mean temperatures for different months of the year, or on mean annual returns for different assets. We also know from experience that it is quite unlikely for a summer day to be 10°F, or for a stock to return 700% in any given year.

Summarizing information

There's little doubt that staring at, for example, ten years of monthly returns will help us little in characterizing the behavior of any asset. The same would happen, in general, if we wanted to assess whether two assets are closely related or not. That's where the magnitudes we discuss in this chapter come in: they help us *summarize* information in a single number.

Before we jump into numbers and statistics, though, a quick comment on two related concepts. A **population** is the *complete* set of observations on any variable of our interest; a **sample**, on the other hand, is a *subset* of the population. To illustrate, if we are interested in the portfolio returns of every Chartered Financial Analyst (CFA) in New York during 2003, and collect information on every and each CFA, we will have obtained the population. If, alternatively, we choose to collect information on a subset of only 500 CFAs, we will have obtained a sample.

The main reason for working with a sample is obvious: it's a lot less costly to obtain a sample than the whole population. However, the only purpose of obtaining a sample is to make inferences about what is really going on in the population. In other words, a sample is simply a convenient tool that is used with the final goal of learning something about the population.

TABLE 27.1

Year	Dow (%)	Footsie (%)
1994	5.0	−6.5
1995	36.9	26.0
1996	28.7	16.9
1997	24.9	28.7
1998	18.1	17.5
1999	27.2	20.6
2000	−4.8	−8.2
2001	−5.4	−14.1
2002	−15.0	−22.2
2003	28.3	17.9

Let's start by taking a look at the numbers in Table 27.1, which contains the returns of the Dow and the Footsie (the familiar names of the indices generally used to describe the behavior of the American and UK markets, respectively) between 1994 and 2003. Now, if we wanted to say something about the behavior of these markets, or how they are related to each other, staring at these numbers would help little. Calculating some statistics, however, would.

The mean

The mean is perhaps the most widely used measure of central tendency. You remember this one, of course. We calculate averages all the time, and at the end of the day the mean is just that, an average. In other words, the (arithmetic) *mean (AM)* is the sum of all the relevant observations, divided by the number of observations. That is,

$$AM = (1/T) \cdot \sum_{t=1}^{T} R_t \qquad (27.1)$$

where R_t represents returns in period t, and T is the number of observations. Given this definition, the mean annual return of the Dow during the 1994–2003 period is given by

$$\frac{5.0\% + 36.9\% + \ldots - 15.0\% + 28.3\%}{10} = 14.4\%$$

Regarding its interpretation, the mean is just an average and there is not much more to it than that. Remember, however, that there is an important distinction, very relevant in finance, between the arithmetic mean and the geometric mean, both of which are discussed in detail in Chapter 2. What we are calling simply the mean in this chapter is in fact the *arithmetic* mean; hence the notation *AM*. (Most books that refer simply to the mean of a distribution also implicitly refer to the arithmetic mean.)

Easy as it is to calculate and interpret, the mean has one problem: it can be markedly affected by extreme values, particularly when the number of observations is small. To illustrate, assume that the return of the Dow in 2003 had been 500% (you wish!). If we recalculate the mean, now we'll find that its value is 61.6%, substantially different from our previously calculated value of

14.4%. In other words, the introduction of an extreme value in our small sample causes our measure of central tendency to more than quadruple! Enter then our next statistic.

The median

The **median** is another measure of central tendency and is calculated in the following way. First, we arrange all the observations in increasing order; then, if the number of observations is odd, the median is the value in the middle; and if the number of observations is even, the median is the average of the two values in the middle. To illustrate, if we arrange in increasing order the ten annual returns of the Dow between 1994 and 2003 we obtain

−15.0%, −5.4%, −4.8%, 5.0%, 18.1%, 24.9%, 27.2%, 28.3%, 28.7%, 36.9%

Then the median is 21.5% (that is, the average of 18.1% and 24.9%), and it can easily be interpreted as the return such that half of the returns are higher, and half of the returns lower, than this value.

Note two things. First, if we considered also the return of the Dow in 1993 (16.9%, not reported in Table 27.1), and reordered all eleven returns, we would obtain

−15.0%, −5.4%, −4.8%, 5.0%, 16.9%, 18.1%, 24.9%, 27.2%, 28.3%, 28.7%, 36.9%

Then the median would be 18.1% (that is, the value in the middle), and again half of the returns would be above, and half below, this number.

Second, and going back to the ten returns between 1994 and 2003, assume again that the return in 2003 had been 500%. As we saw above, that changed the mean from 14.4% to 61.6%. Does it change the median by much? Not at all. You can check for yourself (by reordering the returns and taking the average of the two in the middle) that the median remains at its previous value of 21.5%.

In general, when it's not appropriate to give heavy weight to extreme observations, the median is preferred over the mean. When considering income distributions, for example, a few individuals can have levels of wealth vastly larger than most of the individuals in the sample (think Bill Gates or Warren Buffett). In these and similar cases, the mean is quite a bit higher than the median (the latter being easily interpreted as the level of wealth exceeded, and not reached, by half of the individuals) and would give too rosy a picture of wealth. In short, then, the median is less affected by extreme values than the mean.

The mode

Our final measure of central tendency is not widely used in finance. The **mode** is simply the value that occurs most frequently. If you look again at the returns of the Dow between 1994 and 2003, you'll see that no return appears more than once; hence, that set of observations simply has no mode.

Although, again, this statistic is not widely used in finance, it may actually be useful in other applications. Consider a manufacturer of tennis shoes looking at the distribution of sizes of the shoes he sells. It would obviously be of interest to this entrepreneur to know what is the size in heaviest demand. That number, precisely, would be given by the mode.

The variance

Consider two hypothetical assets, both with the same mean return of 10%. Would you consider these two assets equally desirable if the observed returns of the first asset were tightly clustered between 9% and 11%, whereas those of the second asset were widely dispersed with values as low as –50% and as high as 70%? Of course not. In other words, *dispersion* around the mean matters, and that is precisely what the variance intends to capture.

Now, there's a problem with simply measuring the average distance to the mean. The problem is that if we take the average of the differences between each observation and the mean, above-average distances and below-average distances may cancel out. Consider, for example a mean return of 10% and two returns of –10% and 30%. If we subtract the mean from each return we get –20% in the first case and 20% in the second case; and if we take the average of these two differences we'll get 0%. However, it is obvious that this number would be misleading as a measure of dispersion.

A possible solution is to simply take the average of the *squared* differences between each return and the mean. And that is precisely what the **variance (Var)** measures, the average of the squared deviations from the mean. More formally, the variance is given by

$$Var = (1/T) \cdot \sum_{t=1}^{T} (R_t - AM)^2 \qquad (27.2)$$

and because it is an average of non-negative numbers, it is itself a non-negative number.

Calculating a variance is very simple in Excel (as we will see at the end of the chapter), but just to make sure you understand what's behind the number that Excel throws back at you in the blink of an eye, take a look at Table 27.2. The second column shows the returns of the Dow taken from Table 27.1; the third column simply subtracts the mean from the returns in the second column; and the fourth column squares the numbers in the third column. If we take the average of the numbers in this last column, we will obtain the variance of returns (0.0291 in our case).

TABLE 27.2

Year	R (%)	R–AM (%)	(R – AM)²
1994	5.0	–9.4	0.0088
1995	36.9	22.6	0.0509
1996	28.7	14.3	0.0205
1997	24.9	10.5	0.0111
1998	18.1	3.7	0.0014
1999	27.2	12.8	0.0164
2000	–4.8	–19.2	0.0370
2001	–5.4	–19.8	0.0393
2002	–15.0	–29.4	0.0864
2003	28.3	13.9	0.0193
Average	14.4%		0.0291

Not too difficult, huh? Two brief comments, then. First, you may occasionally see an expression for the variance in which the sum of squared differences from the mean is divided by $T - 1$ instead of by T. Obviously, this has little impact when the number of observations is large, as is usually the case in finance (though not in the tables of this book!). When the number of observations is small, however, dividing by either T or $T - 1$ may lead to fairly different estimates. In these cases, it is convenient to calculate the variance with respect to $T - 1$. (The reasons why this is the case are purely statistical and we won't bother with them here. Just hold on to the fact that in finance we usually deal with large T and therefore whether we divide by T or $T - 1$ is largely irrelevant.)

Second, as a measure of dispersion, the use of the variance is straightforward: the larger this number, the larger the dispersion around the mean. And yet, by looking at the last column of Table 27.2, you couldn't be blamed for wondering, 'And what is a percentage squared?'

The standard deviation

And that's the problem with the variance as a measure of dispersion: it is not measured in the same units as those of the variable we consider. In our case, the variance gives us a percentage squared, which does not have a straightforward interpretation. But don't throw your arms up in despair just yet; we're only one step away from arriving at a more intuitive measure of dispersion.

The **standard deviation (SD)** is simply the square root of the variance (that is, $SD = Var^{1/2}$), and is measured in the same units as those of the variable we are considering. If we take the square root of 0.0291 we will obtain 0.1706 or roughly 17.1%. The standard deviation is also discussed in Chapter 3 and for our current purposes it suffices to highlight that, just as was the case with the variance, the higher the standard deviation, the higher the dispersion around the mean. And, obviously, because the standard deviation is the square root of a non-negative number, it is itself a non-negative number.

The covariance

So far we have focused on summary statistics for a single variable. And yet, in finance, we're often interested in the *relationship* between two variables. We could ask, for example, whether the Dow and the Footsie tend to move closely or loosely together, or whether they move in the same or in opposite directions.

The **covariance** between two variables i and j **(Cov_{ij})** measures the strength of the linear association between them. Formally, it is defined as

$$Cov_{ij} = (1/T) \cdot \sum_{t=1}^{T} (R_{it} - AM_i) \cdot (R_{jt} - AM_j) \tag{27.3}$$

Just in case the notation is messy, let's take a look at what equation (27.3) implies. It basically says that, for each period t, we need to take the difference between the value of each variable and its respective mean (that is, $R_{it} - AM_i$ and $R_{jt} - AM_j$), multiply these two differences, do the same for all the periods, and take the average of these products. Too messy? OK, take a look at Table 27.3 then.

TABLE 27.3

Year	Dow		Footsie		Product
	R (%)	R – AM (%)	R (%)	R–AM (%)	
1994	5.0	–9.4	–6.5	–14.2	0.0133
1995	36.9	22.6	26.0	18.3	0.0413
1996	28.7	14.3	16.9	9.2	0.0132
1997	24.9	10.5	28.7	21.0	0.0221
1998	18.1	3.7	17.5	9.8	0.0037
1999	27.2	12.8	20.6	12.9	0.0166
2000	–4.8	–19.2	–8.2	–15.9	0.0305
2001	–5.4	–19.8	–14.1	–21.7	0.0431
2002	–15.0	–29.4	–22.2	–29.8	0.0877
2003	28.3	13.9	17.9	10.2	0.0142
Average	14.4%		7.6%		0.0286

The second and fourth columns of this exhibit show the returns of the Dow and the Footsie taken from Table 27.2. The third and fifth columns show these returns minus the mean of each respective market. And the last column is simply the product of the third and the fifth columns. The average of the numbers in this last column is, precisely, the covariance.

What does this number mean? Here comes the problem. In fact, there are *two* problems with the covariance. The first is that it depends on the units in which the variables are measured. For example, suppose I wanted to assess the relationship between the height and weight of the students in my corporate finance course. If I took all the heights measured in inches and all the weights measured in pounds, and calculated the covariance, I would obtain a given number. However, if I were to rescale all the weights from pounds to kilos, and recalculated the covariance between height and weight, I would obtain a different number. Of course nothing fundamental has changed in the relationship (students' heights and weights haven't changed), and yet the covariance has changed. Not good.

The second problem is that the covariance is unbounded, that is, it has neither an upper limit nor a lower limit. This implies that, by looking at the number we just calculated (0.0286) we cannot really tell whether the relationship between the Dow and the Footsie is weak or strong. We can tell that these two markets are positively related (that is, when the Dow increases the Footsie tends to increase, and vice versa), but not how strong this relationship is. Too discouraging? Don't worry, help is just around the corner. Enter our next (and final) statistic.

The correlation coefficient

Both problems of the covariance can be easily solved by a simple modification, which will lead us to the last summary statistic we discuss in this chapter. The **correlation coefficient** between two variables i and j (**$Corr_{ij}$**) is obtained by dividing the covariance between the two variables by the product of the standard deviation of both variables. Formally, the correlation coefficient is given by

$$Corr_{ij} = \frac{Cov_{ij}}{SD_i \cdot SD_j} \tag{27.4}$$

This coefficient is also discussed in Chapter 5 and for our current purposes it suffices to highlight a few things. First, it measures the strength of the *linear* relationship between two variables. In other words, two variables may be very closely related in a nonlinear way, and yet the correlation coefficient may indicate a very weak or nonexistent relationship. This is, again, because the correlation coefficient aims to assess linear relationships only.

Second, it can take a maximum value of 1 and a minimum value of −1. When the correlation is positive, the two variables tend to move in the same direction as each other, whereas when it is negative they tend to move in opposite directions. A correlation equal to 1 indicates a perfect positive linear relationship between two variables, and a correlation equal to −1 indicates a perfect negative linear relationship between them. A correlation equal to 0 indicates no *linear* relationship between them.

Perhaps the most intuitive way of thinking about the extreme values of this coefficient is the following. When the correlation between two variables is either 1 or −1, by knowing the value of one variable, we could *perfectly* predict the value of the other variable. This is so because in these cases we could always write the linear equation that deterministically relates the two variables. The lower the absolute value of the correlation between two variables, however, the less precisely we could predict the value of one variable by knowing the value of the other. In the particular case when the correlation between two variables is equal to 0, then there is nothing we can say about the value of one variable by knowing the value of the other (as long as we try to relate the variables in a linear way).

Finally, going back to the Dow and the Footsie, what does the correlation coefficient tell us about them? According to equation (27.4), all we need to compute it is the covariance between these two markets (0.0286, calculated in the previous section), and the standard deviation of returns of both markets (17.1% for the Dow, which we calculated earlier, and 17.5% for the Footsie, as you can easily check for yourself). Then, the correlation between the American and the UK markets is equal to $0.0286/(0.0171 \cdot 0.0175) = 0.96$. In other words, there is a *very* close (linear) relationship between these two markets, which indicates that they move very much in sync.

The big picture

In finance we deal with random variables and information about them must be summarized in order to be interpreted. Measures of central tendency such as the mean and the median are central to financial analysis; so too are measures of dispersion such as the variance and the standard deviation. But we do not always analyze variables in isolation. Sometimes it's important to assess the strength of the relationship between two variables, in which case the concepts of covariance and correlation become critical.

All these statistics are extremely useful and provide critical insight to make financial decisions. But again, they are tools, and like any other tool they should be used with caution.

Excel section

Calculating the summary statistics discussed in this chapter in Excel is very simple. Suppose you have a series of ten returns of one asset in cells A1 through A10 and a series of ten returns of another asset in cells B1 through B10. Then, you do the following:

- To calculate the *mean* of the first asset simply type '**=average(A1:A10)**' in cell A11 and hit 'Enter.'

- To calculate the *median* of the first asset simply type '**=median(A1:A10)**' in cell A11 and hit 'Enter.'

- To calculate the *mode* of the first asset simply type '**=mode(A1:A10)**' in cell A11 and hit 'Enter.'

- To calculate the *variance* of the first asset simply type '**=varp(A1:A10)**' in cell A11 and hit 'Enter.'

- To calculate the *standard deviation* of the first asset simply type '**=stdevp(A1:A10)**' in cell A11 and hit 'Enter.'

- To calculate the *covariance* between the assets simply type '**=covar(A1:A10,B1:B10)**' in cell A11 and hit 'Enter.'

- To calculate the *correlation coefficient* between the assets simply type '**=correl(A1:A10,B1:B10)**' in cell A11 and hit 'Enter.'

As mentioned above, it is not unusual to see an expression for the variance in which the sum of squared deviations from the mean is divided by $T - 1$ instead of by T. Excel provides a way to estimate both the variance and the standard deviation in this way:

- To calculate the *variance* of the first asset simply type '**=var(A1:A10)**' in cell A11 and hit 'Enter.'

- To calculate the *standard deviation* of the first asset simply type '**=stdev(A1:A10)**' in cell A11 and hit 'Enter.'

Challenge section

1 Table 27.4 reports the returns of the stock markets of Argentina and Brazil during the 1994–2003 period. The behavior of these markets is summarized here by the MSCI index of each market, measured in dollars and accounting for both capital gains and dividends. Given these returns, compute:

(a) The mean return of each market.

(b) The median return of each market. Is the median of each market different from the mean of the same market? Why?

(c) The mode of each market. Does it exist? Why?

(d) The variance of returns of each market.

(e) The standard deviation of returns of each market.

(f) The covariance between these markets. How would you interpret it?

(g) The correlation coefficient between these markets. How would you interpret it?

TABLE 27.4

Year	Argentina (%)	Brazil (%)
1994	−23.6	65.7
1995	12.9	−19.2
1996	20.3	42.5
1997	24.6	27.3
1998	−24.3	−39.6
1999	34.3	67.2
2000	−25.1	−11.4
2001	−18.3	−17.0
2002	−50.5	−30.7
2003	101.3	115.0

2 For the sake of completeness, also compute both the variance and standard deviation of returns of each market with respect to $T - 1$. Are these two numbers very different from their respective numbers with respect to T? Why?

28

STATS II: NORMALITY

Frequencies and histograms

The normal distribution

Calculating probabilities

The standard normal distribution

The big picture

Excel section

Challenge section

Appendix

H ave you read the previous chapter? If yes, then you have refreshed your memory with some useful statistics that provide invaluable help in summarizing financial information. Which means you're ready for the second step of our crash course in stats. The heart of this chapter focuses on the normal distribution and some of its applications. But it may be helpful to discuss a couple of issues before we get to this distribution.

Frequencies and histograms

In the previous chapter we argued that not much can be learned by staring at ten years of monthly returns of any given asset. It is better, we argued, to calculate some summary statistics. Having said that, a convenient grouping and subsequent visual display of the data may occasionally be helpful.

In a nutshell, we could do the following. We start by grouping the relevant data in convenient ranges; we then count the absolute and relative number of observations in each range; and finally we display this information in a bar graph. The number of observations in each range is usually called a frequency. An *absolute frequency* refers to the number of observations in each range, and a *relative frequency* refers to the proportion of observations in each range (relative to the total number of observations).

To drive these points home, take a look at Table 28.1. The data in the table refers to the monthly returns of the world market portfolio (usually the returns of the MSCI All Country World index, as is the case here) between January 1994 and December 2003. The first and fourth columns display the ranges in which the data is arranged; these ranges are usually chosen depending on the purpose at hand, and those in the table are convenient for our purpose. The second and fifth columns show the number of returns in each interval, that is, the absolute frequencies. Finally, the third and sixth columns show the number of returns in each interval relative to the total number of observations (120), that is, the relative frequencies.

A quick glance at the table shows, for example, that two-thirds of the returns (80) fall in the interval between –3% and 5%. It also shows that, as the returns depart more and more from the mean (0.7%, not shown in the table), the number of returns in the intervals tends to decrease. High frequencies around the mean return, and decreasing frequencies as returns depart more and more from the mean are, in fact, quite typical of most financial assets.

A histogram is a graphical representation of ranges and (either absolute or relative) frequencies. An example is shown in Exhibit 28.1. This bar chart shows the ranges (in the horizontal axis) and the absolute frequencies (in the vertical axis) that correspond to the numbers in Table 28.1.

TABLE 28.1

Range	Absolute	Relative	Range	Absolute	Relative
(−° ,−10%)	2	1.7%	(0%, 1%)	14	11.7%
(−10%, −9%)	1	0.8%	(1%, 2%)	13	10.8%
(−9%, −8%)	2	1.7%	(2%, 3%)	12	10.0%
(−8%, −7%)	1	0.8%	(3%, 4%)	9	7.5%
(−7%, −6%)	3	2.5%	(4%, 5%)	9	7.5%
(−6%, −5%)	3	2.5%	(5%, 6%)	7	5.8%
(−5%, −4%)	5	4.2%	(6%, 7%)	7	5.8%
(−4%, −3%)	4	3.3%	(7%, 8%)	2	1.7%
(−3%, −2%)	9	7.5%	(8%, 9%)	2	1.7%
(−2%, −1%)	9	7.5%	(9%, 10%)	1	0.8%
(−1%, 0%)	5	4.2%	(10%, °)	0	0.0%

EXHIBIT 28.1
World market, histogram

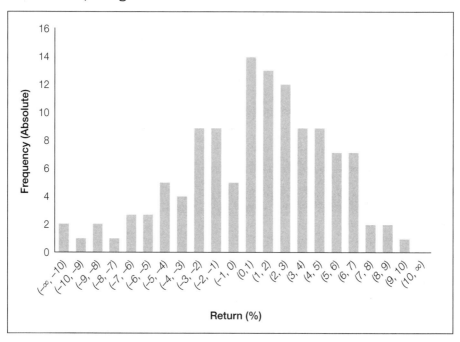

Although histograms are not very widely used in finance, we review them briefly here because stock market returns can occasionally be displayed in this form. They also provide a good visual introduction to continuous probability distributions, the most important of which we now turn to discuss.

The normal distribution

Statistical distributions are widely used in many financial applications. In fact, any time we forecast the return of an asset, we need to make an assumption about its underlying distribution. Because random variables can be, as we discussed in the previous chapter, discrete or continuous, so can statistical distributions.

The normal distribution is a continuous distribution described by a horrifying expression. You may have seen it many times before, but if you don't quite remember it, sit down, take a deep breath, and take a look at the expression

$$f(x) = \frac{1}{\sqrt{2 \cdot \pi \cdot SD^2}} \cdot e^{-\frac{(x - AM)^2}{2 \cdot SD^2}} \qquad (28.1)$$

where x is a particular value of the continuous random variable X, $e = 2.71828$, $\pi = 3.14159$, and AM and SD denote the mean and standard deviation of X, respectively. This expression yields the probability that the random variable X takes the value x, and now that we've seen it, for all practical purposes you may as well forget it. As we will see below, Excel calculates probabilities arising from the normal distribution in the blink of an eye.

For many and varied reasons, this distribution plays a central role in both finance and statistics. We won't get into those reasons here; there are plenty of books that not only discuss this distribution in depth but also give you its history as well. We'll remain faithful to our goal and focus on the practical aspects of this distribution.

So, what can we stress from a practical point of view about the normal distribution? Several things. First, it is bell-shaped and symmetric around its mean. Exhibit 28.2 shows a normal distribution of returns with a mean of 12% (and a standard deviation of 20%). Both the bell shape and the symmetry are clear from the picture.

EXHIBIT 28.2
The normal distribution

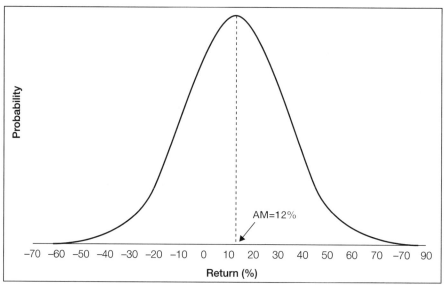

Second, the symmetry of the distribution implies that the mean is equal to both the median and the mode, so the normal distribution is in fact symmetric around all three parameters. The fact that the mean is equal to the median, in turn, implies that in the normal distribution 50% of the observations are below the mean and 50% above the mean. (This is not the case in asymmetric or skewed distributions, as we will see in the next chapter.)

Third, a normally distributed random variable is unbounded. In other words, the numbers on the horizontal axis go all the way from $-\infty$ to $+\infty$. Note that this is a bit problematic when characterizing stock returns because stocks are subject to limited liability, that is, the most we can lose when we buy equity is the amount of our investment, which in turn implies that the minimum possible return is –100%. Having said that, this limitation is, from a practical point of view, virtually irrelevant.

Fourth, the normal distribution is fully defined by only two parameters, its mean and standard deviations. This is just another way of saying that different combinations of *AM* and *SD* generate different normal distributions. Or, put differently, it means that by knowing these two parameters, we know everything we need to know to make probabilistic predictions out of this distribution.

Finally, the probabilities of one, two, and three standard deviations around the mean are well known. As you probably remember, 68.3%, 95.4%, and 99.7% of the observations cluster one, two, and three standard deviations around the mean, respectively. In the normal distribution of returns depicted in Exhibit 28.2, for example, the probability of observing returns in the interval (–8%, 32%) is 68.3%. Similarly, the probability of observing returns in the intervals (–28%, 52%) and (–48%, 72%) is 95.4% and 99.7%, respectively.

Calculating probabilities

Let's go back once again to the normal distribution of returns in Exhibit 28.2, which has a mean of 12% and a standard deviation of 20%. Incidentally, those are, roughly, the mean annual return and the annual standard deviation of the S&P500 from 1926 on.

There are, of course, many interesting questions we could ask, but let's entertain here just a few. Before doing so, note that all questions about probabilities for different values of the random variable of interest (the S&P500, in our case), are actually questions about *areas* under the relevant normal distribution. These areas, in turn, are calculated by integrating equation (28.1) in the relevant intervals. (But don't worry, Excel calculates those integrals for us in the blink of an eye.)

Let's ask, for example, what is the probability that the S&P500 returns, in any given year, 12% or less? That's easy. Because we know that the mean is equal to the median, and 50% of the area is below the median, then the probability is 50%. No sweat.

What about the probability that the S&P500 returns, in any given year, 5% or less? That's only a tiny bit more difficult. Take a look at panel A of Exhibit 28.3. We need to calculate the area below 5%, and that can easily be done in Excel, as we will see at the end of this chapter. There are in fact two ways of doing it, and you will be asked to try both in the Challenge Section. And you should find then that the probability in question is 36.3% .

What about the probability that the S&P500 returns, in any given year, at least 30%? This is another tiny bit more difficult, but again rather easy in Excel. We only need to take into account that Excel gives us areas *to the left* of the target return, and in this case we inquire about an area *to the right* of the target return, as panel B of Exhibit 28.3 shows. Again, you will be asked to calculate this number in the Challenge section, and you should find then that the probability is 18.4%. (You don't need to be reminded that the whole area under *any* probability distribution is 1, do you?)

Finally, what would be the probability that the S&P500 returns, in any given year, between 5% and 20%? Again another tiny bit more difficult, but again

EXHIBIT 28.3

Calculating probabilities (I)

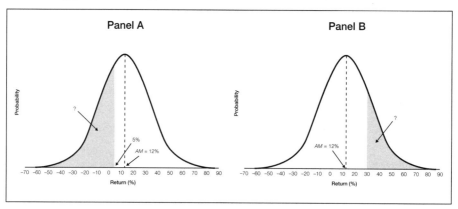

rather easy in Excel. Take a look at Exhibit 28.4. What we need now is the area between 5% and 20%, and you will be asked in the Challenge section to calculate it. And you should find then that the probability is 29.2%.

EXHIBIT 28.4

Calculating probabilities (II)

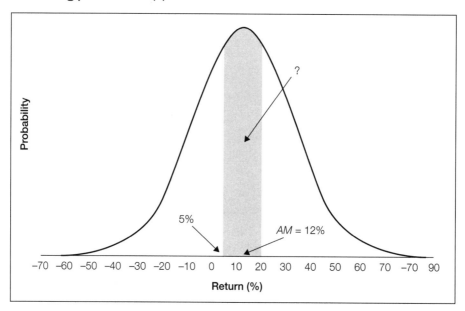

That should do it. We have inquired about probabilities less than a target return, more than a target return, and between two target returns. If, after reading the Excel section at the end of this chapter, you can answer the problems in the Challenge section, you will know just about all you need to know about calculating probabilities out of any normal distribution.

The standard normal distribution

Actually, one more thing. Not incredibly important nowadays given the widespread use of spreadsheets, but you may find it useful at times anyway. Note that anytime we want to calculate a probability for any random variable of interest, we need to know the distribution's mean and standard deviation, and with these two parameters plus a target value for the random variable, we need to calculate an integral (ouch!) using equation (28.1).

That is very easy to calculate in Excel or other computer programs, but very tedious without them. And it gets even more tedious if we need to do this for different variables, with different normal distributions. Enter then the *standard* normal distribution.

This distribution arises from a simple transformation of *any* normal distribution, which consists of subtracting its mean from the random variable of interest, and then dividing by its standard deviation. More precisely, if a random variable X follows a normal distribution with mean AM and standard deviation SD, then the random variable $Z = (X - AM)/SD$ follows a standard normal distribution with mean 0 and standard deviation 1. If we go back to equation (28.1), and set $AM = 0$ and $SD = 1$, we will obtain the expression for the standard normal probability distribution, which is given by

$$f(z) = \frac{1}{\sqrt{2 \cdot \pi}} \cdot e^{-\frac{z^2}{2}} \tag{28.2}$$

where z is a particular value of the continuous random variable Z.

So what's the big deal, you may ask, if equation (28.2) looks just a tiny bit less horrifying than equation (28.1)? Why is it that going from a normal distribution with mean AM and standard deviation SD to another with mean 0 and standard deviation 1 is such a leap forward? For a very simple reason: if we have no computer at hand, it makes a world of difference in terms of computing time and effort.

Suppose we wanted to find out the probability that ten different (normally distributed) assets, all of them with different means and standard deviations, return more than 15% in any given year. No Excel, no computer. Then we would have to calculate ten integrals using equation (28.1), after which we will be awarded a PhD in applied math and a two-week vacation in the Bahamas.

But there's a shortcut. We can subtract from the target return (15%) the mean of each asset, and then divide by the standard deviation of each asset, which would give us ten different values of Z. And here comes the clincher: the standard normal distribution is tabulated, and having our ten values of Z we can easily find the desired probabilities with the help of the table.

Tables for the standard normal distribution are widely available, and you can find one at the end of this chapter. You have probably used them before too. Just in case, let's use it once to find out the probability that the S&P500 returns less than 25% in any given year.

Start by calculating the value of Z by subtracting the mean return of the S&P500 (12%) from the target return (25%) and then dividing by its standard deviation (20%), that is, $Z = (0.25 - 0.12)/0.20 = -0.65$. (This number means that 25% is 0.65 standard deviations above the mean.) Then look up in the table in the appendix at the intersection between –0.6 (in the first column) and 0.05 (on the first row), and you should find the number 0.7.442 or 74.22%.

In short, the wide availability of tables for the cutoff points of the standard normal distribution makes it a convenient way to find out probabilities when no computer is available. (Excel also enables us to calculate probabilities by using the standard normal distribution, and we'll see how in the Excel section.)

The big picture

The normal distribution plays a crucial role in both finance and statistics. It's also very convenient to work with in many ways. Having said that, caution is in order. Remember that, often, the normality of returns is *an assumption*, not a fact. In other words, the returns of an asset may often be *assumed* to be normally distributed, but evidence may tell us otherwise.

To be sure, many assets do follow a normal distribution, but many others do not. The distribution of some assets may be skewed, or have fat tails, both of which imply departures from normality. There are varied ways to test whether normality is an appropriate assumption, and we'll have a bit more to say on this issue in the next chapter. For the time being remember: reality does not necessarily conform to convenient assumptions.

Excel section

Calculating probabilities out of a normal distribution is quite simple in Excel. Consider a series of normally distributed returns r, with mean AM and standard deviation SD. (Note that you don't have to type r_0, r_1, AM, or SD in the following calculations; you have to enter *the actual values* for these magnitudes.)

- To calculate the probability that r takes a value lower than or equal to r_0, you need to use the 'normdist' command. More precisely, type '=**normdist(r_0, *AM*, *SD*, true)**' and hit 'Enter.'

- To calculate the probability that r takes a value larger than or equal to r_0, you still use the same command. In this case you simply type '=**1–normdist(r_0, *AM*, *SD*, true)**' and hit 'Enter.'

- To calculate the probability that r takes a value between two numbers r_0 and r_1, such that $r_0 < r_1$, you still use the same command. In this case you type '=**normdist(r_1, *AM*, *SD*, true)–normdist(r_0, *AM*, *SD*, true)**' and hit 'Enter.'

You can also calculate all these probabilities by using the *standard* normal distribution. Note, however, that you can do so only *after* properly standardizing the random variable of your interest.

- To calculate the probability that the variable r takes a value lower than or equal to r_0, you first need to standardize it. You can do this in two ways. One is simply by calculating $z = (r_0 - AM)/SD$. The other is by using the 'standardize' command. In this case you need to type '=**standardize(r_0, *AM*, *SD*)**' and then hit 'Enter,' which would give you exactly the same z.

- After calculating z in one of the two ways suggested above, to calculate the probability that the variable r takes a value lower or equal than r_0, you need to use the 'normsdist' command. That is, type '=**normsdist(z)**' and hit 'Enter.'

Note that the 'normsdist' command does not require you to input the mean and standard deviation of the distribution because, by definition, these parameters in the standard normal distribution are 0 and 1. Note that you can also use the 'normsdist' command to calculate the probability that the variable r takes a value larger than or equal to r_0, or the probability that r takes a value between any two numbers r_0 and r_1.

Challenge section

1   Considering the returns of US Treasury bills during the 1980s and 1990s reported in panel A of Table 28.2, fill in the blanks of panel B by calculating the absolute and relative frequencies for the ranges indicated. Then make a histogram depicting both ranges and absolute frequencies. Do the returns of US T-bills appear to be normally distributed?

TABLE 28.2

Panel A				Panel B		
Year	Return	Year	Return	Range	Absolute	Relative
1980	11.2%	1990	7.8%	(2%, 3%)		
1981	14.7%	1991	5.6%	(3%, 4%)		
1982	10.5%	1992	3.5%	(4%, 5%)		
1983	8.8%	1993	2.9%	(5%, 6%)		
1984	9.9%	1994	3.9%	(6%, 7%)		
1985	7.7%	1995	5.6%	(7%, 8%)		
1986	6.2%	1996	5.2%	(8%, 9%)		
1987	5.5%	1997	5.3%	(9%, 10%)		
1988	6.4%	1998	4.9%	(10%, 11%)		
1989	8.4%	1999	4.7%	(11%, 12%)		
				(12%, °)		

2   Assume that the annual returns of the S&P500 from 1926 on follow a normal distribution with mean 12% and standard deviation 20%. Then use the 'normdist' command to compute:
   (a)   The probability that the S&P500 returns next year 12% or less.
   (b)   The probability that the S&P500 returns next year 5% or less.
   (c)   The probability that the S&P500 returns next year at least 30%.
   (d)   The probability that the S&P500 returns next year between 5% and 20%.

3   Recalculate all the numbers in question 1, but now using the 'normsdist' command.

Appendix

Cumulative distribution function for the standard normal distribution

Each number in the table below represents an area between $-\infty$ and z^* or, similarly, the probability that $z'' z^*$; that is $P(z'' z^*)$. Each z^* should be read as the *sum* of a number in the first column and a number in the first row. For example, the probability that $z'' 0.22$ is 0.5871, and the probability that $z'' 2.48$ is 0.9934. Probabilities for z^* numbers lower than 0 are calculated as 1 minus the number in the table. For example, the probability that $z'' - 0.75$ is $1 - 0.7734 = 0.2266$; the probability that $z'' - 2.31$ is $1 - 0.9893 = 0.0107$.

z^*	0.0000	0.0100	0.0200	0.0300	0.0400	0.0500	0.0600	0.0700	0.0800	0.0900
0.0	0.5000	0.5040	0.5080	0.5120	0.5160	0.5199	0.5239	0.5279	0.5319	0.5359
0.1	0.5398	0.5438	0.5478	0.5517	0.5557	0.5596	0.5636	0.5675	0.5714	0.5753
0.2	0.5793	0.5832	0.5871	0.5910	0.5948	0.5987	0.6026	0.6064	0.6103	0.6141
0.3	0.6179	0.6217	0.6255	0.6293	0.6331	0.6368	0.6406	0.6443	0.6480	0.6517
0.4	0.6554	0.6591	0.6628	0.6664	0.6700	0.6736	0.6772	0.6808	0.6844	0.6879
0.5	0.6915	0.6950	0.6985	0.7019	0.7054	0.7088	0.7123	0.7157	0.7190	0.7224
0.6	0.7257	0.7291	0.7324	0.7357	0.7389	0.7422	0.7454	0.7486	0.7517	0.7549
0.7	0.7580	0.7611	0.7642	0.7673	0.7704	0.7734	0.7764	0.7794	0.7823	0.7852
0.8	0.7881	0.7910	0.7939	0.7967	0.7995	0.8023	0.8051	0.8078	0.8106	0.8133
0.9	0.8159	0.8186	0.8212	0.8238	0.8264	0.8289	0.8315	0.8340	0.8365	0.8389
1.0	0.8413	0.8438	0.8461	0.8485	0.8508	0.8531	0.8554	0.8577	0.8599	0.8621
1.1	0.8643	0.8665	0.8686	0.8708	0.8729	0.8749	0.8770	0.8790	0.8810	0.8830
1.2	0.8849	0.8869	0.8888	0.8907	0.8925	0.8944	0.8962	0.8980	0.8997	0.9015
1.3	0.9032	0.9049	0.9066	0.9082	0.9099	0.9115	0.9131	0.9147	0.9162	0.9177
1.4	0.9192	0.9207	0.9222	0.9236	0.9251	0.9265	0.9279	0.9292	0.9306	0.9319
1.5	0.9332	0.9345	0.9357	0.9370	0.9382	0.9394	0.9406	0.9418	0.9429	0.9441
1.6	0.9452	0.9463	0.9474	0.9484	0.9495	0.9505	0.9515	0.9525	0.9535	0.9545
1.7	0.9554	0.9564	0.9573	0.9582	0.9591	0.9599	0.9608	0.9616	0.9625	0.9633
1.8	0.9641	0.9649	0.9656	0.9664	0.9671	0.9678	0.9686	0.9693	0.9699	0.9706
1.9	0.9713	0.9719	0.9726	0.9732	0.9738	0.9744	0.9750	0.9756	0.9761	0.9767
2.0	0.9772	0.9778	0.9783	0.9788	0.9793	0.9798	0.9803	0.9808	0.9812	0.9817
2.1	0.9821	0.9826	0.9830	0.9834	0.9838	0.9842	0.9846	0.9850	0.9854	0.9857
2.2	0.9861	0.9864	0.9868	0.9871	0.9875	0.9878	0.9881	0.9884	0.9887	0.9890
2.3	0.9893	0.9896	0.9898	0.9901	0.9904	0.9906	0.9909	0.9911	0.9913	0.9916
2.4	0.9918	0.9920	0.9922	0.9925	0.9927	0.9929	0.9931	0.9932	0.9934	0.9936
2.5	0.9938	0.9940	0.9941	0.9943	0.9945	0.9946	0.9948	0.9949	0.9951	0.9952
2.6	0.9953	0.9955	0.9956	0.9957	0.9959	0.9960	0.9961	0.9962	0.9963	0.9964
2.7	0.9965	0.9966	0.9967	0.9968	0.9969	0.9970	0.9971	0.9972	0.9973	0.9974
2.8	0.9974	0.9975	0.9976	0.9977	0.9977	0.9978	0.9979	0.9979	0.9980	0.9981
2.9	0.9981	0.9982	0.9982	0.9983	0.9984	0.9984	0.9985	0.9985	0.9986	0.9986
3.0	0.9987	0.9987	0.9987	0.9988	0.9988	0.9989	0.9989	0.9989	0.9990	0.9990

29

STATS III: NON-NORMALITY

Moments

Skewness

Kurtosis

An example

The lognormal distribution

Calculating probabilities again

The big picture

Excel section

Challenge section

We concluded the previous chapter with a word of caution, stressing that normality is a convenient assumption that may or may not describe properly the distribution of the asset we want to analyze. We move on now to discuss a few issues that have to do with non-normal distributions, with a special focus on the lognormal distribution.

Moments

All distributions, normal and non-normal, are characterized by parameters called **moments**. The first two moments we already know: the first is the mean and the second is the variance. For a normal distribution, that is all that matters. Remember, once we know the mean and variance of a normal distribution we know everything we need to know to work with it.

Not all distributions, however, are that easy to characterize. In other words, if we want to calculate the probability of obtaining different target returns for an asset with a non-normal distribution of returns, we usually need more information than just the mean and the variance; that is, we need to know more moments. Note, however, that the problem remains essentially the same: we still need to calculate areas (mathematically, integrals) under the relevant distribution.

Having said that, we'll now take a quick look at the third and fourth moments of a distribution, called skewness and kurtosis, respectively. From a practical point of view, moments higher than the fourth are virtually irrelevant. If you know these first four moments (mean, variance, skewness, and kurtosis), you'll be just fine.

Skewness

Not all random variables are characterized by symmetric distributions. In fact, it's not unusual to find assets whose returns are skewed in one direction or another. If you go back to the previous chapter and take another look at the histogram of returns in Exhibit 28.1, for example, you'll notice the lack of symmetry, with the left tail being longer than the right tail.

Exhibit 29.1 shows two asymmetric or skewed distributions. Panel A shows a distribution with a long right tail and panel B another with a long left tail. The former is usually said to exhibit positive (or right) skewness; the latter, on the other hand, is usually said to exhibit negative (or left) skewness.

EXHIBIT 29.1
Skewness

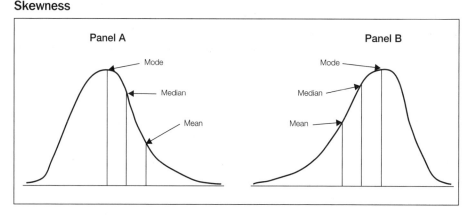

An important characteristic of skewed distributions is that the mean, the median, and the mode are all different. (In symmetric distributions, all three parameters have the same value.) In fact, as Exhibit 29.1 also shows, in distributions with positive skewness, the mean is larger than the median, which in turn is larger than the mode. In distributions with negative skewness, on the other hand, the mode is larger than the median, which is turn is larger than the mean. In both cases, the peak of the distribution is given by the mode.

In order to measure the asymmetry of a distribution we can calculate the **coefficient of skewness (Skw)**, the third moment of a distribution, which is given by

$$Skw = \frac{(1/T) \cdot \sum_{t=1}^{T} (R_t - AM)^3}{SD^3} \tag{29.1}$$

where R_t represents returns in period t, T is the number of observations, and AM and SD represent the mean and standard deviation of the distribution. A positive value of this coefficient indicates that the underlying distribution is positively skewed (a long right tail), and a negative value indicates that the underlying distribution is negatively skewed (a long left tail). In all symmetric distributions, this coefficient takes a value of 0.

In case you're panicking at the look of equation (29.1), fear not. As we will see at the end of the chapter, Excel calculates the coefficient of skewness in the blink of an eye. (Actually, Excel uses a slightly different formula that incorporates a small-sample adjustment, that is, a little correction that gives us a more precise estimate when the number of observations is small. However, because in finance we usually deal with large samples, we don't have to worry about this correction.)

Where does skewness stem from? In a nutshell, positive skewness arises when the mean is pulled up by some unusually high values (outliers), and negative skewness when the mean is pulled down by unusually low values. The negatively skewed distribution of monthly returns displayed in Exhibit 28.1, in the previous chapter, arises largely from a few large negative returns (such as −14% in August 98 and −11% in September 2002).

Positive skewness may also arise naturally from compounding. Consider an investment of $100 in an asset with a mean return of 30% a year, and assume, first, two consecutive years of 50% returns (that is, 20 percentage points above the mean). At the end of these two years we'll have $225, for a cumulative (two-year) return of 125%. Now, assume two consecutive years of 10% returns (that is, 20 percentage points below the mean). After two years we'll end up with $121, for a cumulative (two-year) return of 21%. Finally, note that 125% is 56 percentage points above the expected two-year return (69%), whereas 21% is only 48 percentage points below the expected two-year return. In short, the distribution of compounded (or cumulative) returns, is positively skewed.

Kurtosis

The fourth moment of a distribution, kurtosis, measures its peak and tails, usually relative to those of a normal distribution. A distribution with a higher peak and fatter tails than the normal distribution is called *leptokurtic*; one with a lower peak and thinner tails is called *platykurtic*.

Formally, the **coefficient of kurtosis (*Krt*)** is given by

$$Krt = \frac{(1/T) \cdot \sum_{t=1}^{T} (R_t - AM)^4}{SD^4} \tag{29.2}$$

and takes a value of 3 for the normal distribution. As a consequence, instead of this coefficient, you may often find reported the coefficient of *excess* kurtosis (*EKrt*), which is simply given by $EKrt = Krt - 3$. Thus, a positive value of *EKrt* indicates a high peak and fat tails, and a negative value indicates a low peak and thin tails, in both cases relative to the normal distribution. (What Excel calls kurtosis is, in fact, the coefficient of excess kurtosis. Also, as in the case of skewness, Excel introduces in the calculation a small-sample adjustment that we don't have to worry about.)

Many financial assets exhibit leptokurtosis. Most distributions of daily stock returns, for example, are characterized by fat tails. These indicate that large returns (both positive and negative) are more likely than a normal distribution would lead us to expect. As we discussed and stressed before, normality may be a convenient assumption but it not always is an appropriate characterization of the way the world behaves.

An example

Just to make sure you're on top of the intuition behind the first four statistical moments, let's take a look at the Nasdaq, one of the largest US electronic stock markets. Table 29.1 reports various statistics for the distribution of daily returns of the Nasdaq between January 1, 1994 and December 31, 2003.

TABLE 29.1

Mean	0.05%
Standard deviation	1.81%
Skewness	0.18
Excess kurtosis	4.37
Minimum	−9.67%
Maximum	14.17%

Let's start with the first moment. The mean daily return of the Nasdaq over the past ten years is 0.05%, that is, one-twentieth of 1%. It doesn't look like much, but remember that these are daily returns not annual. (The mean annual return of the Nasdaq during the same period is 16.4%.) The standard deviation is 1.81%, which means that, *if* this distribution were normal, then 99.7% of the returns would be contained in the interval (−5.39%, 5.49%), that is, three standard deviations each side of the mean. We'll get back to this interval shortly.

The coefficient of skewness is positive (0.18), which indicates that the distribution of daily returns of the Nasdaq has a long right tail. This, in turn, indicates that the Nasdaq is more likely to go up than down. The coefficient of excess kurtosis is also positive (4.37), which means that the Nasdaq delivers more large (positive and negative) returns than would be expected if its distribution were normal.

Two quick tests on the coefficients of skewness and kurtosis, which we won't get into, confirm that the departures of normality are substantial. (In statistical terminology, these tests confirm that the distribution of daily returns of the Nasdaq exhibits *significant* departures from normality.) But without getting into technicalities, there's a simple way to see that this distribution is skewed to the right, leptokurtic, and far from normal.

Between the beginning of 1994 and the end of 2003 the Nasdaq traded 2,519 days. If the daily returns of the Nasdaq were normally distributed, then 99.7% of the daily returns should be contained in the interval (–5.39%, 5.49%). That would leave 0.3% of the returns outside this interval; that is, only 8 returns. However, during the past ten years, there were 20 returns above 5.49% and 19 returns below –5.39%, a total of 31 more returns than would be expected under normality. In short, during the 1994–2003 period, the distribution of daily returns of the Nasdaq departed substantially from normality.

The lognormal distribution

Consider a stock that starts a year at $100 and by the end of the year declines to $50, for a –50% return. In order to go back up to $100, this stock needs to return 100%. It's easy then to see the asymmetry in returns: a stock that goes down 50% needs to go up 100% to go back to its initial value. We can replace $100 and $50 for any two values that we like, but we will always find the same: a stock that goes down by x% needs to return *more* than x% to go back to where it started.

If you recall our discussion in Chapter 1 about the difference between simple returns and continuously compounded returns, you will no doubt realize that the returns in the previous paragraph are all simple returns. But what if we calculated continuously compounded returns instead? That's easy. If we want to express simple returns in terms of continuously compounded returns, all we need to do is to take the log of 1 plus the simple returns. Then, our two simple returns, –50% and 100%, turn into $\ln(1 - 0.5) = -69.3\%$ and $\ln(1 + 1.0) = 69.3\%$ continuously compounded returns.

And what does this have to do with lognormality, you may ask? Note that if we express the changes in terms of continuously compounded returns, the positive return and the negative return are symmetric. That is, the absolute value of the return (69.3%) is the same. However, if we express the changes in terms of simple returns, the absolute value of the positive return (100%) is higher than the absolute value of the negative return (50%). In other words, continuously compounded returns are symmetric, but simple returns are positively skewed.

Now, here comes . . . a theorem! I know, you don't even want to hear about it. But this one is simple and we won't prove it; we'll just state it. The theorem says the following: if any random variable $\ln(X)$ is normally distributed, then the random variable X is lognormally distributed. That wasn't so bad, was it?

Now let's see why this is relevant to our discussion. Recall that, if R and r denote simple and continuously compounded returns, respectively, we know that $(1 + R) = e^r$ and $\ln(1 + R) = r$. So, according to the theorem above, if $\ln(1 + R) = r$ follows a normal distribution, then $(1 + R)$ follows a lognormal distribution. In other words, if continuously compounded returns are normally distributed, then simple returns are lognormally distributed. And if the distribution of r looks like that in Exhibit 28.2 in the previous chapter, then the distribution of $(1 + R)$ would look like Exhibit 29.2.

EXHIBIT 29.2
The lognormal distribution

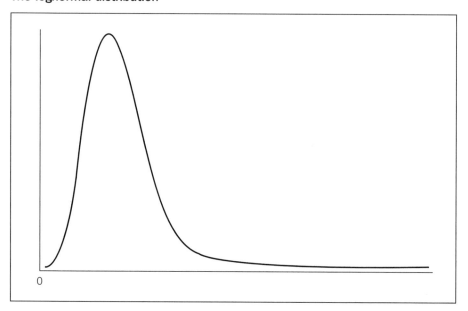

Note that the lognormal distribution is not symmetric but positively skewed. Note, also, that this distribution is defined only for positive values of the variable X. As a consequence, it is common not to focus on the distribution of R but on the distribution of $(1 + R)$. This is simply due to the fact that, because R cannot be lower than –100%, then $(1 + R)$ cannot be lower than 0.

Now, here's a little something that you should know. When academic financial economists deal with returns, they usually deal with continuously compounded returns. When they estimate correlations, or betas, or run econometric analyses, they virtually always do it with these returns. The reasons are many and varied, but an important one is that, as we've just seen, continuously compounded returns are more likely to be normally distributed (owing to their symmetry) than simple returns.

Investors, however, are largely interested in simple returns. This is because investors care about how much money they start with and how much money they end up with, and that can be straightforwardly measured by simple returns. And, as long as we believe (or find out through statistical testing) that continuously compounded returns are normally distributed, then simple returns *must* be lognormally distributed.

As is the case with the normal distribution, Excel returns probabilities out of the lognormal distribution in the blink of an eye (as we will see at the end of the chapter). Which means that the three expressions below are reported only for the sake of completeness. They follow from the fact that the random variable $\ln(X)$ is normally distributed with mean AM and standard deviation SD, which implies that X follows a **lognormal distribution** with probability distribution, mean, and variance, respectively, given by

$$f(x) = \frac{1}{x \cdot \sqrt{2 \cdot \pi \cdot SD^2}} \cdot e^{-\frac{[\ln(x) - AM)]^2}{2 \cdot SD^2}} \tag{29.3}$$

$$E(X) = e^{(AM + SD^2/2)} \tag{29.4}$$

$$Var(X) = e^{(2 \cdot AM + SD^2)} \cdot (e^{SD^2} - 1) \tag{29.5}$$

where x is a particular value of the random variable X, and, as we saw in the previous chapter, $e = 2.71828$ and $\pi = 3.14159$. Equation (29.3) yields the probability that the random variable X takes the value x, and equations (29.4) and (29.5) yield the mean and variance of the (lognormally distributed) variable X as a function of the mean and variance of the (normally distributed) variable $\ln(X)$.

Calculating probabilities again

Let's take a look at the returns of the Dow over the past 50 years. Table 29.2 reports some summary statistics for the distribution of continuously compounded annual returns. These returns do not contain dividends, which if considered would increase the mean annual return by roughly 2–3% but would have little impact on volatility, skewness, and kurtosis.

TABLE 29.2

Mean	7.2%
Standard deviation	15.9%
Skewness	−0.46
Excess kurtosis	−0.50
Minimum	−32.3%
Maximum	36.4%

A bit of simple testing, not discussed or reported here, indicates that the skewness and kurtosis of this distribution are not substantial (not significant, in statistical terms). This means that, for practical purposes, the distribution of continuously compounded annual returns of the Dow can be considered normal, and, therefore, that the distribution of simple annual returns of the Dow must be considered lognormal.

As we discussed above, investors are usually interested in simple returns, and the questions we'll pose refer to those returns. However, in order to get our answers, we need to use the parameters of the distribution of continuously compounded returns. This sounds a bit messy, I know. If we care about one distribution, you may fairly ask, why do we have to deal with the other? Simply because most of the time (perhaps for no good reason) the parameters of a lognormal distribution are defined in terms of the parameters of the underlying normal distribution.

If you take another look at equations (29.4) and (29.5), you'll see that the mean and variance of the lognormal distribution are defined in terms of the mean and variance of the underlying normal distribution (AM and SD^2). Excel, actually, is no exception. If we want to calculate areas (probabilities) under a distribution of simple returns, we have to input the mean and standard deviation of the underlying distribution of continuously compounded returns. Oh well, sometimes we just have to follow the crowd . . .

So, we could start by asking what is the probability that the Dow returns, next year, 10% or less. That is simply the area to the left of 10% under the lognormal distribution curve. As we will see at the end of the chapter, Excel gives us this number in the blink of an eye, and you will be asked to calculate it in the Challenge section. You should find that this probability is 55.8%.

What about the probability that the Dow returns at least 20% next year? That is the area to the right of 20% under the lognormal distribution curve, and again you will be asked to calculate it at the end of the chapter. You should find that it is 24.4%.

Finally, what about the probability that the Dow returns between 5% and 25% next year? That is the area between 5% and 25% under the lognormal distribution curve, and you will also be asked to calculate it at the end of the chapter. You should find that this probability is 38.8%.

If, after reading the Excel section at the end of this chapter, you can answer the problems in the Challenge section, you will know just about all you need to know about calculating probabilities out of a lognormal distribution. In Chapter 12 these ideas are used to forecast the probability of any target return in any target investment horizon.

The big picture

However convenient the assumption of normality may be, many financial assets simply don't follow the normal distribution. Many are skewed, have fat tails, or exhibit other departures from normality. The coefficients of skewness and kurtosis provide critical information about these departures, the former measuring asymmetry and the latter the thickness of the tails.

Of all the skewed distributions, the lognormal is the one that is most widely used in finance. Forecasting the probability of achieving target returns under lognormality is not difficult and, in many cases, is more accurate than forecasts based on the normal distribution.

Excel section

The coefficients of skewness and excess kurtosis are very easy to compute in Excel. Suppose you have a series of ten returns in cells A1 through A10. Then, you do the following:

■ To calculate the coefficient of skewness, you simply type '**=skew(A1:A10)**' and hit 'Enter.'

- To calculate the coefficient of excess kurtosis, you simply type '=**kurt(A1:A10)**' and hit 'Enter.'

As mentioned above, note that Excel introduces some small-sample adjustments to these two coefficients to improve the estimate when the sample is small. And, as also mentioned above, given that in finance we usually deal with large samples, you don't really have to worry about these adjustments.

You may also want to know that you don't have to estimate summary statistics one by one in Excel. In fact, there is a simple way to estimate several summary statistics at once. This is what you do:

- Start by selecting 'Tools' from the menu; then from the options given select 'Data Analysis'; and from the options given select 'Descriptive Statistics.' This will open a dialogue box in which you have to do at least three things. First input the data range (A1:A10 in our case) in 'Input Range'; then, input the cell in which you want the beginning of the output table to be displayed in 'Output Range;' then tick the box of 'Summary Statistics;' and finally click 'OK'.

To calculate probabilities out of a lognormal distribution, the only thing you need to keep in mind is that Excel will ask you for the mean and standard deviation of the associated normal distribution. For example, if you want to calculate probabilities out of a *lognormal* distribution of *simple* returns, Excel will ask you for the mean and standard deviation of the underlying *normal* distribution of *continuously compounded* returns. This obviously means, in turn, that you first have to calculate continuously compounded returns and then their mean and standard deviation.

Assume that the continuously compounded returns $r = \ln(1 + R)$ are normally distributed with mean AM and standard deviation SD, which means that the simple returns $(1 + R)$ are lognormally distributed. We are interested in calculating probabilities out of the distribution of $(1 + R)$. Assume then that you have a series of 10 continuously compounded returns in cells A1 through A10, and that you have calculated their mean and standard deviation in cells A11 and A12, respectively. (Note that you don't have to type $1+R_0$, $1+R_1$, AM, or SD; you have to enter *the actual values* for these magnitudes.) Then, you do the following:

- To calculate the probability that R takes a value lower than or equal to R_0, you need to use the 'lognormdist' command. More precisely, type '=**lognormdist(1+R_0, AM, SD)**' and hit 'Enter.'

- To calculate the probability that R takes a value larger than or equal to R_0, you still use the same command. In this case you simply type '=1–lognormdist(1+R_0, *AM*, *SD*)' and hit 'Enter.'
- To calculate the probability that R takes a value between two numbers R_0 and R_1, such that $R_0 < R_1$, you still use the same command. In this case you type '=lognormdist(1+R_1, *AM*, *SD*)–lognormdist(1+R_0, *AM*, *SD*)' and hit 'Enter.'

Challenge section

1 Consider the same returns of US Treasury bills during the 1980s and 90s reported in panel A of Table 28.2, in the previous chapter. Using these returns, compute:
   (a) The coefficient of skewness by using the 'skew' command.
   (b) The coefficient of excess kurtosis by using the 'kurt' command.
   (c) The statistics displayed when using the 'Tools/Data Analysis/ Descriptive Statistics' option.

2 Go back to the distribution of continuously compounded annual returns of the Dow during the period 1954–2003 in Table 29.2. As we have already discussed, these returns are normally distributed, with a mean of 7.2% and a standard deviation of 15.9% (which implies that the *simple* returns are lognormally distributed). Using this distribution estimate:
   (a) The probability that the Dow returns next year 10% or less.
   (b) The probability that the Dow returns next year at least 20%.
   (c) The probability that the Dow returns next year between 5% and 25%.

30

STATS IV: REGRESSION ANALYSIS

Regression analysis: An overview

Hypothesis testing

Risk, return, and emerging markets

Multiple explanatory variables

The adjusted-R^2

Predictions

A final comment

The big picture

Excel section

Challenge section

We've come to the end of our statistical review. Our last topic, regression analysis, has many and far-reaching applications in finance. It's also very broad and technical, so we will only scratch its surface here. The goal is to get you back up to speed with a quick refresher that involves both interpreting and running regression models.

Regression analysis: An overview

In a nutshell, regression analysis is a statistical technique that enables us to test a model (or theory, or idea) that attempts to explain the behavior of a variable of our interest. It basically works out this way. We start with a variable whose behavior we want to explain; we continue by proposing one or more variables to explain that behavior; we link all the relevant variables in one expression or equation; we collect data on all the relevant variables; we estimate the proposed relationship; and we finally run some tests on the validity of our model.

The variable we want to explain is called the *dependent variable*, and the variables that explain its behavior are called *independent* (or *explanatory*) *variables*. Therefore, there's one dependent variable (y) and k independent variables ($x_1, x_2 \ldots x_k$), where k can be any integer larger than or equal to 1.

A *cross-sectional* analysis attempts to explain the behavior of the dependent variable at a given point in time across different units of observation: for example, mean returns in 2003 across several companies, or income per capita on December 2003 across several countries. A *time-series* analysis, on the other hand, attempts to explain the behavior of the dependent variable over time: for example, the returns of a company over the past ten years, or the income per capita of a country over the last century.

Formally, the **multiple linear regression model** can be expressed as follows:

$$y_i = \beta_0 + \beta_1 \cdot x_{1i} + \beta_2 \cdot x_{2i} + \ldots + \beta_k \cdot x_{ki} + u_i \qquad (30.1)$$

Let's think about this expression a bit. The left-hand side shows the dependent variable (y) that the model attempts to explain. The right-hand side shows a constant or intercept (β_0); the k independent variables ($x_1, x_2 \ldots x_k$) that we believe can explain the behavior of the dependent variable, each multiplied by a constant ($\beta_1, \beta_2 \ldots \beta_k$); and an error term ($u$). The subscript i

runs from 1 through n, where n is the number of observations in the sample. (As a convention, the subscript i, for $i = 1, 2 \ldots n$, is typically used for cross-section analysis, and the subscript t, for $t = 1, 2 \ldots T$, where T is the number of observations, for time-series analysis.)

Let's start with the interpretation of the coefficients. For any independent variable x_j, β_j measures the impact on y of a one-unit change in x_j, holding all the other independent variables constant. In other words, β_j isolates the impact of x_j on y. (Formally, β_j is the partial derivative of y with respect to x_j.) The intercept β_0, on the other hand, is the *expected* value of the dependent variable when all the independent variables take the value 0.

The error term can be thought of as comprising the impact on the dependent variable of all variables other than the ones in the model. In other words, given that no model will be able to explain fully the behavior of the dependent variable, the error term collects its unexplained behavior. The usual assumption is that the *expected* value (average) of the error term is 0, implying that the many influences on the dependent variable of the variables not included in the model cancel each other out.

The standard way of estimating a relationship like (30.1) is by a procedure called ordinary least squares (OLS). We will not get into the details of this technique here, which is covered in detail in most books on statistics or econometrics. We'll stick to our practical goal and just say that the OLS procedure yields the estimates of $\beta_0, \beta_1 \ldots \beta_k$, which we will call $b_0, b_1 \ldots b_k$, respectively.

These estimates, in turn, are the coefficients that we use to predict the expected value of the dependent variable, $E(y)$. More precisely, we predict $E(y)$ with the expression

$$E(y) = b_0 + b_1 \cdot x_1 + b_2 \cdot x_2 + \ldots + b_k \cdot x_k \tag{30.2}$$

Note that, having estimated the coefficients $b_0, b_1, \ldots, b_k$ by OLS, we only need specific values for $x_1, x_2, \ldots, x_k$ to make a prediction on the expected value of the dependent variable.

Finally, after estimating a model that attempts to explain the behavior of an independent variable of our interest, we will surely be interested to know *how much* of that behavior the model actually explains. Enter then the R^2, sometimes called the coefficient of determination. This coefficient, which can take a minimum value of 0 and a maximum value of 1, measures the *proportion* of the variability in the dependent variable that is explained by the model. Obviously, the larger this number, the better the model.

Hypothesis testing

Most models yield some prediction about the value of the coefficients β_0, β_1, . . ., β_k. They may predict the sign of some coefficient (for example, that β_1 should be positive) or a precise value for some other (for example, that β_2 should be equal to 1). However, we cannot really test a model's predictions simply by comparing our estimates to their hypothesized values.

If this sounds a bit confusing, it is important at this point to keep in mind the difference between a sample and a population. Although we're always interested in the true value of the coefficients in the population, we virtually always deal with samples. This means that our estimates are subject to sampling error, which is just a fancy way of saying that our estimates may or may not be equal to the true population coefficients.

And here is, precisely, where hypothesis testing comes in. If you ever heard expressions such as 'this coefficient is significantly different from 0,' or 'this coefficient is not significantly different from 1,' they all mean that, having obtained our estimates and having run a statistical test on them, we can draw some conclusion about the difference between our estimates and their true value in the population.

In order to test any hypothesis about a coefficient, we need both the estimate of the coefficient and its so-called standard error. This is just a number that measures the precision of our estimate. The higher this number, the lower the precision, and the more uncertain we are about our estimate. Each coefficient b_j has its own standard error (SE_j).

A critical hypothesis we always want to test is whether the beta coefficients of our model are significantly different from 0. This is important because, if they are not, then our model does not really explain the dependent variable at all. This hypothesis can easily be tested with the so-called *t-statistic*, which is simply the ratio of our estimate of a beta coefficient and its standard error, that is, b_j/SE_j.

The simplest way to test this hypothesis is to compare the *p-value* (*p*) of the *t*-statistic with a chosen *significance level* (*α*). The former is not trivial to calculate but is part of the output of any program that estimates regressions (including Excel). The latter is a chosen number that measures the probability of rejecting a hypothesis when it is true. By far, the most widely used significance level in finance and economics is 5%.

Having obtained the p-value of the t-statistic of a beta coefficient, and having chosen a significance level, the rule to test the hypothesis that beta is *not* significantly different from 0 is straightforward:

- If $p < \alpha$ $\Rightarrow$ Reject the hypothesis
- If $p > \alpha$ $\Rightarrow$ Do not reject the hypothesis.

If the hypothesis is rejected, we say that beta is significant; that is, the variable associated with this coefficient plays an important role in explaining the behavior of the dependent variable. If, on the other hand, the hypothesis is not rejected, we say that beta is not significant and the opposite is the case. (Unless you want to get into the technical aspects of hypothesis testing, from a practical point of view you'd be wise to just take these two numbers, the p-value given by the output of an OLS estimation and the 5% significance level, as given, and simply apply the rule above.)

So much for the 'theory.' If you were familiar with regression analysis but hadn't dealt with it in a while, hopefully the previous discussion refreshed your memory. If you were not familiar with regression analysis, then you *must* be confused! That's why we're going to move right now to discuss an example in which we'll deal in practice with all the magnitudes we just discussed in theory.

Risk, Return, and Emerging Markets

Table 30.1 shows the 27 emerging markets on the MSCI Emerging Markets Index, the most widely followed benchmark for emerging markets investing. It also shows the mean monthly return (MR), the monthly standard deviation (SD), and the beta (with respect to the world market) of all these markets during the 1999–2003 period.

The variable whose behavior we want to explain is the mean return of these markets. Let's say we believe that we can explain the differences in mean return across markets by differences in risk (volatility), and let's quantify the latter with the standard deviation of returns. Let's also say, rather obviously, that we expect these two variables to be positively related. So now we have . . . a model! Our dependent variable is the mean return, our only independent variable is the standard deviation of returns, and we expect the β_1 coefficient to be positive.

Table 30.2 shows part of the output from an OLS estimation of our model. (At the end of the chapter we'll see how we can run regressions like this in Excel.)

TABLE 30.1

Country	MR (%)	SD (%)	Beta	Country	MR (%)	SD (%)	Beta
Argentina	0.5	13.5	0.7	Mexico	1.4	7.9	1.2
Brazil	1.9	13.3	2.0	Morocco	−0.2	4.7	0.2
Chile	1.1	6.5	0.9	Pakistan	2.9	12.3	0.4
China	0.5	11.1	1.1	Peru	1.9	6.6	0.4
Colombia	1.3	10.3	0.4	Philippines	−0.9	8.9	0.7
Czech Rep.	2.0	9.2	0.5	Poland	0.9	10.5	1.3
Egypt	0.7	8.9	0.7	Russia	4.5	15.6	1.8
Hungary	0.8	8.8	0.9	South Africa	1.4	7.3	1.0
India	1.8	9.1	0.7	Sri Lanka	1.5	12.5	0.1
Indonesia	1.9	14.4	1.0	Taiwan	0.5	10.2	1.1
Israel	1.6	7.3	0.7	Thailand	2.1	13.0	1.5
Jordan	1.1	3.9	0.1	Turkey	3.1	20.9	2.6
Korea	1.9	11.8	1.6	Venezuela	1.4	14.6	0.9
Malaysia	1.8	8.8	0.5				

The model is estimated with 27 observations, 1 mean return and 1 standard deviation for each of the 27 markets in our sample. The R^2 of the model (0.28) indicates that the standard deviation of returns explains 28% of the variability in mean returns. It doesn't look like much, but this is not unusual for this type of model.

TABLE 30.2

Observations:	27		b	SE	t-stat	p-value
R^2:	0.28	Intercept	−0.001	0.005	−0.25	0.80
Adjusted-R^2:	0.25	Variable 1	0.152	0.049	3.13	0.00

The estimate of the β_1 coefficient (0.152) indicates that, for every 1% increase in the standard deviation of returns, mean returns are expected to increase by roughly 0.15%. The output also shows the standard error (0.049) and the t-statistic (3.13) of b_1, which we can use to test the hypothesis whether β_1 is *not* significantly different from 0. Given a 5% significance level, the p-value of the t-statistic provided by the output (0.00), and the fact that $p = 0.00 < \alpha = 0.05$, we can decisively conclude that β_1 is significant. In other words, volatility does in fact explain the behavior of mean returns in emerging markets.

Finally, a word about the constant, which is, remember, the expected value of the dependent variable when the independent variables take a value of 0. Given that $p = 0.80 > \alpha = 0.05$, we accept the hypothesis that this coefficient is not significantly different from 0. In other words, if a market has no volatility, its expected return is 0.

Multiple explanatory variables

The risk variable we chose to explain the behavior of mean returns in emerging markets in our previous model was volatility, measured by the standard deviation of returns. Now, we could have thought of another independent variable, and that is, of course, beta. Table 30.3 reports the output of a regression in which we attempt to explain mean returns in emerging markets with beta as the only independent variable.

TABLE 30.3

Observations:	27		b	SE	t-stat	p-value
R^2:	0.21	Intercept	0.007	0.003	1.99	0.06
Adjusted-R^2:	0.18	Variable 1	0.008	0.003	2.57	0.02

You should have no problem interpreting this output by now. We ran the regression with 27 observations; we are able to explain 21% of the variability in mean returns; when beta increases by 1, mean returns are expected to increase by 0.008, or 0.8%; and we easily reject the hypothesis that beta does not explain mean returns ($p = 0.02 < \alpha = 0.05$).

Now, if we have found that both volatility and beta are important determinants of the variability in mean returns across countries, shouldn't we include *both* of them in our regression? We could (and probably should), and the output of this model, now with two independent variables, is displayed in Table 30.4.

TABLE 30.4

Observations:	27		b	SE	t-stat	p-value
R^2:	0.30	Intercept	−0.001	0.005	−0.12	0.91
Adjusted-R^2:	0.24	Variable 1	0.118	0.068	1.75	0.09
		Variable 2	0.003	0.004	0.73	0.47

Surprised? A quick glance at the p-values of our two independent variables, volatility and beta, shows that neither is significant ($p = 0.09 > \alpha = 0.05$ and p

$= 0.47 > \alpha = 0.05$). How can this be if we had concluded before that both were significant? And how can they not be significant if, taken together, they explain 30% of the variability in mean returns?

This is a rather common problem in regression analysis called *multi-collinearity*. This fancy name simply refers to a situation in which the explanatory variables are highly correlated among themselves. (In fact, in our case, the correlation between the standard deviation of returns and beta is a high 0.7.) This, in turn, usually translates into a situation in which each individual variable appears to be not significant, but the independent variables taken as a group do explain a substantial part of the variability in the dependent variable. Exactly our case.

Intuitively, what happens is the following. As we have seen, both volatility and beta, considered one at a time as independent variables, are important determinants of the variability in mean returns across emerging markets. But because volatility and beta are highly correlated between themselves, when we put them together in the same regression, they basically end up explaining largely the same variability in mean returns. In other words, each adds little explanatory power to the explanatory power already provided by the other.

The adjusted-R^2

Let's now focus for a moment on a coefficient reported in all the outputs above but that we have so far ignored, the *adjusted-R^2*, which is both interesting in itself but also related to the issue we just discussed. Recall that the R^2 measures the proportion of the variability in the dependent variable that we explain with our model. Now, what do you think would happen to the R^2 if, whatever the model we start with, we add one more independent variable?

Obviously, the added variable cannot 'un-explain' the variability in the dependent variable we're already explaining. The worst that could happen is that the new variable does not add any explanatory power at all, in which case the R^2 will not change. In other words, every time we add a variable to a model, the R^2 will either increase or stay the same. (In general, it will increase, however slightly.)

The adjusted-R^2, however, 'penalizes' the inclusion of another variable for making the model less parsimonious. In other words, every time we add a variable to a model, there are *two opposing* effects on the adjusted-R^2. On the one hand, it increases because the new variable will add some explanatory power (however small), but on the other hand, it decreases because it penalizes us for making the model more complicated. Which of the effects dominates will depend on the independent variable we add.

If we add a 'good' variable, meaning one that will help us explain a substantial part of the variability in the dependent variable (*that we've not explained with other variables already included in the model*), then the adjusted-R^2 will go up. If, on the other hand, we add a variable that either has little to do with the dependent variable or is highly correlated to other independent variables already included in the model, the adjusted-R^2 will go down.

In this regard, the adjusted-R^2 provides a 'quick and dirty' check on whether it is convenient to add another variable to a model. As an example, note that if we start by explaining mean returns with volatility, the adjusted-R^2 is 0.25 (Table 30.2). If we then add beta as explanatory variable, the adjusted-R^2 *falls* to 0.24 (Table 30.4). This does not mean that beta is a 'bad' variable when we want to explain the behavior of mean returns. It means that, *if we're already explaining returns with volatility*, making the model more complicated by adding another explanatory variable (beta) does not really pay off. And this is simply because much of what beta can explain of the variability of mean returns is already explained by volatility.

Predictions

One of the main goals of regression analysis is to predict expected values of the dependent variable. Having estimated the coefficients of the model and determined specific values of the dependent variables that may be of interest, it's all about adding and subtracting. Let's make a just a couple of predictions from the model estimated in Table 30.4, whose equation we can write as

$$E(y) = -0.001 + 0.118 \cdot x_1 + 0.003 \cdot x_2 \qquad (30.3)$$

where x_1 and x_2 represent our two independent variables, volatility and beta, respectively.

What would be the expected monthly return of an emerging market with relatively low risk, represented by a monthly volatility of 6% and a beta of 0.5? Simply substitute 0.06 and 0.5 for x_1 and x_2 in equation (30.3) and you should obtain 0.8%. And what would be the expected monthly return of an emerging market with relatively high risk, represented by a monthly volatility of 15% and a beta of 1.3? Again, simply substitute 0.15 and 1.3 for x_1 and x_2 in equation (30.3) and you should obtain a much higher 2.1%.

A final comment

It is possible that you may have heard or read about a simple rule to test hypotheses in which we can simply compare the absolute value of a t-statistic with the number 2. If the absolute value of the t-statistic is larger than 2, then we reject the *non*-significance of the coefficient in question; otherwise, the coefficient is in fact not significant. Is this rule different from the rule based on p-values we discussed above? Not at all.

Given a large sample, as is usually the case in finance, both rules will almost always lead us to the same decision. The 'almost always' is due to the fact that 2 is an approximation of the correct number for large samples, which is actually 1.96. However, in small samples, 2 is not the right number against which to compare the absolute value of the t-statistic. As an example, consider that for the regression in Table 30.4, the correct number is not 2 but 2.064. (Just in case you're curious, this number comes from a Student's t distribution, for a regression with 27 observations and a model with two explanatory variables. Never mind . . .)

In short, the rule we discussed based on p-values is easy to implement and very general. Sure, calculating a p-value is not trivial and you have to rely on the output of some computer program to obtain it. But any program that estimates OLS regressions (including Excel) provides the p-value of the t-statistic of all the coefficients in the regression as part of the default output of the run.

The big picture

Regression analysis is an essential tool in finance. It provides a simple framework to analyze the evidence on a model and to test the hypotheses that follow from it. After having established the reliability of a model, regression analysis is also essential for assessing the impact of a variable on another, as well as for forecasting future values of the variable of our interest. An essential tool in your toolkit, without a doubt.

Excel section

Running regressions in Excel is fairly simple, although it is fair to say that there are far more complete and sophisticated software packages for this purpose. Excel, however, does provide you with the elementary output that is sufficient for many practical applications. You should also know that there are a variety of commands in Excel that provide you with partial information about a regression. (You can calculate, for example, just the slope of a regression with the 'linest' function.) We'll discuss here an option that gives you a fairly comprehensive output.

Let's assume you have three series of ten observations each in cells A1 through A10, B1 through B10, and C1 through C10. Let's also assume that the first column displays the observations for the dependent variable, and the other two columns for the two independent variables. To open the required dialogue box you need to select from the 'Tools' menu the 'Data Analysis' option. From the available options, search for 'Regression,' click it, and then click 'OK.'

Once in the dialogue box, in order to run a regression with just *one* explanatory variable, you do the following:

- Click in the box labeled 'Input Y Range' and then select the range for the dependent variable (A1:A10).

- Click in the box labeled 'Input X Range' and then select the range for the independent variable (B1:B10).

- Finally, from 'Output Options' select 'Output Range,' click the box next to it, and input a cell where you would like *the beginning* of the output to be displayed. (Note that the output is displayed over several cells. For a regression with just one explanatory variable, expect it to take some 18 rows and 9 columns.)

We will not go over the whole output here simply because it displays more information than we have covered in this chapter. Note, however, that you will find in the Excel output the number of observations in the regression, the R^2, the adjusted-R^2, the coefficients estimated, their standard errors, their t-statistics, and their p-values, all of which we have discussed above.

To run a regression with more than one explanatory variable the procedure is the same, with only one difference. In the second step above, after clicking the box labeled 'Input X Range,' instead of selecting the data for one independent variable, you select the data for *all* the independent variables. For example, if you had two independent variables in cells B1 through B10 and C1 through C10, you would click 'Input X Range' and then select the range B1 through C10.

Challenge section

1 Consider the mean monthly returns (MR), monthly standard deviation of returns (SD), and beta with respect to the market (the S&P500) of the 30 companies in Table 30.5, all calculated over the 1999–2003 period. The companies in the list are those that make up the Dow Jones Industrial Average after its latest change of composition on April 8, 2004.

   (a) Estimate a linear regression model in which mean returns are solely explained by volatility measured by the standard deviation of returns.

   (b) What do you make out of the R^2 of this regression?

   (c) Interpret the two coefficients estimated and test their significance. Does volatility seem to be a good variable to explain the variability in mean returns across companies?

TABLE 30.5

Company	MR (%)	SD (%)	Beta	Company	MR (%)	SD (%)	Beta
3M	1.9	7.0	0.6	Honeywell	0.6	13.6	1.3
Alcoa	2.1	12.9	1.8	Intel	1.5	15.7	2.1
Altria	1.1	11.0	0.3	IBM	0.6	11.1	1.4
American Express	1.0	8.1	1.1	Johnson & Johnson	0.7	7.1	0.3
American Intl	0.7	7.8	0.8	JP Morgan Chase	0.6	11.7	1.8
Boeing	1.1	10.1	0.7	McDonald's	-0.3	8.5	0.8
Caterpillar	1.7	10.4	1.0	Merck	-0.1	9.0	0.3
Citigroup	1.8	9.0	1.4	Microsoft	0.5	13.7	1.7
Coca-Cola	0.0	7.9	0.3	Pfizer	0.1	7.0	0.4
DuPont	0.3	8.1	0.9	Procter & Gamble	0.6	7.4	-0.1
Exxon Mobil	0.5	5.3	0.4	SBC Comm.	-0.4	10.4	0.8
General Electric	0.3	8.1	1.1	United Tech.	1.5	9.3	1.1
General Motors	0.8	11.4	1.3	Verizon	0.0	10.4	1.0
Hewlett-Packard	0.9	15.0	1.8	Wal-Mart	0.8	8.4	0.8
Home Depot	0.4	10.8	1.4	Walt Disney	0.1	9.4	1.0

2 Estimate a linear regression model in which mean returns are solely explained by beta.

   (a) What do you make out of the R^2 of this regression?

   (b) Interpret the two coefficients estimated and test their significance. Does beta seem to be a good variable to explain the variability in mean returns across companies?

▶

3 Estimate a linear regression model in which mean returns are explained by both volatility and beta.

(a) What do you make out of the R^2 of this regression?

(b) Interpret the three coefficients estimated and test their significance. Do volatility and beta seem to be good variables to jointly explain the variability in mean returns across companies?

(c) Go back to the regression run in question 1(a) in which mean returns are solely explained by volatility, and compare its adjusted-R^2 with that of the multiple regression model estimated in this question. Does it pay to add beta to a regression in which mean returns are explained by volatility?

INDEX

absolute purchasing power parity 321–22
accounting profits 283–4, 285, 286
adjusted present value (APV) model 156,
185–9, 189, 190, 191, 192
adjusted-R^2 377–8
allocation restriction 125, 127, 130
alpha (Jensen's) 113
American options 274, 293
amortization 169, 170
annualized standard deviation (ASD)
139, 140–2, 144
Apple 60–1
appreciation, currency 319, 320
arithmetic mean returns (AM) 15–17, 18–19,
20, 23, 32, 76
arithmetic returns 5
  see also simple returns

backwardation 308
Bank of America (BoA) 36–9
bearer bonds 215
beating the market 121
benchmarks 207–8, 209, 212
  cross-sectional 206–7, 208, 209
  temporal 206, 207–8, 209
  theoretical 207, 208
beta coefficients 373–4
beta of a stock 62, 69, 70, 71, 72, 73
  CAPM and 77–80, 86, 93
  forward-looking estimates 73
  size 89
  value 88–9
bills see Treasury bills
Black-Scholes model 276, 277, 297–9
bonds 74, 75, 76, 77
  call protected 215
  convexity 245–6, 249
  current yield 221
  deep-discount 244
  discount rate 218–19, 234–5, 243, 244,
    245–6, 249

duration 240, 241–45, 248, 249
  modified 244–5, 246–8, 249
face value or principal 214, 216, 217, 223
floated 214
high-yield (junk) 232, 237
indenture 214
inflation-protected 214, 216
interest rate (coupon) 214, 216–17, 218–19,
    223, 234–5, 243, 244
investment grade 232, 237
maturity
  and duration 240, 242–4, 244
  and market risk 234–5, 237, 244
maturity date 214
pricing 216–19, 235–6, 237, 240, 245–8,
    249
principal or face value 214, 216, 217, 223
returns 219–23
  long-term 137–8, 139, 143–4
risk 228–37, 240
types 214–15
yield to maturity 219–23, 229–30
book-to-market ratios (BtM) 85, 87, 88,
90

call options 274, 275, 293, 301
  at the money 293
  in the money 293
  out of the money 293
  valuation 276–7, 294–9
callable bonds 215
capital
  cost of see cost of capital
  return on (ROC) 285
capital asset pricing model (CAPM) 69–83, 85,
    86, 87, 89, 93–4, 158, 173
capital charge 285
capital free cash flow (CFCF) 169, 170–2,
    174–6, 178, 182–3, 184, 188, 189, 192
capital gain 5
capital loss 5

CAPM *see* capital asset pricing model
cash flow 169–72
    incremental 264–5
    see also capital free cash flow
        (CFCF); discounted cash flow
        (DCF) models; equity free cash
        flow (EFCF)
cash flow return on investment (CFROI) 289
cash value added (CVA) 289
Coca Cola 4, 5, 8–9, 15
coefficient of kurtosis 361, 362, 363, 368
coefficient of skewness 360–1, 362, 363, 367
compounding 5–7, 361
consols 215, 218
consumption assets 309
contago 310
continuously compounded returns 7–11, 146,
        147, 363–5, 366
    multiperiod 9–10
convenience yield 309, 310
convertible bonds 215
corporate bonds 215
corporate value creation 282–91
correlation coefficient 43, 48–9, 54, 342–3
cost of capital 80–2, 173, 174–6, 190, 191, 285
    inflation-adjusted (or real) 289
cost of carry 309–10, 311
cost of debt 80–1, 176–7
cost of equity 70–82, 85, 91–4, 158, 177, 183,
        190
cost of unlevered equity 186–7, 188, 192
coupon of a bond 214, 216–17, 218–19, 223,
        234–5, 243, 244
covariance 43, 60–3, 69, 71, 126, 340–2
credit ratings 232–3, 235, 237
cross-sectional analysis 371, 372
cumulative standard deviation (CSD) 141–42
currencies 318–30

Damodaran, Aswath 287
debentures 215
debt 171, 173
    cost of (required return) 80–1, 176–7
    level of 190, 191
    net benefits of 185–6, 189, 191, 192
    net impact of 185, 191
    tax shields 186, 188
debt/equity ratios 187, 188, 190, 191
default risk 74, 228, 230–2, 237
Dell 174–7, 183–5, 187–9
dependent variables 371
depreciation 169, 170
    currency 319, 320, 325
discount rates 258, 259, 260–67

time-varying 266–7
discounted cash flow (DCF) models 156, 157,
        212
    constant-growth version 194–6, 200
    two-stage version 194–5
    see also adjusted present value
        (APV) mode; dividend discount model
        (DDM); flows-to-equity (FTE) model;
        weighted-average cost of capital (WACC)
        model
discounting 257
Disney 50–2
dispersion, measures of 338–90
distributions
    non-normal 359–69
    normal 349–57
diversification 46–55, 58–60, 62, 63–5, 97
    international 63–4
dividend discount model (DDM) 156, 157–66,
        172, 173, 189
    constant growth 160, 163, 165
    no growth 159, 162–3
    two stages of growth 160–1, 164, 165
dividend payout ratios (DPRs) 165
dividend yield 5, 311
dollar-weighted returns 19–22
downside standard deviation of returns 100–2,
        106, 120

earnings 169–70
earnings before interest and taxes
        (EBIT) 283
economic profits 283–90
economic value added (EVA) 288–9, 290
effective annual yield to maturity 223
effective interest rate 6–7
efficient set 39, 41, 43
Eli Lilly 206, 208, 210–11
emerging markets 49, 72, 374–9
Enron 50, 232
equity
    required return on (cost of) 70–82, 85, 91–4,
        158, 177, 183, 190
    valuation 156–212
equity charge 285
equity free cash flow (EFCF) 169, 170–2,
        182–3, 184, 190, 192
European options 274, 293, 297
exchange rates 318–20, 323–4, 325, 328, 329
    forward 318, 327–8, 329
    purchasing power parity (PPP) 323, 324
    spot 328, 329
exercise (or strike) price 274, 276–7, 293, 296,
        297

explanatory (independent) variables 371
   multiple 376–7
Exxon Mobil 18–19, 27–9, 30, 31

Fama, Eugene 89
feasible set 38, 39, 41, 43
Fed Stock Valuation Model (FSVM) 208
financial options 276, 293–303
   call 293, 294–9, 301
   exercise (or strike) price 293, 296, 297
   expiration date 293
   leverage 300–1
   protection 300, 301–2
   put 293, 294–7, 299–300, 301
   risk-free rate 296
   time to expiration 296
   valuation
      at expiration 294–5
      before expiration 294–300
      value of underlying asset 276, 295–6, 302
Fisher effect 324–5, 329
floating-rate bonds 214
flows-to-equity (FTE) model 156, 182–5, 189,
   190, 192
forward exchange rates 318, 327–8
forward parity (FP) 328
forwards and futures 3053–16, 327, 328
free cash flow to equity 170
free cash flow to the firm 170
French, Kenneth 89, 90
frequencies 347–9
fund styles 121
fundamentals 209–10
futures and forwards 305–16, 327, 328

GARP (growth at a reasonable price) 211
General Electric (GE) 161–65
geometric mean returns (GM) 17–19, 20, 21, 23,
   32–3, 76
government bonds 74, 76, 215
growing perpetuity 157, 160, 183
growth stocks 87

hedgers 306, 312
hedging 312–15
high-yield bonds 232, 237
histograms 347–9
holding period, and risk and return 139–44,
   148–9
holding-period returns *see* simple
returns
Holt Associates 289
Home Depot 60–1
hypothesis testing 373–4

IBM 36–9
immunization strategies 248
income
   net 169–70, 172, 283, 284
   residual 284–9, 290
income immunization 248
indenture 214
independent (explanatory) variables 371
   multiple 376–7
inflation 68
inflation differentials 322, 323–4, 329
inflation-protected bonds 214, 216
inflation rates 318, 322–5, 326, 328
inflation risk 229, 233
initial margin 307
Intel 18–19, 27–9, 30, 31
interest expense 172
interest rate parity (IRP) 327–8, 329
interest rate risk *see* market risk
interest rates 248–9, 257, 318, 326–7, 328
   bonds 214, 216–17, 218–19, 223, 234–5, 243,
      244
   effective 6–7
   nominal 6–7, 324, 325
   real 324, 327
internal rate of return (IRR) 20–1, 82, 220, 230,
   260–8
   bonds 220
   multiple 263
   no 263
international diversification 63–4
international Fisher effect (IFE) 325–7, 329
international parity conditions 318, 328, 329
internet companies 208
   see also Yahoo!
intrinsic value 157, 162, 165, 173, 178, 183,
   189, 191
investment assets 309
investment horizon, and risk and return 137–49
investors, goals 125–6

Jensen index 112–16, 117
junk (high-yield) bonds 232, 237

kurtosis 361–3, 367

law of one price (LOP) 320–2
leptokurtosis 361, 362
leverage 300–1, 308
levered free cash flow 170
liquidity risk 228, 233
logarithmic returns *see* continuously
      compounded returns
lognormal distribution 363–5, 367, 368–9

long run, risk and return in 137–49
luck 110–11, 121
Lynch, Peter 211

Macaulay's duration 246
maintenance margin 307
margin accounts 307–8
margin call 307
marked to market 307
market capitalization 85, 86
market efficiency 157
market (interest rate) risk 74, 228, 233–6, 237, 240, 243, 244, 247
market portfolio 69, 75, 78
market risk premium 70, 87
    CAPM and 71, 72–3, 75–7, 77, 79
    forward-looking estimates 73
    three-factor model and 87, 88, 89–93
market value added (MVA) 288–9
market value weights 191
mean, arithmetic (AM) 336–7, 360, 362
mean compound return *see* geometric mean returns
mean returns 15–23, 31–3, 99
    arithmetic 15–17, 18–19, 20, 23, 32, 76
    dollar-weighted 19–22
    emerging markets 372–7
    geometric 17–19, 20, 21, 23, 32–3, 76
mean reversion 145–6, 149
median 337–8, 360
Merck 209, 210–11
Microsoft 50–2, 101–2
minimum variance portfolio (MVP) 38–9, 41, 43, 50, 51, 127
mode 338, 360
Modigliani, Franco and Leah 118
moments 359
    see also kurtosis; mean; skewness; variance
Moody's rating agency 231
Morningstar 121
multicollinearity 377
multiple linear regression model 371–3
multiples 156, 204–5, 212
mutual funds 53

net income 169–70, 172, 283, 284
net operating profit after taxes (NOPAT) 283–4, 285, 288, 289
net present value (NPV) 82, 259–68, 271–74, 278–9, 280, 282
Nokia 78–9
nominal exchange rate 318–19
nominal interest rate 6–7, 324, 325
normal distribution 349–57

standard 353–4
notes 74, 75, 208, 215

option premium 294
options *see* financial options; real options
Oracle 98–9, 100–2
ordinary least squares (OLS) procedure 372

p-value 373–4, 379
PEG ratio 210–11
perpetuity 159
    growing 157, 160, 183
platykurtic distribution 361
population 335, 373
portfolios
    covariance between stock and 60–3, 69, 126
    diversification 46–55, 58–60, 62, 63–5, 97
    n-asset 41–3
    optimal 125–35
    returns 36–44
        maximization of 125, 128–9, 130
        risk 36–44, 46–55, 57–66, 125–35
        minimization of 125, 127–8
        standard deviation 37, 41–2, 60, 61
        three-asset 39–41
        two-asset 36–9
        variance 60–3, 69
PPP (purchasing power parity) 321–4, 328–9
predictions 378–9
present value 20, 21, 257–8
price immunization 248
price-to-book (P/B) ratios 156, 204, 205
price-to-cash flow (P/CF) ratios 156, 204, 205
price-to-dividend (P/D) ratios 156, 204, 205
price-to-earnings (P/E) ratios 156, 204, 205, 207–8, 210
    adjusted by growth (PEG) 210–11
    trailing and forward 205
price-to-sales (P/S) ratios 204, 205
price(s) 156, 157
    bonds 216–19, 235–6, 237, 240, 245–8, 249
    exercise (or strike) 274, 276–7, 293, 296, 297
    futures 308–11
    law of one price 320–22
    spot 309
probabilities 351–3, 366–7
Proctor & Gamble 60–1
profits
    accounting 283–4, 285, 286
    economic 283–10
purchasing power 68, 71, 73, 256, 257, 319, 324, 325
purchasing power parity (PPP) 321–4, 328–9
put-call parity 299

put options 274, 275, 293, 301
  at the money 293
  in the money 293
  out of the money 293
  valuation 276–7, 294–7, 299–300

R&D 288
random variables 334–5
RAROC (risk-adjusted return on capital) 290
rating agencies 231–2, 237
real cost of capital 289
real interest rate 324, 327
real options 274–80
  call and put 274, 275, 276–7
  exercise price 276–7
  expiration date 274
  misuses of 278–9
  risk-free rate 277
  time to expiration 277
  types of 275–6
  valuation of 276–8
  value of underlying asset 276, 277
registered bonds 215
regression analysis 371–82
reinvestment risk 221, 229, 2331
relative valuation 154, 202–10
required returns 68–82
  CAPM and 69–82, 85, 86, 87, 89, 93–4, 183
  debt 80–1, 176–7
  equity 70–82, 85, 91–4, 158, 177, 183, 190
  three-factor model and 85, 87, 88–93, 94
  unlevered equity 186–7, 188
residual income 284–9, 290
return on capital (ROC) 285
returns 4–13
  bonds 219–23, 137–8, 139, 143–4
  continuously compounded 7–11
    multiperiod 9–10
  downside standard deviation (semideviation)
    of 100–2, 106, 120
  expected 71, 73, 87, 112, 125, 126
    maximization of 125, 128
  in the long-term 137–49
  and luck 110–11, 121
  mean reversion in 145–6, 149
  observed 112–13
  portfolios 36–44, 125, 128–9, 130
  and risk taking 111
  target 127–8, 130, 146–8
  upside standard deviation of 102–3
  volatility of *see* volatility of returns
  see also mean returns; required returns; risk-
    adjusted returns (RAR); standard
    deviation of return (SD)

reverse valuation 194–202
risk 27–33
  bonds 228–37
  default 74, 228, 230–3, 237
  diversifiable 59
  downside 97–106, 120
  inflation 229, 233
  interest rate (market) 74, 228, 233–6, 237
  liquidity 228, 233
  in the long-term 139–49
  minimization of 125, 127–8
  portfolio 36–44, 46–55, 57–66, 125–35
  reinvestment 221, 229, 233
  standard deviation as measure of 30–1, 37, 97
  systematic (market) 57–66, 59, 60, 85, 87,
    97, 117
  target level of 125, 128, 130
  total 27–34, 57–8, 117
  undiversifiable 59
  unsystematic (idiosyncratic) 59, 60, 97
risk premium (RP) 68–9, 69, 70, 71, 77, 85
  see also market risk premium (MRP); size
    risk premium; value risk premium
risk-adjusted performance (RAP) 118–19
risk-adjusted return on capital
(RAROC) 290
risk-adjusted returns (RAR) 52–3, 54, 69,
  111–23
  maximization of 125, 128–9
risk-free rate 68–9, 71, 88
  CAPM and 73–5, 79, 85, 89, 93
  forward-looking estimates 73
  options 277, 296
ROC (return on capital) 285
Russia 16–17, 23

S&P500 208
samples 335, 373
sampling error 373
secured bonds 215
semideviation of returns 100–2, 106, 120
shareholder value 282–91
shareholder value added (SVA) 290
Sharpe ratio 117–18, 119, 120, 129
shortfall probability 142–4, 145
Siegel, Jeremy 137
significance level 373–4
simple returns 4–5, 8–9, 10–11, 361–3
  multiperiod 9–10
  see also arithmetic returns
size beta 89
size effect 87
size risk premium 86–7, 88–93, 94
skewness 103, 359–61, 362, 363, 367

Sortino ratio 120
speculators 306
spot exchange rates 328, 329
spot market 306
spot price 308
stakeholder theory 282
Standard & Poor's (S&P) 231
standard deviation (SD) 340
standard deviation of return (SD) 29–31, 33, 57,
    62, 97–9
  annualized 139, 140–2, 144
  cumulative 139–40
  downside 100–2, 106, 120
  as measure of risk 30–1, 37, 97
  of a portfolio 37, 41–2, 60, 61
  upside 102–3
standard error 373
statistics
  non-normal distributions 359–69
  normal distributions 349–57
  regression analysis 371–82
  summary 334–45
Stewart, Stern 288
stocks
  long-term return of 137–8, 139, 140–2,
    143–4, 149
  valuation 156–212
strike (exercise) price 274, 276–7, 293, 296,
    297
styles, fund 121
Sun Microsystems 22, 23
SVA (shareholder value added) 290
systematic (market) risk 57–66, 59, 60, 85, 87,
    97, 117

t-statistic 373–4, 379
target weights 191
tax shields, debt 186, 188
ten-year notes 74, 75, 208, 215
terminal value (TV) 157, 164–5, 173, 183
three-factor model 85, 87, 88–93, 94
time diversification 144–5, 148–9
time-series analysis 371, 372
total business returns (TBR) 290
total shareholder returns (TSR) 289–90
Treasury bills 68, 74, 76, 77, 215
Treasury Inflation-Protected Securities (TIPS)
    214
Treynor index 115–16, 117, 118, 120

uncertainty 19, 28, 68
unlevered equity, required return on 186–7,
    188, 192
unlevered free cash flow 170

unsecured bonds 215

valuation
  absolute (intrinsic) 156, 212
  bonds 214–51
  financial options 294–300
  fundamental analysis 156
  futures 308–11
  models see adjusted present value (APV)
    model; dividend discount model (DDM);
    flows-to-equity (FTE) model; weighted-
    average cost of capital (WACC) model
  real options 276–8
  relative 156, 204–12
  reverse 194–202
  stocks 156–212
  technical analysis 156
value
  intrinsic 157, 162, 165, 173, 178, 183, 189,
    191
  net present (NPV) 82, 259–68, 271–74,
    278–9, 280, 282
  present 20, 21, 257–8
  terminal (TV) 157, 164–5, 173, 183
  of underlying assets 276, 277–8, 295–6, 302
Value at Risk (VaR) 103–6
value beta 88–9
value creation 282–91
value risk premium 86–7, 88–93, 94
value stocks 87
variance 60–3, 69, 71, 126, 338–40
variance drag 32
venture capital funds 49, 72
volatility
  price (bonds) 235–6, 237, 240, 249
  in value of underlying asset 277–8, 295–6,
    302
volatility of returns 19, 23, 28–9, 31–3, 57, 97
  above the mean 102–3
  below the mean 99, 100–2, 106
  long-term 137, 139
  relative 72
  total 72

weighted-average cost of capital (WACC) model
    80–1, 82, 156, 172–8, 182, 189, 190, 191

Yahoo! 198–99, 201
yield 74–5, 76
  convenience 309, 310
  dividend 5, 311
yield to maturity (bonds) 220–3

zero-coupon bonds 215, 217–18, 244